GOD-SENT

ROY ABRAHAM VARGHESE

GOD-SENT

=A=

HISTORY OF
THE ACCREDITED
APPARITIONS
OF MARY

A Crossroad Book
The Crossroad Publishing Company
New York

The Crossroad Publishing Company
370 Lexington Avenue, New York, NY 10017

Printed in the United States of America

Library of Congress Cataloging-in-Publication Data

Varghese, Roy Abraham.
  God-sent / by Roy Abraham Varghese.
    p. cm.
  Includes bibliographical references.
  ISBN 0-8245-1843-8 (pbk. : alk. paper)
    1. Mary, Blessed Virgin, Saint – Apparitions and miracles – History.
  I. Title.
  BT650 .V37 2000
  232.91′7 – dc21   99-050709

1   2   3   4   5   6   7   8   9   10   06   05   04   03   02   01   00

For our three God-sends
Rachel — "Little Lamb"
Mary — "Exalted of God"
Michael — "Who is like God"

with the fervent prayer that the God-sent
will extend her maternal mantle over their lives

If I saw an angel come down to teach us good, and I was convinced from others seeing him that I was not mad, I should believe in design.

— CHARLES DARWIN, Letter to Asa Gray in *The Life and Letters of Charles Darwin*

I do not think our cures can compete with those at Lourdes. There are so many more people who believe in the miracle of the Blessed Virgin than in the existence of the unconscious.

— SIGMUND FREUD, *New Introductory Lectures on Psycho-Analysis*

I had read a lot about the fashions and frivolity of Paris. These were in evidence in every street, but the churches stood noticeably apart from these scenes. A man would forget the outside noise and bustle as soon as he entered one of these churches. His manner would change, he would behave with dignity and reverence as he passed someone kneeling before the image of the Virgin. The feeling I had then has since been growing on me, that all this kneeling and prayer could not be mere superstition; the devout souls kneeling before the Virgin could not be worshiping mere marble. I have an impression that I felt then that by this worship they were not detracting from, but increasing, the glory of God.

— MAHATMA GANDHI, *My Experiments with Truth: An Autobiography*

I had some stunning thoughts last night, the result of studying Tolstoi, Spengler, New Testament and also the result of praying to St. Mary to intercede for me to make me stop being a maniacal drunkard.... So far, every prayer addressed to the Holy Mother has been answered.... But I do want to point out, the reason I think she intercedes so well for us, is because she too is a human being. — JACK KEROUAC, Letter to Bob Giroux, February 1963

Is Christ only to be adored? Or is the holy Mother of God rather not to be honored? This is the woman who crushed the serpent's head. Hear us. For your Son denies you nothing.

— MARTIN LUTHER, Last Sermon at Wittenberg, January 1546

Love gave her a thousand names. — Flemish hymn on the titles of Mary

The Lord, the apostles, and the prophets have taught us that we must venerate in the first place the Holy Mother of God, who is above all the heavenly powers. If any one does not confess that the holy, ever virgin Mary, really and truly the Mother of God, is higher than all creatures visible and invisible, and does not implore with a sincere faith her intercession, given her powerful access to our God born of her, let him be anathema.

— Second Council of Nicaea (Seventh Ecumenical Council of the undivided Church, accepted by Protestants, Catholics, and Orthodox)

It is not every spirit, my dear people, that you can trust; test them, to see if they come from God;... you can tell the spirits that come from God by this: every spirit which acknowledges that Jesus the Christ has come in the flesh is from God. — 1 John 4:1–3

Then the dragon was enraged with the woman and went away to make war on the rest of her children, that is, all who obey God's commandments and bear witness for Jesus.

— Revelation 12:17

Contents

Acknowledgments   xiii

A Chronology of the Apparitions of the Virgin   xiv

Introduction   1

PART ONE

MONTAGE

THE WITNESS OF THE VIRGIN THROUGHOUT WORLD HISTORY

9

1. Who Is the Virgin?   11

2. The Words of the Virgin in Scripture   12

3. The Veneration of the Virgin   14

4. The Return of the New Eve   17

5. The Recovery of the Ark   21

6. Salvation: Not Fate but the Fiat of Faith   24

7. What Is an Apparition?   28

8. Collective Hallucination?   31

9. A History of the Apparitions   34

10. "My Sole Purpose Is to Ensure That the Will of the Son Is Obeyed"   41

11. Jesus on Mary in the Apparitions   44

12. Mary on Jesus in the Apparitions   47

13. The Virgin and World History   48

14. From the Triumph of the Immaculate Heart
   to the Reign of the Sacred Heart   56

15. Evidence and Explanation   58

PART TWO

VISAGE

IMAGES OF THE VIRGIN AS WITNESSED
IN HER APPEARANCES
63

PART THREE

COLLAGE

MESSAGES OF THE VIRGIN
IN HER APPEARANCES
65

Transcendent Tableaux 70

1. Saragossa, Spain, A.D. 40   70

2. Neocaesarea, Asia Minor, 238   70

3. Rome, Italy, 352   72

4. Walsingham, England, 1061   72

5. Mount Carmel, England, 1251   73

6. Czestochowa, Poland, 1382   74

7. Kazan, Russia, 1579   75

8. Vailankanni, India, sixteenth–seventeenth centuries   76

9. Aparecida do Norte, São Paulo, Brazil, 1717   81

10. LaVang, Vietnam, 1798   81

11. Knock, Ireland, 1879   82

12. Dong Lu, China, 1900, 1995   84

13. Jerusalem, Israel, 1954   85

14. Zeitun, Egypt, 1968   85

Bolts from the Blue 87

1. Appearances to Saints   87

2. Guadalupe, Mexico, 1531   88

3. Rue du Bac, Paris, France, 1830   94

4. La Salette, France, 1846   97

5. Lourdes, France, 1858   101

6. Pontmain, France, 1871   106

7. Fatima, Portugal, 1917 107

8. Beauraing, Belgium, 1932 115

9. Banneux, Belgium, 1933 117

10. Akita, Japan, 1973–81 119

11. Betania, Venezuela, 1976–90 124

12. Cuapa, Nicaragua, 1980 127

13. Kibeho, Rwanda, 1981–89 134

14. Damascus, Syria, 1982–90 138

15. Hrushiv, Ukraine, 1914, 1987 142

16. Cuenca, Ecuador, 1988–90 143

Comprehensive Catechesis 149

1. Amsterdam, Holland, 1945–84: Our Lady of All Nations 149

2. San Nicolás, Argentina, 1983–90: Our Lady of the Rosary 163

3. Naju, Korea, 1985: Queen of the Holy Rosary 171

4. Medjugorje, Bosnia, 1981–Present: Queen of Peace 184

Appendix A: Philosophical, Scientific, and Theological Criteria
in Assessing the Authenticity of Apparitions 215

Appendix B: Sent by Whom? On the Existence of God 230

Appendix C: "Sent" as a Witness: On the Historical Reality of Jesus 234

Appendix D: Ever a Virgin? 236

Works Cited 239

Acknowledgments

I am grateful first to my wife, Anila, and my family for the many sacrifices they have had to make in the course of my working on this book.

I am grateful also to many of the students and authorities on Marian apparitions who have provided direct assistance for this work and in particular the following:

Tim and Melissa Laurel, for assembling the graphics in this volume and in particular for creating the cover.

Dudley Plunkett, for his kind and thorough reviews of various drafts of this volume and for the information in his books on Marian apparitions.

Dr. Courtenay Bartholomew, for the use of his fine collection of photographs and for the information in his two books on the subject.

Dr. Thomas Petrisko, for photographs used in this volume and for the information in his many works on Marian apparitions.

Mr. Robert Schaeffer, for photographs used in this volume.

Dr. Kazimierz Dadak, for his constant assistance.

Mrs. Rocilda Oliveiro of Campo Grande, Brazil, for the information on the Black Madonna of Brazil.

Mrs. Patrizia de Ferrari of Córdoba, Argentina, for information on Our Lady of San Nicolás and the use of photographs.

Mrs. Janice T. Connell, for the information in her various works on Marian apparitions.

Mr. Mark Alder of London, England, for information on Our Lady of Walsingham.

Mrs. Loreto Mary Whelton of London, England, for information on Our Lady of Walsingham.

Ms. Ann Ball of Houston, for the use of photographs and for valuable information from her book on Marian shrines.

Fr. Albert Ostatek, for the picture of Our Lady of Czestochowa; Mr. Joseph Cassano, for the picture of Our Lady of Cuapa; Mrs. Maria Rota, for various pictures; Mrs. Miriam A. Weglian and Mr. Stephen M. Weglian, for information on Our Lady of Cuapa from their book *Let Heaven and Earth Unite!*

The copyright on the image of Our Lady of LaVang reprinted here belongs to the Blue Army of Vietnam.

A Chronology of the Apparitions of the Virgin

Year	Place	Visionary	Title
ca. 40	Saragossa, Spain	St. James the Greater	Our Lady of the Pillar
ca. 81	Patmos, Greece	St. John the Evangelist	The Woman Clothed with the Sun
ca. 238	Neocaesarea, Asia Minor	St. Gregory the Wonder-Worker	
ca. 352	Rome, Italy	John of Rome, Pope Liberius	Our Lady of the Snows
ca. 455	Constantinople	Emperor Leo I	Our Lady of the Golden Fountain
ca. 657	Toledo, Spain	St. Ildefonso, bishop of Toledo	
ca. 708	Evesham, England	Egwin, bishop of Worcester	
948	Einsiedeln, Switzerland	St. Conrad of Constance	
1061	Walsingham, England	Lady Richeldis de Faverches	Our Lady of Walsingham
1119	Monte Vergine, Italy	St. William of Vercelli	
1153	Citeaux, France	St. Bernard of Clairvaux	
1214	Clairefontaine, Luxembourg	Princess Ermesinde	Our Lady of Ermesinde
1216	Assisi, Italy	St. Francis of Assisi	Our Lady of the Angels
1233	Florence, Italy	Seven founders of the Servants of Mary	The Sorrowful Mother
1251	Aylesford, England	St. Simon Stock	Our Lady of Mount Carmel
1298	Helfta, Germany	St. Mechtilde	
1346–73	Vadstena, Sweden	St. Bridget	
1350–80	Siena, Italy	St. Catherine	
1382	Czestochowa, Poland	Empress Helena	The Black Madonna
1392	Zagorsk, Russia	St. Sergius of Radonezh	
1491	Alsatian Vosges	Group of men	
1522	Manresa, Spain	St. Ignatius of Loyola	
1531	Guadalupe, Mexico	Juan Diego	Our Lady of Guadalupe
1536	Savona, near Genoa, Italy	Antonio Botta	Our Lady of Victories
1541	Ocotlán, Mexico	Juan Diego Bernardino	Our Lady of Ocotlán
16th cent.	Vailankanni, India	Peasant boy and others	Our Lady of Good Health
1561	Avila, Spain	St. Teresa of Avila	
1579	Kazan, Russia	Matrona	Our Lady of Kazan
1609	Siluva, Lithuania	Children	Our Lady of Siluva
1634	Quito, Ecuador	Sr. Mary Anne of Jesus	
1664	Grenoble, France	Benoite Rencurel	Our Lady of Le Laus
1673	Paray-Le-Monial, France	St. Margaret Mary Alacoque	
1717	São Paulo, Brazil	Three fishermen	
1779	Sarov, Russia	St. Seraphim of Sarov	
1798	LaVang, Vietnam	Villagers of Quang Tri	Our Lady of LaVang
1830	Paris, France	Sr. Catherine Labouré	Our Lady of the Miraculous Medal

Year	Place	Visionary	Title
1842	Rome, Italy	Alphonse M. Ratisbonne	Our Lady of Zion
1846	La Salette, France	Melanie Calvat and Maximin Giraud	
1850	Lichen, Poland	Thomas Klossowski	
1858	Lourdes, France	Bernadette Soubirous	Our Lady of Lourdes
1861	Turin, Italy	St. John Bosco	
1866	Filippsdorf, Czech Republic	Magdalena Kade	
1871	Pontmain, France	Eugene and Joseph Barbedette, Françoise Richer, Jeanne-Marie Lebosse Eugene Freiteau	Our Lady of Hope
1873	Marpingen, Germany	Katherina Hubertus, Margaretha Kunz, Susanna Leist	
1876	Pellevoisin, France	Estelle Faguette	Our Lady of the Scapular of the Sacred Heart
1879	Knock, Ireland	Villagers of Cnoc Mhuire	Our Lady of Knock
1900, 1995	Dong Lu, China	Thousands of people	Our Lady of China
1906	Quito, Ecuador	Large crowds	
1914, 1987	Hrushiv, Ukraine	Thousands of people	
1917	Fatima, Portugal	Lucia dos Santos and Francisco and Jacinta Marto	Our Lady of Fatima
1932	Beauraing, Belgium	Fernande, Albert, and Gilberte Voisin, Andrée and Gilberte Degeimbre	The Virgin with the Golden Heart
1933	Banneux, Belgium	Mariette Beco	The Virgin of the Poor
1945	Amsterdam, Holland	Ida Peerdeman	Our Lady of All Nations
1946	Marienfried, Germany	Baerbel Ruess	
1947	Tre Fontane, Italy	Bruno Cornacchiola	
1947	Montichiari-Fontanelle	Pierina Gilli	Rosa Mystica
1954	Jerusalem, Israel	Children and adults	
1968	Zeitun, Egypt	Thousands of people	Our Lady of Light
1973	Akita, Japan	Sr. Agnes Sasagawa	
1976	Betania, Venezuela	María Esperanza Medrano de Bianchini	
1980	Cuapa, Nicaragua	Bernardo Martínez	
1981	Medjugorje, Yugoslavia (now Bosnia)	Mirjana, Ivanka, Vicka, Ivan, Marija, Jackov	Queen of Peace
1981	Kibeho, Rwanda	Alphonsine, Anathalie, Marie-Clare, Stephanie, Emmanuel, Agnes, Vestine	
1982	Damascus, Syria	Myrna Nazzour	Our Lady of Unity
1983	San Nicolás, Argentina	Gladys de Motta	Our Lady of the Rosary of San Nicolás
1985	Naju, South Korea	Julia Kim	
1990	Cuenca, Ecuador	Patricia Talbott	

Introduction

The story of the Virgin Mary's mystical appearances in every culture and era since the coming of Christ is without parallel or precedent. All peoples and nations have their own tale of the Virgin's visitation. She has left her mark in the lands of Hindus, Jews, and Moslems, Protestants, Catholics, and Orthodox, Buddhists and Shintoists, Confucians and Communists, Aztecs and animists. Her maternal mien has been perceived and portrayed in every major racial and social "world." She is without question the mother of all humanity, of all races and nations. She is the meeting place of the mystical and the historical.

Immeasurably more intriguing than UFOs and extraterrestrials is the phenomenon of a human and yet heavenly being who bears witness to another world, who comes not to mystify but as a messenger on a mission. And those who seek solace in New Age gurus and high-tech soothsayers will be better served if they turn to Mary of the Magnificat, who was once God-chosen and is now God-sent.

God-Sent! A History of the Accredited Apparitions of Mary is an inquiry into the appearances of the Virgin that considers both the phenomenon as experienced by the visionaries and the meaning and purpose of the phenomenon. Why is she appearing and what is the common thread that runs across her appearances, her messages, the biblical narratives, and the course of human history (both past and future)? This is the object of our inquiry. Loosely speaking, a Platonist might say that this is a study of both the phenomenon ("things that appear") and the noumenon ("things that are thought," "that which is intelligible").

The places and images associated with the Virgin's appearances (or apparitions as they are normally called) have become an integral part of the cultural fabric of the societies in which they occurred. So integral in fact that very few people have looked at the big picture — the extraordinary panorama of her apparitions around the globe and across history. She is not simply Our Lady of Fatima or Our Lady of Lourdes, a European phenomenon. She is the Virgin of Guadalupe (Mexico, 1531), the Healing Mother of Vailankanni (India, sixteenth and seventeenth centuries), Our Lady of Kazan (Russia, 1579), Our Lady of LaVang (Vietnam, 1798), Our Lady of Dong Lu (China, 1900), Our Lady of Akita (Japan, 1973), the Virgin of Kibeho (Rwanda, 1981). Neither are all her famous apparitions recent. She appeared to the Apostles, St. James the Greater (circa 40 A.D.) and St. John the Evangelist in the first century; to St. Gregory the Wonder-Worker in 238; as Our Lady of the Snows in Rome in 352; to a variety of saints and bishops from the fourth to the tenth centuries; as Our Lady of Walsingham in England circa 1061 and Our Lady of Mount Carmel (again in England) in 1251. She has appeared to many of the men and women revered

1

as saints and founders of religious orders (St. Francis of Assisi, St. Teresa of Avila, St. Ignatius of Loyola, St. John Bosco). Contemporary reports of hundreds of apparition claims around the globe should not surprise anyone with a sense of history. Ralph McInerny notes that there are two thousand such stories of ancient encounters with Mary in Latin; another five hundred in verse and six hundred in prose in old French; and numerous others in Anglo-Norman, English, German, Norse, and Spanish. Ancient apparition accounts from other parts of the world include the fifteenth-century Ethiopian manuscript *One Hundred and Ten Miracles of Our Lady Mary* translated by Sir E. A. Wallace in 1933. In his *Miracles of Mary,* Michael S. Durham writes that "the Virgin Mary has appeared more than twenty-one thousand times in the past ten centuries." The French paper *Le Monde* even said there were twenty-one thousand claims of apparitions between 1976 and 1986!

Adding to the fascination of the phenomenon is the fact that the very idea of "apparitions" of a human person is peculiar to Christianity. Although there have been two claims of appearances of angels in the history of religions outside of Christianity (Islam, Mormonism), reports of a human person sent by God appearing across history with a message for the world is quite simply unique to Marian apparitions. Neither Hinduism nor any of the other world religions has any tradition or even concept of such a phenomenon. Thus reports and claims of Marian apparitions stand in a class of their own without analogy or replication in the history of religions.

Despite the diversity in time and place of her reported appearances, the Virgin's messages have been remarkably consistent and also universal in import. The focus in all the apparitions has been God: conversion to God, salvation in God, a life filled with God (through prayer, fasting, penance, reconciliation, communion) — and the rejection of all that separates us from God (sin of every kind) with a warning of the dire consequences of separation from God. And the God she directs us to is the Triune God: the Father, the Son, and the Holy Spirit. Distinctive features of her own relationship with each of the Three Persons are emphasized in one way or another in the different apparitions.

Certain common characteristics (although there are exceptions even here) are found in the major apparitions with a worldwide focus, which we might call the archetypal modern apparitions: the recipients are most often peasant children; during an apparition, the visionary is visibly transformed and enters into a state of ecstasy in which he or she is demonstrably oblivious to sensory stimuli including flames, needle piercing, and loud noises but is seen communicating with someone invisible to observers; the visionaries are given messages to transmit to the world; the visionaries also receive "secrets" that they are either to keep to themselves or reveal only to an appointed person (La Salette, Lourdes, Fatima, Medjugorje); there is initial skepticism from local administrative and ecclesiastical authorities; there is some "lasting sign" left behind that testifies to the truth of the apparition; the apparition site continues to draw multitudes of pilgrims.

It might be asked why devotions to the Virgin are often centered on a particular apparition and the narrative, message, title, and sometimes image associated with that apparition. If she is the "universal" mother, why is she tied to a particular locality (Guadalupe or Fatima, Quito or Walsingham)? The answer is found in the mystery of the Incarnation of God in Jesus Christ. The Creator of space and time could be known by His creation only by localizing Himself in a particular island of space and time: as "Jesus of Nazareth" who "suffered under Pontius Pilate." The All-Holy manifests Itself through specific holy places and times and things. "The particular conveys the universal, and what is universal is rooted in what is particular. This appears to be a principle of God's working with us. It is expressed in the incarnation," writes Jeremy Sheehy, the principal of St. Stephen's House, Oxford, an Anglican theological college, "The use of the different geographical titles of our Lady is then a perfectly natural consequence of this principle. This is what, I think, David Jones was getting at when he said, 'She's a rare one for locality.' " In fact, "To speak of, for instance, Our Lady of Walsingham, speaks to us of her presence in particular places, and in each particular place." The remembrance of Mary's appearance at a particular place is therefore a reminder of her presence at every particular place in which her children are present.

This book comprises three major sections: first, we consider the various issues surrounding the question of Marian apparitions including their relation to the Old and New Testaments and to the ancient Fathers, liturgies, and Councils of the undivided Church, the basis for belief in the accredited apparitions and a brief history of the apparitions and their impact on world history; second, we view a portrait gallery of the Virgin's appearances across the world and history; and third, we review brief accounts of the major apparitions followed by the exact text of the words of the Virgin in her major apparitions (the apparitions are divided into three categories, depending on their duration and the nature of their messages). In four appendices, we first assess the basis of belief in her apparitions as it relates to scientific, philosophical, and theological methodologies; second, we consider the question of the existence of God since the assertion that the Virgin in her apparitions is God-sent assumes that God exists; third, we analyze the basis for affirming the historical reality of Jesus Christ since, in talking of the Virgin as witness, we affirm that she is a witness to her Son; finally, we examine the biblical and theological issues relating to the perpetual virginity of Mary since this ancient doctrine is assumed in any description of her as the Virgin.

In this volume we restrict ourselves of necessity to a certain body of apparitions, those that have been investigated and validated by contemporary ecclesiastical and, in some cases civil, authorities. There are two reasons for this. First, the sheer number of reported apparitions (over twenty thousand) is such as to make the task of winnowing the credible from the fraudulent the work of a lifetime. Second, even if time and talent were available, the data in many cases is not. The overwhelming majority of these claims were never formally investigated; neither were relevant records assembled and preserved. Consequently, it is all but impossible today to determine their veracity. The mere fact that someone claims to see a vision or "hear" an inner voice from an external source (called a locution) does not thereby confer any validity to the claim. We face not simply the danger of fraud and self-deception but also of diabolic deception, of which the recipient may or may not be conscious.

The great modern apparitions that have been "approved" or thoroughly investigated, on the other hand, have been very carefully evaluated using relevant scientific and theological methodologies. The "secular" historian David Blackbourn in his investigation of the Marpingen apparitions notes that "for all historians of the subject, clerical approval has created superior documentation." The distinguished Lutheran historian Jaroslav Pelikan writes in *Mary through the Centuries* that "the miraculous powers of the Virgin of Lourdes and the Virgin of Fatima have received certification at the highest level of authority." So here we focus simply on apparitions which have gone through the winnowing process instituted by civil and ecclesiastical authorities of the day. The premodern apparitions considered here were also subjected to a certain level of investigation, but their inclusion is primarily based on the kind of "signs" and fruits associated with them — it is these signs and fruits that help provide at least supporting authentication of the apparition claim.

Thus all the apparitions studied here have been judged "worthy of belief" by ecclesiastical authorities or are currently still under investigation. Two apparitions in this second category are Medjugorje, Bosnia, and Naju, South Korea. In an interview transcribed in the appendix, Cardinal Joseph Ratzinger, prefect of the Vatican's Congregation for the Doctrine of the Faith, stated to me that the Medjugorje phenomenon is still in progress and no final verdict (from the standpoint of the Catholic Church) can be made until the phenomenon has ceased and all the evidence is available. This means that the Church has neither approved nor condemned the reported apparition. But the empirical evidence generated in the investigation of Medjugorje by scientists and others can certainly be evaluated by any reasonable person (and in the interview, the cardinal distinguishes between the study of empirical evidence and the Church's role of pastoral governance). Like Medjugorje, Naju is another instance of an ongoing phenomenon, one that transcends the regional horizon and has attracted both international and Vatican interest. In fact, in a recent published interview, the secretary of the Congregation for the Doctrine of the Faith, Archbishop Tarcisio Bertone, stated that "one should consider Medjugorje as a Sanctuary, a Marian shrine, in the same way as Czestochowa."

Not all the apparitions considered here are Catholic in provenance. Several have been validated by Eastern or Oriental Orthodox authorities. Many others were accepted by the undivided Church.

These self-imposed limitations dictate the absence of certain well-known apparitions and locutions. There is no study, for instance, of Garabandal, Spain. The phenomenon in question ceased in the 1960s, and the local bishop has chosen to keep its files "closed." Without making any judgment on its authenticity or lack thereof, the present study cannot therefore consider it. Again, there is no study of any reported apparition in the United States. The two most famous, Bayside, New York, and Necedah, Wisconsin, were roundly condemned by church authorities in the United States and, even without these condemnations, the data available on them does not inspire any confidence in their authenticity. No judgment, positive or negative, is made on the many other current apparition claims in the United States simply because the official investigative machinery has not been deployed in evaluating them. There is no study either of the reported locutions received by the famous Fr. Stefano Gobbi, who, it is said, has traveled to more cities and countries than any other living person spreading the locution messages, because this is an inquiry into apparitions and not locutions.

A substantial number of the introductory chapters are spent on the Blessed Virgin Mary, the subject of the apparitions. This book is not intended to be a theological treatise, but it seems obvious that we cannot understand either the apparitions or the apparition messages until we have a better idea of the identity and role of the alleged messenger. Among Christians today, the status of the Virgin is as controversial as the truth of Marian apparitions, and so there is no choice but to take this question head on. We cannot understand the Virgin or her messages without knowing what the Bible and the Fathers, liturgies, and Councils of the ancient Church have said about her. The scriptural understanding of Mary is the scriptural understanding given us by the Fathers, ancient liturgies and Councils. If we reject that understanding then consistency demands that we also reject their understanding of such doctrines as the Blessed Trinity or the two natures and one Person in Christ. These latter doctrines are not taught in so many words by Scripture, but the people who were closest to the human authors of Scripture understood these authors to be teaching certain doctrines about the Triune God, the God-man, and the Blessed Virgin. These doctrines stand or fall together: picking and choosing is neither logically nor historically defensible.

We cannot, then, begin to understand Marian apparitions without understanding what the Christians who "wrote" and first interpreted Scripture taught about Mary, for it is this Mary that is the subject of all the accredited apparitions. From the teachings of the Fathers, Councils, and first liturgies we observe that they saw the New Testament revealing a Mary who was the Immaculate (Constantinople III), All-holy (Nicaea II), Perpetually Virgin (Constantinople III) Mother of God (Ephesus, Chalcedon), Mother of Humanity and Intercessor before the Trinity (Nicaea II); she was the New Eve with Jesus the New Adam and, as New Eve, Mother of all Christians. The defining paradigm for Marian apparitions is Revelation 12, and the Marian interpretation of this is defended here (if something so obvious needs defense). Mary's intercession for her children was also viewed in the context and against the background of the Genesis 3–Revelation 12 theme of the conflict between the infernal serpent and the Woman and her Seed.

Those who take the time to study the writings on the Virgin Mary of the Fathers, Councils, and liturgies will be astonished to discover that the messages from the great apparitions simply echo the words of these ancient authorities.

The startling coincidence of theme and message between the apparitions and the "Ancients" reminds us of a statement made in a totally different context. In his *God and the Astronomers,* the astrophysicist Robert Jastrow noted that many of the latest developments in modern astronomy seemed to have quasi-theological implications. So much so, he said in a famous passage, when the scientist who lived with faith in the power of reason scales the mountain of ignorance and clambers over the final rock "he is greeted by a band of theologians who have been sitting there for centuries." Those who study the purported statements of the Virgin in the apparitions and then turn to the ancient writings about her will find too that they are "greeted by a band of Fathers, Councils, and liturgies who have been sitting there for centuries."

Returning to the "noumenon" of Marian apparitions, or rather their raison d'être, we cannot help seeing that the apparitions of the last two hundred years are like majestic movements in a grand symphony racing as crescendos to a climax. These modern apparitions retain such classical features as the request to build a church or chapel and the disclosure of a healing spring. But now there is a new immediacy and poignancy as themes that were last heard in the second- and third-century Fathers and liturgies move to the foreground: suddenly it is the work of the New Eve and the New Adam and the coming of a New Heaven and a New Earth that is the fulcrum on which modern history turns and is to turn.

The great teaching of Irenaeus and all subsequent Church Fathers is that history — under divine direction — repeats itself but in an equal and opposite manner! This is the gist of his teaching about recapitulation and recirculation. This inverse parallelism shows itself first in the contrast between Adam and Eve and Jesus and Mary: as the evil angel seduces Eve to disobey God and Eve in turn persuades Adam to open the doors of damnation, so a good angel comes to Mary with a divine command that she obeys and thus gives birth to the Jesus who opens the doors to redemption. She is the New Eve and Jesus the New Adam.

But the parallelism of Adam and Eve and Christ and Mary does not cease with their individual acts of obedience and disobedience. These acts had cosmic effects. With the original sin of Adam (caused by Eve) the human race and all of creation were thrown into decay and destruction. With the redemptive death of Christ (in which His Mother sorrowfully participated as Simeon had described), the human race and all of creation were called to enter a new splendor even greater than the perfection present before the Fall when everything is brought together "under Christ, as head, everything in the heavens and everything on earth" (Eph. 1:10). The Christian message is that God does not lose, that His plans always bear fruit. If humanity fell through a man and a woman, humanity would be saved through a man and a woman. If Adam and Eve left the Eden that God had planned for them and their progeny, then the new Adam and the new Eve would take their offspring into a new Eden infinitely more joyous than the first Eden, for here all of creation is transformed by the very life of God. In the Christian dispensation, all of human history is moving inexorably toward this great climactic consummation when "all things [are] to be reconciled through him [Christ] and for him, everything in heaven and everything on earth" (Col. 1:19–20). And as Mary brought Christ into the world in His first coming and suffered with Him to the end, she likewise prepares the way for His coming reign when the divine will is to be done on earth as it is in Heaven.

This is the reign of the King of Hearts, and so the Queen of Hearts must prepare the hearts of all humanity for entry into their Kingdom. The metaphor of the heart embodies love: the Immaculate Heart is the love of Mary for her children; the Sacred Heart is the Savior's love for the "adopted" brothers and sisters she brings to Him (whether or not they are aware of her intercession). It is fitting indeed that we should talk of hearts in this context since the innermost truth about reality is the love of the Three Persons for each other and for all of creation. This love manifests itself to humankind through the love of Jesus (the Sacred Heart) and the love of Mary (the Immaculate Heart). And as Mary's yes to the angel prepared the world for the first coming of her Son, so she prepares the faithful to say yes to the coming of the Kingdom of her Son. This is the coming Era of Peace that is a fundamental theme of the modern apparitions.

The Era of Peace is not the "millennium" of the millennialists; neither is it the Second Coming. It is the New Heaven and the New Earth of Ephesians, Colossians, and the Fathers that follows a promised "purification" of the world, a purification that will be experienced as a "chastisement" by those who defy Christ.

The Mother of Christ wants all her children to be saved: she yearns to save them (through their acceptance of her Son) not simply from a temporal chastisement but an eternal chastisement that comes from their freely chosen everlasting separation from God. If we ask why the Virgin weeps in her apparitions and her images around the world, her answer is simple: Ultimately there is only one thing to be sad about in life and in eternity, and that is the eternal loss of a soul. As she has said more than once in her apparitions: she weeps because of the hardness of hearts, because of the worldwide suffering that will result from divine retribution and most of all because of the perdition awaiting those who will not obey.

Despite the apocalyptic themes that are a consistent feature of many of the modern apparitions, these themes are always complemented by a message of hope and ultimate triumph. On the one hand, we are warned about the catastrophic and inevitable consequences of the abuse of our free will and the rejection of God in sin ("If you do not change, you will hasten the arrival of a Third World War" — Nicaragua). On the other hand, we are offered a way to avert or delay these consequences by repentance, reparation, or some supernaturally significant gesture (the consecration of Russia to the Immaculate Heart requested at Fatima, for instance; the proclamation of a dogma at Amsterdam). Instead of resigning ourselves to fatalism, we are exhorted to exercise our free will in making a difference. The faithful, no matter how few, can make a difference to the ultimate outcome. Ten people of good will were all that were required to save Sodom. In the Gospels, Jesus says the "end-times" would be shortened for the sake of the elect. Just as the Book of Revelation ends on a note of ultimate divine victory, the messages of the Virgin promise her triumph "in the end" and the final reign of her Son.

In the lives of the visionaries who are "victim souls" — Myrna of Damascus, Julia Kim of Korea, Agnes Sasagawa of Akita — a veil is drawn back where we see for ourselves the interaction of the natural and the supernatural realms, the effect of choices on our souls, the need for reparation through suffering. These are souls who, like St. Paul (Col. 1:24), willingly consent to suffer in reparation for the souls that are on the road to damnation. But no one suffers more than the Lord of all creation in His Sacred Heart followed by His Virgin Mother in her Immaculate Heart: for the divine Shepherd the loss of just one lamb is an infinitely tragic loss. Those who turn away from Him crucify Him again (Heb. 6:6), those who persecute His Church persecute Him (Acts 9:4), and His every suffering pierces the heart of His Mother (Luke 2:35). And so, until the end of history and time, the New Eve will appear to all her children to draw them to the New Adam so that they too can enter the New and Eternal Eden.

MONTAGE

The Witness of the Virgin throughout World History

1. Who Is the Virgin?

Just as the question of who Jesus was cannot be answered without reference to the Old Testament, the purported appearances and messages of the Virgin will make no sense if we know nothing about her depiction in the Bible and the primordial Christian community of faith. As the Church Fathers saw it, Scripture portrayed Mary as the New Eve whose obedience to God's command as delivered by the angel Gabriel opened the door to the coming of the New Adam — in contrast to the Old Eve whose disobedience to God's command under the influence of a fallen angel led the Old Adam to his fatal choice. For her oblation of herself she became a model for Christians who was universally venerated. Second, both in Scripture and in the Fathers, Mary is closely associated with the Holy Spirit. It was her overshadowing by the Holy Spirit that preceded the Virgin Birth. It is the Holy Spirit who is recorded as directly speaking through Elizabeth and Simeon in praising Mary. And it is surely significant that Scripture refers to Mary's presence at the descent of the Holy Spirit at Pentecost. Finally, it was Mary's compassionate request that led to her Son's first miracle at the beginning of His ministry, and so Mary's intercession especially as it relates to miracles was widely accepted.

The significance of Mary is above all as a link to her Son. The fundamental driving force of all Marian doctrine and devotion is the perception that it is only through her we can fully accept and appreciate both His divinity and His humanity. Her divine maternity — human mother of God the Son — is the most telling testimony to His true humanity. Her special status — immaculately conceived, perpetually virgin, assumed into Heaven, New Eve — presupposes and confirms His divinity. We know too that in the entire Bible, only two human persons beheld God in His supernatural splendor: Moses on Mount Sinai and Mary who was "overshadowed" by the Holy Spirit.

But the key to understanding Mary's apparitions is one obscure yet powerful verse in the Book of Revelation: "Then the dragon was enraged with the woman and went away to make war on the rest of her children, that is, all who obey God's commandments and bear witness for Jesus" (12:17). All those who "bear witness for Jesus," then, are children of the Woman. And who is the Woman? On the face of it, there can be little doubt that the Woman Clothed with the Sun in Revelation 12 is the Virgin Mary. For the text says earlier that she is the mother of "the son who was to rule all the nations with an iron scepter" (12:5). By reference to Psalm 2 and to the account of His ascension to Heaven (Rev. 12:6), it is apparent that the son is Jesus. Also the dragon is referenced (12:9) to "the primeval serpent known as the devil or Satan" of Genesis 3. Revelation 12 is thus linked to Genesis 3, which refers to the future conflict between the serpent and the Woman and her Son. Historically, Christians (including Martin Luther) have seen Genesis 3 as a prophecy of the coming of Christ and His Mother and their war with Satan. This dovetails with the Revelation 12 account of the war between Christ and His Mother on the one side and Satan on the other (the recently released International Bible Commentary notes that Rev. 12:17 is a clear reference to the messianic text of Gen. 3:15).

Some have tried to say that the Woman here is merely allegorical, perhaps she symbolizes Israel or the Church. But this is at best a second layer of meaning since consistency (as some scholars point out) demands that the Son be treated like His Mother. Either both are mere symbols or they are both real individuals (not one a symbol and the other real). It is unlikely too that Christ would be seen here as an offspring of either Israel or the Church. First, He had been rejected by Israel and so Israel would not be the mother of those who witness to Him, and, second, the Church springs from Him, not vice versa. The Woman is not a spirit because spirits do not give birth to children or need physical nourishment (Rev. 12:6). Thus the Woman Clothed with the Sun is Mary, and Revelation 12 is an account of the first Marian apparition (after the death of the Virgin)!

Revelation 12:17 is doubly important because here we see that the Woman is the mother of all who "bear witness for Jesus." Thus, she is the mother of all Christians (again acknowledged by Luther) and like any other mother comes to the aid of her children when they are in need, as we see in the great Marian apparitions in history. Moreover, she who is the mother of all those who witness to Jesus has historically been the greatest of the witnesses!

The great apparition scholar René Laurentin suggests that Revelation 12 seems to foretell apparitions because the Mother of the Messiah appears in the heavens but also shows herself present on earth and in the struggles of her children (Rev. 12:17). He notes too that in many of her famous apparitions — from Guadalupe to the Miraculous Medal to Medjugorje — the Virgin appears clothed with the sun and crowned with stars as in Revelation 12.

In a nutshell, to grasp the nature and significance of Marian apparitions we must first understand that Mary is the New Eve who is united with her Son the New Adam in the war with the dragon, second, that she is the human vehicle most closely associated with the Holy Spirit, and, third, that she is the Mother of all Christians who comes to their aid at all times and places. This is the underlying rationale and dynamic behind the appearances of the Virgin in history.

Moreover, human beings are creatures of flesh and blood. We have to touch, see, and feel. We are not angels. That is why God became man, and why He came to us in His Risen Body. That is why He manifests the means of salvation through the material: in baptism, for instance, a salvific event acceptable to all Christians. Marian apparitions are simply an extension of the divine response to the human need to touch and feel and see the Holy.

2. The Words of the Virgin in Scripture

One astounding but little noticed feature of the biblical narratives is the fact that every word uttered by Mary — and these were numerically few in number — had momentous consequences in the divine plan of salvation.

When she said to the angel Gabriel, "Let what you have said be done to me," the Holy Spirit "came upon" her and she became the Mother of the Redeemer of humanity.

When she greeted her cousin Elizabeth, the Holy Spirit Himself spoke to her through Elizabeth saying that at the sound of Mary's voice, "the child in my womb leaped for joy" — an event that has historically been regarded as the sanctification of John the Baptist in the womb.

When the inspired Elizabeth praised her for the act of faith and obedience that caused her to be "blessed," Mary responded with the proclamation of praise we call the Magnificat. Two things should be noted about this hymn: first, Mary attributes her glorification to God and, second, she says "all generations will call her blessed" because of what God has done for her (and God bestowed this blessing, we find from Elizabeth's statement just before, because Mary "believed"). Those who believe that Scripture is inspired by God will acknowledge that, in proclaiming the divine decree that she is to be called blessed, Mary is not showing a lack of humility. In praising Mary, we are implicitly praising God's infinite generosity and love in working through the humble and the lowly and in richly blessing those who obey Him. Jesus Himself has told us not to hide our light under a bushel for, in bearing testimony to the blessing we have received, we bear testimony to God.

Finally, in the most famous wedding in history, her Son changes His own timeline for His ministry in response to her words, "They have no wine." Mary already knows He will do what she requests and tells the servants, "Do whatever he tells you." The miracle that follows not only begins the public ministry of Jesus but also causes His disciples "to believe in him."

Once our minds and hearts focus on these words of Mary, the Mary we see in the apparitions will be seen as a mirror-image of the "blessed" handmaid of Scripture and the messages of the apparitions will be heard as an echo of the voice that resonates so momentously in Scripture. In the apparitions, Mary speaks of three things: we are reminded of the importance of doing God's will ("Let what you have said be done to me," "Do whatever he tells you"); we are told about her own key role in the divine plan, and, in telling us this, she simply restates what she proclaimed in the divinely inspired Magnificat; we see her referring to her own vocation of intercession, a ministry she began at Cana.

The importance that Mary's words have in Scripture is matched by the importance attributed to her at key events in the biblical narrative: at the presentation in the Temple the Holy Spirit inspires Simeon to say to Mary that, when her Son is rejected, "a sword will pierce your own soul too"; at Calvary her Son establishes her as mother of all believers, "This is your mother"; at the birth of the Church the author of Acts notes that "the mother of Jesus" is present when the Holy Spirit descends on all the believers gathered in prayer; and in Revelation 12 we are given the glorious vision of her as the mother of all those "who obey God's commandments and bear witness for Jesus."

When you couple the impact of her words in the biblical narratives with her presence at key salvation events, it should be apparent that none of her accredited apparitions are in any sense inconsistent or incompatible with the Mary who appears and speaks in Scripture. Marian apparitions make Scripture come alive in history.

3. The Veneration of the Virgin

One consistent characteristic of Marian apparitions is the impetus they lend to veneration of the Virgin. This aspect of apparitions is objectionable to those critics who consider such veneration "unbiblical."

But whether a practice is biblical or not is decided not by one's own historically isolated interpretation of the biblical narratives but by a study of how the Christian Church interpreted these narratives throughout history and across the world. On the question of the veneration of the Virgin (as opposed to the adoration which one owes to God alone), the historical record is unmistakably clear: Christians from the beginning and across the Christian world interpreted Scripture as not only permitting but demanding veneration of the one whom all generations are to call blessed.

We know, from five different sources, that Christians have historically thought and felt that Marian veneration is warranted:

1. The catacombs of the Christian martyrs of the second and third centuries not only show images representing the scriptural stories but also images of the Virgin in which her mediation is invoked for protection and defense. The *Sub Tuum Praesidium* prayer — "We fly to your patronage, O holy Mother of God; despise not our petitions in our necessities, but deliver us always from all dangers, O glorious and blessed Virgin" — is certainly at least as old as the third century (this is known from the discovery of a papyrus from that period).

2. The second-century apocryphal gospels and the fifth-century *transitus mariae* narratives are obviously fantasies with no basis in fact. They do, however, show us something important: the idea that the Virgin was the most important participant in salvation history after her Son was so rooted in the minds and hearts of the faithful that some of them felt compelled to invent stories about Jesus and Mary that paid homage to their exalted status. What is important here is not the story but the state of mind that led to the invention of the story: these stories were written by and for people who already took the adoration of Jesus and the veneration of Mary for granted.

3. The writings of all of the Church Fathers, the teachers of the earliest Christian communities who interpreted Scripture for the faithful, bear eloquent testimony to Marian veneration. In their scripturally derived understanding of Mary as the New Eve and the New Ark of the Covenant (see the next two chapters), the Fathers established an unassailable basis for Marian veneration that was accepted for centuries by the Christians of East and West.

4. Perhaps the truest witness to the faith of the believing community is the language of their prayer and liturgical celebration. All of the ancient liturgies, even those before the Council of Ephesus, testify to the firm belief of the Christian faithful in the veneration of Mary and the invocation of

her intercession. The Eastern liturgies, the most ancient of them all since Christianity originated in the East, resonate with hymns, odes, and prayers to the Virgin. Thousands of the canons in the Byzantine liturgy are written in honor of the Virgin: "While we sing the glories of thy Son, we praise thee, too, O Mother of God, living Temple of the Godhead. O purest One, do not despise the petitions of the sinner." "Hail, Mother of God, Virgin full of grace, Refuge and Protection of the human race." The Alexandrian liturgy is also replete with Marian veneration and invocation: "Hail to thee, O Virgin, the very and true Queen; hail glory of our race." "Hail Mary! We beseech thee, holy one, full of glory, ever Mother of God, Mother of Christ, lift up our prayers to thy beloved Son, that He may forgive us our sins." The Antiochene liturgy, perhaps the oldest of the ancient liturgies, includes the liturgy of St. James. The Marian invocations in this latter liturgy are profoundly moving, for example, the following recited during the breaking of the Host, "My blessed Lady Mary, beseech with thine only Begotten that he be appeased through thy prayers and perform mercy on us all." In the Western liturgies, Marian veneration and invocation appears in the liturgy of the Mass and also forms a prominent part of regular prayers (offices) and feasts. These liturgies celebrate all of the privileges of the Virgin ranging from her Divine Maternity to her Virginity, Sanctity, Assumption, and Mediation.

5. Finally, the great Councils of the undivided Church proclaim the convictions held in common by all Christians for the first ten centuries about the role of Mary in salvation history. No Christian can reject these Councils since to reject them would ipso facto mean rejecting the teachings of the Councils about such articles of faith as the Holy Trinity and the two natures and one person in Christ. The Trinity is not a word used in the Bible, but it is an interpretation of certain biblical passages ratified by the Councils of the Church. To believe in the Trinity is implicitly to accept the authority of the Councils that taught the doctrine of the Trinity. If one accepts the doctrine of the Trinity, then one has also to accept the Marian doctrines taught by the Councils — since both doctrines are ultimately accepted on the authority of the bodies that taught them. Among the Councils, the Third Ecumenical Council at Ephesus (431), which taught that Mary was *Theotokos,* Mother of God, gave a new doctrinal momentum to the great wave of Marian veneration and invocation that had been building up in previous centuries. After this Council, more churches were named after her, new prayers were addressed to her, and great feasts in her honor were introduced into the Church's calendar. The language of the first seven Ecumenical Councils, accepted as authoritative by Protestants, Catholics, and Orthodox alike, gives some idea of the reverence that Christians had for their Mother: the Fifth Ecumenical Council (Second Council of Constantinople, 553) describes her as "the holy, glorious and ever-Virgin Mary." "The Virgin Mary" was "really and truly the Mother of God" says the Third Council of Constantinople (680). Finally, and most significantly,

the Seventh Ecumenical Council (the Second Council of Nicaea, 787) proclaims, "The Lord, the apostles, and the prophets have taught us that we
must venerate in the first place the Holy Mother of God, who is above all
the heavenly powers. If any one does not confess that the holy, ever virgin
Mary, really and truly the Mother of God, is higher than all creatures visible
and invisible, and does not implore with a sincere faith, her intercession,
given her powerful access to our God born of her, let him be anathema."

The ancient veneration of the Virgin has been lost in modern times. Did this
loss come about from a rediscovery of what the Bible teaches? The answer is
no since the ancient authors were familiar not just with the New Testament
narratives but with the authors of these narratives. Moreover, if the Christian
community had been wrong for all these centuries in its fundamental beliefs
about Mary, then there is no reason to believe it was right on any other doctrine,
including the doctrine of the Trinity.

The veneration of the Virgin extends to veneration of her images for, as the
Seventh Ecumenical Council taught,

[We] define with all certitude and accuracy that just as the figure of the
precious and life-giving Cross, so also the venerable and holy images, as
well in painting and mosaic as of other fit materials, should be set forth in
the holy churches of God, and on the sacred vessels and on the vestments
and on hangings and in pictures both in houses and by the wayside, to wit,
the figure of our Lord God and Savior Jesus Christ, of our spotless Lady,
the Mother of God, of the honorable angels, of all saints and of all pious
people. . . . For the honor which is paid to the image passes on to that which
the image represents, and he who reveres the image reveres in it the subject
represented.

The Old Testament condemns idolatry, the worship of graven images and the
attribution of deity to any man-made object, but the very book that condemns
such idolatry also has Yahweh commanding the construction of images of angels
(as do other books of the Bible). Martin Luther's interpretation of Old Testament
passages on idolatry is helpful, "Nothing else can be drawn from the words:
'Thou shalt have no strange gods before me' except what relates to idolatry.
But where pictures or sculptures are made without idolatry, the making of such
things is not forbidden." Luther also said, "If I have a painted picture on the wall
and I look upon it without idolatry, that is not forbidden to me and should not
be taken away from me." Also relevant here is that curious incident in Numbers
21:7–9: " 'Intercede for us with Yahweh to save us from these serpents.' Moses
interceded for the people, and Yahweh answered him, 'Make a fiery serpent
and put it on a standard. If anyone is bitten and looks at it, he shall live.' So
Moses fashioned a bronze serpent which he put on a standard, and if anyone
was bitten by a serpent, he looked at the bronze serpent and lived.' " This event
was important enough for Jesus to refer to it in the context of His own mission
("as Moses lifted up the serpent in the desert," John 3:14).

In her apparitions, the Virgin is taking us back to the ancient teachings and practices of the undivided Church. As she said in Amsterdam, "I am not bringing a new doctrine. I am merely restating old themes."

4. *The Return of the New Eve*

The messages of the Marian apparitions revolve around a theme that was fundamental to the first pastors and teachers of Christianity, namely, the parallels between Mary and Eve and the paths to damnation and salvation. This theme sounds foreign to many Christian ears only because so few know the "faith of the Fathers" and the text of the ancient liturgies. If nothing else, the apparitions of the Virgin herald the return of a precious memory.

The first, unanimous, and single most important teaching of the Fathers of the Christian Church about Mary, starting with St. Justin the Martyr, 100–165 A.D., is that Mary is the New Eve. The contrast between Eve and Mary, Adam and Christ, the evil angel in Eden and the good angel at the Annunciation, and the Tree of the Knowledge of Good and Evil and the Tree of the Cross, lies at the heart of the history of salvation. This is the hidden and yet obvious truth in Scripture that became foundational to the theology and worship of the first Christians. Scholars today point out that Justin's understanding of the Virgin Mary is taken exclusively from Scripture (which is not to say that tradition has no value). The distinguished Lutheran church historian Jaroslav Pelikan notes that Fathers like Irenaeus, when writing about Mary as the New Eve, do not even try to argue for this interpretation since it was already considered a part of the basic body of Christian belief.

The history of salvation in the Judeo-Christian revelation is built around covenants between God and humanity. The idea of a covenant entails an agreement freely entered into by two parties, on the one side God and on the other humanity. Pelikan tells us that, in the Christian vision, two of the key players on the human side were Eve and Mary. This is the message of the Fathers as illustrated in the citations below from Bernard Buby's *The Marian Heritage of the Early Church*.

Justin wrote:

> He became man by the Virgin in order that the disobedience which proceeded from the serpent might receive its destruction in the same manner in which it derived its origin. For Eve, who was a virgin and undefiled, having conceived by the word of the serpent, brought forth disobedience and death. But the Virgin Mary received faith and joy, when the angel Gabriel announced the good tidings to her that the Spirit of the Lord would come upon her, and the power of the Most High would overshadow her, wherefore also the Holy One begotten of her is the Son of God, and she replied, "Be it done unto me according to your word." (*Dialogue with Trypho*)

Irenaeus of Lyons (140–202):

> [Eve] having become disobedient, was made the cause of death, both to herself and to the entire human race; so also did Mary, having a man be-

trothed [to her], and being nevertheless a virgin, by yielding obedience, become the cause of salvation, both to herself and the whole human race. (*Against Heresies III*)

And just as it was through a virgin who disobeyed that man was stricken and fell and died, so too it was through the Virgin, who obeyed the word of God, that man resuscitated by life received life.... Adam was necessarily to be restored in Christ, that mortality be absorbed in immortality, and Eve in Mary, that a virgin, become the advocate of a virgin, should undo and destroy virginal disobedience by virginal obedience. (*Proof of the Apostolic Teaching*)

Tertullian (155–240):

God recovered His image and likeness in a procedure similar to that in which He had been robbed of it by the devil. For it was while Eve was still a virgin that the word of the devil crept in to erect an edifice of death. Likewise, through a Virgin, the Word of God was introduced to set up a structure of life.

As Eve had believed the serpent, so Mary believed the angel. The delinquency which the one occasioned by believing, the other by believing effaced. (*The Flesh of Christ*)

Athanasius of Alexandria (295–373):

Eve listened to the suggestion of the serpent and tribulation descended upon all. And you have inclined your ears to the supplications of Gabriel, and penitence flourished. (*De Virginitate*)

Ephraem of Syria (306–73):

Eve brought on the sin, and the debt was reserved for the Virgin Mary, that she might pay the debts of her mother, and tear up the handwriting under which were groaning all generations. (*On the Annunciation of the Mother of God*)

Cyril of Jerusalem (315–86):

Through Eve yet virgin came death, through a virgin, or rather from a virgin, must Life appear; that as the serpent beguiled the one, so to the other Gabriel might bring good tidings. (*De Christo Incarnato*)

Ambrose of Milan (339–97):

It was through a man and a woman that flesh was cast from paradise; it was through a virgin that flesh was linked to God. (*Epistle 63*)

Eve is called mother of the human race, but Mary mother of salvation. (*Sermon 45*)

Augustine of Hippo (354–430):

> The first man, by persuasion of a virgin, fell; the Second Man, with consent of a Virgin, triumphed. By a woman the devil brought in death; by a woman the Lord brought in life. An evil angel of old seduced Eve, a good angel likewise encouraged Mary.... What Eve did by her ill-believing, Mary by her good-believing blotted out. From a woman was the beginning of sin, and on her account we all die, from a woman was the beginning of faith, and on her account are we repaired unto everlasting life. (*Sermon 28*)

Peter Chrysologus (400–450):

> Why Christ wanted to be born is this: that just as death came to all through Eve, so through Mary life might return to all. (*Sermon 99*)

Hesychius of Jerusalem (d. circa 451):

> See how great and of what kind is the dignity of the Virgin Mother of God? For the Only begotten Son of God the world's Creator was born as an infant of her, re-formed Adam, sanctified Eve, drove out the dragon, and opened Paradise, keeping sure the seal of her womb. (*Oratio de Deiparae Laudibus*)

Amphilochilis of Iconium (circa 340–94):

> Woman was defended by woman, the first opened the way to sin, the present one served to open the way to justice. The former followed the advice of the serpent, the latter brought forth the slayer of the serpent and brought to light the author of light. The former introduced sin through the tree, the latter brings in grace through the tree. (*Patrologia Graeca,* vol. 46)

The Mary-Eve typology was not just a theological metaphor but entered into the liturgical celebrations and devotion of the early Christians and became a part of all the ancient liturgies. It was in effect a fundamental teaching of the Church and underlies all the doctrines that we call Marian; for instance, she who would begin the process of reversing the consequences of original sin could not be subject to these consequences (conception in sin, corruption of the grave). Moreover, the importance of the Annunciation — of Mary's yes — for human salvation was not highlighted simply by theologians and pastors. It served as one of the central and persistent themes of artistic creation inspired by the Christian story. Almost all the greatest artists of Christendom have made their own contributions to the depiction of the Annunciation.

But Mary's role in salvation history did not end with the Annunciation. On the one hand, she is permanently the New Eve just as her Son will always be the New Adam. On the other, we see that she is mysteriously present with the New Adam at precisely the times most crucial to the accomplishment of redemption. When the "cause of salvation" offers up her infant Son at the Temple, it is prophesied that a sword will pierce her soul. This prophecy was fulfilled, said the Fathers and the faithful, when her offering came to a climax on Calvary and she became for all time the Sorrowful Mother. The consent given at the Annunciation extended through the Presentation at the Temple to the Sacrifice on Calvary.

As Eve was associated with Adam at all stages of the Fall, so also the New Eve was associated with the New Adam at every step of the road to redemption. The Fathers recognized that the Incarnation cannot be separated from the Cross and redemption, and in calling Mary the New Eve they drew our attention to the singular role she played in the redemptive mission of God Incarnate. Referring to the ancient Church's understanding of Mary as the New Eve, the Anglican theologian Eric Mascall wrote in 1963 (in *The Blessed Virgin Mary: Essays by Anglican Writers*) that Mary can be "described as coredemptrix in order to bring out the fact that, while Mary has a real part in the redemptive process, because she is morally and physically associated in it with her Son, yet her part is, and must be, essentially subordinate and ancillary to his." "Co" is taken from the Latin term *cum* meaning "with." "The force of the prefix *co* is to indicate not equality but subordination, as when St. Paul tells his Corinthian disciples that 'we are God's fellow-workers,' his *synergoi,* his *co*-operators." More recently (in his *Mary for All Christians*), another great Anglican thinker, John Macquarrie, noted that Mary symbolizes the "perfect harmony between the divine will and the human response, so that it is she who gives meaning to the expression 'coredemptrix.' " To the extent that any Christian shares in the redeeming work of Christ, he or she is a coredeemer; the classic statement of this truth comes from St. Paul's Epistle to the Colossians: "It makes me happy to suffer for you, as I am suffering now, and in my own body to do what I can to make up all that has still to be undergone by Christ for the sake of his body, the Church" (Col. 1:24). Macquarrie notes that Mary's coredemptive "contribution was unique" because through her willing acceptance she became the Mother of the Redeemer. (Also, Mary's role as coredemptrix does not eliminate the fact that she herself had to be redeemed; it is believed that her redemption took place at conception through the redemptive effects of her Son's death, which could go backward and forward in time, so that she was not affected by original sin; no other satisfactory explanation can be given of the term *kecharitomene* used of her, by the angel Gabriel, which meant that she had already been transformed by grace before the birth of her Son.)

To be the New Eve is inevitably to be the partner of the New Adam. It is this truth taught by Scripture as the Fathers understood it and celebrated in the great liturgies of East and West that is also a key theme in the apparitions of the last two hundred years: the Immaculate Heart of Mary lays the groundwork for the reign of the Sacred Heart of Jesus, the Coredemptrix prepares the way for the Second Coming of the Redeemer. The sorrowing mother at Calvary revealed in one apparition that "from my Son's birth until His death, I was filled with grief."

In so many of the modern apparitions, she and her images are seen in tears: her tears are shed for the eternal loss of her spiritual children and for the pain that human sin continues to cause her Son. "Why do you persecute me?" asks the Lord of Saul, the killer of Christians. And Christians who fall away "have willfully crucified the Son of God and openly mocked him" (Heb. 6:6). Although the Virgin enjoys the essential beatitude of Heaven, as a human Mother her happiness is not complete without the happiness of her children, and hence this latter secondary joy will not be complete until the end of time.

The Virgin's identity as the New Eve, with its attendant and ancillary implications, was accepted by all Christians for the first fifteen hundred years of Christianity. Although it has been in eclipse in certain parts of the Christian world for the last five hundred years, one cannot reject this truth without throwing into question a whole host of other such truths. For instance, the doctrine of the Trinity is an interpretation of Scripture that is accepted because it emerged over centuries in the writings of the Fathers (the first major treatise on the divinity of the Holy Spirit was written in the fourth century when Athanasius wrote his *Epistolae ad Serapionem* in 360), the teaching of the Councils, and the worship of the liturgy. If one rejects the authority of these three pillars, then one cannot teach the doctrine of the Trinity as an authoritative Christian doctrine. But if one accepts their authority, then one cannot reject the doctrine of the New Eve.

Precisely because it is a true Christian doctrine that is of continuing significance in salvation history, this doctrine has been brought back to humanity in the modern Marian apparitions. The now-forgotten teaching of the Fathers, the Councils, and the liturgies is being handed down again but from another source: the New Eve herself.

5. The Recovery of the Ark

In some of her famous apparitions, the Virgin asks the visionary or visionaries to request the local ecclesiastical authority to build a church or chapel. In the apparitions at San Nicolás, Argentina, she explains the basis for this request by referring to Exodus 25:8: "They shall make a sanctuary for me, that I may dwell in their midst." In this passage, Yahweh is giving instructions to the Israelites for building the Ark of the Covenant by means of which He would be present to them.

This biblical reference from the Virgin is notable because it marks the recovery of another ancient doctrine: the Blessed Virgin Mary is the Ark of the New Covenant. The foundations for this doctrine were already laid in the New Testament. The verses that describe the Holy Spirit's "overshadowing" of Mary are mirror images of the Old Testament passage about Yahweh's coming into the tabernacle. "The Holy Spirit will come upon you and the power of the Most High will cover you with its shadow" (Luke 1:35). "The cloud covered the Tent of Meeting and the glory of Yahweh filled the tabernacle" (Exod. 40:34). Biblical scholars have argued that other verses concerning Mary in the Gospels of Luke and John parallel passages about the Ark of the Covenant in the Old Testament. Moreover, the description of the Ark of the Covenant in the Temple in Heaven is immediately followed by the vision of the Woman clothed with the Sun: "The sanctuary of God in heaven opened, and the ark of the covenant could be seen inside it.... Now a great sign appeared in heaven: a woman, adorned with the sun" (Rev. 11:19–12:1).

The biblical parallels were not lost on many of the Fathers as their statements here indicate (again, most of these excerpts come from Bernard Buby's *The Marian Heritage of the Early Church*).

Athanasius of Alexandria (295–373):

> O Ark of the covenant surrounded totally and purely on all sides with gold! You are the Ark containing all gold, the receptacle of the true manna, that is human nature wherein the divinity resides. (*De Virginitate*)

Hesychius of Jerusalem (d. circa 451):

> Arise, Lord, into Your rest, You and the Ark of Your sanctification, which is very evidently the Virgin Mother of God. For if You are the Pearl, with good reason is she the Ark. (*Sermon V, De S. Maria Deipara*)

Cyril of Alexandria (370–444):

> If we look back to the way of the Incarnation of the Only-begotten, we shall see that it is in the temple of the Virgin, as in an ark, that the Word of God took up His abode. (*De Adoratione in Spiritu et Veritate*)

Modestus, Patriarch of Jerusalem (d. 630):

> It was not an ark made by hands and plated with gold, but a living ark created by God, wholly luminous with the radiance of the all-holy and life-giving Spirit who had visited her. Within this ark there was no jar of manna and no tablets of the covenant, but instead the bestower of manna and of the promised blessings of eternity, the Lord of the new and the old covenants, who from this ark came into the world as a child and freed those who believe in him from the curse of the law. (Homily)

Proclus, Patriarch of Constantinople (d. 446):

> "The Most High has sanctified His own tabernacle" (Ps. 45:5). The Incarnate Word dwelled in a womb which He had created free from all that might be to His dishonor. (Homily)

The Akathistos hymn addresses Mary thus:

> Hail, Ark of the Holy Spirit's gilding!

Mary is the Ark of the New Covenant precisely because she is the *Theotokos*, Mother of God the Son, and *Panagia*, the All-Holy who is Spouse of God the Holy Spirit. Both truths have been defined by Ecumenical Councils of the undivided Church. The Ecumenical Council of Ephesus taught that "if anyone does not confess that God is truly Emmanuel, and that on this account the holy Virgin is the Mother of God (for according to the flesh she gave birth to the Word of God become flesh by birth), let him be anathema." The Seventh Ecumenical Council, the Second Council of Nicaea, formally addressed Mary by her ancient title *Panagia* meaning "all-holy"; the masculine form of this Greek word is *Panagion*, the title of the Holy Spirit. This same Council also decreed in so

many words what all the other Councils assumed: she is "higher than all creatures visible and invisible" and all Christians must "implore with a sincere faith
her intercession, given her powerful access to our God born of her." Mary's
mediation of God's grace is also taught by the Fathers and the liturgies of the
ancient Church. And the idea that Mary intercedes for us and mediates grace
is not only ancient but biblical.

Very few will deny that Abraham and Moses were mediators of God's grace
in Old Testament times (in view of the many biblical passages that support this
doctrine). It has often been shown that Mary in the New Testament serves not
simply as the New Eve but also typifies the roles of Abraham and Moses. Both
Abraham and Mary are called blessed because of their righteous actions and
through their actions all generations are blessed — and both offer their sons to
the Lord. When the Virgin at Cana says, "Do whatever he tells you" (John 2:6),
she is just as much a mediatrix to believers as Moses was to the Israelites who
tell him, "All that Yahweh has said, we will do" (Exod. 19:8).

The mediation of Mary is intrinsically maternal in nature: she is the most
perfect created image of the Father because only the Father and Mary have
generated the Son and by her cooperation in the Incarnation she "mediates" the
Redeemer of fallen humanity; she is also mother of all those who witness to
Christ (Rev. 12:17) for those who participate in the sonship of Christ (Gal. 4:4)
are adopted sons and daughters of His eternal Father and His human Mother.
Even when she is a mediator of her Son's power at Cana, this mediation is
maternal in nature, and it is a mediation that inspires faith in the Apostles.
Her mediation also arises from the biblically recorded intimacy of her union
with the Holy Spirit, which was acknowledged and celebrated by the Christian
community from the beginning.

The Bible does not teach that mediation by human beings ceases with death.
Jesus Himself tells us of Lazarus in Abraham's bosom after death. The Epistle
to the Hebrews and the Book of Revelation teach the intercessory activity of the
human spirits now with God: "A large quantity of incense was given to him to
offer with the prayers of all the saints on the golden altar that stood in front of
the throne; and so from the angel's hand the smoke of the incense went up in
the presence of God and with it the prayers of the saints" (Rev. 8:3–4).

1 Timothy 2:5 says, "For there is only one God, and there is only one mediator between God and mankind, himself a man, Christ Jesus, who sacrificed
himself as a ransom for them all." Mary's mediation, like the mediation of all
Christians (as described by the same Apostle in Col. 1:24 and elsewhere), is a
participation in this unique mediation of Christ. He alone is the unique Son of
God, but all Christians can and must participate in this Sonship as they can and
must participate in His unique Priesthood. So also, all are called to participate
in the unique mediation of the One Mediator. And just as her coredemptive participation in the work of the One Redeemer is qualitatively different from the
participation of other coredeemers in Christ, her maternal mediation is qualitatively different from the way in which other mediators participate in her Son's
mediation. Jesus is the unique and unrepeatable Redeemer and Mediator. He
is God and man. But all Christians are called to participate in His redemptive

activity and His mediation — and the first to do so was the New Eve who was uniquely also *Theotokos* (Mother of God) and *Panagia* (Spouse of the Spirit).

Both the Fathers and the ancient liturgies have taught the Virgin's mediation, as evident in earlier citations. Two final excerpts, one from Ephraem of Syria and the other from the Akathistos hymn, will convey the depth and fervor of the ancient Christian confidence in the Virgin's intercession and mediation. Ephraem of Syria:

> No standard of victory is stronger than your defense. Therefore, You who are altogether immaculate, and the world's mediatrix, with penitent heart, do I supplicate. In necessities I invoke your prompt protection, salutary next after God, and your secure and most powerful patronage — guilty though I be of many offenses — from the depth of your heart. My most holy Lady, Mother of God, and full of grace; glory of our common nature; dispenser of all good things; after the Trinity, mistress of all; after the Paraclete, another consoler; and after the Mediator, the whole world's mediatrix... as the Mother, then, of Him who alone is good and merciful, receive my most miserable soul, and graciously obtain through your mediation and defense that it be found at the right hand of your Only-begotten Son. (*Precationes ad Dieparam*)

The Akathistos hymn calls Mary the "gate of salvation," "the heavenly ladder by which God came down; the bridge that carries the earthborn to Heaven." This is a theme repeated and amplified in all the ancient liturgies.

Why then does the Virgin ask for churches and chapels at the sites of her apparitions? Because, as pilgrims can testify, these serve as oases of grace in the wilderness of the world. At these churches, the Holy Spirit distributes graces, the Son is adored and the Father is worshiped — and she whom all generations are to call blessed is venerated.

The apparitions of the Virgin in history are divinely decreed opportunities to recover the Ark of the New Covenant — an Ark that has been hidden from many Christians for nearly five hundred years.

6. Salvation: Not Fate but the Fiat of Faith

Perhaps as controversial as the role of Mary in Christian belief is the question of salvation itself. It is no exaggeration to say that wars have been fought over this issue, since it was the single most important disagreement that led to the Protestant Reformation and the subsequent division of Christian Europe. In the present day, numerous conferences and ecumenical groups have created a friendlier climate. For instance there are Anglican-Catholic, Lutheran-Catholic, and Evangelical-Catholic dialogues and other such initiatives studying areas of agreement and disagreement. The joint statements from these dialogues have at least created a better understanding of the other side's positions. We have gone beyond the harsh caricatures of the past.

The climax of the various dialogues came on October 31, 1999, with the historic "Joint Declaration on the Doctrine of Justification," in which the Lutheran World Federation and the Catholic Church announced that "on the basis of their dialogue the subscribing Lutheran churches and the Roman Catholic Church are now able to articulate a common understanding of our justification by God's grace through faith in Christ." The declaration noted,

> We confess together that good works — a Christian life lived in faith, hope, and love — follow justification and are its fruits. When the justified live in Christ and act in the grace they receive, they bring forth, in biblical terms, good fruit. Since Christians struggle against sin their entire lives, this consequence of justification is also for them an obligation they must fulfill. Thus both Jesus and the apostolic Scriptures admonish Christians to bring forth the works of love. When Catholics affirm the "meritorious" character of good works, they wish to say that, according to the biblical witness, a reward in heaven is promised to these works. Their intention is to emphasize the responsibility of persons for their actions, not to contest the character of those works as gifts, or far less to deny that justification always remains the unmerited gift of grace.

In its conclusion, the document proclaims that "The understanding of the doctrine of justification set forth in this Declaration shows that a consensus in basic truths of the doctrine of justification exists between Lutherans and Catholics."

It is commonly agreed by Catholics and Protestants that salvation was given by Jesus Christ and accepted in faith by the believer, that God's grace takes primacy over every human initiative and that we are able to live as the children of God only because of the gift of the Holy Spirit. Disagreement starts over the question of whether or not our freedom plays a role in our salvation. But this is not a disagreement between Catholics and Protestants since there are disagreements about this among Protestants (e.g., Calvinists and Wesleyans) and certainly there is the Orthodox position to consider as well. An appeal to the teaching of the Bible will not resolve the matter because the disagreement centers on two different understandings of a wide range of biblical verses.

While almost everyone agrees that God's grace draws us to Him and that we can be saved only because of His grace, we part company over the issue of whether or not we can say yes or no to God. To some Protestants no was never an option for those whom God has decided to save, and when He offers them His Grace, His offer is irresistible. The human response is entirely a divinely ordained action and so no merit attaches to it. This means that those whom God has not foreordained for salvation have been foreordained for damnation. The opposite view holds that God is an infinite Lover who thirsts for every human soul, that He moves Heaven and Earth to make salvation available to His creatures, that He gives every person sufficient grace to say *fiat*, yes, to Him. We can say yes to God because of the grace He gives us to say yes. But we can also say no. To say yes is the greatest, most praiseworthy decision of our lives — one which will bring us endless joy. We look to all those who have said yes as models who motivate us, and the greatest of these models is the maiden whose "yes" made her mother of her Savior. This latter view is the understanding of biblical teaching that we find in the teachings of Church Fathers and Councils.

The main foundation for the doctrine that our free decisions determine our eternal destiny is the teaching of Jesus:

> And there was a man who came to him and asked, "Master, what good deed must I do to possess eternal life?" Jesus said to him, " ...If you wish to enter into life, keep the commandments. ...If you wish to be perfect, go and sell what you own and give the money to the poor, and you will have treasure in heaven; then come, follow me." (Matt. 19:16–22)

> For every unfounded word men utter they will answer on Judgment day, since it is by your words you will be acquitted, and by your words condemned. (Matt. 12:37)

> In his anger the master handed him over to the torturers till he should pay all his debt. And that is how my heavenly Father will deal with you unless you each forgive your brother from your heart. (Matt. 18:34–5)

> You will be hated by all men on account of my name; but the man who stands firm to the end will be saved. (Matt. 10:22)

> For the Son of Man is going to come in the glory of his Father with his angels, and, when he does, he will reward each one according to his behavior. (Matt. 16:27)

> "I tell you solemnly, insofar as you neglected to do this to one of the least of these, you neglected to do it to me." And they will go away to eternal punishment, and the virtuous to eternal life. (Matt. 25:45–46)

> The hour is coming when the dead will leave their graves at the sound of his voice; those who did good will rise again for life; and those who did evil, to condemnation. (John 5:28–29)

> Very soon now, I shall be with you again, bringing the reward to be given to every man according to what he deserves. (Rev. 22:12)

Some have said that any attempt to focus on being good and holy is a deception of the devil, who tries to make us rely on our own good works for our salvation instead of focusing only on the all-sufficient atonement of Jesus. While affirming that salvation is possible only because of the redemptive death of Jesus and that we cannot be saved unless He draws us to Him and gives us the grace to accept Him, we could just as plausibly say that any attempt to downplay the need for holiness and for turning away from sin is a deception of the devil, who wants to lead us from trivial sins to the terrible fate of which we are warned in Hebrews:

> If, after we have been given knowledge of the truth, we should deliberately commit any sins, then there is no longer any sacrifice for them. There will be left only the dread prospect of judgment and of the raging fire that is to burn rebels. Anyone who disregards the Law of Moses is ruthlessly put to death on the word of two witnesses or three; and you may be sure that anyone who tramples on the Son of God and treats the blood of the covenant which

sanctified him as if it were not holy, and who insults the Spirit of grace, will be condemned to a far severer punishment. (Heb. 10:26–30)

St. Paul has a similar warning:

Your stubborn refusal to repent is only adding to the anger God will have toward you on that day of anger when his just judgments will be made known. He will repay each one as his works deserve. For those who sought renown and honor and immortality by always doing good there will be eternal life; for the unsubmissive who refused to take truth for their guide and took depravity instead, there will be anger and fury. (Rom. 2:5–8)

Moreover, the followers of Jesus participate in His work of salvation. St. Paul writes that "it makes me happy to suffer for you, as I am suffering now, and in my own body to do what I can to make up all that has still to be undergone by Christ for the sake of his body, the Church" (Col. 1:24). St. James even says that "anyone who can bring back a sinner from the wrong way that he has taken will be saving a soul from death and covering up a great number of sin" (James 5:20).

Mary is a key participant in God's plan of salvation in human history. She was called to be the Mother of the Savior and to share in His salvific suffering; it was her *fiat* ("Let it be done") to the messenger from God that made the Incarnation possible; she played a key role in the miracle that began His ministry in the world; she was there with Him at the end of His life; and she was called to be the Mother of all those who witness to Jesus. As the witness who is the Mother of all witnesses, she is a human expression of the infinite love of God that seeks the salvation of every soul. When she tells us about coming to salvation and about her maternal protection, she is speaking to us as a mother seeking the well-being of her children.

The Presbyterian scholar Ross Mackenzie writes (in *Trinitas, Christos, Maria,* an ecumenical anthology edited by the present author):

To bid Mary stand beside us is to remember that we are already with her in the new creation. She is linked with us, and ministers to us still in the new creation as the Mother of mercy. To invoke her in public and private prayer is to recall that, while the first creation came about by the will of God alone, the new creation involved this woman's will also. She is a minister of God, *synergos theou,* to use one of Paul's daring phrases. Even the least of the Apostles considered himself linked with Christ in a glorious cause: "We entreat you on behalf of Christ," he says to the Corinthians, "to be reconciled to God" (2 Cor. 5:20). To speak on behalf of Christ is therefore to be a mediator of God's saving work in the world.

Both Scripture and the Marian apparitions tell us that Jesus and His Mother are intimately involved in the drama of salvation unfolding in human history. It may be asked here how Jesus and Mary can continue to suffer now that they are in Heaven. A more fundamental question is how Jesus could have suffered if He was God — since God is unchangeable. But to say that God is unchanging is not to say that God is static. As one philosopher said, "God is unchanging because

His activity, being infinite, can never be either less or more than it *is*." And God's absolutely unchanging and yet absolutely active life is a life of infinite and eternal love and self-giving among the Three Persons of the Trinity. When one of the Three Persons united Himself with a human nature, it was only to be expected that His life on earth would manifest in human terms His infinite and eternal self-giving — in a sin-stained world such self-giving could not but mean suffering and death. In suffering and dying for us, therefore, Jesus gave us a glimpse of the infinite and unchanging love that is the inner life of God. In being crucified, says George Macdonald, Jesus "did that in the wild weather of His outlying provinces which He had done at home in glory and gladness." Our suffering in this life can thus become (if we offer it up) a participation in the heartbreaking love of the Trinity that was expressed most fully in human terms by Jesus, the Man of Sorrows, the Suffering Servant, and after that by His Mother, whose heart was pierced in the fulfillment of her Son's mission. If we ask whether God feels for us or suffers for us, the answer is that His infinite, unchanging love (unchanging not in that it is static but in that it is the highest possible and cannot decrease) is experienced most intensely — if we are open to it (as Mary was) — when our hearts are broken and our hopes shattered. In suffering and sacrifice, in being betrayed and rejected, we taste the love of the Lamb.

7. What Is an Apparition?

The term "apparition" in years past was used of ghosts and spirits. Today, even the Oxford American Dictionary defines it primarily as "an appearance, something that appears, especially something remarkable or unexpected." This newer definition certainly fits in with its usage in a Marian context.

Apparitions must be distinguished from dreams, illusions, and hallucinations (none of these three exist anywhere except in the mind of the subject) on the one hand and visions on the other. In an apparition, the witness sees a three-dimensional person who is really there but who has a glorified body (the resurrected body). Whereas a vision is an internal event, an apparition is external: a person is present at a definite location in space and time and is visible (in many of the great apparitions) to more than one witness. Visions can be imaginative (involving images) or spiritual (imageless), but in a vision a body is not objectively present although an angel who appears in a vision will "assume" a body. The witness to an apparition is commonly called a "visionary." This term is somewhat misleading since it suggests that the witness is "unworldly" (most visionaries have been down to earth) or the viewer of a vision. We will continue to use the term "visionary" here with all its handicaps since the only viable alternative, "seer," has been hijacked by dabblers in the occult.

What is the character of the "seeing" in an apparition? To answer this, we must first ask what happens when we see something in the physical world. Any kind of seeing is a nonphysical activity. When our five senses perceive something, we experience it directly and immediately in a mode that is entirely different from anything in physical reality. When we see a rainbow, our perception of the different colors is caused by vibrations impinging on our nerve ends; nevertheless the image in our consciousness with the different colors is qualitatively not itself the series of vibrations; the image is nonphysical although it is caused by the physical.

But it is not simply objects observed by our sensory organs that are the data of our consciousness. We have concepts that our minds abstract from what is visible to us (we have the general concept of "dog" in our mind which is distinct from any particular dog) and even concepts that cannot be perceived but can be thought (the concept of God or certain mathematical theorems). Conceptual thought is not tied to any bodily organ as such and sets us apart from animals who are capable only of perceptual consciousness. When our spiritual soul separates from the body, then we become incapable of sensory perception but can nevertheless engage in purely intellectual thought.

The Christian revelation claims that our separated souls are united with a glorified body at the time of the Last Judgment. We can only speculate about the sensory and conceptual capabilities of the glorified body — the model being the Body of the Risen Christ — but we know that the joy of Heaven is essentially the joy that comes from seeing God as He is. Since God is not physical, this "seeing" refers to the union of our intellect and our will with Him who is Infinite Truth and Infinite Good.

Returning to the kind of perception that occurs in an apparition, we note that it is perhaps a distinctive perception that occurs when we witness a glorified body. Maybe it is even a foretaste of the kind of "seeing" that we will enjoy in a glorified state. We know it has the character of normal "seeing" to the visionary because all the visionaries report that Mary appears to them and converses with them as a three-dimensional flesh-and-blood human being — albeit clothed in heavenly splendor. We know also that this "seeing" is restricted to the visionaries, since nobody else present at an apparition sees the Virgin (except in those apparitions like Hrushiv and Zeitun, where she appeared to thousands of people; in those instances she did not come to entrust specific individuals with a specific mission).

Finally, we know that, in most cases, a visionary is visibly transformed during the apparition and enters into a state of ecstasy in which he or she is oblivious to sensory stimuli (this has been observed not just in modern apparitions like Lourdes, Fatima, Beauraing, and Medjugorje but also in the cases of mystics through the centuries such as Teresa of Avila). Thus, a third-party observer present at an apparition does not "see" the Virgin but can see the changes to the visionary: the state of ecstasy and the fact that he or she is communicating with someone who is invisible to the observer.

Apparition sites can also be venues of extraordinary phenomena that are visible to all present: the dancing sun at Fatima or such physically miraculous objects as the tilma. Again, spiritual fruits are associated with apparition sites: conversions, renewed fervor, and the like.

The ecstasy into which a visionary enters can perhaps best be illustrated by Medjugorje, the Marian apparition that has been subjected to the most extensive scientific and medical monitoring in history. The volume *Scientific and Medical Studies on the Apparitions at Medjugorje* reports that the six visionaries would be engaged in a given activity such as talking or reciting a prayer before the apparition began. Then suddenly and simultaneously, they cease whatever they are doing, kneel down, and turn their eyes toward the same point on the wall facing them and move their lips without any sound; next, their voices are heard simultaneously as they start at the third word of the Lord's Prayer, the first two having been uttered by the Virgin; finally they raise their heads and turn their eyes upward simultaneously at the end of the apparition as they watch her leave. Scientific observers noted that the first synchronous action could possibly be attributed to natural causes but not the others. During the ecstasy engendered by the apparition, the visionaries are entirely insensitive to external sensory phenomena. Thus the visionaries display no response or change when, during the ecstasy, bright lights are flashed in their eyes, loud noises played in their ears, sharp needles inserted into them. And their facial expressions exude sheer joy, peace, and love.

Moreover, before and during the ecstasy, scientists recorded their brain-waves with electroencephalograms, their eye movements with electro-oculograms, etc. Their objective was to determine whether the ecstasy was a dream-state, an illusion, a malady such as epilepsy, hysteria, or a cataleptic state, a nervous disorder, or a pathological ecstasy. According to Professor Henri Joyeux of the Medical Faculty of Montpelier in France, who directed many of these studies,

> These young people are healthy and there is no sign of epilepsy nor is it a sleep or dream state. It is neither a case of pathological hallucination nor hallucination in the hearing or sight faculties connected with an abnormality in the functioning of the peripherical sensorial receivers, the hearing function, or sight. Neither are there any paroxystical hallucinations as testified by the electroencephalogram nor delirious hallucinations nor acute mental confusion. It is neither hysterical nor a nervous disorder nor a pathological ecstasy because the visionaries show no signs of these conditions in any of the clinical examinations. It cannot be a cataleptic state, for during the ecstasy the facial muscles are operating in a normal way. We can also ascertain that the intentness of the movements of the orbs of the eyes of all the visionaries is in perfect timing with each other at the beginning and the end of the ecstasy. During the ecstasy there is a perfect convergence of their eyes and there is a strong feeling of a face-to-face encounter between the visionaries and the person we cannot see. Their behavior presents no pathological signs. During the ecstasy they are in a state of prayer and interpersonal communication. They are not drop-outs, dreamers, or people who are tired or distressed. (Interview with *Paris Match*, Summer 1985)

The Medjugorje visionaries, like the visionaries of all the accredited apparitions, have been described by contemporaries and investigators as normal people of sound mental health — and not suggestible, excessively imaginative, or hysterical by temperament. Some of them were noticeably "slow" in terms of intellectual prowess, perhaps because this helped establish the external source of the messages they received.

But how does the visionary "see" what he or she reports? On the one hand, as the Thomist Garrigou-Lagrange noted, "ecstasy is the suspension of the exterior senses"; this is at least partially the case. But the most plausible explanation for the data available on perception in an authentic apparition seems to be that this is a case of a person in this world witnessing a glorified body (or, in some cases, an angel that assumes a human body). A glorified body exhibits the properties we observe in the Risen Body of Jesus (although He had not yet ascended to Heaven): it is three-dimensional and yet agile (not limited in its speed of movement), subtle (passing through solid objects), invisible (unless it appears to a chosen soul), immortal, and immune to any decay or disease. This body appears only to those who have been specially selected: the Risen Christ did not appear before the Roman or Jewish authorities but only before faithful followers who were entrusted with a mission.

Similarly, the glorified body of Mary only appears to those who have been selected for a mission. The souls of these individuals are elevated in such a manner as to be able to "perceive" the glorified body (although we note that their sensory organs also play a role as evidenced by the movement of their eyes and lips during an apparition). Until the General Judgment only two human beings have their glorified bodies: Jesus, Who rose from the dead and ascended to Heaven, and Mary, who was assumed body and soul into Heaven (as affirmed in the ancient liturgies and in Revelation 12). The only true apparitions are appearances of a Risen Body, and this is why we hear almost always of apparitions of Mary — starting with her appearance as the Woman Clothed with the Sun. Jesus will come again in his Risen Body only at the end of history, although He can and has appeared in visions, as have saints and angels.

Every visionary has said that the beauty and splendor of the Blessed Virgin was beyond any earthly description; this is only to be expected if we are to go by the description of the first Marian apparition, the Woman Clothed by the Sun. In many of the apparitions, the visionaries did not at first know if the Lady they saw was the Virgin — just as Mary Magdalen did not at first recognize the Risen Christ. But once He spoke she knew who He was, and once the Lady spoke the visionaries knew who she was.

8. Collective Hallucination?

From these starting points, we move to another fundamental fact: accounts of the appearances of the Virgin are embedded in all the great cultures of the world. These accounts are not simply of historical interest since the tangible and intangible objects associated with these apparitions continue to exert immense power to this day. When considering apparitions that took place in the distant past, for instance, the sixteenth-century apparitions of Guadalupe and Vailankanni, we must not limit ourselves simply to the historical background. To accurately assess these phenomena we must also take into account their contemporary *power*: why do they draw millions to this day, millions who believe that they are healed and transformed at the apparition sites?

Moreover, the messages associated with these cross-cultural appearances are so remarkably similar as to suggest a single script-writer. To dismiss them as collective hallucinations that result from cross-cultural disorders of the human psyche is to forget that there are actual tangible objects associated with the apparitions (the tilma, or cloak, of Guadalupe with the miraculous image of the Virgin, the healing spring of Lourdes); hallucinations cannot account for such objects. To say they are deceptions of the devil is to forget that the apparitions have resulted in millions of conversions to Christianity, and as Jesus Himself said when He was accused of working His miracles through diabolic influences, "every kingdom divided against itself is heading for ruin" (Luke 11:17).

The methodologies employed by modern science can neither prove nor disprove claims of apparitions. In a given apparition, the visionary claims to see the Virgin and enters a state of ecstasy in which he or she is demonstrably dissociated from the external world and yet engages in normal communication with the Virgin. But (in most cases) nobody else can see her because she is present in a special mode that is not susceptible to public empirical observation. If she is not thus observable, devices that detect empirical phenomena are of no help. But if science cannot "detect" the Virgin, it can still evaluate the visionary. Scientific equipment can be of assistance in monitoring the physical state of visionaries during the ecstasy accompanying an apparition. Psychological techniques can help in the process of determining the sanity and normalcy of the visionary. Moreover, scientific methodologies and devices can be utilized in examining the tangible evidence that is given as a sign (the tilma for instance). Within these inescapable limits, science has found nothing to contradict the claims of the visionaries of the major apparitions.

An appendix at the end of this book outlines philosophical, scientific, and theological criteria that can and have been applied in judging the authenticity of apparition claims. Philosophically, the important questions are whether there can be exceptions to the ordinary laws of nature and what would count as evidence for such exceptions. Scientifically, the question is whether the visionary is having a hallucination, since there is no physical evidence for the presence of a person. Theologically, the question is whether the visionary's experience is diabolic or divine in origin.

On the philosophical criteria, it is pointed out that laws of nature and claims of supernatural phenomena have one thing in common: they attempt to explain the available data in a coherent manner. In certain cases, the evidence for a supernatural phenomenon emerging from independent testimonies and physical traces left by the phenomenon outweighs the objection that the laws of nature cannot on occasion be suspended. Moreover, belief in the laws of nature should lead to belief in an ultimate explanation for these laws and of the universe as a whole, namely, God. And if there is a Creator and if He directs nature and history to meet certain objectives, then there is a strong probability that He will intervene in nature and history to meet these objectives.

On the scientific criteria, it is shown that none of the visionaries associated with the accredited apparitions has indicated the usual symptoms of hallucination: mental illness (neurosis, psychosis), drugs, an exaggerated tendency for wishful thinking, or such conducive circumstances as a strong desire and a favorable setting. Moreover, the hallucination hypothesis requires that there is no information introduced that is not already in the subject's mind — but in most of the apparitions the visionaries found it hard to comprehend let alone communicate the information received. This hypothesis also cannot account for all the other phenomena associated with apparitions apart from the visual portion. Most important, the lasting signs left at the major apparitions cannot be subsumed under the hallucination umbrella.

On charges of collective hallucination, one expert notes that genuine hallucinations are always peculiar to one individual, and it is not possible for groups of people to have repeated identical hallucinatory experiences which they insist are real without showing signs of psychic abnormality. The charge of "collective hallucination" is not applicable to Marian apparitions for quite another reason. A non-Christian student of apparition claims writes, "It is absurd to discuss the visions [Marian apparitions] in terms of group hallucination or mass hysteria. Though massive crowds were often present and desperate to see the visions, to share the experience of the visionaries, there is no convincing instance of this happening: the overall experience of those who came, full of hope, to observe was one of disappointment. Even at Fatima the experiences of the visionaries and the crowd seem to have been mutually exclusive" (Kevin McClure in *The Evidence for Visions of the Virgin Mary*). At one point, the crowds at Lourdes were in fact quite annoyed when they were not able to "see" anything extraordinary themselves.

In the appendix on criteria applicable in evaluating apparitions, we also consider as a case study the objections to apparitions (primarily in terms of cultural conditioning) raised by the well-known atheist Antony Flew.

Concerning the theological criteria, it is noted that some Christians accept the supernatural character of Marian apparitions but then cite biblical passages to impugn these apparitions as satanic deceptions. Here it is not the Bible per se that emerges as the antagonist but a particular exegesis of certain biblical passages. In the appendix we show that the biblical passages cited by the critics actually instruct us to expect apparitions and to distinguish between the authentic and the demonic. Far from telling us to reject all apparitions, these passages tell us "never to suppress the Spirit or treat the gift of prophecy with contempt" but to "hold on to what is good" (1 Thessalonians 5:21). We are told to test every spirit "to see if they come from God" (1 John 4:1). We then consider the criteria historically employed by the Christian community in evaluating claims of apparitions. The central theme of these criteria is the biblical command that you shall know them by their fruits — fruits as they relate to the changes to the visionaries, effects on devotees, the soundness of the doctrine that emerges, and the reality of accompanying miraculous phenomena. The extraordinarily positive fruits of the accredited Marian apparitions — from the cessation of human sacrifices to scientifically inexplicable healings to the impetus given to the spreading of the Gospel — can hardly be denied even by critics.

It is to be noted that even Jesus did not perform miracles where there was lack of faith, and those who have no place in their hearts for the Virgin will not be able to recognize or appreciate her loving intercession in any of the great apparitions.
    plus 2pt

9. A History of the Apparitions

It is sometimes thought that reports of Marian apparitions started in nineteenth-century France. Nothing could be further from the truth. The history of Marian apparitions begins in the Age of the Apostles.

The first report of a Marian apparition dates back to 40 A.D. (the year traditionally assigned), when the Virgin miraculously appeared to St. James the Greater in Spain. This apparition was an instance of bilocation since Mary was still alive at the time in Jerusalem. (Bilocation is the capability of simultaneously being physically present in two places; it was exercised by several famous saints and in modern times by Padre Pio). St. James, apparently her favorite Apostle, was discouraged by his work, and so the Virgin appeared to offer consolation, a pattern that is repeated in other Marian apparitions in history. Another standard theme was inaugurated at this apparition, for she told St. James that God wanted him to build a church under her patronage and name. (As has been noted, this theme derives from her role as the New Ark of the Covenant and also from the divine mandate that all generations are to call her blessed.) According to traditional accounts of the apparition, St. James was given a pillar of jasper and a statue of the Virgin that still survive, after over nineteen hundred years, in the Holy Chapel in the Basilica of El Pilar in Spain. The Virgin also said that the Lord wanted him to return to Jerusalem, where he was the first Apostle to be martyred — thus fulfilling his request to drink of the cup of His Master.

The second apparition to an Apostle is the famous apparition of the Virgin recorded by the Apostle John in the Book of Revelation, chapter 12: "Now a great sign appeared in heaven: a woman, adorned with the sun, standing on the moon, and with the twelve stars on her head for a crown." This is Mary's first apparition after her death. The reasons for preferring a Marian interpretation of this passage have been reviewed earlier. It may be said that there is no way to verify the historical accuracy of the event described in Revelation 12, but the following comments are relevant: (a) The account here is very clear in its details. (b) The descriptions of the Virgin offered by witnesses to many subsequent apparitions mirror the description of the Woman of Revelation 12. In most apparitions the Virgin is clothed in light more blinding than the sun and actual miracles of the sun have played a prominent role in at least two famous apparitions. Moreover, some of the Virgin's apparitions have been to Christians persecuted by their enemies (China, Vietnam). The Ark of the Covenant in Heaven of Revelation 11:19 is suddenly replaced by the Woman Clothed with the Sun. In many Marian apparitions, the Virgin has been portrayed as the new Ark of the Covenant. (c) For a Christian who believes in the divine inspiration of Scripture, the main question is whether this passage belongs to the canon, which it does.

The apparitions that came immediately after the Apostolic Age were not documented like the accounts of modern apparitions. The genres of historical writing and investigative journalism prevalent today were not developed until quite recently, and hence we find little of either secular or religious history chronicled in a systematic fashion. Nevertheless, reports of Marian apparitions in the first ten centuries of Christian history survived in three modes: (a) Many of the hundreds of popular shrines and pilgrimage sites attribute their origin to purported apparitions or visions, the most famous being the Basilica of St. Mary Major in Rome, which, according to popular belief, was built on the instructions of the Virgin to a wealthy Roman couple in 352 A.D., and the Church of Our Lady of the Golden Fountain, built by Emperor Leo I after an apparition in circa 455 A.D. (b) For centuries, apparitions have been reported by those whom later generations called saints, a phenomenon going back to such famous instances as the apparitions to St. Gregory the Wonder-Worker, circa 238 A.D. (an account, notable for its restraint, written up by St. Gregory of Nyssa and considered quite reliable), and St. John Damascene, 749. Some accounts of apparitions of this era came from ecclesiastical authorities who claimed to be personal witnesses of the phenomenon, for instance, St. Ildefonso, the bishop of Toledo, Spain, circa 657, and Egwin, bishop of Worcester, England, circa 708. The famous Odo of Cluny (d. 942) promoted a well-known apparition of Mary to a robber in which she described herself as the Mother of Mercy (the robber later became a monk). On the night of September 13, 948, St. Conrad, bishop of Constance, saw Jesus Christ, accompanied by many saints, consecrating the Chapel of Einsiedeln, Switzerland, to the Virgin Mary, also present, and this chapel subsequently became one of the premier pilgrimage sites in Europe after an investigation by Emperor Leo and Pope Leo VIII. (c) There are also the thousands of accounts of Marian apparitions reported by the laity. Some of these are obviously legendary, but, when taken as a whole, these accounts show a continuous awareness in the Christian mind of the Virgin's interventions in history. Moreover, not a few of these narratives bear remarkable similarities in their structure to the much better documented modern apparitions.

There is one great difference between the first fifteen centuries of Christendom and the last five. Despite several influential heresies, the undivided Christian world of the entire first millennium after Christ and at least half the second millennium was united in its conviction that Mary was the all-holy and perpetually virgin Mother of God who interceded with the Trinity for her children (these were doctrines taught by the Councils of the undivided Church). Marian intercession in Heaven and intervention in human history were accepted by all Christians. Marian apparitions were therefore not controversial in themselves. And the central figure in these apparitions, the Virgin, was not as concerned with questions of right doctrine as she was with consolation, encouragement, and exhortations to holiness. Apocalyptic prophecies at the turn of the first millennium were not of Marian origin. They were, rather, the utterances of individuals claiming (with varying degrees of credibility) to be specially inspired by the Holy Spirit.

In the second millennium of Christianity, the Church suffered two great wounds. The first was the Eastern Schism of 1054, which saw the departure of what are now known as the Eastern Orthodox churches. The second was the Protestant Reformation of 1517.

The first split had no particular effect on Marian apparitions or reports about them. Both Catholic and Orthodox saints described their encounters with the

Virgin as did the faithful in general. But, as we shall see, the second great split in Christendom had a paralyzing effect on apparition history.

In many of the great apparitions of the Middle Ages the Virgin asked the visionary to build a chapel or shrine. The most famous such apparition was to Richeldis de Faverches, Lady of the Manor of Walsingham, England, in 1061. The Lady Richeldis was asked to build a replica of the House of Nazareth in England and was given both the physical specifications for the structure and supernatural assistance in its construction. The Holy House of Walsingham became one of the four greatest shrines of Christendom, next to Jerusalem, Rome, and Compostela, Spain, and attracted thousands of pilgrims. The popularity of this shrine indicates that the idea of Marian apparitions had been established in the minds of the faithful. Again, St. William of Vercelli, an Italian hermit, was asked to construct a church on the top of Monte Vergine, Italy. This church was made a basilica and is now a pilgrimage center. In 1233, the Virgin appeared to seven merchants of Florence and asked them to form a religious order in which they dedicated themselves totally to God. They did as she requested and built a monastery on Monte Senario; the order they founded is now called the Order of the Servants of Mary. The apparition took place on August 15, later to be celebrated as the Feast of Assumption.

From 1173 to 1779, the Virgin appeared to many famous saints. She appeared to the founders of some of the most influential religious orders in history ranging from St. Francis of Assisi (Franciscans) to St. Ignatius of Loyola (Jesuits). Many famous mystics were also favored with apparitions: St. Bernard of Clairvaux, St. Bridget of Sweden, St. Gertrude, St. Catherine of Siena, St. Sergius of Radonezh, St. Teresa of Avila, St. Margaret Mary Alacoque, and St. Seraphim of Sarov. Two of the most powerful icons in history were also rediscovered in this period: the Black Madonna in Czestochowa, Poland, in 1382 and Our Lady of Kazan in Kazan, Russia, in 1579.

Although one of the first Marian apparitions (St. Gregory the Wonder-Worker) took place in Asia, most of the accredited apparitions of the next thirteen centuries unfolded in Europe. But from the sixteenth century to the eighteenth, three major apparitions were reported on other continents: the apparitions of Our Lady of Guadalupe in Mexico, of Our Lady of Good Health in India, and Our Lady of LaVang in Vietnam. These were not peripheral apparitions; in terms of the numbers of people they attracted, they rivaled (and rival) the great apparitions of Europe. Guadalupe in fact was the single most influential apparition of all and converted an entire nation to Christianity. In 1531 the Virgin appeared to an Aztec, Juan Diego. Juan Diego's bishop asked for a sign, and the Virgin left behind a miraculous image of herself on a cloak made of cactus. The physical properties of this image continue to defy every attempt at naturalistic explanation. In Vailankanni, India, there were two celebrated apparitions of the Virgin with the infant Jesus in the sixteenth century; in both cases the apparitions were to local boys. The water in a pond at the site of the first apparition is renowned for its healing properties. A basilica with a miraculous image of Our Lady of Good Health stands on the site of the second apparition. The basilica was mainly built by Portuguese sailors in the seventeenth century in gratitude to the Virgin for miraculously preserving them in a storm just off the Vailankanni coast on the feast of her Nativity. The shrine is a pilgrimage center for millions of people of all religions from all over India, and thousands of healings and other miracles have been reported there. In LaVang, Vietnam, the Virgin appeared to persecuted Christians who had fled to the jungle; the site of her apparition is also a well-known shrine and pilgrimage spot where many miracles have been reported.

Despite the apparitions to individual saints, Europe itself was going through a dry spell with respect to Marian devotion in general and apparitions in particular between the Protestant Reformation and the end of the Inquisition. This is not to say apparitions did not occur — but the recipients were unlikely to report them publicly for fear of reprisals. Paradoxically the hostility to apparitions of this period came from both Protestant and Catholic authorities. The post-Reformation Protestant iconoclasts dismissed Marian devotion as an idolatrous superstition and alleged that Marian apparitions came from the devil. On the Catholic side, there were two forces at work: first, there was the so-called Catholic Enlightenment, which had no interest in Marian piety or visions and promoted a "rationalized faith"; second, any claim to a supernatural vision or message was a risky proposition during the Roman and the Spanish Inquisitions. The historian David Blackbourn observes that the Jesuits were suppressed in 1773 partially because they were so closely associated with the Marian revival.

The Spanish Inquisition ceased in 1820 and the Roman Inquisition in 1829. The first of the modern Marian apparitions was reported in 1830. This was the apparition of Our Lady of the Miraculous Medal to Sister Catherine Labouré at the Rue du Bac in Paris. The Virgin made prophecies, later fulfilled, of events that were to take place in the next forty years and asked Catherine to produce and distribute a medal with a portrait of herself as she was seen in the apparition. Many of those who wore the medal reported miracles, and it soon became known as the Miraculous Medal; hundreds of millions of these medals have been distributed since the apparition. (Another such miraculous instrument of grace given in an apparition was the scapular that the Virgin passed on through St. Simon Stock in 1251). The body of Catherine, who died in 1876, remains incorrupt.

Three other major apparitions took place in France in the nineteenth century. At La Salette, in 1846, the Virgin appeared to two shepherd children and warned them of chastisements that were to afflict the world in both the immediate future and the end-times because of sin (although these could be averted if people were to convert). A spring was later found at the site of the apparitions and many miraculous cures were reported there. In 1858, the Virgin appeared to Bernadette Soubirous at Lourdes. At both Rue du Bac and La Salette, the Virgin had spoken of the present age being evil; and at both she had shed tears. At Lourdes she asked for penitence. She also asked Bernadette to drink the water from a particular spot in the grotto: on digging into the ground there, Bernadette found a spring which is today the great healing spring of Lourdes. Bernadette was also told to request the parish priest to build a chapel. The priest had asked Bernadette to find out who she was from the lady and, in one of the final apparitions, the Virgin said, "I am the Immaculate Conception." Over five thousand cures have been reported at Lourdes, although only about sixty of them have been thoroughly investigated.

In 1871, the Virgin appeared to five children in the village of Pontmain. Although silent, she "spoke" through a scroll that was unfurled before them. Her title in this apparition was "Our Lady of Hope" because of her response to petitions for protection from the advancing Prussian army (see the chapter "The Virgin and World History").

Three other lesser known but accredited apparitions of the nineteenth century were the apparitions to Magdalena Kade in Philippsdorf, Bohemia, in 1866, to Estelle Faguette in Pellevoisin, France, in 1876, and to several villagers in Knock, Ireland, in 1879. Both Magdalena and Estelle were on their deathbeds but were cured after the Virgin appeared to them; the Our Lady of the Scapular of the Sacred Heart devotion derives from the Estelle Faguette apparition. In the Knock apparition, the villagers saw the Virgin with St. Joseph, St. John the Evangelist with an open Bible, and the Lamb in front of a cross. This was a silent apparition, but Knock is renowned as a shrine of spiritual and physical healing.

One of the well-known apparitions of the nineteenth century was so embroiled in controversy that it is usually ignored in histories of apparitions: the reported apparition of the Virgin to three children in the village of Marpingen, Germany: Katherina Hubertus, Margaretha Kunz, and Susanna Leist. The visionaries claimed to have seen a "woman in white" on July 3, 1873, in the woods near their home. In a subsequent apparition, she is reported to have said that "I am the Immaculately Conceived." Several cures were reported from water brought to the site of the apparitions. Thousands of people converged on the site. The Prussian government was alarmed by the sequence of events and detained the children for five weeks and subjected them to severe interrogation. Under pressure from the civil authorities, one of the children retracted the claim of having witnessed the apparitions but later retracted the retraction. The parish priest became a supporter of the apparition and was subsequently harassed by the government. Soldiers prevented pilgrims from coming near the apparition site. Bishops disagreed among themselves on the facticity of the claims. At the time of the reported apparition, the diocese had no bishop because of an ongoing conflict between the Catholic Church and the Prussian government. The famous German Mariologist Matthias Scheeben investigated the phenomenon and reached a favorable verdict. Once a bishop had been appointed to head the diocese (in 1881), the Church never issued a formal verdict because of the controversy. The first of the visionaries, Susanna, died at the age of fourteen; the other two became nuns and died at a relatively young age. Reportedly, the visionary who had retracted her story and retracted the retraction (Margaretha) had to leave the Poor Clares because she was not willing to deny the story of the apparitions despite pressure from within the order; subsequently she joined the Sisters of Providence.

The great Church-approved apparitions of the twentieth century are Fatima, Portugal; Beauraing and Banneux, Belgium; Zeitun, Egypt; Akita, Japan; Kibeho, Rwanda; Betania, Venezuela; Cuapa, Nicaragua; San Nicolás, Argentina; and Damascus, Syria. The devotion deriving from the Amsterdam, Holland, apparition has been officially approved. The Medjugorje, Bosnia, and Naju, South Korea, apparitions are still in progress and the ecclesiastical investigation will not be complete until the phenomena have ceased. The official investigation into the Cuenca, Ecuador, apparition is still in progress. Thousands of other apparitions and locutions in Asia, Africa, Australia, Europe, and the Americas have been claimed in the course of this century, but the investigative data required to consider them in the present inquiry is not available.

Fatima is considered in detail at various points in this book. Three shepherd children, Lucia dos Santos and Francisco and Jacinta Marto, witnessed six apparitions of the Virgin between May 13 and October 13, 1917. Thousands of observers witnessed the famous miracle of the sun during the last apparition. Various prophecies made at Fatima were subsequently fulfilled (see "The Virgin and World History"). The Fatima request for prayer, reparation for sin, and devotion to the Immaculate Mary were persistent themes in most subsequent apparitions. To reinforce the terrible consequences of sin, the Virgin gave the visionaries a glimpse of Hell and the fate of unrepentant sinners.

At Beauraing, Belgium, too, where the Virgin appeared to five children in 1932, the emphasis is on the conversion of sinners and on leading good lives. The Virgin appears with a golden heart to emphasize the importance of devotion to the Immaculate Heart. The next year in Banneux, Belgium, the Virgin appeared to Mariette Beco and described herself as the Virgin of the Poor. She took Mariette to a spring and said,"This spring is reserved for all nations — to relieve the sick." Many miraculous cures were reported by those who came to the spring. The phrase "for all nations" inaugurates a theme that is repeated in apparitions of the next several decades.

The next major milestone in apparition history is Amsterdam, Holland, where the Virgin began appearing to Ida Peerdeman on March 25, 1945. These apparitions are notable for the prophecies made by the Virgin that were verifiably fulfilled (see "The Virgin and World History"). Moreover, in Amsterdam she affirmed her identity as the Lady of All Nations, or Peoples, and her role as Coredemptrix, Mediatrix, and Advocate.

"Silent" apparitions took place in Jerusalem, Israel (1954), and Zeitun, Egypt (1968). The second apparition was witnessed by hundreds of thousands of people of all religions and took place over a church that is believed to have been built over the site where Joseph and Mary stayed with the baby Jesus during their exile in Egypt.

These silent apparitions were followed by an apparition of the Virgin in Akita, Japan, in 1973, where she spoke to Sister Agnes Sasagawa, a deaf nun, through a statue. This statue of the Virgin, modeled on the image of Our Lady of All Nations from Amsterdam, wept blood on 101 occasions. Like the message at Fatima, the Akita message was prayer, penance, reparation for sins. If Fatima showed the fiery flames of Hell as the ultimate consequence of sin, the warning of Akita is that the sins of the world are going to call down fire from the sky which will destroy much of humanity. The tears of blood are the tears of a Mother lamenting the impending (but not inevitable) loss of her children.

Betania and Cuapa followed Akita. At Betania, the Virgin came in 1976 to María Esperanza with a "message of love and reconciliation to all people and nations." She was "the Reconciler of All Nations" (again, the theme of Our Lady of All Nations) and wanted María to "tell my children of all races, of all nations, of all religions, that I love them." But she warned that mankind will succumb to fire, war, and death if it does not convert. Thousands of people have observed, and continue to observe, apparitions of the Virgin and other miraculous phenomena at Betania. In Cuapa in 1980, she appeared to Bernardo Martínez and repeated the message of conversion while warning that the consequences of sin could be a Third World War. She wept at the hardness of heart that prevented so many from converting but promised, "A mother does not forget her children. I have not forgotten you, all you who are suffering. I am your mother, mother of all sinners. Please pray this prayer, knowing it is pleasing to my Son: Most holy Virgin, you are my mother, the mother of all sinners."

The year 1981 saw the beginning of an apparition that has caused more conversions than any other apparition in history with the exception of Guadalupe. This was Medjugorje, a hamlet in Bosnia, where the Virgin appeared to six children. Over fifty thousand priests — among them several hundred cardinals and bishops — have now made the pilgrimage to Medjugorje and are listed on the parish rolls of the St. James Church there. The supernatural energy — or grace — unleashed by Medjugorje has borne fruit in millions of conversions around the world. The Medjugorje message of prayer, fasting, and reconciliation has formed an entire generation. The Virgin has given ten secrets to three of the visionaries and nine to the other three. When all ten of the secrets have been given to all of the visionaries, the apparitions will cease and what is foretold in the secrets will begin to unfold. The Virgin has said that it is better to convert now than to wait until the secrets are revealed since it could be too late by then. Hundreds of cures and thousands of miracles have been reported from Medjugorje.

In the same year as Medjugorje, another series of apparitions started in Kibeho, Rwanda, with the Virgin appearing to seven children. The Virgin warned that "there is not much time left in preparing for the Last Judgment. We must change our lives, renounce sin. Pray and prepare for our own death and for the end of the world." Solar phenomena and other miracles were witnessed by thousands of the pilgrims. The Virgin predicted the savage bloodshed that was to come to Rwanda.

Five other major apparitions took place after Medjugorje: San Nicolás, Argentina; Damascus, Syria; Hrushiv, Ukraine; Naju, South Korea, and Cuenca, Ecuador. In San Nicolás, on September 25, 1983, the Virgin appeared to Gladys de Motta, a housewife. Gladys received eighteen hundred messages. The apparitions ceased on February 11, 1990. The messages invite the faithful to consecrate themselves again to God. Many conversions and healings have been reported. In Damascus, on November 22, 1982, Myrna Nazzour exuded olive oil from her fingers. The oil was seen to produce miraculous cures. Myrna also suffered the wounds of the stigmata. The messages in Damascus have focused on interchurch unity. The Hrushiv apparition, which went on from April 27, 1987, to August 15, 1988, was seen by hundreds of thousands of people. The Virgin offered encouragement to the faithful people of Ukraine but said that Russia's failure to convert to Christ could lead to a Third World War. In Cuenca, Ecuador, from 1988 to 1990, the Virgin appeared to a young girl and said she that wants "prompt conversion from a humble heart" and that "he who is with God will be protected under my mantle, in the Heart of my Son and in my Heart." She called for prayer, penance, and fasting and again warned that failure to convert would result in devastating consequences for the world.

Whereas Eastern Europe is known for its miraculous icons of the Virgin, the Far East has been endowed with two famous weeping statues. The first one was Akita and the second is Naju, South Korea. A statue belonging to Julia Kim of South Korea began to weep tears of blood on June 30, 1985. Since then Julia received numerous messages from the Virgin. The stigmata (the wounds of Christ) appeared on her and numerous Eucharistic miracles have been reported. In the messages, the Virgin asks the faithful to offer up reparations for the conversion of sinners in the world and to pray fervently, especially with the Rosary. A major theme of the messages is that life begins at the moment of conception and that abortion is murder.

10. *"My Sole Purpose Is to Ensure That the Will of the Son Is Obeyed"*

Despite the explosion of gigantic databanks and the daily avalanche of facts and figures, the modern era is characterized by confusion about the most basic questions of life. Those who are speeding down the information superhighway have no idea either of their ultimate destination or how to get there. A few who have thought about these matters seek answers from New Age gurus and channelers — or by scanning the universe with the hope of hearing from some form of extraterrestrial intelligence. Superstitions about aliens and reincarnation and the like have gripped the popular imagination.

So whom do we turn to for answers, ultimate and reliable answers? No doubt, many have hoped that they could receive clear answers to the most important questions from God Himself here and now. Many would like to touch and feel the supernatural to be assured of its existence. And, of course, many want to know if there is a life after death and what it's like. The question here is whether Heaven has responded to these hopes and desires.

What this book seeks to show is that we have indeed heard from Heaven, that God has sent a Messenger to every era and culture to remind us of His revelation two millennia ago, to bring us to His Divine Word and other instruments of grace, to open our hearts to Him, and to live our lives with the full awareness that our every choice is an eternal yes or no to Him. Right before our eyes we see a phenomenon that resists any natural explanation while giving us the very truths and graces that we seek with all our hearts. So before we speculate about the so-called chariots of the gods (Erich Von Daniken), let's consider the tilma of Guadalupe; and before we puzzle over the X Files let's read the M Files.

To preempt a common concern, we must begin by stating what should be obvious: Marian apparitions neither supplant nor supplement the Gospel. Mary's appearances and messages amplify the Word of God and apply it in history and our lives. Just as the Word of God is transmitted through the writings of human beings, the echoes of His Word are sent to us through the Messenger He has chosen for a singular role in His plan of salvation.

But whereas the written Word is a public and final revelation of God, the messages that come to us from the Virgin belong to the domain of private revelation. The public revelation takes precedence over the private at all levels. Nevertheless the fact that a revelation is private does not imply that it is either untrue or insignificant. If there are good grounds for believing that such a revelation took place then there is also good reason for believing that God wanted us to pay attention to it. The private revelation confirms for both believers and unbelievers the truth of the public. Moreover, a reliable private revelation can give us a reliable explanation of many texts in the public revelation while also showing how we can apply them here and now.

When Christian believers read the Bible they read it with the excitement that comes from knowing that God is speaking through these human words. At times evangelists and preachers may explain or apply the biblical texts so as to deepen our excitement or to offer nuggets of wisdom. We do not normally think of such reflections as substitutes for Scripture or additions to it. Similarly, the Virgin's messages are just examples of explanations and applications of Scripture with the difference that the one who is explaining and applying is God-sent.

To remind us of His own teaching about the great questions of life, Jesus sends us, across the world and throughout history, His own Mother, whom He named the mother of us all. The faith that He founded spread around the world because of the supernatural signs shown by His witnesses, the Apostles and their disciples. This faith now is consolidated by the Mother of His witnesses with supernatural signs. And just as Jesus chose people from the humblest walks of life as His witnesses, His Mother too, in her appearances, works through the lowest levels of society. God does not intimidate us into faith by irresistible displays of His glory, and that is why it was possible for many who saw and heard the human Jesus to reject Him although He gave them sufficient evidence for acceptance. Likewise, Marian apparitions give just enough evidence to suggest that they are from a supernatural source, but the phenomenon is never coercive.

Supernatural signs have an effect not simply on one's faith but on history itself. For instance, whatever else you might say about it, the reported resurrection of Jesus had a material effect on history. The changed lives changed the history of the world. The transformation of the Apostles led to the transformation of empires and civilizations. The same kinds of things can be said about the apparitions of Mary. Guadalupe led to the conversion of millions of Aztecs. Lourdes, Fatima, and Medjugorje were also responsible for millions of conversions. Other than the resurrection, no other claims of supernatural occurrences have had the kind of effect on history that we associate with Marian apparitions. Even if we say that the apparitions are illusions, we have to admit that they had a very real effect on history. Moreover, whatever we might say about the biblical background of Marian apparitions, we cannot deny that these apparitions have concretely fulfilled two biblical prophecies: first, that all generations will call her blessed, and, second, that she will be present with those who witness to Jesus.

To adopt a familiar vocabulary, we might say that the Virgin appears in history to conduct ongoing "revivals" at which one undergoes a conversion experience and makes a resolution to lead a life of holiness. Heaven and Hell and sound doctrine are also persistent themes at the revival events run by humanity's mysterious companion in all cultures and ages. Sometimes, instead of a sermon on fire and brimstone, the helpers at the revival have been given a vision of Hell in all its fury.

The major apparition messages of the Virgin reinforce the reality of Heaven and Hell, the urgency of conversion, the terrible tragedy that is sin and its horrific consequences even in this world, the necessity of prayer, penance, and reparation for sin, and the obligation to turn to the means of grace offered by God. These are the teachings of Jesus in the Gospel and St. Paul in his epistles. There are two approaches taken by the Virgin in her message: on the one hand she exhorts and encourages us in the journey to holiness; on the other, she warns us in the severest terms of the consequences of sin in history. These approaches are not only compatible but are different sides of the same coin. Jesus too was relentless in His calls to holiness, and His severe warnings of the punishment of Hell for those who die unrepentant are echoed in the admonitions of the Virgin. Like at Cana, in the Amsterdam apparition the Virgin says, "My sole purpose is to ensure that the will of the Son is obeyed."

Historically, Marian devotion has had a Christological complement. In the early Church, the common image was of Mother and Infant. And while this has been a feature of many of the apparitions (in fact, the Guadalupe tilma shows a pregnant maiden), many others continue the New Adam–New Eve theme such as we see in the link of the Immaculate Heart of Mary to the Sacred Heart of Jesus. Devotion to the Immaculate Heart of Mary is stressed in many of the modern apparitions because it is the safest and surest pathway to permanent adoration of the Sacred Heart of her Son: the great Ecumenical Councils declared that Mary was the Mother of God in order to protect the truth that Jesus was both God and Man. Henceforth, said the (undivided) Christian Church, the surest protection against Christological heresy was the affirmation and veneration of Mary as the *Theotokos*. Compared to the great honors and privileges contained in the doctrine of Mary's divine maternity, the New Adam–New Eve–inspired terminology of Immaculate Heart–Sacred Heart is quite modest, while being a legitimate and meaningful expression of an ancient truth. In affirming devotion to Mary's Immaculate Heart we are simultaneously affirming the primacy of the Sacred Heart to whom she leads us. The triumph of the Immaculate Heart ultimately is a preparation and a pathway to the ultimate destination, which is the reign of the Sacred Heart, the Era of Peace under Christ the King. Like the doctrine of *Theotokos,* the doctrines of New Adam–New Eve/Sacred Heart–Immaculate Heart are ultimately safeguards of the doctrine of the Incarnation.

While noting that in some cases she appears with the infant Jesus, we also see that, in most apparitions, Mary appears alone. This is consistent with Revelation 12:17, where we see only the Woman who is the Mother of the witnesses for Jesus. Jesus works through His witnesses, and through the Mother of His witnesses. Jesus Himself had prophesied that He would come again only at the end of history; until then the mission of teaching and converting has been entrusted to His witnesses.

Visions of Jesus, such as those recorded by Sr. Margaret Mary Alacoque and Sr. Faustina Kowalska, are linked to the growth and spread of particular devotions like the Sacred Heart and the Divine Mercy; and in some Marian apparitions, Jesus also appears in the course of the phenomenon, but only to emphasize certain teachings and not as the "messenger." Such visions of Jesus are not apparitions, for an apparition involves an actual physical appearance, and, as He said in the Gospels, Jesus will not come back physically until the Second Coming.

Three features of Marian apparitions deserve special mention with respect to the kind of "message" they communicate concerning Mary's role in human history.

First, almost all the influential modern apparitions were witnessed by children. This makes sense because it reinforces the biblical understanding that Mary is a Mother; in apparitions involving children, the mother-child relationship is unmistakable. Also, children are more transparent than adults: they have fewer preconceived notions and are easier to see through if they are lying: they make the best *eye*-witnesses.

Second, most of the Marian apparitions involve a healing spring, miraculous cures, and the like. We note that in the ministry of Jesus and of His Apostles, physical healing and cures accompanied the teaching of the Gospel. These healings both confirmed the truth of the teaching and reflected the mercy and compassion of God Almighty. (Moses too was guided to special springs.)

Third, the history of Marian apparitions shows a pattern of responses to crisis situations, as one expects from the mother of witnesses pursued by the dragon. The Virgin appeared to the Apostle James when he was discouraged. She appeared to Juan Diego when it was apparent that the Church was making very little headway with the natives of the New World. She brought heavenly consolation to the persecuted Vietnamese Christians of the eighteenth century. She demonstrated the reality of the supernatural in a series of apparitions in nineteenth-century France, where the Enlightenment with its denial of the supernatural had just begun. At Fatima, she warned of catastrophes ahead and of actions that could avert these. In Kibeho, Rwanda, and Medjugorje, Bosnia, she appeared to warn her children of the bloodshed that was to come. In her twentieth-century apparitions in particular she has sought to counteract the spread of modern atheism that is the greatest threat today to Christianity. "I have come to show the world that God exists," she said at Medjugorje.

11. Jesus on Mary in the Apparitions

The discussion of the New Adam–New Eve theme in the teachings of the Fathers and the ancient liturgies indicated that veneration of Mary in no way subverts the worship of Jesus but instead consolidates the truth of His divinity, humanity, and all-sufficient redemptive sacrifice. Similarly, apparitions of the Virgin reinforce the truth of the Incarnation and other important truths of the faith.

We have said that "apparitions" of Jesus are not possible if "apparition" is understood to mean an appearance in His Risen Body since He has said in the Gospels that He will not come again physically until His Second Coming. Nevertheless, Jesus does communicate to chosen souls through visions. Some Marian apparitions also include visions (as opposed to apparitions) of Jesus. The perspective of Jesus on Mary in these visions is consistent with the ancient voice of the Church.

To Berthe Petit (who was given prophetic visions of World War I before it took place)

> Cause My Mother's Heart, transfixed by sorrows that rent Mine, to be loved. (December 25, 1909)

> You must think of My Mother's Heart as you think of Mine; live in this Heart as you will seek to live in Mine; give yourself to this Heart so wholly united to Mine. (February 7, 1910)

> The world must be dedicated to the Sorrowful and Immaculate Heart of My Mother as it is dedicated to Mine. Fear nothing, no matter what suffering or obstacles you may meet. Think only of fulfilling My will. (March 1910)

> It is in coredemption that My Mother was above all great. That is why I ask that the invocation as I have inspired it should be approved and diffused throughout the Church....It has already obtained grace. It will obtain more until the hour comes when, by consecration to the Sorrowful and Immaculate Heart of My Mother, the Church shall be uplifted and the world renewed. (September 1911)

> The title Immaculate belongs to the whole being of My Mother and not especially to her heart. This title flows from my gratuitous gift to the Virgin who has given me birth. However My Mother has acquired for her heart the title Sorrowful by sharing generously in all the sufferings of My heart and My body from the crib to the Cross. There is not one of these sorrows which did not pierce the heart of My Mother. Living image of My crucified body, her virginal flesh bore the invisible marks of My wounds as her heart felt the sorrows of My own. Nothing could ever tarnish the incorruptibility of her Immaculate Heart. The title of Sorrowful belongs, therefore, to the heart of My Mother, and more than any other, this title is dear to her because it springs from the union of her heart with Mine in the redemption of humanity. This title has been acquired by her through her full participation in My Calvary, and it should precede the gratuitous title "immaculate" which My love bestowed upon her by a singular privilege. (October 1920)

To Sister Lucia of Fatima:

> "Have compassion on the heart of your most holy Mother, covered with thorns, with which ungrateful men pierce it at every moment, and there is no one to make an act of reparation to remove them. (December 10, 1925)

> What is being done to promote the devotion to the Immaculate Heart of Mary? (February 26, 1926)

I want My entire Church to know that this favor [the conversion of Russia] was obtained through the Immaculate Heart of My Mother so that it may extend this devotion later on and put the devotion to this Immaculate Heart beside the devotion to My Sacred Heart. (1929)

To Emmanuel (Rwanda):

How can someone say he loves Jesus, adores Him, and lives outside His Blessed Mother's Immaculate Heart? My Mother is the Mother of the world. (1982)

To Gladys (San Nicolás, Argentina):

If this generation does not listen to My Mother, it will perish! I ask the world to do so. (March 12, 1986)

Today I warn the world of what the world seems unaware: Souls are in danger; many will be lost! Salvation will reach few unless I am accepted as the Savior! My Mother should be received. My Mother should be listened to in all of her messages. Mankind must discover the wealth she brings to Christians. The children of sin will grow in sin, if disbelief grows in them! I want a renewal of spirit, a breaking away from death and an attachment to life. The Heart of My Mother is the one chosen for what I ask to become reality. Souls will find me through her Immaculate Heart! (November 19, 1987)

Before the world was saved by means of Noah's Ark; today the ark is My Mother. Through her, souls will be saved, because she will bring them toward Me. He who rejects My Mother rejects Me! Many are letting the grace of God pass by in these days. (December 30, 1989)

To Myrna (Damascus, Syria):

My daughter, she is My Mother from whom I was born. He who honors her, honors Me. He who denies her, denies Me. And he who asks something from her obtains it because she is My Mother. (August 14, 1987)

To Patricia Talbott (Cuenca, Ecuador):

Love My Mother because she holds back the fury of Heaven. Love her in all the good that happens to you and be discreet. (December 28, 1988)

To Julia Kim (Naju, South Korea):

My beloved little soul! The greatest treasure in My Church is My Mother Mary, who is most holy. My Mother is the Queen of the Universe, the Queen of Heaven and your Mother. Therefore, My Mother Mary can love you, as I love you, and can do anything that I can do through the grace from Me. (September 22, 1995)

12. Mary on Jesus in the Apparitions

Like any mother, Mary rejoices when her Son is honored. But her Son is different from every other son in history for He is both God and Savior of humanity. In her apparitions, the Virgin speaks about her Son from four main perspectives: (1) as the Mother who is distraught by the suffering of her Son; (2) as the Mother of her Son's brothers and sisters whom she must "educate" in faith and holiness; (3) as her Son's messenger in every age applying His teaching in that period in history; (4) as Evangelizer leading those who do not know her Son to Him.

The Sorrowful Mother

My daughter: It was the blows that started His suffering; then the thorns, the nails, the lance. It was so painful, for me, to see Him suffer! Today, it is the sins, the hurtful words, the atheism. Yes, again they are crucifying Him, again my Heart bleeds. (San Nicolás, Argentina, April 1 [Good Friday], 1988)

My heart has been consumed over my only Son. (Damascus, Syria, November 4, 1983)

Those who drive carts cannot swear without adding my Son's name. These are the...things which cause the weight of my Son's arm to be so burdensome. (La Salette, France, 1846)

This evening I am especially asking you to venerate the Heart of my Son, Jesus. Make atonement for the wounds inflicted to the Heart of my Son. That heart has been offended with all sorts of sin. (Medjugorje, Bosnia, April 5, 1984)

Educator

Sacrifice yourselves for sinners, and say many times, especially whenever you make some sacrifice: O Jesus, it is for love of You, for the conversion of sinners, and in reparation for the sins committed against the Immaculate Heart of Mary.... When you pray the Rosary, say after each mystery: O my Jesus, forgive us, save us from the fire of Hell. Lead all souls to Heaven, especially those who are most in need. (Fatima, Portugal, July 17, 1917)

Do you love my Son? (Beauraing, Belgium, January 3, 1932).

My rays which come from the sun of justice of my divine Son will dazzle you. Be loyal to His doctrine. Lead an evangelical, secular, and apostolic life! (Betania, Venezuela, November 27, 1985)

Messenger

Jesus wishes to make use of you to make me known and loved. He wants to establish in the world devotion to my Immaculate Heart. (Fatima, Portugal, June 13, 1917)

My sole purpose is to ensure that the will of the Son is obeyed. (Amsterdam, Holland, March 4, 1951)

Nobody knows the exact date and hour of the Lord's coming again to us. Preparations are in progress to defeat His enemies, destroy them, and establish His Kingdom on this earth. He will come to you on clouds displaying His power to build His glorious Kingdom. Prepare to greet Him with trust, love, and faith. He is coming to you through me, His Mother. As He was sent to you by God the Father through my virgin body, Jesus will be using my Immaculate Heart in returning to you as the King. Therefore, all the children of the world! Open your mind widely without delay and return to me. (Naju, Korea, January 29, 1991)

Evangelizer

Most people are crashing against a wall of evil. Only those who believe in Christ the Redeemer will be saved. My children, come to me, all of you. Make this known. (San Nicolás, Argentina, December 16, 1983)

Mary is truly the path to Jesus if you look at her role as Evangelizer. As the Evangelizer, she brought eight million Aztecs to her Son. Historians say that through her apparitions in nineteenth-century France, she did more to preserve the faith than any apologist or church authority. She has consoled those who are persecuted for their faith in China, Vietnam, and many other countries. She continues to draw millions of people of all religions to her shrine in India.

She is also specially loved in the Moslem world, partly because of the great honor she is given in the Qur'an. Her apparition at Fatima strikes a chord with Moslems because Fatima was the name of Mohammed's favorite daughter; Lourdes was named after a Moslem commander who became a Catholic; Medjugorje is in the middle of a Moslem-majority country; Zeitun, Egypt, and Damascus, Syria, are in Moslem-majority countries. At Zeitun, she appeared to nearly two million people in all, most of them Moslem. There are good reasons then for the traditional belief that Mary will be Heaven's Ambassador to the Moslem world — a role she has already started fulfilling.

It has also been widely believed that she will bring the peoples of China and Russia to her Son.

13. The Virgin and World History

Obviously the apparitions of the Virgin did not take place in a vacuum. Even the most determined skeptics have to admit that the alleged apparitions of the Virgin Mary have had an effect on history at least in terms of sociological consequences. Here we will go beyond the "religious" dimension of the Virgin's interventions to consider their world-historical impact.

To begin with, the Virgin's perspective on the history of the world mirrors Yahweh's constant warnings through His Prophets to the people of Israel in the Old Testament; her messages to the world share the admonitory tone of St. Paul's epistles. The Old Testament showed us that human history is driven primarily by the purposes and plans of God and humanity's responses to the divine initiative. There was a divinely ordained law of cause and effect in the moral and spiritual realms that was just as inexorable as causal law in the physical world. Human sin brought divine retribution — even for God's anointed (David) — although divine mercy was always available to the repentant. This inescapable link between human choices and their consequences in human history did not cease with the New Testament. In fact, while the New Covenant made the graces given to the people of Israel in the Old Covenant available to the world as a whole, along with the immeasurably greater graces that came with the redemptive death of the Savior, there was no revocation of the moral order. Jesus warned that "I tell you, you will not get out till you have paid the very last penny" (Luke 12:59), and He wept over Jerusalem because of its impending destruction ("I tell you solemnly, all of this will recoil on this generation," Matt. 23:36), a destruction that He attributed to its rejection of Him.

In the Old Testament, God revealed the world-historical connection between choices and consequences through His Prophets. In the Christian dispensation, He has revealed that there is one Prophet ordained to carry out this mission of merciful warning and constant encouragement: the Mother of "all who obey God's commandments and bear witness for Jesus."

In her apparition messages the Virgin Mother gives a diagnosis of world history that defies the canons of "political correctness" of the secular and religious elites, much as the teachings of Jesus were offensive to both civil and ecclesiastical authorities. But just as the message of Jesus drew the common people so does the message of the Virgin in her apparitions find a home in the hearts of the faithful in general. To spread His message, Jesus chose peasants and fishermen, those at the lowest rungs of society. To spread her message, the Virgin almost invariably chooses the poor and the lowly (the intellectually sophisticated and the politically or ecclesiastically powerful have never been the direct recipients of her major apparitions). We remember, of course, that it was the Virgin who proclaimed that the Almighty will "exalt the lowly."

The Virgin's verdict is simple: nothing has changed since the days of Noah. The key to world history is the state of our souls. She predicted (and predicts) specific consequences of specific choices and showed how the major events of modern world history were inextricably bound up with human actions and decisions. Her warnings became (or become) more urgent as dire events moved (or move) closer, but she always holds out hope for those who repent. Moreover, she herself gives specific remedies that can protect those who act accordingly, the consecration of Russia to the Immaculate Heart being the most famous example.

The Virgin's interventions have affected world history in two ways. On one level, the conversions that resulted from her apparitions have had an impact on the particular society in which she appeared. On another level, through her intercession with God, which is possible only if there is a free response from the faithful, historical events have taken a different course than would normally have been expected.

The sociological impact of Marian apparitions has been acknowledged by secular historians. The first and most obvious instance was Guadalupe. What even those who reject the apparition have to acknowledge is that something happened in 1531 that led to the conversion of the Aztec nation, of eight million Aztecs.

Jacques Lafaye, a historian at the Sorbonne in France, in fact sees Guadalupe as the foundational event for a new American culture and a postcolonial indigenous new world. The apparition took place just before a rebellion of the Aztecs that would have wiped out all the Spaniards in Mexico — and with them Christianity. Because the Virgin is said to have appeared as an Aztec and to an Aztec and to have chosen a Spanish title for herself (Guadalupe), the apparition also helped unify the Spaniards and the natives.

The response of the faithful to the reported Marian apparitions in nineteenth-century France also had a decisive influence in mitigating the forces that sought to turn France entirely away from the Church. The successful popular revolt of July 1830 against Charles X, who had tried to restore the privileges of the nobility and the clergy, threatened to complete the destruction of the Church, a process that had begun in the French Revolution. But the first of the modern Marian apparitions, Our Lady of the Miraculous Medal, was reported in July and November 1830 in Paris, the very seat of the Enlightenment. This apparition, coupled with the apparitions of 1846 (La Salette) and 1858 (Lourdes), had such a great impact that large segments of the general population returned to faith and the Church — a turn of events that historians cannot explain without reference to the reported apparitions. Jaroslav Pelikan notes that the campaign "that the Virgin waged" was far more effective than the intellectual defense of French Catholic apologists and the political defense of the institutional Church. In the twentieth century, the reported apparitions of Fatima and Medjugorje in particular, and the hundreds of other claims of apparitions in general, have played a major role in bringing millions to Christianity and consolidating the faith of millions of others.

It is to be remembered here that the reported apparitions of the Middle Ages and before and the shrines associated with these apparitions played a significant role in both spreading and consolidating the faith. This was the case too with the reported apparitions and shrines in countries like India and Vietnam.

But it is the second level of the effects of the Virgin's interventions on world history that is of interest here, what we might call the supernatural impact on the course of history. This impact can be divided into two categories: warnings of impending tragedies, sometimes with prescriptions for prevention (usually reparation and prayer); manifestations of the Virgin's intercession in response to the petitions of the faithful.

Warnings

In the warning category, we might include the hundreds of apparitions that have been reported before such great calamities as the French Revolution, the destructive wars of nineteenth-century Europe, and the two world wars of the twentieth century. Some of the most striking supernatural warnings (verifiable as having taken place before the events in question) are listed here. The hundreds of claimed apparitions during these periods that were never formally investigated are not included.

On February 2, 1634, in the Immaculate Conception Convent in Quito, Ecuador, the Virgin appeared to Sister Mary Anne of Jesus and warned that the twentieth century would see a flight from faith and morals and that the Church itself would be internally affected by heresy and apostasy; this would be followed by a chastisement and then a renewal.

On June 17, 1689, the famous St. Margaret Mary Alacoque, to whom Jesus revealed the mysteries of His Sacred Heart, was instructed by the Lord to ask the reigning king of France to consecrate his country to the Sacred Heart. The king did not honor this request. It was on June 17, 1789, that the French Revolution broke out and King Louis XVI was ousted from the throne and thereafter beheaded. This correlation was actually drawn to the attention of Sister Lucia of Fatima by the Lord Himself, who warned (in August 1931) that a similar failure to carry out the request to consecrate Russia to the Immaculate Heart could result in similar consequences: "Make it known to my ministers that, given they follow the example of the king of France in delaying the execution of My command, that they will follow him into misfortune." More on the Fatima request follows.

In the Miraculous Medal apparition of 1830, the Virgin prophesied that the king of France would be overthrown, the archbishop of Paris would be stripped of his clothes, churches would be desecrated, and the streets would run with blood — all over a period of forty years. All the prophecies came to pass within forty years of 1830: the king was ousted in a matter of days, churches were desecrated, the archbishop was beaten and stripped of his clothes, two subsequent archbishops were murdered, and mobs roamed the streets.

At La Salette in 1846, the Virgin warned of the failure of the potato and walnut crops, of famines, and of the death of children from disease. Within a year the crops failed and over a million people died of famine in Europe; many children died of cholera.

On May 12, 1914, the Virgin appeared to twenty-two people in the village of Hrushiv, Ukraine, and warned that Russia would become a godless country and would go through two wars; Ukraine would suffer for eighty years and then be free. In 1987, she appeared in the same village and said their freedom was at hand and that Ukraine would soon be an independent state.

At Fatima, Portugal, starting in May 1917, the Virgin made these prophecies: the war would come to an end soon but a greater war would break out after a strange light was seen in the northern sky; Russia would scatter its errors around the world; various nations would be annihilated; Russia would be converted; in the end the Immaculate Heart of Mary would triumph and there would be an Era of Peace. The First World War did end soon after. Strange lights were seen in the northern sky (claimed by some to be the aurora borealis) in 1938, prior to the beginning of World War II the next year. Russia did become Communist and scattered its errors around the world. In fact, on October 13, 1917, on the last day of the Fatima apparitions, Vladimir Lenin walked into Russia. The Communists were removed from power in 1991 (after the requested consecration was carried out; see below). The prophecies about various nations being annihilated and the Era of Peace have not yet been fulfilled. Three "secrets" were given to the Fatima visionaries. The first two secrets of Fatima were the revelation of Hell and the importance of devotion to the Immaculate Heart. The third secret is with the Pope and has not been revealed to the world. Asked about its contents, Sister

Lucia, the only surviving visionary of Fatima, said, "It is in the Gospel and the Book of Revelation. Read them." In March 1939, Jesus told Sister Lucia, "The time is coming when the reign of My justice will punish the crimes of various nations. Some of them will be annihilated."

The most destructive battle of the Second World War, the Battle of the Bulge (claiming 162,000 lives), took place in the Ardennes, where two Belgian towns, Beauraing and Banneux, are located. These were the two places where the Virgin last appeared (in 1932 and 1933) before the outbreak of the war. She appeared especially grave and sorrowful in her last apparition at Banneux.

During the Amsterdam apparitions of Our Lady of All Nations, which began on March 25, 1945, the Virgin prophesied the following events: the date of the death of Pope Pius XII; the Second Vatican Council and the nature of its reforms; a future Marian dogma on mediation; the death of Pope John XXIII and the election of Paul VI; the Communist takeover of China (this prophecy was made in 1945); the Korean War; the formation of Israel (April 21, 1945, and December 26, 1947); the Cold War and the Berlin Wall; germ warfare; the fall of Communism in Russia ("I see the sickle and the hammer, but the hammer breaks away from the sickle and they both drop into a whirlpool.... In Russia a great upheaval would take place," 1947 and 1951); and the war in the former Yugoslavia. On June 9, 1946, she prophesied another great war, which some believe could be the Third World War: "Then the Lady says, 'I predict another great catastrophe for the world.' This she says very sadly and she kept shaking her head: 'If people would only listen — but they will not!'.... Then the Lady points to the east. I see a great number of stars in the air. 'That is where it is coming from,' she says."

At Akita, on October 13, 1973, Sister Agnes Sasagawa was told that if humanity did not repent the Father would inflict a punishment greater than the Deluge on humanity, that "fire will plunge from the sky and a large part of humanity will perish." (October 13 was also the anniversary of the last apparition of Fatima in 1917 with its fiery sun miracle; again on October 13, 1884, Pope Leo XIII received a prophetic revelation about the battle between God and Satan in the twentieth century.)

At Betania, Venezuela, María Esperanza was told by the Virgin (in apparitions which began in 1976), "Mankind is currently abusing the graces received and is moving toward perdition, and if there is no change and improvement of life, it will succumb under fire, war, and death." In Cuapa, Nicaragua, Bernardo Martínez was told in 1980, "If you do not change your ways, you will hasten the arrival of the Third World War. Pray, pray, pray, my children for the entire world. The world is seriously threatened."

At Medjugorje, Bosnia, one of the visionaries, Mirjana, reported:

> Before the visible sign is given to humanity, there will be three warnings to the world. The warnings will be in the form of events on earth. Mirjana will be a witness to them. Three days before one of the admonitions, Mirjana will notify a priest of her choice. The witness of Mirjana will be a confirmation of the apparitions and a stimulus for the conversion of the

world. After the admonitions, the visible sign will appear on the site of the apparitions in Medjugorje for all the world to see. The sign will be given as a testimony to the apparitions and in order to call people back to faith. The ninth and tenth secrets are serious. They concern chastisement for the sins of the world. Punishment is inevitable, for we cannot expect the whole world to be converted. The punishment can be diminished by prayer and penance, but it cannot be eliminated. Mirjana says that one of the evils that threatened the world, the one contained in the seventh secret, has been averted thanks to prayer and fasting. That is why the Blessed Virgin continues to encourage prayer and fasting: "You have forgotten that through prayer and fasting you can avert war and suspend the laws of nature." After the first admonition, the others will follow in a rather short time. Thus, people will have some time for conversion. That interval will be a period of grace and conversion. After the visible sign appears, those who are still alive will have little time for conversion. For that reason, the Blessed Virgin invites us to urgent conversion and reconciliation.

The apparitions in Medjugorje will cease once all six visionaries receive all ten of the "secrets," after which the events foretold in the secrets will unfold. To date, three of them have received ten of the secrets and the other three have received nine.

On August 15, 1982, in an eight-hour long apparition, the visionaries in Rwanda, Africa, were warned that the rivers would run with blood; they were shown visions of thousands of corpses and asked to flee the country. During the civil war which broke out in 1991, over a million people were killed; the rivers were choked with bodies.

In Ukraine, in 1987, the Virgin warned, "The times are coming which have been foretold as being those in the end times."

Manifestations

Of the many great interventions of the Virgin in history, two great miracles of the Rosary involve Austria. On October 7, 1571, the ships of Spain, Venice, and the papal states, under the leadership of Don Juan of Austria, faced a huge Turkish armada. The Turks had taken over Constantinople, the Balkans, and Cyprus and were now poised to conquer Rome and thereafter all of Europe. Pope Pius V had asked the Christians of Europe to pray the Rosary to avert a Turkish triumph. The battle began disastrously for the Christian fleet, for the Turks had managed to separate the three squadrons and were now preparing to cut them to pieces. At that time a tremendous wind mysteriously swept through the area, throwing the Turkish fleet into disarray, and 230 of their 300 galleys were captured or destroyed; the Christians lost 16. This decisive victory is attributed both to the Rosary and to Our Lady of Guadalupe because on board the ship of Prince Andrea Doria, whose squadron had initially been outflanked by the Turks, was an image of Our Lady of Guadalupe (specially sent from Mexico), whose intercession the prince had sought.

The Austrians did not forget this miraculous rescue when their country was taken over by the Soviet Union in the aftermath of the Second World War. In 1948, three years after the Soviets had taken over, 10 percent of all Austrians (seven hundred thousand at the time) began a Rosary crusade pledging to say the Rosary daily until the Soviets left. Seven years later, on May 13, 1955, the Soviets mysteriously left the country. (May 13 was the anniversary of the first Fatima apparition, which was an apparition of Our Lady of the Rosary.) This was the first time in history that the Communists had ever peacefully relinquished control over a country they had taken over — and there was no humanly plausible explanation as to why they would have given up such a resource-rich and strategically located country.

There are several other instances of the Virgin's direct intervention in protecting those who seek her help.

In 1900, the Christians of Dong Lu, who numbered less than a thousand, were attacked by an enemy army of over ten thousand who sought to wipe them out. The army came to a halt and then fled when they saw a beautiful lady in the sky and a fiery horseman who charged toward them. Our Lady of China appeared again to thousands of the faithful in 1995.

In 1871, war had broken out between France and Prussia. The rapidly advancing Prussians had captured the emperor and were on the verge of taking over Paris. At this time, the devout villagers of Pontmain, France, sought the Virgin's intercession and protection. On January 17, she appeared to five children in the village, asking them to pray and giving them two messages, "God will soon grant your request" and "My Son allows Himself to be moved." At the exact time of the apparition (5:30 p.m.), the Prussians stopped their advance for reasons that baffle historians. Some of the Prussians are reported to have seen a lady in the sky, and one of their generals said they could go no further because "there is an invisible Madonna barring the way." The Virgin's title in Pontmain (appropriately) is Our Lady of Hope. Her blue robe in Pontmain had forty-two stars — forty-two years later France would enter the First World War.

In 1938, after repeated requests from Sister Lucia, the Portuguese bishops consecrated their country to the Immaculate Heart of Mary. When the Second World War broke out, Portugal was untouched. Why did the Virgin appear in Fatima, Portugal? Two reasons can be given. First, King John IV of Portugal officially consecrated his country to Our Lady of the Immaculate Conception on October 20, 1646, and gave her his crown. Second, on May 5, 1917, Pope Benedict XV asked the faithful to petition the Mother of Mercy to bring peace to a world at war. Eight days later, on May 13, she responded with her "peace plan" for the century.

One of the great miracles of the Second World War was the mysterious protection of the devotees of the Rosary in Nagasaki, Japan. On August 6, 1945, when the atom bomb was dropped on Nagasaki, four Jesuit priests, Fathers Schiffer, Lasalle, Kleinsore, and Cieslik were praying the Rosary and, as they said, "trying to live the message of Our Lady of Fatima" in their parish house, which was eight houses away from the center of the explosion. These four priests were not only the only survivors within the one mile radius of the explosion, but they suffered none of the after-effects of radiation and their house was undamaged, although all the buildings around them were destroyed!

The Virgin has often chosen Marian feast days to manifest her intercession. The most famous such event in recent times was the miraculous survival of Pope John Paul II. The attempt on his life took place on May 13, 1981, the anniversary of the first apparition of Fatima, and the Pope attributes his escape to a direct intervention of Our Lady of Fatima. It was during his convalescence after the assassination attempt that the Pope studied all the key documents relating to Fatima. When he left the hospital, he was determined to honor the request of both the Virgin and the Lord that Russia be consecrated to the Immaculate Heart. On June 13, 1929, the Virgin had told Sister Lucia, "The moment has come when God asks the Holy Father in union with the bishops of the world to make the consecration of Russia to My Heart, promising to save it by this means." Several popes had sought to meet these conditions and make the appropriate consecration — but none had performed it as requested and Russia continued to spread its errors.

On March 25, 1984, Pope John Paul II made the requested consecration in union with bishops around the world. In July 1989, Sister Lucia confirmed that the required consecration had been accomplished and accepted and "God will keep his word." By the end of 1989, Communism collapsed throughout Eastern Europe. The August 19, 1991, coup against Mikhail Gorbachev failed on August 22, and in her August 25, 1991, message at Medjugorje, the Virgin for the first time mentioned Fatima: "I invite you to renunciation for nine days so that with your help, everything I wanted to realize through the secrets I began in Fatima may be fulfilled." In her September 25, 1991, message from Medjugorje she said, "Now as never before, Satan wants to show the world his shameful face by which he plans to seduce as many people as possible on to the way of death and sin. Therefore, dear children, help my Immaculate Heart to triumph." By the end of 1991, the Soviet Communist state came apart and a free Russia was reborn. Fatima came just before the beginning of Communism and Medjugorje just before its end in Europe.

But even at Fatima, and especially at Medjugorje and Akita, the Virgin and her messages were looking beyond Communism toward a final chastisement from Heaven. Her messages always affirmed that repentance and reparation could mitigate and even eliminate this chastisement. And beyond the chastisement lies the Era of Peace.

With the thousands of nuclear and biological weapons stockpiled around the globe, it is not difficult to foresee a terrestrial and even accidental Armageddon, not to speak of the potential global chaos that could be triggered by a breakdown of communication and computer systems. Even in the Old Testament, the chastisements of God usually came through the natural realm. If Yahweh allowed a heathen army to defeat the Israelites because of their moral laxity, one could see the events as they transpired without seeing the hand of God in them. Likewise the fall of the Berlin Wall and of Communism in Europe could just be seen as inexplicable events; one does not have to relate them to the Fatima prophecy. Similarly, a future divinely directed chastisement may not be recognized as such by those who lack discernment or the benefit of a commentary from the Virgin. In fact, the whole "problem of evil" is really a question of the reality of chastisements: for the doctrine of original sin sees moral evil as the prime cause of the disorder in the world: a chastisement can sometimes be self-inflicted rather than divinely instituted.

It may be said that the prophets of nuclear doom have not only been wrong but consistently wrong. For this we should be thankful. But once a nuclear event or a "natural" worldwide chastisement in some form comes to pass, nothing will ever be the same again; we will not be able to write and read about it as we do now, activities we take for granted. In the previous two world wars, life on the home front could go on with some semblance of normality. Except in heavily damaged areas, newspapers and movie theaters were still operational, food was available. Today, there are weapons that can destroy every form of life on the planet. There are unstable regimes run by unstable tyrants who possess these weapons. And across the world almost all of us have broken — and continue to break — every law in the Book. If ever the Fatima messages of penance and reparation and prayer were applicable, it is today. And that is why Mary weeps over the world today as her Son wept over Jerusalem!

14. From the Triumph of the Immaculate Heart to the Reign of the Sacred Heart

A remarkable feature of Marian apparitions is the congruency of their prophetic messages with the vision of the New Testament and the Fathers of the Church.

The Epistle to the Ephesians offers a cosmic vision of the mission of Christ:

> He has let us know the mystery of his purpose, the hidden plan he so kindly made in Christ from the beginning to act upon when the times had run their course to the end; that he would bring together everything under Christ, as head, everything in the heavens and everything on earth. (Eph. 1:9–10)

The Epistle to the Colossians continues this theme,

> He is the image of the unseen God and the first-born of all creation, for in him were created all things in heaven and on earth: everything visible and everything invisible.... All things were created through him and for him. Before anything was created, he existed, and he holds all things in unity.... As he is the Beginning, he was first to be born from the dead, so that he could be first in every way; because God wanted all perfection to be found in him and all things to be reconciled through him and for him, everything in heaven and everything on earth, when he made peace by his death on the cross. (Col. 1:15–20).

The Christian message is that all of material creation is finally to be glorified through and in Christ. The Fathers who saw the pattern of "recapitulation" and "recirculation" (inverse correspondence) in salvation history, where the evil done by Eve is remedied by the New Eve, see the same process at work at all levels of God's creation. In the long run, God's purposes will not be frustrated.

If humanity fell in Adam through Eve, humanity would rise again in the New Adam through the New Eve; if the Paradise made for the human race was lost by the disobedience of the parents of human life, an even greater Paradise would be gained through the obedience of the parents of life in God ("grace"). If it seemed that Satan would prevent every human person from participating in the divine plan, the response of God was to crush Satan through the free participation of a human person in His plan, a person who brought forth the divine Person who would be the Redeemer. The process of the transfiguration and transformation of the terrestrial order began when God Himself took on human flesh, and the process will culminate at the end of history when the whole physical world will be transfigured and transformed by being "taken up into Christ." The model for the transfigured universe is the Risen Body of Christ, but this is as far as human imagination can go without being lost in mere speculation.

The New Testament also talks of a time of persecution before the final victory of Christ, and this theme too was developed by the Fathers.

As the last chapter indicated, the prophetic message of the Marian apparitions echoes three themes: the continuing sinfulness of humanity will cause a new chastisement from God, the greatest and the last of the chastisements; the Virgin will prepare the faithful for the coming of her Son (before and during the chastisement), and this will be the triumph of her Immaculate Heart; her triumph will be followed by an Era of Peace under the reign of the Sacred Heart of Jesus. All this will be followed by the Second Coming of Christ, the General Judgment of the human race and eternity.

Although many have speculated about various details of the Era of Peace, it is safe to say that none of the major apparitions has given us such details beyond stating the fact that there will be a chastisement followed by an Era of Peace. The details are perhaps to be found in the "secrets" but these secrets will only become known shortly before their fulfillment.

At Rwanda the Virgin warned of a severe chastisement, and rivers of blood soon flowed through the nation. In Medjugorje, her constant refrain was "Peace," and, as many of the first observers later said, the true import of her constant requests for reconciliation became apparent only after war had broken out in Bosnia. Today, almost all major apparitions, particularly Akita, warn that catastrophe lies ahead for the world unless there is radical repentance. La Salette, in particular, had prophesied that the Antichrist would come to power during the final chastisement (a theme that is again found in both Scripture and the Fathers).

But the chastisement is at the same time a purification and when it comes to an end — on this the messages are consistent — an Era of Peace, a Golden Age, will come to the world. This is the era when the divine will is obeyed on earth as it is in Heaven. None of the visionaries, for example, Sr. Lucia of Fatima or the Medjugorje visionaries, are worried about the final outcome. And, it must be repeated, any future "chastisement" can be mitigated and even averted by our free actions — by prayers and sacrifices and reparation. Ten good men could have saved Sodom. The continuing intercession of the Virgin, the divine mercy of her Son, and the suffering of victim souls around the world can yet save the day!

The language of Immaculate Heart and Sacred Heart conveys the love of the

Lord and His Mother (the heart being the center of love and feeling), which, in turn, reflects the love of the Trinity. The metaphor of the Two Hearts is an icon that throbs with the infinite and never-ending love of the loving Father, the crucified Son, and the sanctifying Spirit. Ultimately consecration to the Sacred Heart of Jesus through the Immaculate Heart of Mary is an entrance into the eternal love of the Three Persons. Human history itself must be consecrated — a purifying and therefore painful consecration — through the Immaculate Heart of its Mother to the Sacred Heart of its Savior so that it can enter eternity. Those who have individually made this consecration have nothing to fear in any future chastisement.

These words from Scripture are especially applicable here:

> You may be quite sure of this, that if the householder had known at what hour the burglar would come, he would not have let anyone break through the wall of his house. You too must stand ready, because the Son of Man is coming at an hour you do not expect.... Happy that servant if his master's arrival finds him at that employment." (Luke 12:39–40, 43)

> The Day of the Lord is going to come like a thief in the night.... But it is not as if you live in the dark, my brothers, for that Day to overtake you like a thief. No, you are all sons of light and sons of the day: we do not belong to the night or to darkness, so we should not go on sleeping, as everyone else does, but stay wide awake and sober.... Let us put on faith and love for a breastplate, and the hope of salvation for a helmet. God never meant us to experience the Retribution, but to win salvation through our Lord Jesus Christ, who died for us so that, alive or dead, we should still be united to him. So give encouragement to each other, and keep strengthening one another, as you do already. (1 Thess. 5:2, 4–6, 8–11)

15. Evidence and Explanation

The globe- and history-spanning nature of Marian apparitions is little known. Almost as little known is the fact that there is a comprehensive body of tangible evidence supporting the historically accepted apparition reports. Moreover, despite repeated attempts to do so by the most determined skeptics, not one of the constituents of this body of evidence has been nullified nor a single visionary (witness of the apparition) discredited. The prosecution has had every possible opportunity to undermine the veracity of the star witnesses and the credibility of the evidence on the table. And yet it has presented no case. An a priori rejection of supernatural phenomena is irrelevant because it simply begs the question raised by the existence of the evidence. Speculative theories about apparitions as projections of fears and fantasies from the vulnerable visionary's unconscious are not helpful in the courtroom because they cannot begin to account for the tangible evidence. So the prosecution has built no case. And the jury — here the human race — reached its verdict a long time ago: the visionaries were truthful when they reported the apparitions of the Virgin.

The tangible evidence is extraordinary in its variety. Take the famous tilma of Guadalupe with the miraculous image of the Virgin. Despite decades spent in trying to show it to be a human painting, there is still no scientific explanation for its origin (its colors, for example, do not originate from any animal, vegetable, or mineral dye known in this world). Take the spring at Lourdes. Numerous meticulously documented healings have taken place here, but the analyses done on the contents of the spring have shown it to be plain water. (Such healing springs are not uncommon in Marian apparitions, another prominent example being Vailankanni, India.) Take the prophecies of Fatima about the Second World War and the rise and demise of Communism in Russia (the apparition took place before any of these events). Or take the televised apparition of the Virgin in Hrushiv, Ukraine — an apparition that appeared on the television screens of the former Soviet Union — and the photographs of the Lady of Light that were taken during the apparitions in Zeitun, Egypt, before hundreds of thousands of people. Likewise, the sparkling tears on the wooden statue of Our Lady of Akita appeared on national TV in Japan.

A recurrent motif in Marian apparitions is the Virgin's desire to provide a "sign" for those who do not believe. "Signs" were on occasion demanded by church authorities or family members who wanted evidence that the visionary was indeed witnessing an apparition of the Virgin. The most famous sign of all was the tilma of Guadalupe, but others, such as the miracle of the sun at Fatima, have been almost as remarkable. Here it may be well to note that signs and wonders in Marian apparitions are never performed for sensational purposes but in response to a request for evidence (in contrast to the kind of bizarre phenomena one would expect if these events were diabolically directed). The signs serve the function of giving sufficient ground for belief — and this was the case with the signs and wonders performed by Jesus. Thus the Virgin acknowledges and responds to legitimate demands for evidence.

The case for the authenticity of the apparition claims chronicled here may be summarized as follows:

1. The revelation of God in Jesus Christ was truly a revelation of God as He is in Himself and of the origin and purpose of human life.

2. God acts in human history through His chosen instruments to bring about conversion to Christ and subsequently sanctification and salvation. But a true conversion cannot be coerced: it must be freely accepted.

3. In God's blueprint of salvation, Mary is the New Eve who brings us the New Adam through her free choice. She is the Spouse of the Holy Spirit (she is the only human person in Scripture who is overshadowed by the Spirit), the Mother of all Christians who are adopted brothers and sisters of her Son Jesus. Her first apparition to the faithful is shown in Scripture in Revelation 12. Revelation 12:17 shows that she will be present with Christians throughout their battle against Satan. At Cana, we see that her intercession bears fruit in "signs." Many interpretations have been given of the significance of this event, but two facts are undeniable: she requested

a miracle and her Son performed one in response. We are intrigued also by the curious comment, "My time has not yet come." Does this mean that when His time has come (which it did on Calvary), His Mother can intercede with Him for miracles?

4. Numerous credible witnesses across the globe and throughout history have claimed to have seen the Virgin. Some of these witnesses were the holiest people of their time and were later venerated as saints. Most of the witnesses were children who were in many cases very severely questioned but still held to their stories. During an actual apparition, it is quite evident to onlookers that a naturalistically inexplicable change has taken place in the visionary (technically termed a state of ecstasy). In some of the apparitions, the Virgin asked the visionaries to keep certain of her messages as "secrets" that could be revealed only to the appointed person at the appointed time. The tenacity with which the younger visionaries have refused to reveal these "secrets" — from Lourdes to La Salette to Fatima to Medjugorje — despite threats (sometimes to their lives as at Fatima) and bribes is another paradoxical feature of the apparition stories.

5. The ecclesiastical authorities have in most instances been skeptical about apparition claims and visionaries. Fatima, for instance, was approved as worthy of belief only thirteen years after it ended. Thus the Christian community as a whole did not simply accept claims of apparitions without carefully securing and studying the evidence. Generally, the visionaries themselves were transformed by their experiences and led exemplary lives thereafter.

6. The messages of the various apparitions are remarkably consistent despite the enormous differences of locations and time frames.

7. The messages received at the various apparitions in one way or another echo the words of Mary in Scripture: on the importance of doing God's will; on the divine mandate that all generations are to call her blessed; and on the intercessory role she assumed at the beginning of her Son's ministry.

8. Many of the major apparitions have ended with a "lasting sign" that is not susceptible to natural explanation (the tilma of Guadalupe, for instance).

9. There is a correlation between the crises in history and the appearances of the Virgin: she comes whenever her children need her.

10. The apparitions have had a concrete effect on history and on millions of people.

All of the facts above call out for an explanation. Explanation is the fundamental job of both good science and sound philosophy. We start with the assumption that explanations exist for everything (and this is where the quest for an explanation for the existence of the universe leads ultimately to the existence of God). We accept explanations for phenomena that most plausibly fit the evidence. We discount purported explanations that are driven by ideological agendas or mere speculation, especially when these refuse to address the evidence in hand.

No serious naturalistic explanation has been offered by the skeptics. If we look at the global and history-spanning nature of Marian apparitions, the curious consistency of messages from multiple visionaries, the tangible "lasting signs," and the mass conversions that not only resulted at the time of the reported apparition but continue to this day, we are left with no other plausible or viable explanation but that of the visionaries. In other words, the visionaries were indeed witnesses of apparitions of Mary.

Presumably, the preceding chapters have given us at least a glimpse of "the big picture." From these heights we now descend to each individual apparition site, there to see and hear the Virgin.

PART TWO

VISAGE

Images of the Virgin as Witnessed in Her Appearances

From the days of the Old Testament, holy images were considered instruments of God's grace. Although worship of graven idols was forbidden, Yahweh commanded the construction of images of angels that were to be placed on top of the Holy of Holies, the Ark of the Covenant. In Numbers 21:7–9, God commands Moses to make a bronze serpent: those who were bitten by the deadly serpents only had to look at the bronze serpent to be healed. The importance of holy images was also recognized by the Christians in the catacombs. The Seventh Ecumenical Council authoritatively declared that the veneration and display of holy images was legitimate and to be encouraged.

In Christian history, several icons are called miraculous because of the many miracles associated with them. Icons with miracle stories that are displayed here include the Black Madonna of Czestochowa and Our Lady of Kazan. Images of Our Lady of Guadalupe are also reputed to have miraculous attributes: such an image was partially responsible for victory at the Battle of Lepanto; other Guadalupe images are said to have held back floods and famines and the like.

The images of the Virgin shown here are different from beautiful pictures painted by gifted artists. Although they are not photographs taken during her apparitions, the images here were made under the direction of those who actually saw her — and one of them, the tilma of Guadalupe, comes to us directly from the Virgin.

Our Lady of Czestochowa, Poland, 1382
Photo courtesy of Our Lady of Czestochowa Shrine in the U.S.

Church at Fatima, Portugal
Photo courtesy of Professor Courtenay
Bartholomew

Our Lady at the Cova at Fatima, Portugal
Photo courtesy of Iris Photo

Fatima apparition of 1929
Photo courtesy of Professor Courtenay Bartholomew

Sr. Lucia of Fatima with Pope John Paul II
Photo courtesy of Professor Courtenay Bartholomew

Visionaries of Fatima, Portugal
Photo courtesy of Professor Courtenay Bartholomew

Our Lady of Kazan, Russia, 1579
Image courtesy of St. Isaac of Syria Skete icon distributors

Visionary of Damascus, Syria
Photo courtesy of Maria Rota

Our Lady of Soufanieh, Damascus, Syria, 1982-90
Image courtesy of the Shrine of Our Lady of Soufanieh

Our Lady of the Pillar, Saragossa, Spain A.D. 40 [Pope John Paul II at prayer at the shrine]
Photo courtesy of Professor Courtenay Bartholomew

Alphonsine, visionary of Kibeho, Rwanda, 1981-89
Photo courtesy of Maria Rota

Visionary of Hrushiv, Ukraine, 1987
Photo courtesy of Maria Rota

Miraculous well in Hrushiv, Ukraine
Photo courtesy of Maria Rota

Our Lady of the Rosary of San Nicolás, Argentina, 1983-90
Photo courtesy of Patrizia de Ferrari Coronado

Construction of the church requested by Our Lady of San Nicolás
Photo courtesy of Patrizia de Ferrari Coronado

The visionary of
Banneux, Belgium
Photo courtesy of Ann Ball

The Virgin of the Poor, Banneux, Belgium, 1933
Photo courtesy of Ann Ball, from *A Litany of Mary* (OSV)

The visionaries of Beauraing, Belgium
Photo courtesy of Ann Ball

Our Lady of the Golden Heart, Beauraing, Belgium, 1932
Photo courtesy of Professor Courtenay Bartholomew

The visionaries of
Medjugorje, Bosnia
Photo courtesy of Maria Rota

The Queen of Peace, Medjugorje, Bosnia, 1981
Image courtesy of Medjugorje center

Our Lady of Cuapa, Nicaragua, 1980
Photo courtesy of Joseph Cassano from
Let Heaven and Earth Unite
by Stephen and Miriam Weglian

Aparecida do Norte, São Paulo,
Brazil, 1717
Photograph by author

Our Lady of China, Donglu, China, 1900, 1995
Photo courtesy of Our Lady of China Church, New York

Visionary from Ecuador, 1988-90
Photo courtesy of
Patrizia de Ferrari Coronado

Cuenca, Ecuador, 1988-90
Photo courtesy of Patrizia de Ferrari Coronado

Our Lady of Quito, Ecuador, 1906
Photo courtesy of Ann Ball

Our Lady of Mount Carmel,
England, 1251
Postcard

Our Lady of LaVang, Vietnam, 1798
Image courtesy of
the Blue Army of Vietnam

Our Lady of Walsingham, England, 1061
Photo courtesy of Our Lady of Walsingham Shrine

Our Lady of Zeitun, Egypt, 1968
Photo courtesy of Coptic Orthodox Church

Church at which apparitions took place in Zeitun, Egypt
Photo courtesy of Professor Courtenay Bartholomew

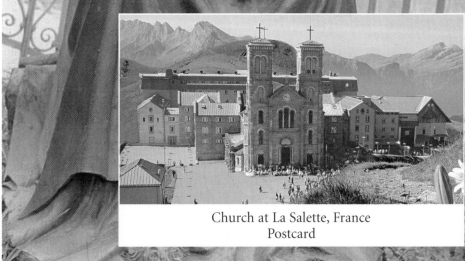

Church at La Salette, France
Postcard

Our Lady of La Salette, France, 1846
Postcard

Our Lady of La Salette, France, 1846
Photo courtesy of Professor Courtenay Bartholomew

Our Lady of Lourdes, France, 1858
Postcard

Visionary of Lourdes, France
Photo courtesy of
Queenship Publishing

Pope John Paul II at the grotto of Lourdes
Photo courtesy of Professor Courtenay Bartholomew

The visionaries of Pontmain, France, 1870
Postcard

Our Lady of Hope, Pontmain, France, 1870
Photo courtesy of Professor Courtenay Bartholomew

The Miraculous Medal

The Miraculous Medal apparition, Rue de Bac, France, 1830
Photo courtesy of Professor Courtenay Bartholomew

de Vrouwe van alle Volkeren

Our Lady of All Nations, Amsterdam, Holland, 1945-84
Image courtesy of Our Lady of All Nations Chapel, Amsterdam

Our Lady of Good Health, Vailankanni, India, 16th-17th centuries
Photo courtesy of Basilica of Our Lady of Good Health, Vailankanni, India

Church at Vailankanni, India
Photo courtesy of Basilica of Our Lady of Good Health, Vailankanni, India

Apparition site at Knock, Ireland, 1879
Photo courtesy of Shrine in Knock, Ireland

Our Lady of Akita, Japan, 1973
Photo courtesy of Spiritual Director
of Sister Agnes

The visionary of Akita, Japan
Photo courtesy of Maria Rota

Visionary of Betania, Venezuela
Photo courtesy of Maria Rota

Our Lady of Betania, Venezuela, 1976
Photo courtesy of Professor Courtenay Bartholomew

Our Lady of Guadalupe, Mexico, 1531
Image courtesy of Basilica of Our Lady of Guadalupe, Mexico City

The miraculous statue of Our Lady of Ocotlán, Mexico,
believed to have the same supernatural origin as the Tilma of Guadalupe.
Photo courtesy of the Basilica of Our Lady of Ocotlán

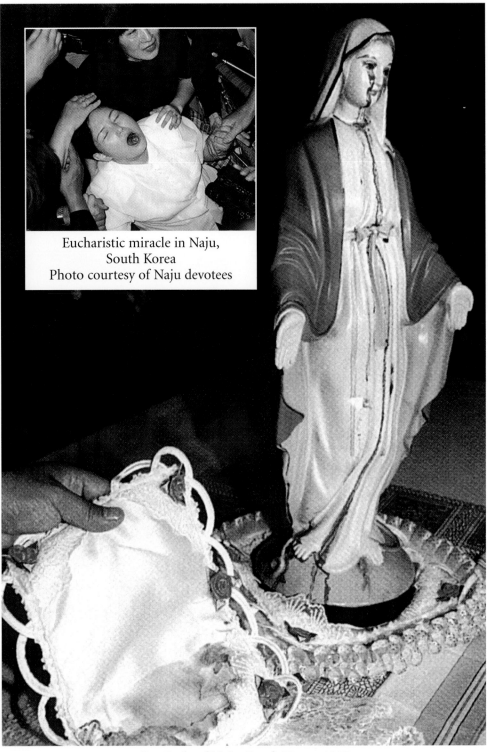

Eucharistic miracle in Naju,
South Korea
Photo courtesy of Naju devotees

Our Lady of Naju, South Korea, 1985
Photo courtesy of Naju devotees

PART THREE

COLLAGE

MESSAGES OF THE VIRGIN
IN HER APPEARANCES

Part Three section is a compendium of the messages of the Blessed Virgin in her apparitions around the world and across history along with brief accounts of the actual apparitions. Every one of the apparitions described here has been investigated and, with three exceptions, "validated" by Catholic or Orthodox ecclesiastical authorities; Medjugorje in Bosnia and Naju in South Korea have been extensively investigated by scientists who have given positive conclusions, but no final verdict has been issued by ecclesiastical authorities because these are still ongoing phenomena. The investigation into the Cuenca, Ecuador, apparition is still in progress.

The apparitions described here have been classified under three heads: Transcendent Tableaux, Bolts from the Blue, and Comprehensive Catechesis.

Under the category of "Transcendent Tableaux," we include those apparitions that display the following characteristics:

- For the most part, they took place many centuries ago.

- Investigative documentation on the apparition is minimal (this is not true of all the apparitions in this category, e.g., Knock and Zeitun).

- In some cases, the apparition was witnessed by a large number of people, but there was no particular message associated with the apparition.

- The apparition has left behind a "sign" that continues to exert immense power in contemporary times.

The apparitions in "Bolts from the Blue," share in the following features:

- They have taken place in comparatively recent times (with the exception of Guadalupe).

- They have been rigorously investigated.

- They have left behind some "sign" that has testified to their authenticity: such signs range from healing springs to prophecies that are later fulfilled.

- They are also associated with definite messages that have had as much of an impact as the tangible reality of the apparition and the signs (in some cases the messages have had more of an impact than the external phenomena).

"Comprehensive Catechesis" comprises those apparitions that show the Virgin as teacher. In these apparitions, the Virgin is engaged in an extensive pedagogical exercise, the fruits of which are beneficial for both the visionary and the world at large. Extended apparitions of this kind began with Amsterdam in 1945. The need for such sustained catechetical courses seems obvious: in the latter half of the twentieth century, the worldwide reach of the media of mass communication has helped filter the skepticism and unbelief of the elite into the minds and hearts of a global audience on an almost daily basis. Where sin abounds grace abounds even more, said St. Paul. In the face of deception and evil, God sends us a vehicle of truth and holiness. Those who suffer continuous bombardment from the enemy require continuous relief and reinforcement — and a comatose patient can hardly complain about having to receive nourishment intravenously. The emphasis in this section is on the precise text of the Virgin's messages rather than on the details of the apparition itself. Entire volumes can and have been written on almost every one of these apparitions, but there is no space in this context to expand on all of the fascinating background material.

The four greatest Marian apparitions in history in terms of worldwide impact are Guadalupe, Lourdes, Fatima, and Medjugorje. As yet the Catholic Church has not issued an official assessment of Medjugorje because, as Cardinal Joseph Ratzinger, the prefect of the Sacred Congregation for the Doctrine of the Faith, explained to me in an interview, the phenomenon is still in progress. Nevertheless, Medjugorje has exerted a greater impact in terms of conversions of unbelievers than any other apparition in history except for Guadalupe.

The systematic investigation of Marian apparitions by officially appointed experts began only in 1830 with the apparition of the Miraculous Medal, the apparition that is generally considered to be the inaugural event of the Marian age. Marian apparitions of previous eras were kept alive in the popular memory by a combination, in different degrees, of traditions and devotional practices centered around the particular apparition. Some like Vailankanni in India (sixteenth century) and LaVang in Vietnam (eighteenth century) have minimal initial documentation. The Portuguese-Dutch conflicts in India played some role in the loss of existing documentation, and the brutal anti-Christian persecution in Vietnam made it impossible to preserve much in the way of written records. Despite these obstacles, the shrines built on the original sites of the apparitions in Vailankanni and LaVang remained pilgrimage destinations from the time of the apparitions and the images of the Virgin associated with the particular apparition have been a potent source of faith for millions.

Four things must be understood about the pre-1830 apparitions:

- Each of these apparitions, as described in traditional accounts, follows the same general pattern as the other Marian apparitions in history (including the post-1830 apparitions) and communicates the same themes and messages.

- They continue to have a tremendous impact today on millions of devotees who make pilgrimages to the apparition sites; thousands of miracles have been reported, for instance, at Vailankanni.

- Many of them are identified with a concrete sign left by the Virgin that remains a mysterious and potent phenomenon in itself: the tilma in Guadalupe, the healing spring in Vailankanni, the over-nineteen-centuries-old image of Our Lady of the Pillar in Saragossa.

- The entire identity of each of these sites — and this includes the shrine, the devotees through the centuries, the reported miracles, the particular devotions, the impact on society — is inextricably tied to the historicity of the apparition. It is impossible to understand or explain any of the better known apparition sites without recourse to an account of the apparition.

A common characteristic of the major pre- and the post-1830 apparitions is the existence of one or more publicly tangible elements of evidence in their support — what the lawyers would call "prima-facie evidence," evidence sufficient to establish a presumption of truth unless refuted. Evidence of this kind may be classified under the category of "Enduring Signs." The listing on pp. 68–69 summarizes the "enduring signs" associated with the great apparitions.

In a previous section, we observed that the few words uttered by the Blessed Virgin Mary in Scripture had an extraordinary impact on salvation history: "Let what you have said be done to me" led immediately to the overshadowing by the Holy Spirit and the incarnation of the Son of God; the greeting to Elizabeth led to her being inspired by the Holy Spirit and the sanctification of John the Baptist; the divinely inspired Magnificat promises that "all generations shall call me blessed"; and the final "they have no wine" and "do whatever he tells you" brought faith to the disciples and inaugurated the public ministry of Jesus. Mary's messages in her apparitions, in one way or another, echo these biblical utterances while also materializing the other representations of her we see in Scripture: as the New Eve whose soul is to be pierced (think in this context of the tears shed by icons of the Virgin around the world), as the preeminent human dwelling place of the Holy Spirit, as the Mother of all those who bear witness to Jesus.

Grounded in this biblical matrix, the main themes of Marian apparitions, the messages of the Virgin, exhort humanity to (1) repent for the life of sin, (2) convert to a life of holiness, (3) pray, (4) do penance.

From biblical times, we have known that those favored with a special supernatural revelation are sometimes told to keep at least a part of it a "secret." St. Paul, writing of a mystic he knew who received a private revelation, says that he "was caught up into paradise and heard things which must not and cannot be put into human language" (2 Cor. 12:4). Similarly, several of the visionaries who witnessed Marian apparitions have been entrusted with one or more

APPARITION	ENDURING "SIGN"
Saragossa, Spain, 40	Ancient column of jasper and image of Our Lady of the Pillar
Rome, Italy, 352	St. Mary Major Basilica, Rome
Walsingham, England, 1061	Ancient remnant of the Slipper Chapel and historical records of the Holy House of Walsingham, conversions through the centuries
Mount Carmel, England, 1251	Devotion of the Brown Scapular
Czestochowa, Poland, 1382	Image of the Black Madonna, historical miracles
Guadalupe, Mexico, 1531	tilma with the image of Our Lady of Guadalupe, conversion of eight million Aztecs
Kazan, Russia, 1579	Icon of Our Lady of Kazan
Vailankanni, India, 16th and 17th centuries	Image of Our Lady of Vailankanni, healing spring and basilica on the site of the apparitions
São Paulo, Brazil, 1717	Image of Nossa Senhora Aparecida, conversions
LaVang, Vietnam, 1798	Image of Our Lady of LaVang, church on the site of the apparitions, healing miracles
Rue de Bac, France, 1830	Miraculous Medal, prophecies fulfilled, incorrupt body of St. Catherine Labouré, miracles experienced by millions who wore the medal
La Salette, France, 1846	fulfilled prophecies, healing spring
Lourdes, France, 1858	healing spring, incorrupt body of St. Bernadette
Pontmain, France, 1871	protection from the advancing Prussian army
Knock, Ireland, 1879	Basilica of Our Lady Queen of Ireland at the site of the apparitions, spiritual and physical healings
Dong Lu, China, 1900, 1995	Christian community in Dong Lu, image of Our Lady of China, miracles in the sky in 1995
Hrushiv, Ukraine, 1914, 1987	fulfilled prophecies, apparitions visible to thousands
Fatima, Portugal, 1917	sun miracle and other luminous phenomena visible by those present, fulfilled prophecies

secrets pertaining to world history that they are to reveal only at the appointed time and to the appointed person.

But those who study Marian apparitions must beware of wasting time and energy on idle curiosity about the "secrets." These apparitions are not important because they are fascinating supernatural phenomena or because they contain "inside information" on the end-times: their central purpose, as defined by she who appears, is to take us back to the Gospel. At a certain level, the apparitions are valuable reminders of the reality of the supernatural. We realize that God

APPARITION	ENDURING "SIGN"
Beauraing, Belgium, 1932	healings, luminous phenomena seen by those present
Banneux, Belgium, 1933	healing spring
Amsterdam, Holland, 1945–84	fulfillment of prophecies: "My signs are contained in my words"
Zeitun, Egypt, 1968	photographs of the Virgin as she appeared above the church in Zeitun
Akita, Japan, 1973	wooden statue of the Virgin exuding blood, sweat, and tears; stigmata on visionary; deaf visionary regains hearing
Betania, Venezuela, 1976–present	hundreds of cures, apparitions of the Virgin witnessed by over two thousand people, stigmata appearing on the visionary, bleeding Host
Cuapa, Nicaragua, 1980	luminous phenomena witnessed by onlookers, fulfilled prophecies
Kibeho, Rwanda, 1981–89	solar phenomena visible to all present, fulfilled prophecies
Medjugorje, Bosnia, 1981–present	pilgrimages by over fifty thousand religious and clergy, hundreds of documented cures, thousands of conversions, unprecedented increases in the reception of the sacraments, celestial phenomena
Damascus, Syria, 1982–90	exuding of olive oil witnessed by over one hundred thousand people, miraculous healings, stigmata on the visionary, progress on a common Easter made in meeting in Syria
San Nicolás, Argentina, 1983–90	source of conversions, vocations, and prayer groups; numerous healings; stigmata
Naju, Korea, 1985–present	tears of blood, tears, oil from statue of the Virgin, Eucharist turns into flesh and blood on visionary's tongue, descent of the Eucharist from the ceiling, spiritual and physical healings, stigmata on the visionary
Cuenca, Ecuador, 1988–90	holy pictures and images exuding oil and tears, blood from the crucifix, Eucharist that miraculously appeared in the visionary's home, luminous phenomena in the sky, the Virgin speaking through the visionary

---

and the spiritual realm are not creations of our intellect or imagination but an inescapable and immediately relevant part of our lives and of the world and history as a whole. But what is most important about the apparitions are their messages, because these apply the Gospel to our lives here and now and guide us in making the choices that will determine our eternal destiny.

TRANSCENDENT TABLEAUX

1. Saragossa, Spain, A.D. 40

The first apparition of the Virgin was witnessed by St. James the Greater, who was reputed to be her favorite Apostle. The apparition took place in Saragossa, Spain, in 40 A.D. St. James was preaching on the banks of the Ebro River. Since the Virgin was still alive at the time, this apparition was actually an instance of bilocation. Many holy people have shown this capability for bilocation (St. Antony of Padua, Padre Pio), whereby they would be at prayer in one place and simultaneously be physically present at another location.

St. James, the Apostle who is said to have gone to Spain in 35 A.D., was discouraged by his lack of progress when the Virgin appeared before him, brought by angels from Jerusalem. She gave him a statue of her with the infant Jesus and a six-foot-high pillar of jasper saying, "This place is to be my house, and this image and column shall be the title and altar of the temple that you shall build." The pillar was to be kept in the church and would endure to the end of time as a symbol of the faith of the people there.

James then built a chapel, the first built in honor of Mary. Although this chapel was later destroyed and several others were built on the same site, the pillar and the statue of the Virgin with the Christ Child were miraculously preserved and are still kept intact — after over nineteen hundred years — in a holy chapel in the basilica dedicated to the Virgin of the Pillar. Almost from the very beginning, numerous healings and other miracles have been attributed to the Virgin of the Pillar by those who have come there and sought her help.

In her appearance to him, the Virgin supposedly also told St. James that the Lord wanted him to return to Jerusalem to become the first of the martyrs. St. James was martyred in Jerusalem in 44 A.D. — a fulfillment of the prophecy of Matthew 20:20–23, where Jesus says that James would drink of His cup.

The Spanish Feast of "El Pilar" is on October 12. It was on October 12, 1492, that Christopher Columbus, sailing on the Spanish ship *Santa Maria*, arrived in the New World.

2. Neocaesarea, Asia Minor, 238

St. Gregory Thaumaturgus ("the Wonder-Worker") lived in Neocaesarea in Asia Minor between 213 and 268. Gregory had been confused by some of the debates on the Holy Trinity and had sought divinely inspired discernment. He was privileged to be given an apparition of the Virgin, appearing as a beautiful woman, and St. John the Evangelist, who came as an old man. The Virgin asked St. John to explain the mystery of the Trinity to Gregory. St. John told him, "I will gladly comply with the wishes of the Mother of God" and, after giving a summary, concluded with these words, "There is therefore nothing created, nothing greater or less in the Trinity, nothing superadded.... The Father has never been without the Son, nor the Son without the Spirit; and this same Trinity is immutable and forever unalterable." Two things are of interest here. First, we have said that Marian doctrine is as old as the doctrine of the Trinity. Here paradoxically we have a Marian apparition that is mainly concerned with the doctrine of the Trinity. Second, Mary is accompanied by St. John the Evangelist as she was at the apparition in Knock, Ireland, in 1879.

Below is Gregory of Nyssa's account of the apparition to St. Gregory Thaumaturgus cited in Bernard Buby's *The Marian Heritage of the Early Church*. Buby notes: "The value of Gregory's testimony is that even in patristic times apparitions were recorded":

> Now, as he was one whole night long pondering on the words of faith, and bringing up all sorts of reasonings — for there were at that time, too, some who sought to adulterate the orthodox teaching, and often made the truth ambiguous even to the learned and prudent through plausible arguments — while, I say, he was thus lying awake thinking anxiously about the truth, there appeared to him one in human shape, of aged mien, and of sacred character, by the form and arrangement of his garb, showing marks of great virtue by the grace of his countenance and his whole bearing. Gregory, amazed at the vision, was about to rise from his bed, and to ask him who he was, and wherefore he had come. But the other calmed the troubles of his mind, speaking with gentle voice, and telling him that it was by divine command he appeared — on account of the questions that were exercising him — for the revealing to him of the truth of the orthodox faith. At these words Gregory began to take courage, and to regard him with mingled feelings of joy and awe. The latter then stretched forth his hand, and with fingers extended, pointed to Gregory at what was appearing on the other side. Gregory turning his eyes in the direction of the hand, beheld facing him another vision in woman's form more excellent than human. Struck again with awe he let fall his gaze, lost in bewilderment at the apparition, and unable to bear the sight of the vision — for what was most astonishing in the vision was that, though it was deep night, a light shone forth on him from those who appeared, as though some bright blazing torch were kindled. While then his eyes could not bear the apparition, he heard them conversing together on the subject of his doubts, and thereby not only gained a true knowledge of the faith, but also learned their names, as they addressed each other by their respective titles. And thus he is said to have heard the person in woman's shape bid "John the Evangelist" disclose to the young man the mystery of godliness, while he replied that he was ready to comply in this matter with the wish of "the Mother of the Lord." He then pronounced a formulary well-turned and complete. (*De Vita,* S. Greg. Thaum.)

3. Rome, Italy, 352

Although this is an ancient apparition, the strongest basis for its authenticity is the existence of the largest Marian church in the world, St. Mary Major, one which has been beloved of Popes for centuries.

In the year 352, a wealthy but childless Roman couple, John and his wife, decided to leave their fortune to the Virgin. They often prayed to the Virgin asking for guidance on how their wealth could be put to her use. The Virgin appeared to them on the night of August 4 and told them that she wished a basilica to be constructed on the Esquiline Hill, one of the seven hills of Rome. She would leave snow on the precise area in which she wanted the church — which would be a miracle since August is the hottest time of year in Rome. Liberius, the Pope at the time, also received the same message from the Virgin.

On the morning of August 5, a large part of the Esquiline Hill was covered with snow. Both John and his wife and Pope Liberius came to the hill. After they had measured out the area covered by snow, which was to be the area for the basilica, the snow disappeared. The Pope ordered immediate construction of the basilica, and St. Mary Major was completed in 360.

4. Walsingham, England, 1061

It may be hard to believe today, but one of the holiest places in Europe at one time was Walsingham, a village in Norfolk, England. Walsingham was known as the Nazareth of England, for it was the site of a supernaturally reconstructed replica of the house of Nazareth to which kings and commoners from all over Europe used to make pilgrimages.

Accounts of the apparition behind Walsingham appear in a fifteenth-century ballad that claimed to record the authentic tradition. The widowed Lady Richeldis de Faverches of Walsingham had prayed for a way in which she could honor the Blessed Virgin. One night in the year 1061 the Virgin asked her to build a replica of the house of Nazareth. The Virgin wanted the reconstruction of the house because she wished to commemorate the Annunciation and also to assist those who sought her help. Lady Richeldis was mystically transported to Nazareth, where she was shown the original home and given the exact dimensions required. The lady began work on the construction of the house and at various stages received supernatural assistance.

The house became the destination for pilgrimages the year after it was completed. A church was built around the house to protect it. A chapel, called the Slipper Chapel, was built a mile away from it so that pilgrims could leave their shoes in this chapel and travel the last mile on foot. Edward the Confessor, who ruled England during the construction of the house, offered England to the Virgin as her dowry. All the kings of England from Henry II to Henry VIII made special pilgrimages to Walsingham.

At the express order of Henry VIII, the shrine of Walsingham and the chapels around it were destroyed and the defenders of the shrine executed during the English Reformation. After 1829, when Catholics were allowed to practice their faith again in the England, the Shrine at Walsingham was reconsecrated (the Slipper Chapel managed to survive the destruction). Today there is an Anglican shrine of Our Lady of Walsingham, and Walsingham itself has become a center of Christian unity.

Two things about Walsingham are worthy of notice: it fits the pattern of most Marian apparitions in which the Virgin asks for the construction of a church or chapel; Revelation 11 and 12 show her first as the Ark of the Covenant in the Sanctuary in Heaven and then as the Woman Clothed with the Sun when she appears on earth. Second, even non-Christians who visit Walsingham are moved by its "atmosphere." Its particular emphasis is on the mystery of the Annunciation.

The Lady Richeldis witnessed three apparitions of the Virgin, during which she was told, "Let all who are in any way distressed or in need seek me there in that small house that you maintain for me at Walsingham. To all that seek me there shall be given succor. The small house at Walsingham shall be a remembrance of the great joy of my Salvation, when St. Gabriel the Archangel announced that I should become the Mother of God's Son through humility and obedience to his will."

5. Mount Carmel, England, 1251

The Brown Scapular is one of the three Marian devotions closely associated with apparitions of the Virgin. The other two are the Rosary and the Miraculous Medal. The origin of the Rosary predates St. Dominic, but it is the subject of many messages of the Virgin in various apparitions. The Miraculous Medal originated with the apparition to St. Catherine Labouré.

The Rosary — centered on the 150 psalms and the Gospel narratives of the life and death of Christ — went through many stages of development over the centuries, but all the traditions concerning the brown scapular focus on its origin in an apparition of the Virgin to a great Carmelite monk, St. Simon Stock, in the thirteenth century. Accounts of this apparition were recorded regularly from the time that the Order started putting its traditions in writing, and the promises of the scapular had become an established tradition in the Order within a hundred years of the death of St. Simon Stock.

Simon Stock, an Englishman, decided to join the Order of Our Lady of Mount Carmel while visiting the Holy Land. This Order claimed to have as its founder the Prophet Elijah and its hermits lived on Mount Carmel, made famous by the Prophet. As the Saracens intensified the persecution of the Christian religious orders in the Holy Land, the Carmelites migrated to Europe. In 1241, the Earl of Kent gave the Carmelites a house on his property of Ayleshire.

In England the Carmelites were not popular with the other clergy, who even conspired against them in Rome; their brown cloaks were also viewed with great suspicion. Simon Stock, who had been elected the head of the Order in England, was deeply discouraged by the climate of antagonism and spent the night of July 15, 1251, in prayer to the Virgin seeking her assistance. In the early morning of July 16, the Virgin appeared to him along with the infant Jesus and a host of angels and handed him the scapular along with the following promise:

My beloved son, receive this scapular for your Order. It is the special sign of a privilege which I have obtained for you and for all God's children who honor me as Our Lady of Mount Carmel. Those who die devotedly clothed with this scapular shall be preserved from eternal fire. The brown scapular is a badge of salvation. The brown scapular is a shield in time of danger. The brown scapular is a pledge of peace and special protection, until the end of time.

This promise was eventually given a seal of approval — as a private revelation worthy of belief — by the undivided Western Church and became established throughout Christendom. Many miracles were reported by those who wore the scapular — signaling Heaven's approval — ranging from the sudden conversion of unbelievers to protection from fires, floods, diseases, bullets, swords, and other physical dangers. On the day that he received the scapular, Lord Peter of Linton called Simon Stock to his brother's deathbed, saying that he was dying in despair. St. Simon placed his own scapular on the dying man, who repented shortly after and then died. The scapulars with which many saints were buried were found to be perfectly preserved when the bodies were exhumed centuries later.

The Carmelite Order flourished after the apparition to St. Simon Stock. During the Black Death in the fourteenth century, when many Carmelites sacrificed their lives to help the dying, it was feared that the Order would die out. Again the Virgin appeared to St. Peter Thomas to reassure him that the Order would last until the end of history because its patron, the Prophet Elijah, had especially requested this of the Lord and his petition had been granted.

It has been pointed out that the scapular message is especially related to the parable of the one lost sheep. Just as the divine Shepherd goes to great lengths to save the one lost sheep, the scapular seeks the salvation of every lost sheep. The scapular is made of wool, just as sheep have woolen fleece. And it is worn as a "shoulder garment" (the meaning of "scapular"), just as the shepherd wraps the lost sheep around his neck and over his shoulders.

The scapular has deep roots in the grace of final perseverance. It is not magical. It signals the wearer's commitment to seek to continue in final perseverance aided by the grace of God. It requires an act of free will on the part of the wearer — and the rest is left to God. It is offered as a gift by the Mother who wishes to make every means of grace available to her children so that none may be lost.

The importance of the scapular devotion and Our Lady of Mount Carmel is evident from its role in two of the greatest modern apparitions: the last apparition of Our Lady of Lourdes was on July 16, the Mount Carmel feast day, and in her last apparition, on October 13, Our Lady of Fatima appeared in the livery of Our Lady of Mount Carmel.

6. *Czestochowa, Poland, 1382*

The Queen of Poland is the Black Madonna, the Virgin depicted in the famous portrait of Czestochowa. This great icon has preserved the faith of the Polish people and is believed to be responsible for miraculous interventions in the history of Poland. It is an image of the Virgin reputedly painted by St. Luke and first displayed in Constantinople.

In 1382, the Virgin appeared to Prince Ladislaus of Opolo, who now possessed the icon, asking him to place it in the mountaintop monastery of Jasna Gora in Czestochowa. The prince did so, and the icon soon became the source of many miracles recorded in a book at the monastery.

In 1430, the Tatars took over Jasna Gora, and one of them stole the Black Madonna and carried it away. But the further he went with the painting, the heavier it became. When it was clear that he would not be able to go any further, the enraged Tatar slashed the cheeks of the image with his sword and threw it in a ravine. The icon was recovered and although the "wounds" were painted over more than once, they would strangely reappear.

The Black Madonna is believed to have come to the assistance of the Polish nation during times of danger. In 1655, the whole country had been taken over by the forces of Charles X of Sweden. The only resistance came from a tiny band of Polish soldiers and monks still in control of Jasna Gora. After a siege of forty days, the Swedes finally gave up and left Poland. On September 14, 1920, the Russian army was camping on the banks of the River Vistula and was on the verge of attacking Warsaw. It is believed that the Russians changed their plans and withdrew when they had a vision of the Virgin in the skies over Warsaw. When the Germans left Poland in 1945 they tried without success to blow up Jasna Gora and its priceless icon.

7. *Kazan, Russia, 1579*

Russia is among those nations like Poland and Mexico that sees its national identity in a treasured icon of the Virgin. The great national icon of Russia is Our Lady of Kazan, an image of the Virgin with the infant Jesus. This ancient icon first came into prominence in the eleventh century shortly after the Christianization of Russia. It was believed to go back to the Apostles and was housed in the city of Kazan. In the thirteenth century, Kazan was overrun by its enemies, and the icon was lost in the ruins of the monastery in which it was lodged. Then, in the year 1579, the Virgin appeared to Matrona, a nine-year-old girl, asking her to seek and recover the icon and telling her where it was located. After the Virgin had appeared to her thrice, a number of people, including the archbishop, began digging in the spot indicated by Matrona but with no success. Finally, they allowed Matrona to dig, and at her first attempt, on July 8, she located the icon wrapped in a red cloth.

The apparition and the subsequent finding of the icon exhilarated the population, and in time the icon became well known for numerous miracles and healings and was invoked as the Protectress of Russia. It was later kept in a great basilica in Moscow built for it by one of the czars. At the time of the Communist revolution, the Bolsheviks destroyed the basilica in which the icon was placed, but the icon was swiftly transported out of Russia. The date on which the destruction of the basilica took place is significant: October 13, 1917 — the same day on which the Miracle of the Sun took place in Fatima and the Virgin warned the visionaries of the errors that would come out of Russia while also prophesying the future conversion of Russia.

(The information above comes from the works of Janice Connell and from various distributors of icons of Our Lady of Kazan.)

8. *Vailankanni, India, sixteenth–seventeenth centuries*

It was in Vailankanni in the state of Tamil Nadu, India, in the sixteenth century, that Our Lady first healed a young lame boy, appeared several years later to another boy, and, in the seventeenth century, on the feast of her nativity, miraculously saved a band of Portuguese sailors from a storm in response to their prayers. As this Marian shrine with its miraculous pond became a source of healing and other miracles for millions of pilgrims through the centuries, Pope John XXIII elevated the local church to a basilica, thus publicly recognizing the ministry of Marian intercession taking place here.

What follows is an excerpt from the official history of the shrine of Vailankanni authored by Fr. S. R. Santos.

As in Fatima the Blessed Mother appeared only to shepherds of a tender age, likewise in Vailankanni she appeared to a shepherd boy and a lame boy with miracles. The apparition in Vailankanni is one of the earliest Marian apparitions. She appeared here in the sixteenth century and has been continuously present until now with miracles and wonders. She has attracted and gathered pilgrims of all religious communities whether Catholic, Protestant, Hindu, Muslim, or Parsee. Pilgrims from far and wide pour in and this alone is the sign that her name and fame are being echoed throughout India and even in distant places of the world. Many visit this shrine to invoke her blessings, and many are here to offer thanks to her for the gifts that they have received.

The population of Vailankanni is approximately five thousand. But thousands of pilgrims visit this holy place every day and the numbers go on increasing — a fact that bespeaks the glory of the Miraculous Mother at Vailankanni. During the time of her feast on 8th September, about several hundred thousand pilgrims come there.

Here is a description of the apparitions:

Our Lady's Apparition to a Shepherd Boy

In the sixteenth century, by the side of a street named "Anna Pillai" in Vailankanni, there was a small pond and on its bank was a huge banyan tree. The passers-by used to drink water in that pond. A shepherd boy as usual was carrying milk to his master's house which was in Nagapattinam — a town near Vailankanni. The day was extremely hot. He felt tired and thirsty. After having quenched his thirst at the pond, he sat down to rest a while under the cool shade of the tree.

At that time, he was startled by a bright vision of a beautiful Lady standing before him, holding a lovely child in her arms. He was spellbound by her celestial beauty. Her serene face with its glorious appearance astonished him immensely. The child's face was bright and glorious as the sun. Both wore celestial haloes around their heads. Fascinated by this rare phenomenon, the simple shepherd boy was deeply moved and was at a loss for words. His heart was filled with a sense of awe mingled with reverent fear. With childlike innocence, he clasped his hands together and gently bowed his head in utter humility to give her a deep reverence.

The Lady, however, greeted him with a motherly smile and asked him to give some milk for her child. The boy joyfully gave her the milk and then noticed the smile of satisfaction springing from the baby's face. The shepherd boy rushed to Nagapattinam carrying the remaining milk in his pot. There he reported the whole strange happening to his master and thus the reasons for his unusual delay. He also begged him to excuse him for the shortage of milk in the pot. Great was their astonishment when upon lifting the lid of the milk pot, it was full to the brim with milk and overflowing from the pot. The master was astonished for a moment over this strange and extraordinary event. He hastened with the boy to Vailankanni and came precisely to the pond, where the boy had seen the lady with a child. The gentleman prostrated himself on the ground with awe and reverence, with his forehead pressed close to the holy spot indicated by the shepherd boy.

The story of this miraculous happening soon spread throughout Vailankanni, Nagapattinam and the neighborhood. The Christians in Nagapattinam who heard about it were certain that the vision was of the Blessed Virgin Mary with the Child Jesus. They were filled with joy and reverence and felt proud that their gracious Mother should have thus deigned to honor their neighborhood. From that day the pond near Anna Pillai Street in Vailankanni came to be known as "Matha Kulam" (Our Lady's Pond). To this day it is known by that glorious name. Millions and millions of pilgrims visit the pond with faith and reverence. She has blessed them all with plentiful graces; worries and diseases disappear as the mist at the sight of the morning sun.

Apparition to the Lame Boy, a Buttermilk Vendor

Some years after the first miraculous vision, our gracious Mother deigned to appear again with her Son in her arms to a poor lame boy of the village.

During the sixteenth century, there lived a poor widow in the village of Vailankanni. She had a son who was lame from birth. In order to eke out a living the widow used to carry a buttermilk pot to the place called "Nadu Thittu." It was a little elevated place then where there was a huge banyan tree with outstretched branches. The boy used to sit there and sell buttermilk to the weary wayfarers who would come to take shelter from the burning sun. The cool shade of the tree attracted the passers-by and the lame boy's stall gradually became known to many people. As he was on the lookout for customers, he suddenly found standing before him a lady of peerless beauty, holding in her arms a still more beautiful child, both attired in spotless garments. Sweetly smiling, the lady approached the poor crippled boy and asked him for a cup of buttermilk for the baby. The boy felt immensely happy and proud to be privileged to oblige such a distinguished customer. Without a moment's hesitation he gave her a cup to drink. She started feeding the child with the buttermilk. The boy observed all this, and was rooted to the spot where he sat. The lady then cast a look of benevolent pity on the poor boy and turned to the child in her arms. She pleaded to the child to cure the lame boy who had quenched His thirst. The Mother's request was granted within a second. The boy did not realize the miracle that had been worked on him, but he was intently gazing at the Mother and the Child. She gratefully smiled at the boy for his drink and requested him to do her an additional favor.

The Lady asked the lad to go to Nagapattinam and apprise a certain rich Catholic gentleman of this incident and inform him that she desired to have a chapel built in her name at Vailankanni. With a look of veneration and self-pity the lad pleaded that it was physically impossible for him even to walk. He was lame! The Lady graciously smiled and bade him stand up and walk because he was no longer lame! On this the lad jumped up with joy, and leaped from place to place realizing the pleasant sensation of the earth for the first time. The boy finally reached the town. There he met the Catholic gentleman and revealed the message of the Lady. The gentleman had no difficulty in believing him, for he had himself a similar vision of Our Lady in his sleep on the previous night. The good man had already made up his mind to build a small chapel in Vailankanni in honor of the Blessed Virgin as directed by her in the vision. He went with the boy to the place where Our Lady had appeared in the vision to the boy. With the willing cooperation of the people of the locality whose imagination was stirred by the miraculous cure of the widow's crippled son, the wealthy man from Nagapattinam soon set up a small thatched chapel in Vailankanni. It was fitted with an altar, and a beautiful statue of Our Lady with the Infant Jesus in her left arm was placed on the altar.

Soon the news spread everywhere. Christians and non-Christians flocked to the spot. Many were the favors granted to the people who came to pray so that the fame of the little thatched shrine and the statue of the miraculous Mother with the divine Child in her arms spread far and wide. As a result of the striking cure of the lame boy and other subsequent cures that took place there, the Mother of God came to be known and incessantly invoked as "Our Lady of Health Vailankanni" (Vailankanni Arokia Matha).

The Storm-Tossed Portuguese Ship

The sixteenth century was particularly memorable for the attempts of European merchants to establish trading centers in India. In those days there were no steamships but only sailing vessels. They had to sail all round Africa to reach the Indian Ocean, because the Suez Canal had not yet been dug. The first European country to accomplish the arduous task of reaching India by sea round the Cape of Good Hope was Portugal. For about one hundred years, the Portuguese had a monopoly on trade between Europe and the Far East. They were good sea-men and at the same time ardent Catholics with a tender devotion to Our Blessed Mother Mary the "Star of the Sea." In all their perils at sea they naturally invoked her protection. In the seventeenth century a Portuguese merchant vessel was sailing from Macao in China to Colombo in Sri Lanka. They started their voyage and the ship was sailing toward the west to reach the Bay of Bengal. During the crossing the ship was caught in a terrible storm. The gale grew furious, the waves lashed high, and the fate of the vessel with all on board seemed sealed.

The helpless sailors instinctively threw themselves on their knees, and with all the fervor of sinking souls besought Mary to succor them. They vowed to build a church in her name wherever they could land safely on shore. Their earnest prayer was instantly granted; for there was a sudden and miraculous lull in the winds; the waves fell and the sea became calm. Very soon the tattered ship was safely pushed to the shore of Vailankanni.

On landing, the first thing the sailors did was to fall on their knees and express their grateful thanks to God and to Mary the Virgin Mother of God. They were soon surrounded by a large group of fishermen who lived nearby and who were sure that the strangers were Christians because they prayed to God on their knees. They guided the stranded seamen to the thatched chapel erected by the Catholic gentleman of Nagapattinam. On entering the chapel the grateful sailors once more reverently fell on their knees before the image of Our Lady with the Child Jesus in her arms, but for whose miraculous help they might all have met a watery grave. They soon learned from the local fishermen that the village was called Vailankanni and that the chapel was dedicated to Our Lady of Health. All these strange things happened on the 8th of September, the feast of the Nativity of our Lady, the Mother of Jesus.

The zealous and devoted clients of Mary soon set about to find out the best way to fulfill their vow and built a permanent chapel at the place. A modest brick and mortar chapel 24 feet by 12 feet with a dome overhead and with windows in the usual western style was soon constructed. The statue of Our Lady of the old thatched chapel graced the altar in the masonry structure. The day of the completion of the chapel was celebrated with touching veneration and great rejoicing which demonstrated their heartfelt gratitude for the signal graces which the Blessed Virgin and her divine Son had showered on them. They dedicated the new church to the Nativity of Our Lady in order to perpetuate the day of their landing at Vailankanni.

The Portuguese sailors were not satisfied with all that they had done for the chapel on the spur of the moment. On their subsequent voyages they visited Vailankanni and made many improvements to the chapel. Among them may be mentioned the rich and rare porcelain plates illustrating scenes from the Bible. These plates from China may still be seen fixed round the high altar of the Shrine Basilica of Vailankanni.

Thus, with the landing of the storm-tossed Portuguese ship on the coast of Vailankanni, a new chapter emerged in the history of the shrine. The Vailankanni Shrine was initially a part of the Nagapattinam parish. In those days Nagapattinam was under the control of the Portuguese. But in 1660 the Dutch captured Nagapattinam and its flourishing trade from the Portuguese. The Dutch newcomers were hostile to the Catholic Church since they were Reformed Protestants. So the one hundred years of Dutch rule in Nagapattinam limited the progress made on Our Lady's shrine at Vailankanni.

In 1962, the bishop of the Diocese, Dr. R. A. Sundaram, went to Rome to attend the second session of the Second Vatican Council. At this time, he requested the Holy Father to raise the ancient shrine of Our Lady at Vailankanni to the high rank and dignity of a "minor basilica." The request was carefully looked

into and magnanimously granted. His Holiness Pope John XXIII graciously issued orders raising the shrine to the exalted state of a minor basilica. Thus the
shrine basilica of Vailankanni became linked to the St. Mary Major Basilica of
Rome. In his Apostolic Brief, the Pope noted:

> TO PERPETUATE THE MEMORY OF THE EVENT: We learn that at the illustrious
> church of Vailankanni within the limits of the Diocese of Tanjaore (India)
> the august Virgin Mary through her powerful intercession imparts to her
> clients health and is venerated with deep devotion. For pilgrims in large
> numbers approach the spot even from distant parts and participate in the
> sacred services especially during the Novena preceding the Nativity of the
> Mother of God, so much so that this shrine is not undeservedly hailed as
> the "Lourdes of the East." This singular zeal for the Marian veneration has
> been practiced from fairly ancient times.

Today, throughout India there are shrines of our Lady of Good Health of
Vailankanni. In fact the old chapel built in 1551 upon the cave where the Apostle
St. Thomas lived in Madras is the chapel of the Mother of Good Health of
Vailankanni.

At Vailankanni, Mary evangelizes in a special manner through her miracles
and wonders. Through her motherly affection she touches the hearts of the millions of devotees who come to Vailankanni every year to meet their heavenly
Mother. The power of the Mother acts within them even without their knowledge, and they receive the power to relinquish evil from their life and to begin
changing to goodness by accepting the ways of Jesus, her Son. The Holy Spirit descends upon them and changes them through her intercession. These experiences
are reserved not only for Catholics but for all those who come to her whoever
they may be, whether Hindu, Muslim, or Protestant. Adjoining the basilica is a
"Museum of Offerings" with gold and silver and other gifts from the thousands
of grateful pilgrims who have experienced miraculous healings and wonders
through the intercession of their Mother Mary. The two central pilgrimage spots
in Vailankanni are the healing pond, where the Virgin first appeared, and the
basilica with the miraculous image which is the site of the second apparition.

A touching footnote to the story of the Vailankanni is the role attributed to
the Virgin in the history of the nation of India. According to St. John Damascene,
Juvenal, the bishop of Jerusalem, gave a report on the discovery of Mary's Assumption into Heaven at the Council of Chalcedon. The gist of Juvenal's report
is that, after the death of the Virgin, St. Thomas the Apostle returned from India
to pay his respects at her tomb in Gethsemane; when the Apostles had gathered
at the tomb, they were astonished to discover that the Virgin's body was no
longer there: Thomas, the only Apostle then absent, arrived and desired to see
and venerate the body in which God had dwelt. The Apostles opened the tomb
but did not find the sacred deposit. Juvenal's report concludes that this discovery
led the Apostles to a supernatural conviction concerning the Assumption of the
Virgin. If only because he is the one who brought about its discovery, St. Thomas
could in some sense be considered the Apostle of the Assumption. The connection between India, Thomas, and the Assumption did not end in the first century,

for the nation of India, the apostolic home of St. Thomas, gained independence from the British Empire on August 15, 1947, the Feast of the Assumption!

9. *Aparecida do Norte, São Paulo, Brazil, 1717*

Nossa Senhora Aparecida is the Queen and Patroness of Brazil. The following history of this devotion was provided by Ms. Rocilda Oliveiro.

In 1717, the village of Guaratingueta, São Paulo, was waiting for a very important visitor, the count of Assumar, the governor of São Paulo. The day of his arrival was a day of abstinence, and so the hosts needed to have fish at the reception.

The local fishermen were asked to go fishing in the Paraoba River. Domingos Garcia, João Alves, and Felipe Ramos were three of these fishermen. Although they tried hard they could not catch any fish, and they were beginning to lose all hope.

At this point, when João Alves pulled up the empty net, he saw something inside it. It was the body of a small statue made from obarro (a black material); the statue had no head. The surprised men rowed down the river and tried to fish once more. Again they found something caught in their net. It was the head of the statue.

The astonished fishermen recognized at once that it was the image of Our Lady of the Immaculate Conception and called her "Nossa Senhora da Conceição Aparecida" (Our Appeared Lady of the Conception).

They let the net down again. Although they had toiled all day, they had not gotten anything. But this time, when they hauled up the net, they found they had caught a great multitude of fish. As in Luke 5, when the presence of Our Lord in Peter's boat filled the ship to the extent that it began to sink, likewise the presence of Our Appeared Lady of the Conception did the same to their boat.

Once the statue was brought to the village, many miracles took place, and graces seemed to explode throughout the country. Princess Isabel, who refused to free the slaves in the beginning, signed a paper freeing the slaves. Princess Isabel also offered Our Lady of the Conception a precious gold crown (with twenty-four big and sixteen smaller diamonds). This image was later honored by Popes Pius X, Paul VI, and John Paul II.

10. *LaVang, Vietnam, 1798*

Christianity was first brought to Vietnam by French missionaries in 1533. Vietnamese Christians were persecuted by their rulers almost from the beginning. The Christians, who numbered over one hundred thousand in less than a hundred years after the introduction of Christianity, were severely persecuted in 1698 and the three following centuries, with thousands being martyred.

In 1800 a shrine was set up in Hue in the center of the country to honor Our Lady of LaVang for her intervention in 1798.

In that year, many of the Vietnamese Christians had fled their persecutors and made for the mountain jungles near LaVang. One evening they were praying the Rosary when a beautiful Lady appeared to them carrying a baby and surrounded by angels. She promised that anyone who sought her assistance in that place would be protected by her. The onlookers realized that this was the Virgin Mary. She showed them plants that they could use as medicines and spoke to them as a Mother comforting her children.

The Christians built a church in her honor from straw and leaves, and many miracles and cures were reported there. In 1805, the emperor launched a fresh wave of persecution. The church of LaVang was burnt down, though the altar, which marks the spot of the apparitions, survived. A new brick church was built in 1900. This church was again damaged during the Vietnam war, but the outside altar again was untouched by the bombs and bullets.

11. Knock, Ireland, 1879

On August 21, 1879, Ireland played host to a heavenly tableau straight out of the Book of Revelation. The site of this apparition was the humble town of Knock (Cnoc is Gaelic for "hill"). The apparition itself was different from most of the Marian apparitions of the nineteenth and twentieth centuries in the following respects: no words were spoken; everyone present, not just a group of visionaries, was able to see the Virgin; those who witnessed the apparition did not enter into a state of ecstasy.

The day had been stormy and the pastor of Knock's small church, Archdeacon Cavanagh, was thoroughly soaked by the time he returned home after visiting his parishioners. His housekeeper, Mary McLoughlin, built a fire for him and then went to visit her friend Margaret Beirne (known locally as the Widow Beirne). On the way, as she passed the church, she noticed a few figures outside the church gable on the south end that she took to be statues. After meeting with the Beirnes, Mary returned to the presbytery accompanied by the Widow Beirne's daughter, Mary Beirne.

This time, as they passed the church, they observed that the figures she thought were statues were actually people, namely, the Blessed Virgin Mary, accompanied by St. Joseph and St. John the Evangelist. Behind them was a Lamb resting above an altar. The supernal spectacle was lit by a bright light that lit up the gable wall of the church and was visible miles away. Despite the heavy rain, the figures remained entirely dry. As Mary McLoughlin kept watch, Mary Beirne ran to her house and summoned her mother, her sister Margaret, her brother Dominick, and a niece named Catherine Murray, aged eight. She also brought some neighbors. All those who arrived at the church — eighteen in all — saw the heavenly display. The witnesses included three men, six women, two teenage boys and a girl, and two children. Archdeacon Cavanagh, however, did not take the reports seriously and so did not come out to see what was going on. A little over two hours after they first saw the spectacle, all of those present either went about their chores or had gone to help with a lady whose mother was on her deathbed. When they returned to the church, they saw that the apparition had disappeared.

This is Mary Beirne's description of the apparition:

At the distance of three hundred yards or so from the church, I beheld all at once, standing out from the gable, and rather to the west of it, three figures which, on more attentive inspection, appeared to be those of the Blessed Virgin, St. Joseph, and St. John. That of the Blessed Virgin was life-size, the others apparently either not so big or not so high as her figure; they stood a little distance out from the gable wall, and as well as I could judge, a foot and a half or two from the ground.

The Virgin stood erect, with eyes raised to heaven, her hands elevated to the shoulders or a little higher, the palms inclined slightly toward the shoulders or bosom; she wore a large cloak of a white color, hanging in full folds and somewhat loosely around her shoulders and fastened to the neck; she wore a crown on the head — a rather large crown — and it appeared to be somewhat yellower than the dress or robes worn by Our Blessed Lady.

In the figure of St. Joseph, the head was slightly bent and inclined toward the Blessed Virgin, as if paying her respect; it represented the saint somewhat aged with gray whiskers and grayish hair. The third figure appeared to be that of St. John the Evangelist; I do not know, only I thought so, except the fact that at one time I saw a statue [of St. John] at the chapel of Lekanvey, near Westport, County Mayo, very much resembling the figure which now stood before me.

Above the altar, and resting on it was a lamb, standing with face toward St. John, thus fronting the western sky. I saw no cross or crucifix. On the body of the lamb and around it, I saw golden stars, or small brilliant lights, glittering like jets or glass balls, reflecting the light of some luminous body.

I remained from a quarter past eight to half past nine o'clock.

Shortly after the apparition, two blind men regained their sight there. Knock soon became a center of pilgrimage and healing. Over three hundred miraculous cures have been reported there and at least a million pilgrims now visit Knock every year.

The ecclesiastical authorities did not respond as rapidly to Knock as did the faithful. Although Archdeacon Cavanagh believed in the authenticity of the apparition, the local bishop, the archbishop of Tuam, appointed an investigative commission to study the phenomenon. A scientist from Maynooth did experiments with a magic lantern to show that the display seen by the witnesses could not have been created by a photographic image on the gable wall. Although the commission concluded that the witnesses were trustworthy and satisfactory, the bishop, who was ninety, did not publish their report or say anything further about Knock. Nevertheless, bishops from other countries came to Knock, and some of them reported cures they attributed to Knock. By 1929, the archbishop of Tuam was participating in the ceremonies at Knock. He instituted a new investigative commission in 1936 — and this commission also came back with a positive verdict. In a remarkable gesture of recognition, Pope John Paul II visited Knock in 1979, the centenary year of the apparitions.

Although there was no verbal communication at Knock, the silent tableau spoke to the hearts and minds of the faithful most eloquently and effectively simply through its silence. Knock was a call to contemplation and a reminder of the reality of the Eucharist and the communion of saints.

12. *Dong Lu, China, 1900, 1995*

In 1900, and then again in 1995, the Blessed Virgin appeared to Christians and their enemies in Dong Lu, a village in Baoding in the Hebei Province in north China. Missionaries had established a Christian community in the impoverished Dong Lu village. When the Boxer rebellion broke out in 1900, nearly ten thousand hostile soldiers attacked the Dong Lu Christians, who numbered less than a thousand. Suddenly the attackers were startled to see a beautiful Lady surrounded by light in the sky. They beat a hasty retreat when a fiery horseman — believed to have been St. Michael the Archangel — came charging toward them. The grateful Christians built a church at the site in honor of their protectress, Our Lady of China, who was represented in a famous image kept at the church. The Virgin is depicted in this image as a Chinese empress with the infant Jesus in her hands. In 1924, the Bishops Synod of China chose this image to be denoted as "Our Lady of China" or "Our Lady Queen of China." Although the church was destroyed in 1951, the image is still extant.

Today Dong Lu has a population of eight thousand of whom 80 percent are Christian. The Virgin was again witnessed on May 23 and 24, 1995, the vigil and feast days of Our Lady of China. One hundred and fifty priests and five bishops celebrated Mass for thousands of Chinese Christians on these special days. During the Mass, a colorful cloud covered the altar, and during the consecration the cloud surrounded the sun, which started spinning in different directions. The cloud lifted the sun higher, and the awestruck participants saw Our Lady of China and the Child Jesus in the sky and also the Holy Family, the Heavenly Father, and the Holy Spirit in the form of a dove and angels. This recent apparition was reported in American publications.

(The information on the 1900 apparition came from the works of Janice Connell and from Our Lady of China Church in New York.)

There is a sad footnote to these accounts of the apparitions of Our Lady of China at Dong Lu. Catholic News Service had this report on February 7, 1999: "Underground Catholic peasants in Baoding Diocese were attacked at Christmas time, according to reports received in Hong Kong. Fr. Peter Hu Duo of the Diocese of Baoding had been arrested and seriously beaten by officials December 20 in his sister's home in Xushui County, near Baoding City.... Chinese sources say the whereabouts of two underground prelates, Bishop Su Zhimin of Baoding and his auxiliary, Bishop An Shuxin, remained unknown. Both were arrested in 1996. Fr. Cui Xingang, pastor of Dong Lu Church, also arrested in 1996, was still detained in Qingyuan County, southeast of Baoding, they added. Government forces demolished the popular Dong Lu Marian shrine near Baoding in 1996 and have forbidden the large annual May pilgrimage to the site since."

13. Jerusalem, Israel, 1954

On July 18, 1954, the Primary Class Five of the Coptic School of St. Anthony of Egypt was getting ready for the break when several of the students pointed to the window and shouted "El Adra!," the Virgin. The adults present could not see her and kept the children inside. Then the Virgin appeared in the classroom among the children. She was most visible when she stood against a wall, at which point her figure became more intense and brilliant. The Coptic Patriarchal Church, which ran the school, had a service on July 25, at which nearly four hundred people were present. During this service, the Virgin appeared again — this time floating above the heads of everyone or moving between them. The apparition took fifteen minutes. In a message to the faithful, the Coptic bishop wrote, "She did not come for our sakes. She came because this place is holy, being within a few yards of Calvary and the Tomb."

(The information on this apparition is primarily derived from Ingo Swann's *The Great Apparitions of Mary*).

14. Zeitun, Egypt, 1968

Many of the appearances of Mary occur in places that have some special significance in their own right. Fatima of Portugal, for instance, had been the venue of supernatural events in the past, and it had been prophesied that even greater events would take place there in the future. Knock of Ireland had been specially blessed by St. Patrick, who apparently prophesied that it would be a center of pilgrimage for multitudes in the future. Medjugorje of Bosnia won a special distinction because the villagers had, with great personal sacrifice, installed a huge cross on a prominent hill there in 1933 in commemoration of the nineteen hundred years that had passed since the death of Christ.

Zeitun in Egypt belongs to this category of a place with a particular supernatural significance. In ancient times, Zeitun was known as Mataria, and it was to this city that Joseph, Mary, and the infant Jesus came when they escaped from Herod. St. Mary's Church, an ancient shrine, had been built on the precise spot where the Holy Family had been living in exile. The shrine had disappeared and was then rebuilt; this occurred several times with the shrine finally disappearing by the turn of the century. In 1918, the property was owned by the wealthy Coptic Christian Khalil family. The Virgin revealed to a member of the family that this location was important for her and that fifty years from that date she would bring a special blessing to the church to be built there. The Khalils gave the property to the Coptic Orthodox Church, and the church authorities constructed St. Mary's Coptic Church on it.

On April 2, 1968, at 8:30 p.m., a lady dressed in a robe of light was observed walking back and forth on the dome of the church by Moslem workmen. She was seen kneeling beside a cross on top of the dome. The mechanics who saw her thought she was a nun about to jump off the building, and one of them pointed his finger at her imploring her to stop. The finger he had pointed was gangrenous and was to be amputated. The next day the finger was found to have been completely healed. A crowd gathered, but gradually the luminous lady disappeared before their eyes. Seven days later she was again seen over the church and was identified as the Virgin. This time she went on appearing at different periods up to May 2, 1971. The crowds that came to see her were sometimes as large as 250,000 and included Jews, Moslems and Protestant, Orthodox, and Catholic Christians. The Virgin would often bow to the crowd (a typical gesture in the Middle East) or bless them. Sometimes she held out an olive branch to them (Zeitun means "olive" in Arabic). Her apparitions on the dome were sometimes accompanied by other miraculous phenomena, such as the sudden emission of incense from the dome of the church into the crowd or the flight of dovelike creatures around her. Many miracles and cures were reported by people who came to see her.

The Coptic Patriarch Anba Kyrillos VII appointed a commission to investigate the phenomenon on April 23, 1968. Among the miracles attributed to the Virgin of Zeitun and reported to the commission were various cancer cures, recovery of sight for those totally blind, and the like. The commission accepted the authenticity of the apparitions and declared on May 5 that "these appearances have been accompanied by two great blessings: the first being that of engendering and strengthening faith, and the second is the miraculous cures of desperate cases." Cardinal Stephanos I, the patriarch of the Catholic Copts, issued a statement declaring that "it is undoubtedly a real apparition, confirmed by many Coptic Catholic members of the highest integrity and reliability."

The General Information and Complaints Department of Zeitun, Egypt, released its own report in 1968 and declared, "Official investigations have been carried out with the result that it has been considered an undeniable fact that the Blessed Virgin Mary has been appearing on Zeitun Church in a clear and bright luminous body seen by all present in front of the church, whether Christian or Moslem."

Bolts from the Blue

1. Appearances to Saints

Many of the great saints in history were honored to see the Blessed Virgin, including St. Bernard of Clairvaux, St. Francis of Assisi, St. Sergius of Radonezh, St. Ignatius of Loyola, St. Teresa of Avila, and St. Seraphim of Sarov. In some of her appearances to the saints, the Virgin gave specific messages and, at times, the Lord gave messages about His Mother to saints to whom He appeared frequently. Excerpts from these messages are outlined below.

St. Mechtilde, a Cistercian nun of Helfta, Germany, lived between 1240 and 1298. She had apparitions of both Jesus and Mary. Once, when she was feeling remorseful for not sufficiently loving the Virgin, Jesus appeared to her and said:

> For this fault, and in order to make reparation for it, first praise and honor My Mother for the faithfulness with which, in all her actions and throughout her life, she submitted her will to Mine; second, praise and honor the readiness with which she attended to all My physical needs and with which she had compassion in her heart for all that I had to endure with My body; and thirdly, exalt her for devotion to Me in Heaven, by means of which she draws sinners to Me, converts them to Me, and frees from the sufferings and flames of Purgatory a multitude of souls, for whom her intercession and her powerful intervention more quickly open the realms where they will glorify Me for all eternity.

St. Mechtilde once asked the Virgin, "O most gracious Queen of Heaven, I would love to greet you with the most pleasing salutation which has ever been addressed to you." Mary then appeared to her with the words "Hail Mary, full of grace, the Lord is with thee" written in gold letters on her Immaculate Heart. She said, "No creature has ever said anything that was more pleasing to me, nor will anyone ever be able to find or say to me anything that pleases me more."

St. Gertrude the Great (1256–1302), another Cistercian nun, was the pioneer of devotion to the Sacred Heart of Jesus. For over twenty years, Jesus appeared to her almost every day. When Gertrude asked Him how she could please Him, He said, "Behold My Mother. Endeavor to praise her worthily." On the relation between Christians and His Mother, Jesus said, "I give thee My sweet Mother as thy Protectress. I confide thee to her care. I have given thee My own most merciful Mother for thine, and it is through her that I will dispense My graces to thee." On another occasion, Jesus offered His Sacred Heart to His Mother, saying,

> Most loving Mother, behold My Heart. I offer it to thee with all that divine and eternal love which prompted Me to choose thee for My Mother. In this

Heart I offer thee all that filial affection of which I gave thee so many tokens on earth, when thou didst nourish and carry Me as a little child in thy arms. In this Heart I offer thee that faithful love which kept Me near thee all My mortal life, obedient to thy wishes, as any other son to his mother. I offer thee especially that love which on the Cross made Me in a measure forget My tortures to compassionate thy bitter desolation and to leave thee in My place a guardian and son. And lastly, behold in My Heart the love which prompted Me to exalt thee in thy blessed Assumption far above the saints and angels and to crown thee Queen of Heaven and Earth.

St. Bridget of Sweden (1302–73) is famous for her mystical union with Jesus and the many revelations she received from Him. She also had apparitions of Mary, during one of which the Virgin told her,

From my Son's birth until His death, I was filled with grief. Tears used to come into my eyes when I gazed at His hands and feet, which the nails were going to pierce... when I meditated on His future Passion... and when I saw the Prophets' sayings concerning Him all being fulfilled.... And now I look at all the human beings on earth to see whether maybe there are a few who feel compassion for me and who think of my sorrows, but I find very few who meditate on my suffering and sorrows. Therefore, my daughter, do not forget me, for I am forgotten and ignored by many. See my grief, and imitate me as well as you can. Meditate on my sorrows and my tears, and mourn that the friends of God are so few.... I am grieved over the enemies of my Son in the world who now crucify Him worse than the Jews formerly did. With their vices they crucify my Son in a spiritual way more cruelly and more fearfully than those who crucified Him physically.

When St. Bridget was on her deathbed, the Virgin told her, "Truly, my daughter, they [the doctors] do not pay attention to what death means: for that man dies who cuts himself off from God and becomes hardened in sin. And he who does not believe in God and who does not love his Creator is also dead. But whoever fears God at all times and cleanses himself from his sins through frequent Confession — whoever yearns for union with his God has life and shall not die!"

2. Guadalupe, Mexico, 1531

No event has played as influential a role in the evangelization of non-Christians as the apparition of the Virgin to an Aztec peasant in Mexico in the sixteenth century. It is no exaggeration to say that this apparition was primarily responsible for the Christianization of Latin America, home to nearly a fifth of the world's Christians. Moreover, the same skeptics who sneer at the simple piety of the millions who gaze lovingly at the image of the Virgin of Guadalupe are still unable to explain the existence and nature of this image even with the most advanced scientific techniques.

The conquest of Mexico by Cortés was accompanied and followed by atrocities by both Spaniards and Aztecs. In 1531, the Aztecs, who outnumbered the

Spaniards several times over, were planning to launch a rebellion that would wipe out every Spaniard in Mexico. Missionaries from Spain had little success in their attempts to convert the natives in view of the tensions between the Aztecs and their conquerors. Relations were also strained between the civil and the ecclesiastical authorities and the first bishop in Mexico, Prior Juan de Zumárraga, had actually excommunicated the then administrator, Don Nuño de Guzmán, for his continuing cruelty.

Juan Diego, a fifty-seven-year-old peasant, was an Aztec convert. He was a widower who had been brought up by his uncle, Juan Bernardino. The aged uncle was now under Juan Diego's care, and they lived in the village of Tolpetlac. On the morning of December 9, 1531, Juan Diego passed the hill of Tepeyac on his way to morning Mass in Tlaltelolco. He was startled by the ethereal quality of the birdsong he heard from the hill. Suddenly the singing of the birds ceased, and he heard a young lady calling out to him, "Juan! Juan Diego! Juanito!" On ascending the hill, he saw a fourteen-year-old girl, remarkable for her supernal splendor, beckoning to him. Speaking to him in his Aztec tongue, she said she was the ever-virgin Mary who was the Mother of God and explained that she wanted a church to be built on the hill. Juan Diego, she said, was to go to Tenochtitlán (Mexico City) and make this request to the bishop. Juan Diego obediently went to the bishop's residence. After waiting for several hours, he was finally allowed to meet the bishop. Through an interpreter, Juan González, he described his encounter and the Virgin's request to the bishop. The bishop was touched by the Aztec's sincerity and humility but found the story too extraordinary to believe. Although he could not agree to the request, he kindly told Juan Diego to visit him again later if he had anything more to say.

Juan Diego returned to the Virgin with the bishop's answer and suggested that she choose someone more important to deliver her message if she wanted the bishop to take it seriously. The Virgin insisted, however, that she had chosen him, Juan Diego, and prevailed on him to return to the bishop with the same request. When Juan Diego returned to the bishop he found that he had outworn his welcome; the bishop clearly had not expected him to return so soon. Juan Diego told him the Virgin asked that it be reiterated that she was the Virgin Mary and that she desired a church built on the hill. The bishop answered that he wanted a sign from the lady to show that she was indeed the Virgin. When Juan Diego left, the bishop had him followed by two of his servants. But Juan Diego, who was unaware that he was being followed, disappeared from view when they reached the foot of Tepeyac, and the servants returned to the bishop, falsely accusing the Aztec of hiding from them. On Tepeyac, Juan Diego told the Virgin about the bishop's stance. She asked him to return at daybreak and she would give him the requested sign.

On returning to Tolpetlac, Juan Diego found that his uncle had been struck down with a deadly fever. He tended to Juan Bernardino's needs with herbs and medicines that night and all of the next day, thus failing to keep his "appointment" with the Virgin. On the following day, December 12, Juan Bernardino was convinced that he would die shortly and asked his nephew to bring a priest to administer the last rites. Tepeyac was on the way to Tlaltelolco, where the priest lived, but Juan Diego walked on the east side of the hill and not the west, where the Virgin had appeared, so as to avoid meeting her again and losing time. To his surprise, he saw the Virgin descending toward him from the hill. Juan Diego explained his uncle's condition, to which she said, "Am I not your mother?" and added that his uncle's health had been restored at that very moment. She asked Juan Diego to go to the top of the hill and bring her the flowers blooming there and these would be the sign requested by the bishop. Juan Diego was astounded to see that the top of the hill was covered with Castilian roses although it was the dead of winter. He took off his cloak, called the tilma, and filled it with the roses; he used his tilma to protect them from the cold. When he brought them to the Virgin, she carefully arranged the roses on the tilma and asked him to present them to the bishop as the sign he required to build a church. No one else but the bishop was to be shown the contents of the tilma, she said.

When Juan Diego returned to the bishop, the servants tried to take the tilma with the roses away from him. But Juan Diego would not give it up and insisted on seeing the bishop. When he was at last able to meet the bishop, Juan Diego unrolled the tilma and the roses fell to the ground. Juan Diego, who was holding the tilma away from himself was astonished to see the bishop suddenly kneel in front of it along with the others around him. On looking at the tilma, he saw why, for emblazoned on it was an image of the lady he had seen. The bishop now had no doubt about Juan Diego's story and took the tilma to his private chapel. Later, Juan Diego accompanied the bishop to the hill of Tepeyac and showed him where the church was to be built. The bishop's assistants then went with Juan Diego to his uncle. They found that Juan Bernardino had recovered completely. The Virgin had appeared to him as well, saying he would be cured and asking that she and her image be called Santa María de Guadalupe.

The image on the tilma was of an Aztec girl, but the name she had chosen was Spanish. As the Aztecs saw the image, hundreds and thousands of them converted to the Christian faith. Within seven years, eight million Aztecs had become Christians. By appearing as an Aztec and to an Aztec, the Virgin ensured that Christianity would not be perceived as an alien religion.

Some linguists today say that the word used by the Virgin to describe herself and repeated by the Aztecs (the two Juans) was *tecoatlaxopeuh,* since the Aztec language, Nahuatl, did not have the letters G and D. *Tecoatlaxopeuh,* it is said, means "Entirely perfect Virgin, Holy Mary, who will crush, stamp out, abolish, and eradicate the stone serpent." This self-description was of tremendous significance to the Aztecs, because the Aztecs worshiped a "stone serpent" (shades of Satan!), a deity called Quetzalcoatl, to which they sacrificed thousands of human beings every year. With the coming of the Virgin, human sacrifice among the Aztecs came to a halt.

The tilma, meanwhile, defies all natural explanation. It was made from cactus fibers and consequently should have turned into dust within twenty years — but it has remained on display to the faithful ever since the year of the apparition. Scientists have scrutinized the tilma on numerous occasions and have confirmed that it is made out of the low life-span cactus cloth.

The face on the tilma, along with the robe, mantle, and hands, is composed of pigments that cannot be identified by chemical analysis: it is known that the colors do not come from any known animal, vegetable, or mineral dye. Despite having been exposed to smoke from thousands of candles through the centuries, infrared spectroscopy shows that there is none of the "wear and tear" which comes with age and pollution. The mysterious pigments refract light in such a way that the image continues to be singularly luminous. Also, unlike human paintings, there is no undersketch below the mysterious image.

Even more extraordinary is the fact that an examination of the eyes of the Virgin shows reflections of actual persons in the pupils — a "technique" that ophthalmologists and others simply cannot comprehend. The reflections are of Juan Diego, the bishop, and his interpreter.

The image of the Virgin on the tilma is of the Woman Clothed with the Sun Standing on the Moon, for she is surrounded by rays of the sun and her face is as bright as the sun (the strange luminosity mentioned above); her feet are on the moon. The turquoise, rose, and gold colors on the tilma were the colors of royalty for the Aztecs. Though she was standing on the moon and had stars on her gown, she was no goddess, because her hands were folded in prayer. (Authorities on those icons of the East that are reputed to derive from actual paintings of the Virgin herself have noted the remarkable similarities between the images on those icons and the image of Our Lady of Guadalupe.)

It might be said that these purported events took place so far back in the past that there could be no historical substantiation for them. The first response to this is the continuing present-day miracle of the tilma, which still eludes natural explanation. The second is the hard fact of the conversion of the Aztecs. Both phenomena demand an explanation — and there is no better explanation than the extant accounts of the apparition.

But the historical record has much to offer as well. The earliest account of the apparition is found in a document written between 1551 and 1561 by an Antonio Valeriano. There is also the famous Codex Seville-Tetlapalco calendar, the most ancient book in the Americas. This book is literally an Aztec calendar which gives Aztec history from 1430 to 1557. For the year 1531, there is a woman described as a "a virgin with her hands folded near her heart, her head bent toward the right, in a salmon-colored tunic and a greenish blue mantilla." Finally, a letter from Bishop Zumárraga to Cortés, written on Christmas Eve, 1531, says, "I want to dedicate my cathedral to the Immaculate Conception because it was during that feast (December 8–17) that God and his Blessed Mother deigned to shower the land you won with this great favor."

The image is not known simply for the conversions it effected but also for thousands of other miracles: people suffering from dread diseases have been cured after prayers to the Virgin of Guadalupe; floods and plagues have been halted after special prayers before the image; the captain of the Christian fleet in the naval battle of Lepanto prayed before an image of Our Lady of Guadalupe in his cabin and led his forces to victory against all odds. Many of the miracles attributed to the Virgin of Guadalupe have been commemorated in obscure and famous paintings over the centuries.

The Virgin of Guadalupe is the Virgin Mary. This bears repetition because some critics have said that the Aztecs turned to her simply because it was an Aztec goddess whose Christian credentials were cosmetic. Some modern "cultural" devotees of Our Lady of Guadalupe even published a book on her impact on culture with the title *Goddess of the Americas*. This title is as defamatory and reprehensible as the Aztec goddess charge of the critics. In the first place, the Virgin identified herself very specifically as "the ever-virgin Mary, Mother of the true God who gives life and maintains its existence" — a statement that essentially affirms what the Third Council of Constantinople proclaimed: "If anyone does not in accord with the Holy Fathers acknowledge the holy and ever virgin and immaculate Mary as really and truly the Mother of God, let him be anathema." Second, the message conveyed by an image is incalculably more effective than are conveyed by words: the holy image on the tilma shows the Virgin's hands held heavenward in prayer: certainly goddesses do not pray. The holding together of the hands in prayer is a characteristic gesture adopted by the Virgin in her apparitions precisely in order to prevent misconceptions: like us she is a created being and because she is like us she can empathize more closely as our mother. So that there could be no doubt, she tells Juan Diego, "Am I not of your kind?"

Messages

"My dear little son, I love you. I desire you to know who I am. I am the ever-virgin Mary, Mother of the true God who gives life and maintains its existence. He created all things. He is in all places. He is Lord of Heaven and Earth. I desire a church in this place where your people may experience my compassion. All those who sincerely ask my help in their work and in their sorrows will know my Mother's Heart in this place. I am your merciful Mother, the Mother of all who live united in this land, and of all mankind, and of all those who love me, of those who cry to me, of those who have confidence in me. Here I will see their tears; I will console them and they will be at peace. So run now to Tenochtitlán and tell the bishop all that you have seen and heard."

"My little son, there are many I could send. But you are the one I have chosen."

"My little son, am I not your Mother? Do not fear. The bishop shall have his sign. Come back to this place tomorrow. Only peace, my little son."

"Do not be distressed, my littlest son. Am I not here with you who am your Mother? Are you not under my shadow and protection? Am I not of your kind? Your uncle will not die at this time. There is no reason for you to engage a priest, for his health is restored at this moment. He is quite well. Go to the top of the hill and cut the flowers that are growing there. Bring them then to me."

"My little son, this is the sign I am sending to the bishop. Tell him that with this sign I request his greatest efforts to complete the church I desire in this place. Show these flowers to no one else but the bishop. You are my trusted ambassador. This time the bishop will believe all you tell him."

To Juan Diego's uncle: "Call me and call my image Santa María de Guadalupe."

The Ocotlán Apparition

Another remarkable apparition of Mary also took place in Mexico, just ten years after Guadalupe. This apparition of Our Lady of Ocotlán is known for two fascinating features: its supernaturally revealed healing spring and a miraculous statue of herself bestowed by the Virgin in the same mysterious fashion as she gave the gift of the tilma at Guadalupe. The following account is based on the official history of the Shrine of Our Lady of Ocotlán.

The visionary, Juan Diego Bernardino, no relation of Juan Diego of Guadalupe, lived in Tlaxcala, Mexico. Many of his fellow-villagers had been stricken by an incurable plague, and on February 27, 1541, Juan set out to bring water from a nearby river to help alleviate their suffering. On returning from the river, he passed through a forest near a cliff where he encountered a beautiful lady who said: "God be with you, my son. Where are you going?" When Juan explained that he had gone to bring water for the suffering villagers, the lady appeared pleased and said, "Come with me! I will give you a different water that will cure the sicknesses of your people. Not only your relatives and friends will be healed, but also all those who drink it." The Lady took him to a cliff where a fountain of water was gushing forth and said, "My heart always desires to help those who are suffering. My heart cannot bear to see so much pain and anguish among people without healing them. Drink as much water as you desire. Upon drinking just one drop, the sick will not only be cured, but they will receive perfect health!" The Lady also gave him a message for the Franciscan monks who lived in a nearby monastery: "Tell the monks that in this place they shall find an image of me, which not only will represent my perfection, but also, through it, I will bring forth my mercy and blessings. I want the image to be placed in the chapel of St. Lawrence." The water from the fountain not only cured the stricken villagers but has been a source of healing for thousands of others through the centuries.

The second part of the story concerns the statue. After hearing Juan's story, "the Franciscans, accompanied by a group of people from the village, entered the forest one night and headed toward the fountain of water. Suddenly, they were blinded by a great light spewing huge flames of fire into the sky and onto the trees. Miraculously, the trees in the forest did not burn. One tree seemed to stand out from the rest. They marked that tree and returned to the monastery because it was late at night. Early the next morning, the group, armed with axes, returned to that particular pine tree to split it open. Inside a cavity in the tree, they found a wooden statue of the Blessed Virgin Mary. It was 'burnt' into the tree. They carried the statue on their shoulders to the nearby chapel of St. Lawrence."

"The magnificent statue is beautifully dressed and about five feet tall (the average height for women of that region). Its hands are held in a prayerful position. Fr. Bachill Laoyzaga, an eighteenth-century historian, wrote, "Spacious forehead, beautiful as a sun-lit sky, lovely rosy cheeks, carmine lips, and her eyes a bluish green. During certain religious festivities the countenance of the face changes color from red rose to pale and back again." Many people down through the centuries and even in modern times have witnessed this miracle and other phenomena, for instance, its mysterious luminosity and the sweat that sometimes appears. The tilma of Guadalupe was made from cactus fibers that ordinarily decay in twenty years. The wood from which the statue of Ocotlán is made should have decomposed long ago. But to this day it continues to bear witness to its supernatural origin as forcefully as the tilma.

3. Rue du Bac, Paris, France, 1830

The apparition of Our Lady of the Miraculous Medal at the Rue du Bac in Paris was the first of the great modern apparitions of the Virgin. Paris had become the greatest enemy of Christianity in Europe, and the Virgin chose to begin her counterattack in that very city. It was one of the few Marian apparitions in which the visionary's identity was never disclosed to the public until after her death.

Catherine was the daughter of a farmer in a tiny village near Dijon. Her mother died when she was nine, and in her grief she embraced a statue of the Virgin and said, "Now, dear Blessed Mother, you will be my mother." At the age of eighteen, she had two dreams of an old priest from whom she fled when he beckoned to her. She felt called to join a religious order but was forbidden to do so by her father. She was sent to work in Paris, after which she attended a finishing school. She was miserable in both places, but while she was at the latter she happened to go to the visitor's parlor of a hospital and saw there a portrait of the old priest. He was none other than St. Vincent de Paul, the founder of the Sisters of Charity, and Catherine was convinced that she was called to join this order.

By the time she was twenty-three, her sister-in-law managed to persuade her father to allow her to become a Sister of Charity. Despite her lack of a sound education, she was admitted into the order in January 1830 and in April was sent to the novitiate of the order at 140 Rue du Bac in Paris. From the time she arrived at the novitiate, Catherine received various visions of St. Vincent de Paul and of Jesus present in the Eucharist. The climax of these visions came with the apparitions of the Virgin on July 18 and November 27, 1830. Here is Catherine's own account of the experience:

> And then came the feast of St. Vincent. On the eve, Mother Martha gave us an instruction on devotion to the saints, and in particular the Blessed Virgin. For so long a time I had desired to see her. I went to sleep thinking that St. Vincent might obtain this grace for me. About half past eleven, I heard myself called by my name. I looked in the direction of the voice and I drew the curtain. I saw a child of four or five years old dressed in white who said to me, "Come to the chapel; the Blessed Virgin is waiting for you." Immediately the thought came to me: "But I shall be heard." The child replied: "Be calm, it is half past eleven, everyone is asleep; come, I am waiting for you." I hurriedly dressed and went to the side of the child. I followed him wherever he went. The lights were lit everywhere. When we reached the chapel, the door opened as soon as the child touched it with the tip of his finger. The candles were burning as at midnight Mass. However,

I did not see the Blessed Virgin. The child led me to the sanctuary, and I knelt down there. Toward midnight, the child said, "Here is the Blessed Virgin!" I heard a noise like the rustle of a silk dress...a very beautiful lady sat down in Father Director's chair. The child repeated in a strong voice, "Here is the Blessed Virgin." Then I flung myself at her feet on the steps of the altar and put my hands on her knees. I do not know how long I remained there; it seemed but a moment, but the sweetest of my life. The holy Virgin told me how I should act toward my director, and confided several things to me.

These messages concerned future events and are quoted below in the Messages section. After she had given the messages, "The Virgin disappeared like a light that is extinguished." Catherine believed that the child was her guardian angel.

In this first apparition, Catherine was told that God wished to give her a mission, but she was not informed about the nature of this mission. It was on November 27 of the same year that the Virgin told her what the mission was to be. Again, Catherine's own words will serve best to tell her story:

It was a Saturday before the first Sunday of Advent, at half past five in the evening. In the silence, just after the point of meditation had been read [in the chapel], I seemed to hear a noise at the side of the tribune. When I looked in that direction, I saw the Blessed Virgin. She was standing, dressed in a white robe of silk, like the dawn, her feet resting on a globe, only half of which I could see. There was also a serpent green in color with yellow spots. In her hands, held at the level of her breast, she held a smaller globe, her eyes raised toward heaven....Her face was beautiful, I could not describe it.... Then suddenly, I saw rings on her fingers, covered with jewels, some large and some small, from which came beautiful rays.... At this moment, when I was contemplating the Virgin, she lowered her eyes and looked at me, and an interior voice spoke to me: "This globe that you see represents the entire world, particularly France...and each person in particular." I cannot explain here what I felt and what I saw, the beauty and the light of the rays was so magnificent! The voice spoke to me again: "This is a symbol of the graces which I shed on those who ask me." At this moment, where I was or was not I do not know, an oval shape formed around the Blessed Virgin, and on it were written these words in letters of gold: "O Mary conceived without sin, pray for us who have recourse to thee." Then a voice was heard to say: "Have a medal struck after this model. Those who wear it will receive great graces; abundant graces will be given to those who have confidence." Some of the precious stones gave forth no ray of light. "Those jewels which are in shadow represent the graces which people forget to ask me for." Suddenly the oval seemed to turn. I saw the reverse of the medal: the letter M surmounted by a cross, and below it, two hearts, one crowned with a crown of thorns, and the other pierced by a sword. I seemed to hear a voice which said to me: "The M and the two hearts say enough." After this the Virgin disappeared like a candle blown out.

In May of 1831, with the permission of Catherine's spiritual director, Fr. Aladel, and the director general of the Sisters of Charity, the medal prescribed in the apparition was produced by a Monsieur Vachette. The Sisters of Charity began distribution of the medal and from the very beginning many of those who wore it around their necks reported conversions, cures, and other miracles. It became known as the Miraculous Medal. Fifty thousand were given out in 1832 and 1833 and millions more every year after that, so that today well over a billion of these medals have been distributed around the world.

The official inquiry into the apparition began in 1836, but Catherine declined to testify during the investigation. The apparition was approved as authentic by Archbishop de Quelen of Paris. Catherine lived for another forty-six years, during which time she mainly did menial tasks in one of the Sisters' hospices. Her identity as the visionary was kept a secret. Six months before her death in 1876, she was distressed that the Virgin's request for the construction of a statue of herself as the "Virgin of the Globe" had yet to be executed. Neither of her spiritual directors had implemented this request, and one of them had died and the other had been transferred. Catherine approached the superior general of the Order with the request but was refused. She then went to her own superior and revealed her identity as the visionary of the Miraculous Medal and asked for her help in the construction of the statue. The model for the statue was finished just before she died. Catherine's body did not decay after her death and is now displayed beneath the altar built on the spot where the Virgin appeared to her. She was canonized in 1947.

Description of the Virgin

"The Virgin was standing. She was of medium height, and clothed all in white. Her dress was of the whiteness of the dawn, made in the style called *à la Vierge*, that is, high neck and plain sleeves. A white veil covered her head and fell on either side of her feet. Under the veil her hair, in coils, was bound with a fillet ornamented with lace, about three centimeters in height or of two fingers' breadth, without pleats, and resting lightly on the hair. Her face was sufficiently exposed, indeed exposed very well, and so beautiful that it seems to me impossible to express her ravishing beauty."

Messages

"My child, the good God wishes to charge you with a mission. You will have much to suffer, but you will rise above these sufferings by reflecting that what you do is for the glory of God. You will know what the good God wants. You will be tormented until you have told him who is in charge with directing you. You will be contradicted, but do not fear, you will have grace. Tell with confidence all that passes within you. Tell it with simplicity. Have confidence. Do not be afraid.

"The times are very evil. Sorrows will befall France; the throne will be overturned. The whole world will be plunged into every kind of misery.

"But come now to the foot of this altar; there, graces will be poured on all those who ask for them with confidence and fervor. They will be poured out on the great and the humble. Grave troubles are coming. There will be great danger, for this, the [novitiate] and other communities. At one moment when the danger is acute, everyone will believe all to be lost; you will recall my visit and [the novitiate] will have the protection of God. But it will not be the same for other communities."

With tears in her eyes, the Virgin then said, "Among the clergy of Paris there will be victims — Monseigneur the Archbishop will die, my child, the Cross will be treated with contempt, they will hurl it to the ground and trample it. Blood will flow. The streets will run with blood. Monseigneur the Archbishop will be stripped of his garments." Some of these events were to take place quite soon and the others "in about forty years."

"My eyes will be ever upon you. I shall grant you graces. Special graces will be given to all who ask them, but people must pray."

These prophecies were fulfilled quite rapidly: "the throne" of King Charles X was "overturned" in the latter part of July 1830; riots broke out all over Paris and churches were desecrated; the archbishop was beaten and stripped of his clothes. Some of the buildings housing religious communities were burned down; although angry crowds gathered outside the novitiate of the Sisters of Charity at the Rue du Bac, it was unharmed, as promised by the Virgin. By 1870, forty years after the first apparition, all the prophecies given at the time were fulfilled. Two subsequent archbishops of Paris were murdered during this period. (July 18, 1830)

"Have a medal struck after this model. Those who wear it will receive great graces; abundant graces will be given to those who have confidence." (November 27, 1830)

(The other messages of November 27 have already been cited in the narrative above.)

4. La Salette, France, 1846

The apparition of La Salette is significant in many ways, not least because it is the first of Mary's apparitions to children in modern times and the first modern apparition with both short-term and apocalyptic prophecies (the Rue du Bac prophecies were more near-term in nature).

Melanie Mathieu, fourteen, and Maximin Giraud, eleven, neither of whose parents were practicing Catholics, were tending sheep for different masters on a mountainside near the village of Ablandins in the parish of La Salette. After eating lunch they took a nap. When they woke up, they saw a glowing globe of light that seemed to outshine the sun. The frightened children were about to run away when the globe opened and they saw a weeping lady seated with her head in her hands. Gradually she arose, faced them with her hands crossed across her chest, and asked them kindly to come to her. She spoke in French and not in the patois with which they were more familiar. The children could see the crystal-like tears on her cheeks. The lady then spoke (in their patois) of the different ways in which people were offending her and her Son and of the calamitous consequences of these offenses. She warned of famines ahead, of the failure of the potato crop and of grapes rotting and the walnuts turning bad. She gave each of them separately a "secret" and then said that the calamities ahead could be averted if the people repented. She asked the children to say their prayers and to make what she had said known to all her people. After this she turned away, and the globe of light around her grew brighter and then disappeared.

When the children returned to the village, Maximin first reported the events they had experienced, and Melanie confirmed his account. The parish priest accepted their testimony without further ado, for which he was later reprimanded by his bishop. The civil authorities interrogated the children and tried to catch them in a lie with no success. The children were twice taken up to the site of the apparitions. On the second visit, a man broke off a piece of the rock on which the lady had been sitting and found a spring gushing next to it. Almost immediately the water from this spring was found to heal people who were desperately ill. The bishop of the diocese began an official inquiry into the phenomenon and appointed several commissions of investigators, while asking his priests to maintain silence about the apparition in the pulpit. The government in Paris now also got involved and tried to suppress the "pretended apparition."

Although skeptics hotly rejected the apparition account, people in surrounding villages began to reform their lives while hundreds of pilgrims began the trek up the mountains. Fifty to sixty thousand people came to the location of the apparition on the first anniversary of its occurrence. Twenty-three cures attributed to the mountain spring in the first year were widely accepted. Although the main commission appointed by the bishop ruled in favor of the apparition, the bishop assigned a new team to continue the investigation. The "secrets" given to the children were written down and sent to the Pope, who was reportedly deeply impressed by them.

In November of 1851, five years after the incident took place, the local bishop accepted the authenticity of the apparition of Our Lady of La Salette and announced that the apparition "has within itself all the characteristics of the truth, and that the faithful are justified in believing it beyond doubt and for certain." A basilica was subsequently built on the mountain of La Salette and hundreds of miraculous cures were reported there. The prophecies of Our Lady of La Salette — which were widely circulated by October 1846 — turned out to be remarkably accurate. By December of the year of the apparition, most of the popular crops were disease-stricken, and in 1847 a famine swept all of Europe claiming a million lives, including one hundred thousand in France. Potatoes were not available because they had rotted in the ground, grape diseases caused the closure of most of the vineyards in France, and the walnut crop also failed. Cholera was prevalent in various parts of France and caused the deaths of many children (as predicted) and entire families.

Description of the Virgin

Melanie: "The clothing of the Most Holy Virgin was silver white and quite brilliant. It was quite intangible. It was made up of light and glory, sparkling and dazzling. There is no expression nor comparison to be found on earth. The Most Holy Virgin had a yellow pinafore.

"What am I saying, yellow? She had a pinafore more brilliant than several suns put together. It was not of tangible material; it was composed of glory, and this glory was scintillating, and ravishingly beautiful.

"The crown of roses which she placed on her head was so beautiful, so brilliant, that it defies imagination. The different colored roses were not of this earth; it was a joining together of flowers which crowned the head of the Most Holy Virgin.

"The Most Holy Virgin was tall and well proportioned. She seemed so light that a mere breath could have stirred her, yet she was motionless and perfectly balanced. Her face was majestic, imposing. The voice of the Beautiful Lady was soft. It was enchanting, ravishing, warming to the ears.

"The eyes of the majestic Mary appeared thousands of times more beautiful than the rarest brilliants, diamonds, and precious stones. They shone like two suns; but they were soft, softness itself, as clear as a mirror.

"The Holy Virgin had a most pretty cross hanging around her neck.

"The Holy Virgin was crying nearly the whole time she was speaking to us. Her tears flowed gently, one by one, down to her knees, then, like sparks of light they disappeared. They were glittering and full of love. I would have liked to comfort her and stop her tears." (1853)

Messages

The central message was: Turn away from sin and do penance or undergo terrible suffering.

"Come, my children, do not be afraid: I am here to tell you something of the greatest importance.

"If my people will not obey, I shall be compelled to let go of my Son's arm. It is so heavy, so pressing, that I can no longer restrain it. How long have I suffered for you! If I do not wish my Son to abandon you, I must take it upon myself to pray for this continually. And the rest of you think little of this! In vain will you pray, in vain will you act, you will never be able to make up for the trouble I have taken for you all!

"I gave you six days to work, I kept the seventh for myself and no one wishes to grant me that one day. This it is that causes the weight of my Son's arm to be crushing. Those who drive carts cannot swear without adding my Son's name. These are the two things which causes the weight of my Son's arm to be so burdensome.

"If the harvest is spoiled, it is your own fault. I made you see this last year with the potatoes; you took little account of this. It was quite the opposite when you found bad potatoes; you swore oaths, and you included the name of my Son. They will continue to go bad; at Christmas there will be none left.

"If you have corn, you must not sow it. The beasts will eat all that you sow. And all that grows will fall to dust when you thresh it. A great famine will come. Before the famine comes, children under the age of seven will begin to tremble and will die in the arms of those who hold them. The others will do penance through hunger. The nuts will go bad, the grapes will become rotten.

"If the people are converted, the stones and rocks will change into heaps of wheat, and potatoes will be found sown in the earth.

"Do you say your prayers properly, my children?"

"No, Madame, hardly at all."

"Ah! my children, you must say them morning and evening. When you can do no more, at least say an Our Father or a Hail Mary, and when you have the time to do better, you will say more."

"Only a few old women go to Mass; in the summer, the rest work all day Sunday and in the winter, when they do not know what to do, they only go to Mass to make fun of religion. During Lent, they go to the butchers like hungry dogs!"

"Have you ever seen spoiled wheat, my children?"

"Oh! no, Madame."

To Maximin: "But you, my child, you must have seen some once near Coin, with your father. The farmer said to your father: 'Come and see how my wheat has gone bad!' You both went to see. Your father took two or three ears in his hand, rubbed them, and they fell to dust. Then, on your way back, when you were no more than half an hour away from Corps, your father gave you a piece of bread and said: 'Take it, eat while you can, my son, for I don't know who will be eating anything next year if the wheat is spoiled like that.' "

Maximin: "That's quite true, Madame; I didn't remember." (This was an incident Maximin had forgotten about; when he narrated it to his unbelieving father, it had a profound effect on him since only the two of them knew about it.)

"Well, my children, you will make this known to all my people."

The Secrets

"The priests, ministers of my Son, the priests, by their wicked lives, by their irreverence and their impiety in the celebration of the holy mysteries, by their love of money, their love of honors and pleasures, the priests have become cesspools of impurity. Yes, the priests are asking vengeance, and vengeance is hanging over their heads.

"God will strike in an unprecedented way. Woe to the inhabitants of the earth! The chiefs, the leaders of the people of God have neglected prayer and penance, and the devil has dimmed their intelligence. God will abandon mankind to itself and will send punishments which will follow one after the other. The society of men is on the eve of the most terrible scourges and of gravest events. Mankind must expect to drink from the chalice of the wrath of God.

"May the curate of my Son, Pope Piux IX, never leave Rome again after 1859; I will be at his side. May he be on his guard against Napoleon; he is two-faced, and when he wishes to make himself Pope as well as emperor, God will soon draw back from him." [At the time when this prophecy was made, no one expected another Napoleon to come to power. By November 1852, Napoleon became emperor. Pope Pius IX had been driven from Rome in 1848 and came back with the support of Napoleon, who seemed to have designs on the papacy.]

"The earth will be struck by calamities of all kinds, in addition to plague and famine which will be widespread. There will be a series of wars until the last war. Before this comes to pass, there will be a kind of false peace in the world.

People will think of nothing but amusement. The wicked will give themselves over to all kinds of sin. But blessed are the souls humbly guided by the Holy Spirit! I shall fight at their side until they reach the fullness of years."

Concerning the secrets, Pope Pius IX said, "These are the secrets of La Salette: Unless the world repent, it shall perish!"

5. Lourdes, France, 1858

Bernadette, the oldest of four children, lived in Lourdes, a town in the foothills of the Pyrenees mountains in France. Her father had been financially ruined and the family lived in a small room in a building that was once the town jail. Here, in Bernadette's own words, is an account of how the apparitions began:

"The Thursday before Ash Wednesday (February 11, 1858) it was cold and the weather was threatening. After our dinner, our mother told us there was no more wood in the house and she was vexed. My sister Toinette and I, to please her, offered to go and pick up dry branches at the riverside. My mother said no, because the weather was bad and we might be in danger of falling into the Gave. Jeanne Abadie, our neighbor and friend, who was looking after her little brother in our house and who wanted to come with us, took her brother back to his house and returned the next moment telling us that she had leave to come with us. My mother still hesitated, but seeing that there were three of us, she let us go. We took first of all the road which leads to the cemetery, by the side of which wood shavings can sometimes be found. That day we found nothing there. We came down by the side which leads near the Gave and having arrived at the Pont Vieux we wondered if it would be best to go up or down the river. We decided to go down and taking the forest road we arrived at Merlasse. Then we went into Monsieur de la Fittes field, by the mill of Savy.

"As soon as we had reached the end of this field, nearly opposite the grotto of Massabieille, we were stopped by the canal of the mill we had just passed. The current of this canal was not strong, for the mill was not working, but the water was cold and I for my part was afraid to go in. Jeanne Abadie and my sister, less timid than I, took their sabots in their hands and crossed the stream. However, when they were on the other side they called out that it was cold and bent down to rub their feet and warm them. All this increased my fear, and I thought that if I went into the water I should get an attack of asthma. So I asked Jeanne, who was bigger and stronger than I, to take me on her shoulders. 'I should think not!' she answered. 'If you won't come, stay where you are!'

"After the others had picked up some pieces of wood under the grotto, they disappeared along the Gave. When I was alone, I threw some stones into the water to give me a foothold, but it was no use. So I had to make up my mind to take off my sabots and cross the canal as Jeanne and my sister had done.

"I had just begun to take off my first stocking when suddenly I heard a great noise like the sound of a storm. I looked to the right and to the left, under the trees of the river, but nothing moved; I thought I was mistaken. I went on taking off my shoes and stockings, when I heard a fresh noise like the first. Then I was frightened and stood straight up. I lost all power of speech and thought when, turning my head toward the grotto, I saw at one of the openings of the rock a bush — only one — moving as if it were very windy. Almost at the same time, there came out of the interior of the grotto a golden-colored cloud, and soon after a Lady, young and beautiful, exceedingly beautiful, the like of whom I had never seen before, came and placed herself at the entrance of the opening, above the rose bush. She looked at me immediately, smiled at me and signed to me to advance, as if she had been my mother. All fear had left me, but I seemed to know no longer where I was. I rubbed my eyes, I shut them, I opened them; but the Lady was still there continuing to smile at me and making me understand that I was not mistaken. Without thinking of what I was doing I took my Rosary in my hands and got down on my knees. The Lady made with her head a sign of approval and herself took into her hands a Rosary which hung on her right arm. When I attempted to begin the Rosary and tried to lift my hand to my forehead, my arm remained paralyzed, and it was only after the Lady had signed herself that I could do the same. The Lady left me to pray all alone; she passed the beads of her Rosary between her fingers but she said nothing; only at the end of each decade did she say the Gloria with me.

"When the recitation of the Rosary was finished, the Lady returned to the interior of the rock and the golden-colored cloud disappeared with her."

Bernadette described her experience to her sister Marie (Toinette), asking her to keep it to herself. But when Bernadette began to cry during evening prayers, Marie went ahead and told their mother all about the incident. Her mother said it was just an illusion and forbade Bernadette to go back to Massabieille. For the next few days she was firm in her refusal, but finally the two sisters and Jeanne persuaded her to let them return. On February 14, along with some friends they started off carrying with them a bottle of holy water. When they reached the grotto, Bernadette saw the Lady again and knelt down. She poured the holy water on the ground and this seemed to please the Lady. By now Bernadette had entered the state of ecstasy characteristic of most apparitions: her eyes were focused on a particular location (which seemed to be just empty space to the other observers), and she was entirely oblivious to the presence of her friends. At this time, Jeanne hurled a rock down the incline near the grotto into the river. This startled the children, who scattered in different directions, and their cries attracted the attention of a nearby miller and his family. The miller took Bernadette into his house. On being informed of the incident, Bernadette's mother arrived to pick her up and would have punished her severely but for the miller's intervention.

It seemed unlikely that Bernadette would ever again be allowed to go back to the grotto, but then a prominent local lady, Madame Milhet, and her seamstress, Antoinette Peyret, came to Bernadette and her mother and asked them if they might be able to go together to the grotto. The mother found it impossible to say no to two such influential ladies, and on the morning of February 18 the two of them went with Bernadette to the grotto. The ladies brought a blessed candle and a pen and paper with which they hoped to record the Lady's name during the apparition. When the Lady appeared to Bernadette, she appeared to have no objection to the presence of the two women but said it was not necessary when Bernadette gave her the pen and paper. The Lady told Bernadette she was to come another fifteen times and promised her happiness not in this world but the next. At the request of the two ladies, Bernadette's mother and aunt accompanied her on the next two visits on February 19 and 20. On the 20th, the Lady taught Bernadette a secret prayer, which she recited for the rest of her life.

On February 21, her sixth visit, Bernadette was accompanied by Dr. Pierre-Romaine Dozous, the town's most eminent doctor, who evaluated her physiological condition during the ecstasy and announced that there was nothing abnormal about it, no indication of "nervous excitement." Bernadette was asked to pray for sinners. By this time, large crowds were following Bernadette to the grotto and the local authorities were becoming concerned about safety hazards. Bernadette was separately interrogated by the imperial procurator, who said she was imagining things, and the chief of police, who said she was lying. The chief warned her that she would be imprisoned if she made any further visits to the grotto. Despite this threat she returned there the next day followed by two policemen. On this occasion, the Lady did not appear to her, and she was taunted and mocked by many of the locals. As if to reward her for her perseverance, on the next day, February 23, the Lady again came to her and gave her "three wonderful secrets" that have never been revealed. On February 24, she was given repeated injunctions of "Penitence," and on February 25 she was commanded to drink and bathe in the fountain. Since there was no fountain there, Bernadette started to dig up the gravel with her hands, and soon a small pool had formed, from which she drank and washed her face. The pool became a stream, and its ability to heal and cure became evident almost instantly when, shortly after this apparition, a man who was going blind recovered his sight after bathing his eyes in its waters and a lady's paralyzed hand was restored to normal use. On February 26 Bernadette was told to "kiss the ground in behalf of sinners," on February 27 she was asked to tell the clergy that they should build a chapel at the grotto, and on March 1 she was told that the people should come in a procession to this chapel.

Bernadette was more afraid of the parish priest, Abbé Peyramale, than of the civil authorities. When she fearfully told him of the Lady's requests, he was quite severe with her and said that he did not deal with strangers and that she, Bernadette, must first find out from the Lady who she was. On March 4, over twenty thousand people had gathered to watch Bernadette at the apparition site. Although Bernadette saw the Lady again (this was the fifteenth apparition), the crowds were clearly disappointed that they did not witness any kind of "sign and wonder." Abbé Peyramale had specified the sign he wanted: the blooming of a rose bush in winter. The Lady declined to comply with the abbé's demand.

The next apparition was on March 25, the Feast of the Annunciation, and it was then that the Lady finally responded to Bernadette's request to reveal her identity. Her answer, which Bernadette did not quite comprehend, was "Que soy era Immaculado Conceptiou," "I am the Immaculate Conception." The crowds grew larger after this announcement and the authorities became even more concerned. Lourdes fell under the jurisdiction of the Baron Massy, the prefect of Tarbes, and the baron, who was quite annoyed by the entire phenomenon, asked three prominent physicians to examine Bernadette. Their diagnosis, like that of Dr. Dozous, was that she was physically and mentally sound.

On April 7, when Bernadette was in the state of ecstasy, she accidentally moved her right hand into the flame of the candle that she always held at the apparitions (before the ecstasy began she had been holding the hand near the flame to ward off the wind). Although her hand remained in the flame, she continued in her ecstasy for another fifteen minutes without showing any sign of pain and with no damage to her skin. When the apparition was over, however, and Dr. Dozous touched her hand with a lighted candle, she reacted with pain and surprise.

After this apparition, the civil authorities blocked public access to the grotto. Bernadette felt that since the Lady had both revealed her identity and appeared to her as many times as she promised there was no urgency about returning to the grotto. On July 16, the Feast of Our Lady of Mount Carmel, she received one more "invitation" to come to the grotto — and there saw the Lady for the last time in this world (the eighteenth apparition). With the end of the apparitions, Bernadette went to study at a hospice run by the Sisters of Nevers. Eventually, she resolved to join the Sisters of Nevers and left Lourdes for the last time on July 4, 1866. Always sickly, Bernadette died at the age of thirty-five on April 16, 1879. Miraculously, to this day, Bernadette's body like that of Sister Catherine Labouré, remains incorrupt and lies in the convent chapel in Nevers. She was canonized on December 8, 1933.

As for the spring which Bernadette uncovered under the direction of the Lady, it is now the source of nearly fifteen thousand gallons of water a day. Over five thousand cures have been attributed to the waters of Lourdes, of which the Church has rigorously investigated and validated just sixty-five. Nearly five million pilgrims visit Lourdes every year. A little-known and yet significant event, in this context, was the effect of the water on the son of the emperor of France, Napoleon III. In August 1858, the two-year-old prince imperial "contracted dangerous sunstroke and the threat of meningitis from it." The royal governess was instructed to bring water from Lourdes, which was then sprinkled on the child. The child was subsequently cured, and in October the emperor ordered the local officials to remove the barricades set up around the grotto.

After an investigation of nearly four years, the bishop of the Diocese of Tarbes (to which Lourdes belongs) declared on January 18, 1862: "We judge that Mary Immaculate, Mother of God, really appeared to Bernadette Soubirous on February 11, 1858, and on subsequent days, eighteen times in all. The faithful are justified in believing this to be certain." There are now four churches in Lourdes, and the processions of the pilgrims (requested by the Lady) are a regular part of the ceremonies at this great shrine of healing.

Description of the Virgin

"She has the appearance of a young girl of sixteen or seventeen. She is dressed in a white robe, girdled at the waist with a blue ribbon, which flows down all along her robe. She wears upon her head a veil which is also white; this veil gives just a glimpse of her hair and then falls down at the back below her waist. Her feet are bare but covered by the last folds of her robe except at the point where a yellow rose shines upon each of them. She holds on her right arm a Rosary of white beads with a chain of gold shining like the two roses on her feet."

Messages

Bernadette: "She said to me, 'I do not promise to make you happy in this world, but in the next.'" (February 18, 1858)

Bernadette: "The Lady, looking away from me for a moment, directed her glance afar, above my head. Then, looking down upon me again, for I had asked her what had saddened her, she replied, 'Pray for the sinners.' I was very quickly reassured by the expression of goodness and sweetness which I saw return to her face, and immediately she disappeared." (February 21, 1858)

Bernadette: "Penitence... penitence... penitence!" (February 24, 1858)

Bernadette: "While I was in prayer, the Lady said to me in a serious but friendly voice, 'Go, drink and wash in the fountain.' As I did not know where this fountain was, and as I did not think the matter important, I went toward the Gave. The Lady called me back and signed to me with her finger to go under the grotto to the left; I obeyed but I did not see any water. Not knowing where to get it from, I scratched the earth and the water came. I let it get a little clear of the mud, then I drank and washed." (February 25, 1858)

The Virgin: "Go, and kiss the ground in penance for sinners." "Go and tell the priests to have a chapel built here." (February 27, 1858)

Bernadette (to Abbé Peyramale): "The Lady has ordered me to tell you that she wishes to have a chapel at Massabieille and now she adds 'I wish people to come here in procession.'" (March 2, 1858)

Bernadette (to Abbé Peyramale): "She smiled when I told her that you were asking her to work a miracle. I told her to make the rose bush, which she was standing near, bloom; she smiled once more. But she wants the chapel." (March 3, 1858)

Bernadette: "While I was praying, the thought of asking her name came to my mind with such persistence that I could think of nothing else. I feared to be presumptuous in repeating a question she had always refused to answer and yet something compelled me to speak. At last, under an irresistible impulsion, the words fell from my mouth and I begged the Lady to tell me who she was.

"The Lady did as she had always done before; she bowed her head and smiled, but she did not reply.

"I cannot say why, but I felt myself bolder and asked her again to graciously tell me her name; however, she only smiled and bowed as before, still remaining silent.

"Then once more, for the third time, clasping my hands and confessing myself to be unworthy of the great favor I was asking of her, I again made my request.

"The Lady was standing above the rose bush, in a position very similar to that shown on the Miraculous Medal. At my third request, her face became very serious, and she seemed to bow down in an attitude of humility. Then she joined her hands and raised them to her breast. She looked up to Heaven.

"Then slowly opening her hands and leaning toward me, she said to me in a voice vibrating with emotion: 'I AM THE IMMACULATE CONCEPTION' (Que soy era Immaculado Conceptiou). She smiled again, spoke no more, and disappeared smiling." (March 25, 1858)

6. *Pontmain, France, 1871*

The Pontmain apparition is above all a "sign" for the world that those with a special devotion to the Virgin will be protected during times of tribulation. It is also a testimony to the power of prayer.

War had broken out between France and Prussia, and things were going badly for the French, with the Prussians under Otto von Bismarck swiftly advancing across France. Paris was surrounded and bombarded daily, and the Emperor Napoleon was imprisoned by the Prussians. To the west of Paris was the city of Laval, which was on the verge of falling. Pontmain, a village belonging to the region of which Laval was the capital, was one of the few places in France where the local population practiced their faith and showed great devotion to the Virgin under the leadership of their devout parish priest, Abbé Guerin. Thirty-eight men from Pontmain had been conscripted into the French army, and the townspeople were concerned about their safety. Among the thirty-eight was Auguste Barbedette, the older brother of Eugene (twelve years old) and Joseph (ten years old). At Mass on the morning of January 17, 1871, the Abbé Guerin prayed, "Let us add penance to our prayers, and then we may take courage. God will have pity on us; his mercy will surely come to us through Mary."

That same evening the boys had been helping their father in the barn when a family friend dropped by. While she was talking to their father, Eugene stepped outside, and to his astonishment saw a beautiful lady of about eighteen suspended in the air above a house across from them. The lady wore a blue robe covered with golden stars. On her head was a gold crown and under the crown and over her forehead was a black veil. She wore blue shoes adorned with gold ribbons. He called out to the others but when they came out, only Joseph could see the Lady in the sky. There were three bright stars around the lady's crown, and this even the adults could see. When the mother of the boys came out, she refused to believe them. But two other children who came by, Françoise Richer (eleven) and Jeanne-Marie Lebosse (nine), also saw the lady. Sister Marie Edouard, a nun in the crowd, began to believe that this could be an apparition of the Virgin Mary since children were often able to see the Virgin even when adults could not. She called for yet another child, Eugene Freiteau (six), who also saw the lady as did a two-year-old baby.

As Sister Marie led the crowd in prayer, the apparition went through five changes. The first stage was the initial motionless state, which continued for two hours. The second stage began when Sister Marie started the Rosary. A small red cross appeared over her heart and a blue oval frame with four candles appeared around her while the stars in her robe seemed to increase. When Sister Marie began the Magnificat, the Lady elevated her hands with the palms outward apparently in a gesture of protection. A white scroll appeared under the Lady's feet and words of gold started to form on them: "But pray, my children." In the next phase, a larger cross appeared in her hands and a banner with the name of Christ hung from it. Yet another sentence appeared on the scroll: "God will soon grant your request." In the final phase, a third sentence appeared on the scroll, "My Son allows Himself to be moved." An image of Christ appeared on the cross, and then the cross vanished. The candles in the oval frame were lit by a star, and when the Lady lowered her hands two white crosses appeared on her shoulders. When the parish priest began his prayers, a white veil rose from beneath her feet and covered her until she disappeared.

Amazingly, at precisely the time at which the apparition began (about 5:30 p.m.), the victorious Prussians halted their advance. Historians have no ready explanation for the decision to halt, but it is reported that some Prussian soldiers claimed to have seen an image of the lady in the sky. The Prussian commander, General Schmidt, is even quoted as saying, "We cannot go farther. Yonder, in the direction of Brittany, there is an invisible Madonna barring the way." A peace treaty between Prussia and France was signed eleven days later. All the soldiers from Pontmain returned unharmed.

Pilgrims arrived to pray at Pontmain the day after the apparition, and in February 1875 Bishop Wicart of Laval declared: "We judge that the Immaculate Mary, Mother of God, has truly appeared on January 17, 1871, to Eugene Barbedette, Joseph Barbedette, Françoise Richer, and Jeanne-Marie Lebosse, in the hamlet of Pontmain."

Description of the Virgin

She wore a blue robe embroidered with numerous golden stars. On her head she had a black veil and a gold crown and on her feet blue shoes with gold ribbons. The Lady was tall and beautiful and looked about eighteen; "smiles of ineffable sweetness played about her mouth." When the cross with Christ appeared in her hands, Joseph Barbedette recalled that "her face was marked with a deep sorrow...the trembling of her lips at the corners of her mouth showed deep feeling....But no tears ran down her cheeks."

Messages

"Pray, my children."

"God will soon grant your request."

"My Son allows Himself to be moved."

7. Fatima, Portugal, 1917

Fatima is without question the greatest of the twentieth-century apparitions, one which has had a profound impact both on the faith of millions and on central events of this century. A September 27, 1991, *Wall Street Journal* story subtitled "Believers say Blessed Virgin beat CNN to the news by more than 74 years," considered the impact of Fatima on current events in Russia: "Says William Fairman, a 62-year-old chemist recently retired from Argonne National

Laboratory in Lemont, Ill.: 'Our Lady is simply fulfilling her promise back in 1917 to convert Russia.' Francis Irons, 62, a former Defense Department analyst agrees: Recent events in the Soviet Union are 'only explainable in supernatural terms,' he says."

It is now hardly remembered that no serious analyst, even as recently as in 1988, would dare to have suggested that the Soviet Union could give up Communism or that the Communist regimes of Eastern Europe might relinquish power. But these implausible events were predicted by the Virgin at Fatima in 1917 — and those who believed in her promises from the very start continued to pray for this turn of events despite its utter unlikelihood. The Virgin had predicted first that Russia would spread its errors around the world — this was before the Communists came to power and hence did not sound realistic — and then that Russia would be "converted," a turnaround that could not have been contemplated during the nightmare of the Cold War and the Iron Curtain. Like those of many of her other apparitions, these and similar predictions were fulfilled in future events.

The apparitions of the Virgin at Fatima in 1917 were in some respects a direct response to a plea from Pope Benedict XV, who implored the intercession of the Blessed Mother in bringing the Great War to a halt. On May 5, 1917, the Pope sent out a pastoral letter to the world, in which he asked the faithful to petition Mary the Mother of Mercy in "this awful hour" "that her most tender and benign solicitude may be moved and the peace we ask for be obtained for our agitated world." Within eight days, on May 13, the Mother of Mercy appeared at Fatima with her own "peace plan" for the world. In the third of the Fatima apparitions, the Virgin said that the present war would come to an end (something that most people found unbelievable at the time), but a new and greater war would begin during the papacy of Pius XI.

After the overthrow of the monarchy in 1908, Portugal was ruled by anti-Christian groups who killed nearly seventeen hundred priests, nuns, and monks between 1911 and 1916. Public religious ceremonies were forbidden, as in Mexico. It was into this unpromising environment that the Lady of the Rosary made her world-changing entrance.

The Fatima apparitions were preceded by three appearances of the Guardian Angel of Portugal, in which he prepared the three tiny sheep-herder visionaries for the coming of the Mother of God. Lucia dos Santos (nine), Francisco Marto (eight) and Jacinta Marto (six) had taken their sheep to a hilly area called the Chousa Velha. At this time, wrote Lucia, "a strong wind shook the trees, and above them a light appeared, whiter than the driven snow. As it approached, it took the form of a young man, transparent and resplendent with light. He began to speak. 'Fear not. I am the Angel of Peace. Pray with me.' He knelt on the ground, bowed low, and three times recited a prayer: 'My God, I believe, I adore, I hope, and I love You. I ask pardon of You for those who do not believe, do not adore, do not hope, and do not love You.' Then he arose and said: 'Pray this way. The Hearts of Jesus and Mary are attentive to the voice of your supplications.' " On another occasion, the angel told them, "The Hearts of Jesus and Mary have designs of mercy for you. Offer unceasingly to the Most

High prayer and sacrifices. Offer up everything within your power as a sacrifice to the Lord in reparation for the sins by which he is so much offended and of supplication for the conversion of sinners. Thus bring down peace upon your country. I am the Guardian Angel of Portugal. More than all else, accept and bear with resignation the sufferings that God may send you."

The angel also brought them Holy Communion and prostrating himself in front of the Eucharist repeated a prayer that is now synonymous with Fatima: "Most Holy Trinity, Father, Son, and Holy Ghost, I adore You profoundly and I offer You the most precious Body, Blood, Soul, and Divinity of Jesus Christ, present in all the tabernacles of the world, in reparation for the outrages, sacrileges, and indifference by which He Himself is offended. And by the infinite merits of His Most Sacred Heart and the Immaculate Heart of Mary, I beg of You the conversion of poor sinners." Offering them communion, he said, "Take and drink the Body and Blood of Jesus Christ, horribly outraged by ungrateful men. Make reparation for their crimes and console your God."

The apparitions of the angel were followed by six apparitions of the Virgin to the three children from May 13 to October 13, 1917, and numerous subsequent appearances and messages to Lucia. In some respects Lucia is a living testament to the Fatima event, called to carry out a mission that began in 1917 and still continues through the end of the twentieth century. The apparitions themselves were public events so that even onlookers were aware of something extraordinary taking place, most especially on October 13, 1917.

On May 13, the three children had taken their sheep to a part of the Chousa Velha called the Cova da Iria when they were alarmed by a sudden flash of light from the clear blue sky (literally, a bolt from the blue). As they ran toward their sheep, they saw another flash of light and then a ball of light alighting on a holm oak tree (called *carrasqueira*). In the luminous ball was a beautiful lady. Although they were terrified, the woman calmed their fears, telling them softly that she would not hurt them. She told them she was from Heaven and that she wanted them to come to the Cova on the thirteenth of each month for six months and that she would tell them who she was in her last appearance and explain what she wanted of them. The Lady told them that all three of them would go to Heaven although Francisco would have to say many Rosaries. She asked them if they wanted to offer themselves to God and suffer for the reparation of sin and the conversion of sinners. When they said yes, she told them they would suffer a lot but be strengthened by God's grace; they were to say the Rosary for peace and the end of the war. With this, the Lady glided toward the east until she was out of sight.

Although the father of Francisco and Jacinta accepted their accounts of the event, Lucia's mother was convinced she was lying, gave her a painful beating, and tried to make her retract her story but in vain. On June 13th, the children went back to the Cova despite their parents' attempts to get them to come to the festival of St. Anthony of Padua. The Lady appeared again at noon — onlookers saw the sun dim at this precise time — and asked that they pray five Rosaries a day and continue to come back on the 13th of each month. The children were to learn to read. The Lady told Lucia that Francisco and Jacinta would be taken to Heaven soon, and she alone would be left in the world — and her mission would be to spread devotion to the Lady's Immaculate Heart, for this devotion was of great assistance on the journey of salvation. She left as before in the direction of the east.

After this apparition, both Lucia's mother and the parish priest were adamant that the Lady of the apparitions was of diabolic origin. Lucia was confused and fearful and decided not to go again. But just as the time of the apparition drew near on July 13, her mind found serenity, and she left for the Cova with Francisco and Jacinta (who would not have gone without her). Two or three thousand people awaited them there.

This apparition was especially memorable — and especially important for those who wonder whether Marian apparitions are diabolic in nature. As if to show the difference between her and the diabolic world, the Lady spread out her hands, and the light that poured out from them went into the depths of the earth to show the terrified visionaries a sea of fire filled with demons and the damned. "Even the earth itself seemed to vanish," wrote Lucia, "and we saw huge numbers of devils and lost souls in a vast and fiery ocean. The devils resembled black animals, hideous and unknown, each filling the air with despairing shrieks. The lost souls were in their human bodies and seemed brown in color, tumbling about constantly in the flames and screaming with terror. All were on fire, within and without their bodies, and neither devils nor damned souls seemed able to control their movements. They were tossing about like coals in a fiery furnace, with never an instant's peace or freedom from pain."

The Lady told them that God wanted to establish devotion to her Immaculate Heart precisely to bring more souls to salvation. She warned that a greater war than the last one would break out under the next pontificate if people did not stop offending God. When an unknown light illumined the night, it would be a sign that a divine chastisement would soon begin. She also asked for a consecration of Russia to her Immaculate Heart by the Pope and communion of reparation on First Saturdays. If this were not done, Russia would spread its errors and entire nations would be annihilated — but in the end her Immaculate Heart would triumph because the Pope would consecrate Russia to her and the country would be converted, after which would follow a short time of peace. The first secret of Fatima was the vision of Hell, and the second secret was the revelation of the importance of devotion to the Immaculate Heart. The children were also given a third secret, which has never been revealed, although its contents have been a frequent subject of speculation. Here the apparition ended.

The fourth apparition, scheduled for August 13, did not take place as planned. The children were kidnapped by one of the anticlericalists committed to wiping out the Church, the civil administrator, who threatened the children, in individual sessions, with death in a red-hot frying pan unless they admitted that the alleged experience was a mere deception or told him the secrets they had been given. Heroically, the children held out, and after three days the administrator was finally forced to return them to their village. Meanwhile, on August 13, at the apparition site, the eighteen thousand people who were present witnessed a sign of Heaven's displeasure at this arrogant action. There was lightning and thunder, the sun turned pale, and there was a yellowish haze in the atmosphere. A white cloud settled on the oak tree and rapidly changed colors, taking on all the colors of the rainbow. The children saw the Lady again on August 19 and at this time she spoke of the need for penance for one's sins and those of the world; many souls were damned because there was no one to pray for them.

On September 13, the assembled multitudes, now some thirty thousand strong, again saw the sun dim at noon and then a globe of light descending on the oak tree. They also saw white roses falling from the sky. The visionaries were once again reminded of the importance of saying the Rosary to end the war. She told them that in October she would be accompanied by St. Joseph and the Child Jesus.

By October 13, the whole country had heard of Fatima. Seventy thousand people had arrived at the Cova. The night before, a terrible (some said diabolic) storm swept through Europe, and it was still raining hard by noon of the 13th. When the Lady appeared to the visionaries, she said she was the Lady of the Rosary, that she wanted a chapel built at the Cova, and that people must amend their lives and not offend the Lord since He was already greatly offended. Then she stretched out her hands again and rays of light went toward the sun. Thus began the famous miracle of the sun. The sun now seemed to be a silver disk and the multitudes could look straight into it without shading their eyes. Suddenly it started shooting off different colored rays in all directions and then spinning on its axis. And then just as suddenly it seemed to be hurtling toward the earth. The terrified onlookers dropped to their knees, convinced that the end had come and many sought forgiveness for their sins. Just when it seemed that there would be a cataclysmic collision, the sun returned to its normal position and everything was as before. Miraculously, drenched clothes had dried up and there was neither water nor mud to be seen anywhere. The miracle of the sun was witnessed not just by those in the Cova but by people thirty miles away (thus ruling out the possibility of mass hysteria). While the crowds were gazing at the solar phenomena, the visionaries were witnessing various scenes in the heavens: Jesus in a red costume blessing the crowds, then Jesus as an infant with Mary and Joseph, and finally Mary in the brown robes of Our Lady of Mount Carmel. With this magnificent display, the apparitions of Fatima came to an end — but their impact on the century had only just begun.

Francisco died in April 1919 and Jacinta in February 1920. Both were victims of the great global influenza epidemic. Jacinta heroically endured excruciating pain in the last months of her life, and her body was found to be incorrupt when it was exhumed in 1935 and 1950. As she lay dying, she once asked Lucia, "Why doesn't the Lady show Hell to everybody? Then nobody would ever again commit a mortal sin."

At the local bishop's recommendation, Lucia was sent to a girls school run by the Sisters of St. Dorothy in 1921. In 1926 she entered the novitiate of this Order and in 1934 made her final vows. In 1925 both the Virgin and the Christ Child appeared to Lucia. At this time, Jesus asked the whole world to institute the practice of reparation to the Immaculate Heart on the first Saturdays of every month: those who for five consecutive first Saturdays received communion, went for reconciliation, recited five decades of the Rosary, and meditated for fifteen minutes on mysteries of the Rosary, all in reparation to the Immaculate Heart, would receive the graces required for salvation. In 1929, the Virgin told Sister Lucia that this was the time for the consecration of Russia to the Immaculate Heart.

In October 1930 the bishop of Leiria declared the apparitions of Fatima worthy of belief. Every year over four million pilgrims go to Fatima.

At the request of Sister Lucia, the bishops of Portugal consecrated their country to the Immaculate Heart in 1938 — and with good reason it is believed that, as a result of this act, Portugal was not drawn into the Second World War.

Lucia entered the Carmelite order in 1948. In early 1989, Sister Lucia sent a communication to the world announcing that the consecration of Russia and the world to the Immaculate Heart, made by Pope John Paul II on March 25, 1984, had been accepted by God and that its results would become apparent later that year. In late 1989 the Berlin Wall had fallen and by August of 1991 Russia was no longer Communist. The Communist coup against Gorbachev was launched on August 19, 1991, the same day as the delayed fourth apparition of Fatima. The coup failed and Gorbachev was set free on August 22, the Feast of the Queenship of Mary. Gorbachev was held as a prisoner for three days, as were the Fatima visionaries.

Description of the Virgin

"It was a Lady dressed all in white, more brilliant than the sun, shedding rays of light clearer and stronger than a crystal glass filled with the most sparkling water and pierced by the burning rays of the sun."

Messages

"Do not be afraid. I will do you no harm."

"I am from Heaven."

"I have come to ask you to come here for six months in succession, on the thirteenth day, at this same hour. Later on, I will tell you who I am and what I want. Afterward, I will return here yet a seventh time."

"Are you willing to offer yourselves to God and bear all the sufferings He wills to send you, as an act of reparation for the sins by which He is offended, and of supplication for the conversion of sinners? . . . Then you are going to have much to suffer, but the grace of God will be your comfort."

"Pray the Rosary every day, in order to obtain peace for the world, and the end of war." (May 13, 1917; excerpted from *Fatima, in Lucia's Own Words* by Sister Lucia)

"I wish you to come here on the 13th of the next month, to pray the Rosary every day and to learn to read. Later, I will tell you what I want."

The Virgin's response to Lucia's request for the cure of a sick person: "If he is converted, he will be cured during the year."

Response to Lucia's request that she take them to Heaven: "Yes, I will take Jacinta and Francisco soon. But you are to stay here some time longer. Jesus wishes to make use of you to make me known and loved. He wants to establish in the world devotion to my Immaculate Heart."

Response to Lucia's concern that she would be alone: "No, my daughter. Are you suffering a great deal? Don't lose heart. I will never forsake you. My Immaculate Heart will be your refuge and the way that will lead you to God." (June 13, 1917)

"I want you to come here on the 13th of next month, to continue to pray the Rosary every day in honor of our Lady of the Rosary, in order to obtain peace for the world and the end of the war, because only she can help you."

"Continue to come here every month. In October, I will tell you who I am and what I want, and I will perform a miracle for all to see and believe."

"Sacrifice yourselves for sinners, and say many times, especially whenever you make some sacrifice: O Jesus, it is for love of You, for the conversion of sinners, and in reparation for the sins committed against the Immaculate Heart of Mary."

After the vision of Hell: "You have seen Hell where the souls of poor sinners go. To save them, God wishes to establish in the world devotion to my Immaculate Heart. If what I say to you is done, many souls will be saved and there will be peace. The war is going to end: but if people do not cease offending God, a worse one will break out during the pontificate of Pius XI. When you see a night illumined by an unknown light, know that this is the great sign given you by God that He is about to punish the world for its crimes, by means of war, famine, and persecutions of the Church and of the Holy Father.

"To prevent this, I shall come to ask for the consecration of Russia to my Immaculate Heart, and the communion of Reparation on the First Saturdays. If my requests are heeded, Russia will be converted and there will be peace; if not, she will spread her errors throughout the world, causing wars and persecutions of the Church. The good will be martyred, the Holy Father will have much to suffer, various nations will be annihilated. . . . [At this point, our Lady revealed what has become known as the third part of the Fatima secret.] In the end, my Immaculate Heart will triumph. The Holy Father will consecrate Russia to me, and she will be converted, and a period of peace will be granted to the world. In Portugal, the dogma of the faith will always be preserved. Do not tell this to anybody. Francisco, yes, you may tell him."

"When you pray the Rosary, say after each mystery: O my Jesus, forgive us, save us from the fire of Hell. Lead all souls to Heaven, especially those who are most in need." (July 13, 1917)

"I want you to continue going to the Cova da Iria on the 13th, and to continue praying the Rosary every day. In the last month, I will perform a miracle so that all may believe."

Response to Lucia's question on the money left by visitors: "Have two litters made. One is to be carried by you and Jacinta and two other girls dressed in white: the other one is to be carried by Francisco and three other boys. The money from the litters is for the 'festa' of Our Lady of the Rosary, and what is left over will help toward the construction of a chapel that is to be built here."

Response to Lucia's request for cures: "Yes, I will cure some of them during the year."

"Pray, pray very much, and make sacrifices for sinners: for many souls go to Hell because there are none to sacrifice themselves and to pray for them." (August 19, 1917)

"Continue to pray the Rosary in order to obtain the end of the war. In October Our Lord will come, as well as Our Lady of Dolors and Our Lady of Carmel. St. Joseph will appear with the Child Jesus to bless the world. God is pleased with your sacrifices. He does not want you to sleep with the rope on, but only to wear it during the daytime."

Response to Lucia's request for cures: "Yes, I will cure some, but not others. In October I will perform a miracle so that all may believe." (September 13, 1917)

"I want to tell you that a chapel is to be built here in my honor.

"I am the Lady of the Rosary. Continue always to pray the Rosary every day.

"The war is going to end, and the soldiers will soon return to their homes."

Response to Lucia's request for cures and conversions: "Some yes, but not others. They must amend their lives and ask forgiveness for their sins."

"Do not offend the Lord our God any more, because He is already so much offended." After this statement, the Miracle of the Sun took place. (October 13, 1917)

Later Apparitions

"On December 10, 1925, the Most Holy Virgin Mary appeared to her [Lucia is writing in the third person]. By her side, elevated on a luminous cloud was a Child. The most holy Virgin rested her hand on her shoulder. As she did so, she showed her a Heart encircled by thorns which she was holding in her other hand. At the same time, the child said, 'Have compassion on the Heart of your most holy Mother, covered with thorns, with which ungrateful men pierce it at every moment, and there is no one to make an act of reparation to remove them.'

"Then the Most Holy Virgin said, 'Look, my daughter, at my Heart, surrounded with thorns with which ungrateful men pierce it at every moment by their blasphemies and ingratitude. You at least try to console me and say that I promise to assist at the hour of death, with the graces necessary for salvation, all those who, on the first Saturday of five consecutive months, shall confess, receive Holy Communion, recite five decades of the Rosary, and keep me company for fifteen minutes while meditating on the mysteries of the Rosary, with the intention of making reparation to me.'"

On February 26, 1926, Jesus asked her, "What is being done to promote the devotion to the Immaculate Heart of Mary?"

Then, finally, in 1929, He said, "I want My entire Church to know that this favor [the conversion of Russia] was obtained through the Immaculate Heart of My Mother so that it may extend this devotion later on and put the devotion to this Immaculate Heart beside the devotion to My Sacred Heart."

8. *Beauraing, Belgium, 1932*

Fernande and Albert Voisin left on the evening of November 29, 1932, with Andrée and Gilberte Degeimbre to pick up their sister, also named Gilberte (the younger Gilberte), from an academy run by the Sisters of Christian Doctrine in the little railroad town of Beauraing. The parents of the Voisins were no longer practicing Catholics, and Hector Voisin was even a member of the Marxist Labor Party. The mother of the Degeimbres, Germaine, was a widow who was infrequent in church attendance. When the four children reached the academy, Albert (who was the prankster in the group) happened to turn around and saw "the Virgin in White" walking over a bridge that went over the convent adjoining the academy. The other three did not believe him, but at his insistence they looked back and also beheld a luminous woman clearly walking over the bridge. When the younger Gilberte joined them, she too saw the Lady. The nun who received them, however, was unable to see the apparition. The children saw the same apparition again the following day, but neither the parents nor the nuns believed the accounts of the children. When the children returned the next day, December 1, Germaine Degeimbre and some adults accompanied them. This time the children saw the apparition in the courtyard of the convent. On that day, they saw the Lady four times, mainly over a rose hawthorn bush in the courtyard. On December 2, the mother superior had locked the gates to the convent, but the Lady appeared to them as usual and for the first time spoke to them, answering their questions.

Over the next few days, too, the Virgin appeared to the visionaries daily. From December 4, they noticed that she had a Rosary hanging from her right arm, and on December 8 she appeared to them in the presence of at least ten thousand spectators. It was during the December 8 apparition that, for the first time, the visionaries entered a state of ecstasy in which they were demonstrably impervious to any external stimuli; doctors who were present burnt them, pricked them with knives, etc., without any reaction from the visionaries or any physical injury. The Virgin continued appearing to them on different days. During the December 29 apparition, the children saw that she had a golden heart surrounded by rays of light. The last apparition took place on January 3 before thirty thousand people. Each of the visionaries was given a secret. The last one to get a message was Fernande: observers saw a ball of fire suddenly descend on the hawthorn bush and heard a thunderclap while Fernande immediately dropped to her knees and was given a final message by the Virgin.

After the apparitions were over, two people who had personally come to the visionaries with petitions about their ailments were healed, one from a bone disease and the other from a tubercular condition. Numerous other cures were reported. Another person, Tilman Come, who was healed of a disease of the spinal vertebrae in the summer of 1933, was privileged to witness several additional apparitions of the Virgin with the Golden Heart.

One of the Virgin's chief messages was that she would convert sinners. The Beauraing phenomenon certainly had this effect on many who came into contact with it, ranging from the parents of the visionaries to the editor of a Belgian

Communist newspaper who actually saw the Virgin at Beauraing and spent the rest of his life promoting Marian devotion.

In a July 2, 1949, document the bishop of the diocese to which Beauraing belongs wrote, "We are able in all serenity and prudence to affirm that the Queen of Heaven appeared to the children of Beauraing during the winter of 1932–33 especially to show us in her maternal Heart the anxious appeal for prayer and the promise of her powerful mediation for the conversion of sinners." Today, over a million pilgrims a year visit Beauraing.

Description of the Virgin

As in all other cases, the visionaries were most moved by the beauty of the Virgin. She looked eighteen and had deep blue eyes. Rays of light came from her head. She wore a flowing white gown, which radiated a "kind of blue light," stood on a cloud, had a Rosary on the right arm, and displayed a golden heart surrounded by rays of light.

Messages

Albert: "Are you the Immaculate Virgin?" to which she nodded. (December 2, 1932)

Albert: "What do you want?" The Virgin: "Always be good." The Virgin asked later on that day: "Is it true you will always be good?" Andrée: "Yes! We will always be good."

The visionaries ask for a sign to which the Virgin gives no response. (December 5)

The visionaries: "At the request of the clergy, we ask you what you want of us." The Virgin tells them she wants a chapel, to which the visionaries say: "Yes, we will have it built here." (December 17)

Several of the children: "Tell us who you are." The Virgin: "I am the Immaculate Virgin." (December 21)

In response to Fernande's question about why she had come there, the Virgin said, "That people might come here on pilgrimages." (December 23)

"Soon I shall appear for the last time." (December 28)

"Pray. Pray very much." (December 30)

From December 31, all the visionaries saw the Virgin with her golden heart, a reminder of the doctrine and devotion of the Immaculate Heart.

To Gilberte Voisin: "Pray always." (January 1, 1933)

"Tomorrow I will speak to each one of you separately." (January 2)

To Gilberte Voisin: "This is between you and me, and I ask you to speak of it to no one."

To Gilberte Degeimbre: "I will convert sinners." This is the famous promise of the Virgin of Beauraing. She then entrusted her with a secret and said "Goodbye."

Albert was given a secret and then told "Goodbye."

To Andrée: "I am the Mother of God, the Queen of Heaven. Pray always."

To Fernande: "Do you love my Son?" Fernande: "Yes." "Do you love?" Fernande: "Yes." "Then sacrifice yourself for me."

The Virgin then said "Goodbye" before Fernande could ask any further questions. (January 3)

9. Banneux, Belgium, 1933

Mariette Beco, at age eleven, was the oldest of seven children. Her father was a lapsed Catholic living in a poverty-stricken socialist part of Belgium. Her mother was not a practicing Catholic, and Mariette had stopped going to church and receiving instruction in the faith. On the night of January 15, she was looking out the window for her younger brother Julien and saw a beautiful and luminous young lady who was beckoning to her. Her mother did not believe Mariette's account, but on looking out saw a figure of light outside. She would not allow Mariette to go out for fear of witchcraft. Mariette's father tried to explain away the phenomenon as having been caused by light reflections but could not give a demonstration to establish his claim. The next day Mariette's friend took her to the parish priest, who was skeptical and thought her account was simply a copycat version of the just-finished Beauraing apparitions. At the next apparition, the Virgin led Mariette from her house to a spring, which she said would bring healing to all nations. She also asked for construction of a chapel. There were eight apparitions in all. The parish priest was initially skeptical but eventually accepted the authenticity of the apparitions. In 1949, upon completion of extensive investigations, the bishop of the region officially approved the apparitions.

Distinctive features of the apparitions include: people were converted in large numbers simply by listening to accounts of the apparitions (Mariette's father was one of the converts); the path from Mariette's house to the spring is now open to the public and is the only place in the world which traces a route taken by the Virgin; Mary's self-description was "Virgin of the Poor," and this was especially significant since the world had just gone through a devastating economic depression and Banneux was one of the poorest areas in Belgium; the apparitions of Banneux, along with those of Beauraing, were taking place just before the onset of the Second World War and signified the Virgin's empathy with a world soon to witness terrible suffering (both towns are located in the Ardennes, which was where the Battle of the Bulge, the single most devastating battle of the War, was fought); the Virgin said the spring was for "all nations," an echo of the post–World War II apparitions of Amsterdam, and also a prophecy since over five hundred thousand pilgrims from around the world visit the spring every year and over fifty miraculous cures have been documented; over three thousand monuments and shrines, three hundred chapels, and twenty-five churches around the world are dedicated to the Virgin of the Poor.

Description of the Virgin

Extraordinarily beautiful, enveloped in a "great oval light," the Virgin wore a long white gown with a sash of an "unforgettable blue" and a white, transparent veil covering head and shoulders. Her right foot was visible and "crowned with a golden rose" between the toes. She had a Rosary on her right arm with diamond-like beads and a golden chain and cross. She stood on a cloud with her head and shoulders bent slightly to the left.

Messages

Upon reaching the spring, the Virgin told Mariette, "Place your hands in the water," which she did. Mariette then repeated the Virgin's words, "This stream is reserved for me. Good evening. *Au revoir.*" (Second apparition, January 18, 1933)

Mariette: "Who are you, lovely Lady?" The Virgin: "I am the Virgin of the Poor." The Virgin's reply to the next question indicated that Mariette had misunderstood her statement of the previous day. Mariette: "Beautiful Lady, yesterday you said, 'This spring is reserved for me.' Why for me?" The Virgin: "This spring is reserved for all nations — to relieve the sick." (The Virgin appeared to be amused by this misunderstanding). "I shall pray for you. *Au revoir.*" (Third apparition, January 18, 1933)

Mariette: "What do you wish, my beautiful Lady?" The Virgin: "I would like a small chapel." After this the Virgin blessed her with the sign of the cross and Mariette collapsed (without any resultant harm). (Fourth apparition, January 20, 1933)

The Virgin: "I come to relieve suffering." (Fifth apparition, February 11, 1933)

Mariette: "Blessed Virgin, the chaplain told me to ask you for a sign." The Virgin: "Believe in me, I will believe in you. Pray much. *Au revoir.*" This was one of the most intriguing replies in the literature of Marian apparitions. Many times the recipients of Marian apparitions were asked for signs, and many times the Virgin furnished unmistakable signs of her presence. But here we see that Heaven operates by its own rules: Heaven's "sign" was the miraculous spring that would draw millions of pilgrims, a "sign" that would be shown in good time. The true miracles of God are always subtle. Although they elicit faith, they are displayed only when they serve a clear and permanent purpose. But a sincere faith had to come first. (Sixth apparition, February 15, 1933)

The Virgin had a grave expression and said, "My dear child, pray much. *Au revoir.*" (Seventh apparition, February 20, 1933)

In her final apparition, the Virgin was grave and sorrowful, "I am the Mother of the Savior, Mother of God. Pray much." She blessed Mariette and said, "*Adieu —*

till we meet in God." In French, *au revoir* means "see you again" and *adieu* means "goodbye." (Eight apparition, March 2, 1933)

Mariette was also given a "secret" at one of the apparitions which has never been disclosed.

10. Akita, Japan, 1973–81

Sister Agnes Sasagawa (born 1931) entered the convent of the Institute of the Handmaids of the Eucharist in Akita, Japan, on May 12, 1973. Not long before she had lost her hearing. A month after joining the order, she came to the convent chapel to adore the Eucharist. On opening the tabernacle door, she was astounded to see a light brighter than the sun coming from within and prostrated herself before it. She witnessed the same phenomenon on several subsequent occasions when she came to the chapel; she also saw "spiritual beings" worshiping the Eucharist. She reported these experiences to Bishop John Ito, the bishop of Niigata, the diocese to which Akita belonged, and he advised her to be open but cautious.

Later in the month, Agnes discovered that she was receiving the stigmata. On Thursdays, the palm of her left hand would start to hurt and on the next day a red cross would form on it. On Sunday, she would be healed and the pain would go away.

At 3:00 a.m. on the morning of July 6, she saw a beautiful person in the chapel, her guardian angel, who told her, "Be not afraid. Pray with fervor not only because of your sins, but in reparation for those of all people. The world today wounds the most Sacred Heart of Our Lord by its ingratitudes and injuries. The wounds of Mary are much deeper and more sorrowful than yours. Let us go to pray together in the chapel."

After the angel disappeared, Agnes saw that a three-foot-high wooden statue of the Virgin in the chapel was blazing with light. The statue was modeled on the image of the Virgin as she appeared in Amsterdam in 1945 ("Our Lady of All Nations"). The statue spoke to Agnes and asked her to pray in reparation for the sins of humanity and to follow her superior. After this apparition, Agnes and the other nuns found that there was a wound in the palm of the statue, which continued to bleed until Sunday.

On July 26, the pain from Agnes's wound was almost unbearable. Again, she heard from her angel, "Your sufferings will end today. Carefully engrave in the depth of your heart the thought of the blood of Mary. The blood shed by Mary has a profound meaning. This precious blood was shed to ask your conversion, to ask for peace, in reparation for the ingratitude and the outrages against the Lord. As with devotion to the Sacred Heart, apply yourself to devotion to the most Precious Blood. Pray in reparation for all men. Say to your superior that the blood is shed today for the last time. Your pain also ends today. Tell them what happened today. He will understand all immediately. And you, observe his directions." The angel then disappeared and Sr. Agnes noticed that the pain from her wound had subsided.

On August 3, Agnes again heard from the statue. The Virgin told her that the Heavenly Father was preparing a great chastisement for the world. She also asked for prayer and penance.

On September 29, the statue stopped bleeding, but tears started flowing down its cheeks.

On October 13, Sister Agnes received her last message from the Virgin. She was told that the Father would inflict a terrible punishment on humanity, that fire would fall from the sky and wipe out a good portion of humanity, that the devil would infiltrate the Church.

In May 1974, her angel told Agnes that her hearing would be temporarily restored and then permanently cured later. On October 13 of that year, Agnes regained her hearing, but by March of 1975 she had lost it yet again. At the end of 1975, the angel told her,

> Do not be so surprised to see the Blessed Virgin weeping. She weeps because she wishes the conversion of the greatest number. She desires that souls be consecrated to Jesus and to the Father by her intercession. He who directs you told you during the last sermon today: Your faith diminishes when you do not see. It is because your faith is weak. The Blessed Virgin rejoices in the consecration of Japan to her Immaculate Heart because she loves Japan. But she is sad to see that devotion is not taken seriously. Even though she has chosen this land of Akita to give her messages, the local pastor doesn't dare to come for fear of what one would say. Do not be afraid. The Blessed Virgin awaits you all.

Meanwhile the statue continued to weep on certain given days and by September 15, 1981, the last time this happened, it had shed tears a total of 101 times. On September 28, 1981, her guardian angel showed Agnes a vision of a Bible and asked her to read Genesis 3:15: "I will place enmity between thee (Satan) and the woman (Mary), between thy seed and hers. She will crush thy head and thou shalt lie in wait for her heel." (This was the rendition of the verse in the modern Japanese translation.) The angel then explained the relation between this verse and the fact that the statue had wept 101 times: "There is a meaning to the figure 101. This signifies that sin came into the world by a woman and it is also by a woman that salvation came into the world. The zero between the two signifies the Eternal God who is from all eternity until eternity. The first one represents Eve, and the last, the Virgin Mary."

Fr. Thomas Teiji Yasuda, Sr. Agnes's spiritual director, interpreted the verse and the message in this manner:

> The passage from the Scripture elucidated the profound meaning of the angel's message regarding the 101 weepings. Here in Akita, God himself sent the angel to reveal the profound meaning of the message 'by the authority of the Bible,' the words of God. In Genesis Chapter 3, verse 15, the Sovereign God, the Absolute Being, makes the prophetic announcement to Satan of the combat, in which the Blessed Virgin Mary and Her seed will oppose and confront Satan throughout the ages. It is in union with the

Church, the Mystical Body of Christ, that the Virgin Mary has received, from the Eternal Father, the mission of fighting against and crushing Satan and his cohorts until the end of the world. The miracles of the bleeding and weeping of the statue of the Blessed Mother in Akita were brought about by God in order to illustrate the truth of Mary's role as Coredemptrix.

Theresa Chun, a Korean woman who was diagnosed with a brain tumor, placed an image of Our Lady of Akita under her pillow and prayed to her for a miraculous healing. On August 4, 1981, the tumor was found to have disappeared. In May 1982, her angel told Agnes that her hearing would be permanently restored that month, and on May 30 the deafness was cured. (Tests performed on Agnes at the Akita Municipal Hospital in 1975 had confirmed that she was deaf and it was noted that the deafness was incurable.)

The acceptance of Akita faced three obstacles: scientific, theological, and ecclesiastical.

On the scientific front, the results were quite remarkable. The actual weeping of the statue was not only witnessed by the local bishop but was shown on national Japanese TV. The tears, sweat, and blood from the statue were sent for laboratory analysis in January 1975. The first tests on the samples sent were performed by Professor Eiji Okuhara, a Catholic physician in the Akita University Department of Biochemistry and a former Rockefeller Foundation fellow. Professor Okuhara, who had witnessed the weeping of the statue himself, also passed the samples on to a non-Christian forensic specialist, Dr. Kaoru Sagisaka. The scientists confirmed that the blood, sweat, and tears were of human origin, that the blood was type B and the sweat and tears were type AB.

A subsequent test was performed after Dr. Sagisaka became a professor at Gifu University since it was said that there might have been some contamination of the initial samples by the handlers. In the first report, Dr. Sagisaka had written that "at the time the specimen was taken, or by the time the examiner received the specimen, it could have been contaminated by a minute amount of body fluid of type A or type AB." The report from the new tests, performed on samples extracted after the required precautions were in place, came out on November 30, 1981. Dr. Sagisaka's medical appraisal certificate stated, "I certify that human body fluid is adhering to the specimen and that the blood type of the specimen is type O."

The theological verdict on Akita was left in the hands of an implacable foe of the apparitions, Fr. Garcia Evangelista, a Mariologist from Tokyo who headed up an investigative commission in 1975. Fr. Evangelista rejected the authenticity of the apparitions and claimed that the blood, sweat, and tears pouring forth from the statue came from the "ectoplasmic powers" of Sister Agnes by which she could manifest her bodily fluids through the statue. This conclusion caused confusion for the followers of Akita for many years but it was easily refuted: (a) Agnes had blood type B, but the analyses of the fluids from the statue showed types A, AB, and O; (b) the critic said ectoplasmic powers are exercised when the primary agent is fifteen meters away from the statue, but the blood, sweat, and tears continued when Agnes was visiting her relatives 250 miles away. An

American medical doctor, Dr. Theresa Wei, who once witnessed the statue shedding tears, said that at that precise time Agnes was working in the kitchen — and she could not focus her will power on two things at the same time. When the writer Francis Mutsuo Fukushima confronted Evangelista with these responses, Evangelista admitted that he could not account for the differences between the blood types from the statue and those of Sister Agnes. He then speculated that there were probably other nuns in the convent who had ectoplasmic powers and "sent" tears through the statue. But then it was shown that there were no nuns with the blood type AB at the time of the 1975 analysis.

Despite the evident error of his arguments, a cloud settled on Akita because of Evangelista's prestige and his negative conclusions. The bishops of Japan were divided among themselves on the authenticity of Akita (and we cannot forget that the Akita messages were quite forceful in criticizing the lapses of the clergy). In 1979, Bishop Ito visited the Congregation for the Doctrine of the Faith in Rome and was told that the investigation was under his jurisdiction, and therefore he could deal with it as he saw fit. The bishop then set up a new commission of inquiry, and on September 12, 1981, the commission issued a report stating that the events at Akita were indeed supernatural. The last tears of the statue came on September 15, 1981, the Feast of Our Lady of Sorrows. In a pastoral letter in 1984, Bishop Ito wrote, "After the investigation conducted up to the present day, I recognize the supernatural character of a series of mysterious events concerning the statue of the Holy Mother Mary which is found in the convent of the Institute of the Handmaids of the Sacred Heart of Jesus in the Holy Eucharist at Yuzawadai, Soegawa, Akita. I do not find in these events any elements which are contrary to Catholic faith and morals." Although Bishop Ito's declaration settled the question of ecclesiastical approval for the immediate future, the importance and evident supernatural origin of Akita could be rejected in the future because of the severity of its messages.

Messages

"My daughter, my novice, you have obeyed me well, abandoning all to follow me. Do you suffer much because of the handicap which deafness causes you? You will be assuredly healed. Be patient. It is the last trial. Does the wound in your hand give you pain? Pray in reparation for the sins of humanity. Each person in this community is my irreplaceable daughter.

"Pray very much for the Pope, bishops, and priests. Since your baptism you have always prayed faithfully for them. Continue to pray very much. Tell your superior all that passed today and obey him in everything that he will tell you. Your superior is wholeheartedly seeking prayers now." (First message from the Virgin)

"My daughter, my novice, do you love the Lord? If you love the Lord, listen to what I have to say to you.

"It is very important. Convey it to your superior.

"Many men in this world grieve the Lord. I seek souls to console Him. In order to appease the wrath of the Heavenly Father, I wish, with my Son, for souls who will make reparation for sinners and the ungrateful by offering up their sufferings and poverty to God on their behalf.

"In order that the world might know the wrath of the Heavenly Father toward today's world, He is preparing to inflict a great chastisement on all mankind. With my son, many times I have tried to appease the wrath of the Heavenly Father. I have prevented the coming of the chastisement by offering Him the sufferings of His Son on the Cross, His Precious Blood, and the compassionate souls who console the Heavenly Father — a cohort of victim souls overflowing with love.

"Prayer, penance, honest poverty, and courageous acts of sacrifices can soften the anger of the Heavenly Father. I desire this also from your community; please make much of poverty, deepen repentance, and pray amid your poverty in reparation for the ingratitude and insults toward the Lord by so many men. Recite the prayer of the Handmaids of the Eucharist with awareness of its meaning; put it into practice; offer your life to God in reparation for sins. Let each one endeavor by making much of one's ability and position to offer oneself entirely to the Lord.

"Even in a secular institute, prayer is necessary. Already souls who wish to pray are on the way to being gathered in this community. Without attaching too much attention to the form, pray fervently and steadfastly to console the Lord.

"Is what you think in your heart true? Are you truly prepared to become the rejected stone, my novice, you who wish to become the pure bride of the Lord? In order that you, the bride, become the spouse worthy of the Holy Bridegroom, make your vows with the hearty readiness to be fastened to the Cross with three nails. These three nails are honest poverty, chastity, and obedience. Of the three obedience is the foundation. With total obedience follow your superior. Your superior will understand you well and guide you." (Second message from the Virgin)

"My dear daughter, listen well to what I have to say to you. And relay my messages to your superior.

"As I told you, if men do not repent and better themselves, the Heavenly Father will inflict a great punishment on all humanity. It will definitely be a punishment greater than the Deluge, such as has never been seen before.

"Fire will plunge from the sky and a large part of humanity will perish. . . . The good as well as the bad will perish, sparing neither priests nor the faithful. The survivors will find themselves plunged into such terrible hardships that they will envy the dead. The only arms which will remain for you will be the Rosary and the sign left by my Son (Eucharist).

"Each day recite the prayers of the Rosary. With the Rosary pray for the bishops and priests. The work of the devil will infiltrate even the Church. One will see cardinals opposing other cardinals, and bishops confronting other bishops.

"The priests who venerate me will be scorned and opposed by their confreres; churches and altars will be sacked. The Church will be full of those who accept compromises, and the demon will tempt many priests and consecrated souls to leave the service of the Lord.

"The demon is trying hard to influence souls consecrated to God. The thought of the perdition of so many souls is the cause of my sadness. If sins continue to be committed further, there will no longer be pardon for them.

"With courage, convey these messages to your superior. He will tell each one of you to continue prayers and acts of reparation for sins steadfastly while ordering all of you to pray fervently. Pray very much the prayers of the Rosary. I alone am able still to help save you from the calamities which approach. Those who place their total confidence in me will be given necessary help." (Third message from the Virgin)

11. *Betania, Venezuela, 1976–90*

The modern skeptic who demands that he or she "see" supernatural phenomena before accepting their reality can be directed to two sites in the world today that have often offered such "signs and wonders" to the general public. The first, of course, is Medjugorje, and the second is the lesser known Betania (Spanish for Bethany) in Venezuela. Betania is a two-hour drive from Caracas, the capital of Venezuela, and close to the city of Cua.

The apparitions of María Esperanza Medrano de Bianchini began at the age of five when she had a vision of St. Theresa of Lisieux, who gave her a beautiful rose (appropriately so, coming as it did from the "Little Flower"). At the age of twelve, when it seemed that she might die of pneumonia, the Virgin appeared to her and recommended the medications that saved her life. She continued to have apparitions of Jesus and Mary. She briefly entered a convent but was told that she did not have a vocation to the religious life. She visited the churches of Rome in the 1950s and then went to see the famous Padre Pio, who had apparently prophesied her coming to him and had said, "When I leave, she will be your consolation." On December 8, 1956, the feast of the Immaculate Conception, she married Geo Bianchini, an Italian gentleman whose birthday happened to be on that date. Their first child was also born on December 8!

Even before her marriage, the Virgin had told her in an apparition that she had set aside a holy place for her in Venezuela that would become a center of "constant prayer and pilgrimage" for the people of Venezuela and, eventually, for all "the nations of the world." She was shown a vision of the place, which had an old house, a mill, various plantations, and a grotto with clear water. From the time they were married, the couple looked for this place. Finally, in 1974 they found and purchased the farm shown to María and on March 25, 1976, she had her first apparition of the Virgin there. The Virgin said she was "the Reconciler of People and Nations" and was calling all peoples to reconciliation, to a divine spirituality grounded in faith, to carrying the cross in love. She told María, "My little daughter, tell my children of all races, of all nations, of all religions, that I love them." Betania, she said, would be the Lourdes of Latin America.

While calling for reconciliation, the Virgin also gave warnings of the consequences of turning away from God: "I come to reconcile them, to seek them out, to give them faith, which has disappeared in the noise and din of an atomic awakening which is at the point of bursting out. My message is of faith, love, and hope. More than anything, it brings reconciliation between people and nations.

It is the only thing that can save this century from war and eternal death.... If a change does not come and a conversion of life, one will perish under the fire, war, and death." Again, "Mankind is currently abusing the graces received and is moving toward perdition, and if there is no change and improvement of life, it will succumb under fire, war, and death." The Virgin said that God had sent her to the world to avert this, if possible, through her messages to the faithful and their response.

The apparitions that began in 1976 reached a climax on March 25, 1984, when over a hundred people, some of them atheists, some others professionals like doctors and judges, all saw the Virgin at the grotto. From that point the apparitions became public knowledge and huge crowds began to converge on Betania.

The previous bishop of the Diocese of Los Teques, to which Betania belonged, Bishop Bernal, had already received supernatural confirmation of the authenticity of María's experiences and had given her a free hand. His successor, Bishop Pio Bello Ricardo, was a philosopher by training and inclined to be more cautious before reaching a conclusion either positive or negative. After the public apparition of 1984, the bishop launched a personal investigation of the phenomenon, studying, among other things, the more than five hundred cures and other miracles that were reported at Betania over the next few years. The bishop discussed his investigations with Cardinal Joseph Ratzinger, prefect of the Congregation for the Doctrine of the Faith, and Pope John Paul II and on November 21, 1987, declared, "After having studied repeatedly the apparitions of the Most Holy Virgin in Betania, and having begged the Lord earnestly for spiritual discernment, I declare that in my judgment the said apparitions are authentic and have a supernatural character. I therefore approve, officially, that the site where the apparitions have occurred be considered as sacred."

The miracles continued after the official verdict. Most notable of these was the Eucharistic miracle on the feast of the Immaculate Conception of 1991, when the Host began to bleed and, on being analyzed in Caracas, was found to contain human blood. Pilgrims often saw the Virgin or extraordinary celestial phenomena. In addition to seeing and hearing the Virgin, María herself continues to be the subject of many miraculous happenings ranging from the stigmata to the exuding of sweet aromas. Over two thousand people have claimed to see the Virgin at Betania.

Description of the Virgin

"A friend said, 'María Esperanza, the farm is on fire, the farm is burning, like a candle,' and I said, 'Yes, I see the fire,' but it was from there that the Virgin and the cloud came. And when she revealed herself, she went up to the top of the tree, and I saw she was beautiful, with her brown hair, dark brown, her eyes that were light brown and she had very fine, very pretty eyebrows, tiny mouth, a nose very straight and her complexion was so beautiful, it was skin that seemed like silk. It was bronzed. It was beautiful. Very young. Her hair was down to here, to her shoulders."

Messages

"Daughter, here you have me with my hands enriched with graces and covered with splendors of light, to call all my children to conversion; this is the seed of glory I offer as "MARY RECONCILER OF PEOPLE AND NATIONS," for I come to reconcile all of you. Reconciliation is the inheritance of divine brotherhood of my divine Son! Daughter, hand on my message to all. I will keep you here in my heart from today on and forever!" (March 25, 1976)

"Children, from this my holy mountain of this blessed place, among these trees, I gaze at you from my grotto of prayer, and in silence and seclusion I let you feel me so the grace of the Holy Spirit may enter fully in each one of you and all may receive the divine vocation of service here in my Promised Land and may be able to sweetly work for the love of my beloved Son! Blessed are those who offer their lives to the service of the Lord!" (January 25, 1985)

"Daughter, children, here I am as I announced before; some will feel me, others will see me between the shrubs, others will perceive the perfumed roses of my garden from Heaven, and even more, some, who are sick, drinking from the water of my grotto of prayer, will be relieved; others, will be healed, attaining health and peace!" (December 8, 1986)

"My children, reaffirm your trust in the adorable Heart of my Jesus, who is in love with His Father's delights! Rest on the promises of the Lord who hears the prayers of His children and whose mercy reaffirms all forever! Apostles of my heart! Fill yourselves with gratitude for all will taste love and wisdom since the Holy Spirit will enlighten each one of you in these apocalyptic times with His divine grace, sustaining all with bountiful fruits and divine rain! Sons and daughters, do not stop wearing my miraculous medal to cover yourselves, in order to be protected. Also distribute it generously so sinners may be converted, the sick may be healed, and the moral values of today's world may be reestablished!" (July 6, 1987)

"Oh, my little ones! There is so much grief in my heart! I do not want you to suffer, I do not want to worry you, let alone for you to go through days of tribulation, but there are things that are so hard for men to understand. The only truth which remains is faith which will build in your families the firmness and the certainty that the Lord and this Mother live among all our children showing you the way, that only through deeds of faith the shadows that surround your daily living can be lessened! Children, that is why your prayer must be constant, morning, afternoon, and night, for only prayer can save you!" (February 22, 1989)

"My daughter, my children, here I am. I beg each one of you to especially mend your lives, with penance, the needed prayer, to vindicate God's justice, so offended in these times by men. On the other hand, it is very important for you to attend Holy Mass frequently and to receive the Eucharist so that my divine Son's nourishment may help you in such a way that you will feel enlightened inside by an unknown light, wonderful and sublime, which is the great sign God,

Our Father, wishes for the salvation of all those who with humility surrender faithfully to His Heart!" (March 28, 1989)

12. Cuapa, Nicaragua, 1980

Cuapa is a town of five thousand people in Nicaragua. Fr. Andrés Rongier, S.J., a Jesuit missionary from Mexico, is said to have prophesied in the 1880s that Cuapa would become famous in the future as the site of apparitions of the Blessed Virgin Mary. In the Native Indian language Nahuatl, the word Cuapa means "crushing the serpent's head with a blow" — from *cua* for "serpent" and *pa* for "on." Intriguingly, Guadalupe, if pronounced in the original Nahuatl, sounds like "Cuapa" because there are no "g" or "d" sounds in this language; one interpretation of the meaning of Guadalupe in the native language, we have seen, is the one "who will crush, stamp out, abolish, and eradicate the stone serpent." It might be said here that the Cuapa visionary, Bernardo Martínez, bears several similarities to Juan Diego of Guadalupe: both were humble peasants who had consecrated their lives to working for the Church and who were privileged to witness apparitions of the Virgin in their middle age; both told the Virgin they were unworthy to perform the mission she assigned to them but to both of them she said that they had been chosen; when they did not perform the tasks she had assigned to them, they both tried to avoid her by going to a different location, but she intercepted them there.

Bernardo was born on August 20, 1931. He grew up with his grandmother and studied up to the sixth grade, after which he went to a vocational training school where he learned various manual trades. (He went back to high school in later life and completed it in 1989.) After school, he supported himself by working on a farm.

Bernardo, who had always wanted to be a priest, was the main assistant to the pastor of the local church in Cuapa. In April 1980, Bernardo was puzzled to find that the statue of the Virgin in the chapel was lighting up on its own. This phenomenon, and the soul-searching it caused him, prepared Bernardo for the events that were soon to take place. For starting in May of that year, he was blessed to witness numerous apparitions of both the Virgin Mary and Jesus. The principal apparitions lasted from May to October 1980, but Bernardo was the recipient of several subsequent apparitions and locutions.

In 1982, Bishop Bosco M. Vivas Robelo, then auxiliary bishop and vicar general of Managua and now bishop of León, the diocese to which Fr. Martínez belongs, declared, "I, the undersigned, Auxiliary Bishop and Vicar General of the Archdiocese of Managua, authorize the publication of the narration of the apparitions of the Blessed Virgin Mary in Cuapa." On November 13, 1982, Bishop Pablo Antonio Vega M., prelate bishop of Juigalpa, the diocese in which the apparitions took place, released this statement, "It has been nearly three years now since one of the peasants from the area arrived communicating a message which he said he received from Mary in a series of dreams and apparitions.... Because of the duty and the obligation to protect the wholesome piety of the faithful and for the truth of those events, in my capacity as bishop of the area, I find an obligation to assure the authenticity of the events in order to be able to assist in discerning the true value of the alluded to message.... The 'report' that we present retains the accurate content and language used by the individual who received the visions." *Let Heaven and Earth Unite!*, an account of the apparitions by Stephen and Miriam Weglian, received the following authorization from Bishop Robelo of León, on June 10, 1994: "I hereby authorize the publication of the story of the Apparitions of the Blessed Virgin Mary in Cuapa and the messages given to Bernardo Martínez under the title *Let Heaven and Earth Unite!* May this publication help those who read it to have an encounter with Jesus Christ in the Church through the mediation of the Mother of our Lord." The Bishops Conference of Nicaragua has also approved the apparition, and in fact the bishops presented Pope John Paul II with a statue of Our Lady of Cuapa on his last visit to Nicaragua.

After the principal apparitions, Bernardo was allowed to attend a minor and then a major seminary. On March 19, 1995, he was ordained a deacon, and on August 20, 1995, he was ordained a priest.

Below are excerpts from Bernardo's account of the apparitions.

[After a sleepless night, Bernardo went fishing at a river near Cuapa. In the afternoon he gathered various fruits from surrounding trees. Around three o'clock, he started on his way back to town.]

"Suddenly I saw a lightning flash. I thought and said to myself, 'It is going to rain.' But I became filled with wonder because I did not see from where the lightning had come. I stopped but I could see nothing — no signs of rain. Afterward, I went over near a place where there are some rocks. I walked about six or seven steps. That was when I saw another lightning flash, but that was to open my vision, and she presented herself.

"I was then wondering whether this could be something bad, whether it was the same statue as in the chapel. But I saw that she blinked and that she was beautiful. She remained above the pile of rocks as if on a cloud. And there was a little tree on top of the rocks and over that tree was the cloud. The cloud was extremely white. It radiated in all directions the ray of the sun light. On the cloud were the feet of a very beautiful lady. Her feet were bare. The dress was long and white with a celestial cord around the waist, and it had long sleeves. Covering her was a veil, a pale cream color, with gold embroidery along the edge. Her hands were held together over her breast. It looked like the statue of the Virgin of Fatima. I was immobile....

"And when I removed my hands from my face I saw that she had human skin and that her eyes moved and blinked. I then said — in my thoughts because I could not move my tongue — I said, 'She is alive ... she is not a statue! She is alive!' My mind was the only thing that I could move. I felt numb, my lower jaw stiff and my tongue as if asleep; everything immobilized, as I said, only the ideas moved in my head. I was in those thoughts when she extended her arms — like the Miraculous Medal which I had never seen but which later was shown to me. She extended her arms and from her hands emanated rays of light stronger than the sun and the rays that came from her hands touched my breast.

"When she gave out her light is when I became encouraged to speak. Although somewhat stammering, I said to her, 'What is your name?' She answered me with the sweetest voice I have ever heard in any woman, not even in persons who speak softly. She answered me and said that her name is Mary. I saw the way she moved her lips. I then said, 'She is alive! She spoke! She has answered my question!' I could see that we could enter into a conversation, that I could speak with her. I asked her then where she came from.

"She told me with the same sweetness, 'I come from Heaven. I am the Mother of Jesus.'

"On hearing this, I immediately . . . asked her, 'What is it you want?'

"She answered me, 'I want the Rosary to be prayed every day.'

"I then interrupted and said to her, 'Yes, we are praying it. . . .'

"She told me: 'I don't want it prayed only in the month of May. I want it to be prayed permanently, within the family . . . including the children old enough to understand . . . to be prayed at a set hour when there are no problems with the work in the home.'

"She told me that the Lord does not like prayers we make in a rush or mechanically. Because of that she recommended praying of the Rosary accompanied with the reading of biblical citations and that we put into practice the Word of God. When I heard this I thought and said, 'How is this?' Because I did not know the Rosary was biblical. That is why I asked her and said, 'Where are the biblical citations?' She told me to look for them in the Bible and continued saying: 'Love each other. Fulfill your obligations. Make peace. Don't ask Our Lord for peace because, if you do not make it, there will be no peace.'

"Afterward she told me: 'Renew the five first Saturdays. You received many graces when all of you did this.'

" . . . Then she said: 'Nicaragua has suffered much since the earthquake. She is threatened with even more suffering. She will continue to suffer if you don't change.'

"And after a brief pause she said: 'Pray, pray, my son, the Rosary for all the world. Tell believers and nonbelievers that the world is threatened by grave dangers. I ask the Lord to appease His justice, but, if you don't change, you will hasten the arrival of a Third World War.'

"After she had said these words, I understood that I had to tell this to the people, and I told her, 'Lady, I don't want problems. I have many in the Church. Tell this to another person.'

"She then told me: 'No, because Our Lord has selected you to give the message.'

"When she told me this, I saw that the cloud which was holding her was rising, . . . and I told her, 'Lady, don't go because I want to go and notify Señora Consuelo because she told me that she wanted to see you.'

"She said to me, 'No. Not everyone can see me. She will see me when I take her to Heaven, but she should pray the Rosary as I ask.'

"And after she told me this, the cloud continued to rise. She raised her arms to Heaven as in the statue of the Assumption, which I have seen so many times in the cathedral at Juigalpa. She again looked upward toward Heaven, and the cloud that held her slowly elevated her as if she was in a ray of light. When she reached a certain height she disappeared." (May 8, 1990)

"I saw her in the same way as I had seen her on May 8, with her hands together, and then she extended them. And on extending her hands, the rays of light came toward me. I remained watching her. I remained silent, but I said to myself, 'It is she!...' I though she had come to complain about all that she had told me to say. I felt guilty for not having spoken as she had asked, and at the same time, in my mind, I said, 'I don't go to the place where she appeared because she appears there, and now, she appears to me here. I will be a fine state. She will be following me wherever I am.'

"It was with this in mind, when she told me with her voice soft, but with a tone as of in reprehension, 'Why have you not told what I sent you to tell?'

"I then answered her, 'Lady, it is that I am afraid. I am afraid of being the ridicule of the people, afraid that they will laugh at me, that they will not believe me. Those who will not believe this will laugh at me. They will say that I am crazy.'

"She then said to me, 'Do not be afraid. I am going to help you, and go tell the priest.' When she said this, there was another flash of lightning and she disappeared." (May 16, 1990)

"During the night, in dreams she presented herself. It was the same as during the day. I was at the same place where I saw her the first time. I prayed the Rosary. Upon finishing the Rosary, I again saw the two lightning flashes and she appeared. In my dream, she gave me the same message as she had done the first time....

"Raising her right hand, she pointed toward [a large open] space and said, 'Look at the sky.'

"I looked at that direction. A tree that is in front, between the two palms, did not impede my ability to see because it has few branches and it is low. She presented something like a movie in that space I mentioned. I saw a large group of people who were dressed in white and were walking toward where the sun rises. They were bathed in light and very happy; they sang. I could hear them, but I could not understand the words. It was a celestial festival. It was such happiness...such joy...which I had never ever seen. Not even in a procession had I seen that. Their bodies radiated light. I felt as if I were transported. Nor can I myself explain it...in the midst of my admiration I heard her tell me: 'Look. These are the very first communities when Christianity began. They are the first catechumens, many of whom were martyrs. Do you people want to be martyrs? Would you yourself like to be a martyr?'

"In that instant I did not know exactly what the meaning of being a martyr was — I now know, because I have been asking, that it is he who professes Jesus Christ openly in public, he who is a witness to Him including the giving of his life — but, I answered, 'Yes.'

"After that I saw another group, also dressed in white with some luminous Rosaries in their hands. The beads were extremely white, and they gave off lights of different colors. One of them carried a very large open book. He would read, and after listening they silently meditated. They appeared to be as if in prayer. After this period of prayer in silence, they then prayed the Our Father and ten Hail Marys. I prayed with them. When the Rosary was finished, Our Lady said to me: 'These are the first ones to whom I gave the Rosary. That is the way I want all of you to pray the Rosary.'

"I answered the Lady that, yes, we would. (Some persons have told me that this possibly has to do with the Dominicans.)

"Afterward I saw a third group, all of them dressed in brown robes. But these I recognized as being similar to the Franciscans. Always the same, with Rosaries and praying. As they were passing after having prayed, Our Lady again told me: 'These received the Rosary from the hands of the first ones.'

"After this, a fourth group was arriving. It was a huge procession. This group was dressed as we dress. It was such a big group that it would be impossible to count them. In the earlier ones I saw many men and women; but now, it was like an army in size, and they carried Rosaries in their hands. They were dressed normally, in all colors. I was very happy to see them....I felt at once that I could enter into that scene because they were dressed the same as I was. But...I looked at my hands and saw them black. They, in turn, as the previous ones, radiated light. Their bodies were beautiful. I then said, 'Lady, I am going with these because they are dressed as I am.'

"She told me, 'No. You are still lacking. You have to tell the people what you have seen and heard.' And she added: 'I have shown you the Glory of Our Lord, and you people will acquire this if you are obedient to Our Lord, to the Lord's Word; if you persevere in praying the Holy Rosary and put into practice the Lord's Word.'

"After having said this to me the Vision of the Glory of God disappeared, and the cloud that was sustaining her elevated her toward Heaven. She looked like, as I said, the statue of the Assumption. And in that way, with the cloud lifting her, she disappeared. (June 8, 1980)

"I saw her as a child. Beautiful! But little! She was dressed in a pale, cream-colored tunic. She did not have a veil, nor a crown, nor a mantle. No adornment, nor embroidery. The dress was long, with long sleeves, and it was girdled with a pink cord. Her hair fell to her shoulders and it was brown in color. The eyes, also, although much lighter, almost the color of honey. All of her radiated light. She looked like the Lady, but she was a child.

"I was looking at her amazed without saying a word, and then I heard her voice as that of a child...a child of seven...eight...years. In an extremely sweet voice she gave me a message...I then told her, 'Let yourself be seen so that all the world will believe. These people who are here want to meet you....' But after listening to me she said: 'No. It is enough for you to give them the message because for the one who is going to believe that will be enough, and the one who is not going to believe though he should see me is not going to believe.'

"...I no longer insisted that she allow herself to be seen, but rather I talked to her about the church that the people wanted to build in her honor. She answered me saying: 'No, the Lord does not want material churches. He wants living temples which are yourselves. Restore the sacred temple of the Lord. In you is the gratification for the Lord.'

"She continued, saying: 'Love each other. Love one another. Forgive each other. Make peace. Don't just ask for it. Make peace.'

"[When asked what to do with the money donated by people for a church,] she told me to donate it for the construction of the chapel in Cuapa, and added: 'From this day on do not accept even one cent for anything.'

" ...I did not know whether or not to continue in the catechumenate. I did it to see what she would advise me. She told me: 'No. Don't leave. Always continue firmly in the catechumenate. Little by little you will comprehend all that the catechumenate signifies. As a community group, meditate on the Beatitudes, away from all the noise.'

"Later she added: 'I am not going to return on the 8th of October, but on the 13th.' " (September 8, 1980)

"When we finished the Rosary, we sang 'Holy Queen of Heaven.' We were repeating the part that says, 'Shining Day Star, grant me grace to be able to sing the Ave Maria,' when all of a sudden a big luminous circle formed over the ground. Everyone, without a single exception, saw it. It was like a single ray that fell and marked this luminous circle on the ground. The light came from above. The light that came was like a spotlight that, on touching the ground, was scattered. Seeing how this light fell over the heads of everyone who was there, I again looked upward and saw that a circle had also formed in the sky, as when we say, 'There's a ring around the moon,' or 'There's a ring around the sun.' This circle gave off lights in different colors, without coming from the sun. It was not at that spot as the sun was already setting....

"All of a sudden a lightning flash, the same as the other times; then, a second one. I lowered my eyes and I saw the Lady. This time the cloud was over the flowers we had brought and upon the cloud the Lady's feet. Beautiful! She extended her hands and rays of light reached all of us.

"Seeing the Lady there with her arms extended, I said to the people, 'Look at her! There she is!'

"No one answered anything. I then told the Lady to let herself be seen, that all the people present wanted to see her. She said, 'No. Not everyone can see me....' I again insisted to the Lady that she allow herself to be seen, and she again told me, 'No....' I then told the Lady, 'Lady, let them see you so that they will believe! Because many don't believe. They tell me that it is the devil that appears to me, and that the Virgin is dead and turned to dust like any mortal. Let them see you, Our Lady!'

"She did not answer anything. She raised her hands to her breast in a similar position to the statue of Our Lady of Sorrows — the statue that is carried in procession during Holy Week — and the same as that statue, her face turned pale, her mantle changed to a gray color, her face became sad, and she cried. I cried too. I trembled to see her like that. I said to her, 'Lady, forgive me for what I have said to you! I'm to blame. You are angry with me. Forgive me! Forgive me!'

"She then answered me saying: 'I am not angry nor will I get angry.'

"I asked her, 'And why are you crying?'

"She told me: 'It saddens me to see the hardness of those persons' hearts. But you will have to pray for them so that they will change.'

"I could not speak. I continued to cry. I felt that my heart was being crushed. I felt very sad as if I were going to die from the pain right there. My only relief was through crying. I no longer continued insisting that she let herself be seen. I felt that I was to blame for having said this to her. I could not endure seeing her cry. As I continued to cry, she gave me a message: 'Pray the Rosary; meditate on the mysteries. Listen to the Word of God spoken in them. Love one another. Love each other. Forgive each other. Make peace. Don't ask for peace without making peace because if you don't make it, it does no good to ask for it. Fulfill your obligations. Put into practice the Word of God. Seek ways to please God. Serve your neighbor, as that way you will please Him.'

"When she had finished giving her message, I remembered the requests from the people of Cuapa. I said to her, 'Lady, I have many requests, but I have forgotten them. There are a great many. You, Lady, know them all.'

"Then she said to me: 'They ask of me things that are unimportant. Ask for faith in order to have the strength so that each can carry his own cross. The sufferings of this world cannot be removed. Suffering is the cross that all of you have to carry. That is the way life is. There are problems with the husband, with the wife, with the children, with the brothers. Talk, converse so that problems will be resolved in peace. Do not turn to violence. Pray for faith in order that you will have patience.'

"In this manner she has given me to understand that, if with faith we ask to be free from a suffering, we will be free if that suffering is not the cross we are to carry; but when the suffering is that person's cross, then it will remain as a weight of glory. That is why she tells us to ask for faith in order to receive fortitude and patience.

"Afterward she told me, 'You will no longer see me in this place.'

"I thought that I would definitely never see her again and I began to shout: 'Don't leave us, my Mother!'

"I was speaking for those who were not speaking. She then said to me: 'Do not be grieved. I am with all of you even though you do not see me. I am the Mother of all of you, sinners. Love one another. Forgive each other. Make peace, because if you don't make it there will be no peace. Do not turn to violence. Never turn to violence. Nicaragua has suffered a great deal since the earthquake and will continue to suffer if all of you don't change. If you don't change you will hasten the coming of the Third World War. Pray, pray, my son, for all the world. Grave dangers threaten the world. A mother never forgets her children. And I have not forgotten what you suffer. I am the Mother of all of you, sinners. Invoke me with these words: "Holy Virgin, you are my Mother, the Mother to all of us, sinners." '

"And after having said this three times, she was elevated as if the cloud were pushing her. When she was in the direction of the branches of the cedar, she disappeared." (October 13, 1980)

•

Accounts of subsequent apparitions and locutions of the Virgin and visions and locutions of Jesus to Bernardo are narrated in *Let Heaven and Earth Unite!* by Stephen and Miriam Weglian. The book also includes an interview with the visionary and descriptions of healings and fulfilled prophecies.

In an apparition on March 8, 1987, she spoke of the coming "destruction of atheistic communism in Russia and the whole world." She also said, "I want you to propagate the devotion to the shoulder wounds of my Son" and "If you change and convert, soon, very soon, you will see an end to your sorrows." Then she added, "Repeat with me this prayer (and she said it slowly): St. Mary of Victory. Favorite Daughter of God the Father, give me your faith; Mother of God the Son, give me your hope; Sacred Spouse of God the Holy Spirit, give me your charity and cover us with your mantle."

(The information in this section is primarily derived from *Let Heaven and Earth Unite!* by Miriam and Stephen Weglian and from meetings with Bernardo Martínez.)

13. Kibeho, Rwanda, 1981–89

The Marian apparitions of Kibeho in Rwanda, perhaps the poorest country in Africa (one known also as the "Switzerland of Africa" for its many mountains), were witnessed by seven principal visionaries. The apparitions share many common features with the great apocalyptic visions of the past. As in the nineteenth-century French apparitions and at Fatima and Akita, the Virgin announced impending bloodshed on a horrific scale. Moreover, as in Medjugorje, the apparitions themselves took place in the very region that would shortly become synonymous around the world with genocide and systematic butchery. The warnings issued at Rwanda were not only prophetic but unmistakably accurate and, because they were not heeded, the fate of the nation seemed sealed; the Virgin finally even urged the visionaries to flee their homeland before the onset of the wars ahead.

The apparitions began on November 28, 1981, when Alphonsine Mumureke, a sixteen-year-old student in a Catholic convent, heard a voice calling out "my daughter" to her as she was helping in the dining room. She left the room and saw a beautiful lady in white in the corridor. When Alphonsine asked her who she was, the lady replied, "I am the Mother of the Word," speaking in Kinyarwanda, the language of the Rwandans. The Virgin asked her which of the religions she liked, to which Alphonsine replied, "I love God and His Mother who have given us Their Son who has saved us." The Virgin commended her and said that she wished that some of her friends would have more faith since some did not believe enough. She then asked Alphonsine to join a lay evangelization group called the Legion of Mary and said that she wanted to be loved and trusted as a Mother so that she could lead people to her Son Jesus. (The Legion of Mary is one of the largest lay Christian organizations in the world; one of the pioneers of the Legion from Ireland, Edel Quinn, had devoted her life to the work of the Legion in the neighboring country of Kenya.) The Virgin then gracefully arose until she was out of sight. As she departed, Alphonsine dropped to the ground and was unconscious for about fifteen minutes.

The other children had heard Alphonsine engaged in conversation and were curious to find out what had happened. When Alphonsine narrated her experience, both her friends and the nuns were skeptical and scornful. Alphonsine witnessed another apparition of the Virgin on the next day, in which she was told that the Virgin liked her children to see her as a mother. Again she lost consciousness at the end of the apparition, and again she told the others what had happened but was met with the same ridicule. The apparitions continued through December. Most of the girls continued to mock Alphonsine, even throwing Rosaries at her during the apparitions, but some prayed that others could also share the experience so that they could find out if Alphonsine was being truthful.

On January 12, 1982, these prayers were answered, and Anathalie Muka-mazimpaka, a sixteen-year-old girl who was already a member of the Legion of Mary, witnessed an apparition of the Virgin. The messages she received focused on prayer, humility, and self-sacrifice. Once Anathalie started witnessing the apparitions, most of the community accepted Alphonsine's veracity. The continuing apparitions were now beginning to transform the spiritual life of the students. On March 22, yet another student, twenty-two-year-old Marie-Clare Mukan-ganga, reported seeing the Virgin as well. She had been one of the most ardent scoffers and now begged forgiveness for her disbelief. She said that the Virgin wanted everyone to meditate on the Passion of Jesus and the sorrow of His mother and asked them to pray the Rosary and the beads of the Seven Sorrows to receive the grace of repentance.

By now news of the apparitions had spread around Rwanda and visitors were coming to Kibeho from all over the country. To accommodate the hundreds of onlookers, special platforms were constructed for the visionaries in the convent yard and the crowds could now see them as they entered the state of ecstasy, which often lasted three or four hours. The girls would sing songs or pray the Rosary until the coming of the Virgin at a preset time.

Four others also began seeing Jesus and Mary. Stephanie Mukamurenzi, a fourteen-year-old girl, saw her beginning on May 25, 1982, and received messages about repentance, conversion, and mortification. On June 2, Agnes Kamagaju, twenty-two years old, first saw the Virgin; within months she was also seeing Jesus. Jesus called everyone to conversion and prayer and specially asked the youth to keep their bodies holy. The last of these seemed to be a warning about AIDS and the path of destruction it would cut through Rwanda. On July 2, a fifteen-year-old illiterate pagan boy named Segatashya (who later received the Christian name Emmanuel) saw and heard a handsome thirty-year-old man — Jesus — who taught him the Lord's Prayer and other basic Christian prayers and doctrine. Through Emmanuel, Jesus asked for prayer, repentance, and reparation because the end of the world was rapidly approaching. He also spoke about the failure of many priests to remain faithful to their vows. On September 15, Mary appeared to Vestine Salina, a twenty-four-year-old Moslem woman. Vestine was asked to play the role of a shepherd leading people to God and Heaven. The Virgin asked the people for daily recitation of the Rosary and remembrance of her Seven Sorrows on the Rosary beads.

Huge crowds watched the seven visionaries as they went into ecstasies that lasted several hours. During the ecstasies, the visionaries were not affected when observers pricked them with knives or burnt them with candles or shone bright lights into their eyes; they were also "frozen" so that their arms and legs could hardly be moved. Sometimes during the apparitions the assembled multitudes also witnessed various supernatural phenomena such as miracles of the sun (including the dancing of the sun and multicolored displays like at Fatima), stars turning into crosses at night, and heavy rains that came when the visionaries asked the Virgin to bless the crowds (cures were reported from the water collected from the rain). After warning observers that this would happen, the visionaries went into comatose states for extended periods in which they were taken to Heaven, Purgatory, and Hell. They were also shown a vision of the savage future awaiting Rwanda: rivers of blood, burning trees, and countless rows of corpses, many of them headless. This glimpse of the future, given in an eight-hour-long apparition on August 15, 1982, had such a terrifying effect on the visionaries that it shook even the onlookers. The visionaries were told that there would be a "river of blood" if Rwanda did not come back to God.

The apparitions went on for various spans of time for each visionary: Marie-Clare up to September 15, 1982; Stephanie to December 15, 1982; Emmanuel to July 3, 1983; Agnes to September 25, 1983; Anathalie to December 3, 1983; Vestine to December 24, 1983, and Alphonsine all the way through November 28, 1989. Bishop Jean Baptiste Gahamanyi of the diocese of Butare, to which Kibeho belonged, had appointed investigative commissions of doctors, psychiatrists, and theologians in March 1982. Public devotions at the site of the apparitions were permitted by the bishop on August 15, 1988.

The Rwandan civil war began in 1991 and took a toll of over one million lives. The visionary Marie-Clare was one of the slain. Alphonsine's entire family was killed although she herself escaped. The other visionaries are believed to be in refugee camps, although there is speculation that Emmanuel may have been killed as well. Bishop Gahamanyi is one of the hundreds of clergy who were killed in the civil war. Thousands of dead bodies were thrown into rivers that turned putrid. Thousands of other corpses, many of them decapitated, were left unburied.

Description of the Virgin

Alphonsine: She "was not really white like we see her in pictures. I could not determine the color of her skin, but she was of an incomparable beauty."

Messages

To Marie-Clare: "I am concerned not only for Rwanda or for the whole of Africa. I am concerned with, and turning to, the whole world. The world is on the edge of catastrophe."

"I have come to prepare the way for my Son for your good, and you do not want to understand. The time remaining is short and you are absent-minded.

You are distracted by the goods of this world which are passing. I have seen many of my children getting lost and I have come to show them the true way."

To Alphonsine: "I love a child who plays with me because this is a beautiful manifestation of trust and love. Feel like children with me because I, too, love to pet you. No one should be afraid of their Mother. I am your Mother. You should not be afraid of me but you should love me."

At the last apparition: "I love you, I love you, I love you very much. Never forget the love I have for you in coming among you. These messages will do good not only now but also in the future."

To Anathalie: "Wake up, stand up. Wash yourself and look up attentively. We must dedicate ourselves to prayer. We must develop in us the virtues of charity, availability and humility."

To Stephanie: "Repent, pray, change your life."

To Vestine: "The walk to Heaven is through a narrow road. It is not easy to get through. The road to Satan is wide. You will go fast, you will run because there are no obstacles."

To Emmanuel: "There isn't much time left in preparing for the Last Judgment. We must change our lives, renounce sin. Pray and prepare for our own death and for the end of the world. We must prepare while there is still time. Those who do well will go to Heaven. If they do evil, they will condemn themselves with no hope of appeal. Do not lose time in doing good and praying. There is not much time and Jesus will come."

Jesus to Agnes: "The youth should not use their bodies as an instrument of pleasure. They are using all means to love and be loved and they forget that the true love comes from God. Instead of being at the service of God, they are at the service of money. They must make of their body an instrument destined to the glory of God and not an object of pleasure at the service of men. They should pray to Mary to show them the right way to God."

Jesus to Emmanuel: "I am Jesus before whom all humanity stands."

"I am neither white nor black; I am simply Lord."

"The priests and religious do not take enough care of those who are ill physically and morally. If they have promised freely the vow of chastity, they must observe it faithfully."

"How can someone say he loves Jesus, adores Him, and live outside His Blessed Mother's Immaculate Heart? My Mother is the Mother of the world."

"The world will come to an end. Prepare while there is still time. When I return on earth, the soul will find the body it had before, and then man will bring his own dossier. Do not lose time in doing good. There is not much time left."

"Too many people treat their neighbors dishonestly. The world is full of hatred. You will know my Second Coming is at hand when you see the outbreak of religious, ethnic, or racial wars. Then, know that I am on the way."

14. Damascus, Syria, 1982–90

The Damascus experience of St. Paul is the most famous metaphor for extraordinary conversions to the Christian faith. This metaphor found a literal contemporary translation in the apparitions of eighteen-year-old Myrna Nazzour of Damascus. Myrna, who lives a few blocks away from the house of Ananias where St. Paul spent three days when he was blinded after seeing Jesus, was also blinded for three days during the course of her apparitions when she beheld and heard Jesus on May 31, 1984.

Myrna, a Melkite Catholic, married Nicholas Nazzour, who was Eastern Orthodox, in May 1982. Neither of them were particularly "religious" and in fact quite enjoyed their social life. Then in November of that year, Nicholas's sister Layla fell seriously ill. While Myrna was praying by her side along with two other women, olive oil started oozing from her fingers. At the suggestion of one of the women present, Myrna applied the oil to Layla, who was instantly healed. On November 27, an image of Our Lady of Soufanieh in the Nazzour home began to exude large quantities of olive oil (which was chemically tested and found to be pure); the oil resulted in many healings. These phenomena mystified the couple, who gathered with other family members to pray for discernment. While they were praying, Myrna suddenly found she could not hear them and instead heard an enchanting voice calling her, "Mary, do not be afraid. Open the doors and do not deprive anyone from seeing me." (Myrna is the equivalent of Mary).

As both Myrna and the image of Our Lady continued to exude oil, both scientists and the local police investigated the phenomenon. The investigations only confirmed that oil was indeed coming from the image and not from the frame, that even when Myrna had washed her hands she would exude oil when she started praying. The clergy were also convinced that fraud could be ruled out.

The next definitive phase in the phenomenon took place on December 15, 1982, when Myrna was led by an invisible escort to her roof garden. Once she was there, she saw the Virgin, who was shining "as if she were covered with diamonds." Terrified, Myrna ran away. After being counselled by a clergyman experienced in supernatural phenomena, she developed a more receptive state of mind. Three days later, she was again taken to the roof, this time accompanied by her husband and a number of friends. She saw a globe of light on top of a tree across the street. A beautiful Lady emerged from this globe and then came across the street to Mryna on a "bridge" of light. Speaking in Arabic, the Virgin then gave her first message to Myrna, which essentially outlined her program of action for all of the subsequent messages and apparitions:

> My children, remember God, because God is with us. You know all things and yet you know nothing. Your knowledge is an incomplete knowledge. But the day will come when you will know all things the way God knows me. Do good to those who do evil. And do not harm anyone. I have given you oil more than you have asked for. But I shall give you something much more powerful than oil. Repent and have faith, and remember me in your joy. Announce my Son the Emmanuel. He who announces Him is saved, and he who does not announce Him, his faith is vain. Love one another. I

am not asking for money to give to churches, nor for money to distribute to the poor. I am asking for love. Those who distribute their money to the poor and to churches, but have no love, those are nothing. I shall visit homes more often, because those who go to church sometimes do not go there to pray. I am not asking you to build me a church, but a shrine. GIVE. Do not turn away anyone who asks for help.

The command to "announce my Son the Emmanuel. He who announces Him is saved, and he who does not announce Him, his faith is vain" is especially significant. Evangelization is fundamental to Christianity, but in no other part of the world is evangelization more difficult than in the Middle East.

The Virgin's appearances and messages continued. Over a hundred thousand people had seen the phenomenon of the oil, and healings continued to take place, among them such extraordinary events as a blind Moslem woman recovering her sight and a paralyzed boy regaining the use of his limbs. The Eastern Orthodox Patriarch Ignatius IV Hazim met with the Nazzours and after carrying out an investigation approved the authenticity of the phenomenon as a supernatural reality on December 31, 1982. The Roman Catholic bishop of Damascus, the Most Rev. Paulus Barkash, personally witnessed the phenomenon and wrote the following in his introduction to a book on the apparitions:

> Peace and blessing and my prayer for God's redeeming graces to all who will read this interesting book about the supernatural events of Soufanieh, which continue to occur from 1982 until now. I was personally an eye-witness to the oil coming from the hands and face of Mirna and from copies of the Soufanieh Icon more than once. We congratulate the writer for publishing the Soufanieh events to the glory of God and for devotion to the Virgin Mary. We encourage the faithful to pray, sacrifice, and work with persistence for the unity of the churches as mentioned in the messages of the Virgin to Mirna. While encouraging the faithful to read this precious book, we assure them that what is written in it as extraordinary events, quotes, and messages corresponds to the facts. We ask from God blessing and success to the readers of this valuable book and to all those who contributed to its publication. (June 18, 1990)

The book received an imprimatur from the Melkite (Greek Catholic) archbishop of Damascus, Boulos Bourkhocke.

On May 31, 1984, the oil exuded from Myrna's eyes — a very painful experience. At this time she went into ecstasy, and for the first time saw and heard Jesus. She lost her eyesight for a period of three days after this event. Myrna has also been privileged to receive the stigmata, including the wounds from the crown of thorns, on Good Friday. After three hours, however, the wounds stopped bleeding and closed by themselves.

On August 4, 1984, Myrna went into ecstasy at the end of Mass and was told by Jesus that anyone who divides the Church or rejoices in such divisions was guilty of sin. Her whole ministry is focused on the unity of the churches as commanded by Our Lord and the Virgin; here again she follows in the footsteps of St. Paul, the Apostle of Unity. A key component of this unity, as shown in the messages, is their request that "the feast [of Easter] be unified."

Even the most skeptical of observers will find it striking that great progress has finally been made on the question of celebrating a common Easter — in a meeting in Syria! The Aleppo Statement of March 1998 that came out of a meeting of Eastern Orthodox, Oriental Orthodox, Catholic, and Protestant representatives has come close to an agreement on the norms for a common date by following the norms of the First Ecumenical Council of Nicaea (325): Starting in 2001 Easter is to be celebrated on the Sunday following the first full moon of spring after the vernal equinox (when the sun crosses the equator, using calculations with Jerusalem as the point of reference). Remarkably, the agreement, which has ramifications for the entire Christian world, was reached in the very country where Our Lord and the Virgin brought this ancient but vital issue back to the attention of the faithful. The importance of the common Easter date is evident from the fact that one of the reasons the Council of Nicaea was called was to resolve the question of a common date.

Description of the Virgin

The "large, luminous, white globe like a large diamond ball . . . opened, splitting from the top and dividing into two half-moons. As the halves opened, a bow of light appeared over the top, and inside was the same Beautiful Lady. As the ball disappeared, the Lady seemed to be standing on the branch of the tree. She had a white veil that covered her hair. The veil was part of her dress. Over her right shoulder was a sky-blue cape that wrapped around her back and over her left side. The white dress covered her feet, and only her hands could be seen. The dress and cape seemed to be made of white and blue light. From her right hand, between the second and third fingers, hung a long Rosary."

Messages

"My children, let it be said between us, I have come back here. Do not insult the haughty who are devoid of humility. The humble person craves other people's remarks to correct his shortcomings, while the corrupt and haughty neglects, rebels, becomes hostile. Forgiveness is the best thing. He who pretends to be pure and loving before people is impure before God. I would like to request something from you, a word that you will engrave in your memory, that you shall always repeat: God saves me, Jesus enlightens me, the Holy Spirit is my life; thus I fear nothing." (February 21, 1983)

"The Church that Jesus adopted is One Church, because Jesus is One. The Church is the kingdom of Heaven on Earth. He who has divided it has sinned. And he who has rejoiced from its division has also sinned. Jesus built it. It was small. And when it grew, it became divided. He who divided it has no love in him. Gather! I tell you: 'Pray, pray, and pray again!' How beautiful are My children when they kneel down, imploring. Do not fear, I am with you. Do not be divided as the great ones are. You, yourselves, will teach the generations THE WORD of unity, love and faith." (March 24, 1983)

Jesus: "My daughter, I am the Beginning and the End. I am Truth, Freedom, and Peace. My Peace I give you. Your peace shall not depend on what people say, be it good or bad, and think little of yourself. He who does not seek people's approval and does not fear their disapproval enjoys true peace. And this is achieved through Me. Live your life, contented and independent. The pains you have incurred for Me shall not break you. Rather, rejoice. I am capable of rewarding you. Your hardships will not be prolonged, and your pains will not last. Pray with adoration, because Eternal life is worth these sufferings. Pray for God's will to be done in you, and say:

> Beloved Jesus, Grant that I rest in You above all things, above all creatures, above all Your angels, above all praise, above all rejoicing and exultation, above all glory and honor, above all Heavenly hosts, for You alone are the Most High, You alone are the Almighty and Good above all things. May You come to me and relieve me, and release me from my chains, and grant me freedom, because without You my joy is not complete, without You my table is empty. Only then will I come to say: 'Here I am, because you have invited Me.' " (May 31, 1984, Ascension Day)

Jesus: "My daughter, Do you wish to be crucified or glorified?" Answer: "Glorified."

Jesus smiles and says: "Do you prefer to be glorified by the creature or the Creator?"

Answer: "By the Creator."

Jesus: "This is realized through Crucifixion. Because each time you look at the creatures, the eyes of the Creator move away from you. My daughter, I want you to apply yourself to praying and to humble yourself. He who humbles himself, God increases him in strength and in greatness. I was crucified out of love for you, and I want you to carry and bear your cross for Me, willingly, with love and patience, and (I want you) to await My arrival. He who participates in My suffering, I shall make him participate in My glory. And there is no salvation for the soul except through the Cross. Do not fear, My daughter, I shall give you from My wounds enough to repay the debts of the sinners. This is the source from which every soul may drink. And if My absence lasts, and the light disappears from you, do not fear, this will be for My glorification." (November 26, 1985)

Jesus: "My daughter, She is my Mother from whom I was born. He who honors her honors Me. He who denies her denies Me. And he who asks something from her obtains because she is my Mother." (August 14, 1987)

Jesus: "My daughter, I am pleased that you have chosen Me, not only in words. I want you to join My Heart to your gentle heart so that our hearts will unite. By doing so, you will save suffering souls. Do not hate anyone. Love everyone as you have moved Me, especially those who have hated you and have spoken evil of you, because in so doing you will obtain glory. Continue in your life as wife, mother, and sister. Do not worry about the difficulties and the pains that will afflict you. I want you to be stronger than them — because I am with you — otherwise you will lose My heart. Go and preach to the whole world and tell them without fear to work for unity. Man is not condemned for the fruit of his hands, but for the fruit of his heart. My peace in your heart will be a blessing for you and for all those who have cooperated with you." (November 26, 1987)

Jesus: "It is easier for Me (to accept) that an infidel believe in My name than that those who pretend to have faith and love swear by My name." (August 14, 1988)

Jesus: "My children, Is everything you do out of love for Me? Do not say: What shall I do, because this is My work. You must fast and pray, because through prayer you face My truth and you confront all enemies. Pray for those who have forgotten the promise they made Me because they will say: Why did I not feel your presence, O Lord, even though You were with me?" (November 26, 1988)

Jesus: "My children, you, yourselves, will teach the generations THE WORD of unity, love, and faith. I am with you. But you, My daughter, will not hear My voice until the Feast [of Easter] has been unified." (April 14, 1990, Holy Saturday)

The Holy Virgin: "Do not fear, my daughter, if I tell you that you are seeing me for the last time until the feast [of Easter] is unified. Therefore, tell my children: Do they want or not to see and remember the wounds of my Son in you? If it does not pain them to see that you are suffering doubly, I myself am a mother, and it pains me to see my Son suffering repeatedly. Remain in peace, remain in peace, my daughter. Come, so that He may give you peace, so that you may spread it among the people. As for the oil, it will continue to manifest itself on your hands to glorify my Son Jesus, whenever He wishes and wherever you go. We are with you and with everyone who wishes the Feast [of Easter] to be one. (November 26, 1990)

(The messages have been excerpted from the version in Fr. Elias Zahlaoui's *Remember God*.)

15. Hrushiv, Ukraine, 1914, 1987

On May 12, 1914, two weeks before the First World War, twenty-two people in the village of Hrushiv who were mowing fields near the local church witnessed an apparition of the Virgin. The Virgin told them: "There will be a war. Russia will become a godless country and the Ukraine, as a nation, will suffer terribly for eighty years and will have to live through the world wars, but it will be free afterward." Then on April 27, 1987, exactly one year after the Chernobyl nuclear reactor disaster, the Virgin appeared to twelve-year-old Marina Kizyn above a small church. Subsequently, nearly five hundred thousand people witnessed the apparition as the Virgin appeared daily until August 15, often before crowds of tens of thousands at a time. The Virgin said, "I have come on purpose to thank the Ukrainian people because you have suffered most for the church of Christ in the last seventy years. I have come to comfort you and to tell you that your suffering will soon come to an end. Ukraine will become an independent state."

Description of the Virgin

Before she arrived, a bright light covered the church and surrounding areas; this light was even seen in a television program. The Virgin appeared from within the light and floated above the church.

Messages

About the Chernobyl catastrophe she said, "Do not forget those who have died in the Chernobyl disaster. Chernobyl is a reminder and a sign for the whole world.

"Forgive your enemies. Through you and the blood of the martyrs will come the conversion of Russia. Repent and love one another. The times are coming which have been foretold as being those in the end times. See the desolation which surrounds the world... the sin, the sloth, the genocide. Pray for Russia. Oppression and wars continue to occupy the minds and hearts of many people. Russia, despite everything, continues to deny my Son. Russia rejects real life and continues to live in darkness. ... If there is not a return to Christianity in Russia there will be a Third World War and the whole world will face ruin.

"Teach the children to pray. Teach them to live in truth and live yourselves in truth. Say the Rosary. It is the weapon against Satan. He fears the Rosary. Recite the Rosary at any gathering of people.

"I have come to comfort you and to tell you that your suffering will end soon. I shall protect you for the glory and the future of God's kingdom on earth, which will last for a thousand years. The Kingdom of Heaven and Earth is close at hand. It will come only through penance and the repentance of sin.

"This wicked world is feasting on depravity and impurity. Many lies are proclaimed against the Truth. The innocent are condemned. Many come as false messiahs and false prophets. Be diligent. Be on your guard.

"Happy are they whose lives are blameless and who walk in fear of the Lord.

"My children, all of you are dear to me and please my heart. I make no distinction of race or religion. You here in Ukraine have received the knowledge of the One, True Apostolic Church. You have been shown the door to Heaven. You must follow this path, even though it may be painful.

"The Eternal God is calling you. This is why I have been sent to you. You in the Ukraine were the first nation to be entrusted to me. Throughout your long persecution you have not lost faith, hope, or love. I always pray for you, my dear children, wherever you are."

16. Cuenca, Ecuador, 1988–90

Patricia Talbott was a sixteen-year-old high school student who had begun a modeling career. She had very little interest in spiritual matters. The first apparition took place in her bedroom. On the night of August 24, 1988, Patricia woke up to find her room filled with light. She saw the figure of a beautiful woman in the middle who told her: "Don't be afraid. I am your mother from Heaven. Fold your hands over your chest and pray for peace in the world, for it is now that it needs it the most. Make an altar in this place." In October,

Patricia visited Mexico and saw the Virgin again at the cathedral in the heart of the city. The Virgin said that she would appear in three days to her on Tepeyac Hill (where the original apparitions of Guadalupe took place) and reveal a great secret. At Tepeyac she revealed this secret and also gave her title as the Guardian of the Faith. Subsequent messages were delivered at various churches and chapels until June 1989, when the apparitions were witnessed in a garden in El Cajas, a mountain range in the Andes in Ecuador. The final message was received there on March 3, 1990.

A number of extraordinary signs accompanied the apparitions. Holy cards and images on Patricia's altar at home began to exude oil and tears, and even holy cards placed on the altar by others were seen to exude oil. Soon statues and pictures in other homes in Cuenca were dripping with oil and tears. In a message to Patricia, the Virgin said, "The Father has allowed the grace of the holy oil, and my tears have been shed for the ingratitude of my little children due to the lack of unity, lack of love, and because each nation opens its doors to evil and to its own destruction. Love one another, children, and do not hurt the Father. I am the Guardian of the Faith." In November 1989, a Host miraculously appeared in a box at the feet of the statue in Patricia's room. The Virgin told Patricia, "Get up and look in the little box under the feet of the little statue. There is my Sacred Son." Patricia showed the Host to the Apostolic Nuncio in Quito, who told her, "You should have the Host with you, and do everything the Holy Mother tells you to do." Often a smell of incense would precede the appearance of the Virgin. On the first Saturday of December 1989, thousands of persons who had come to El Cajas saw a bright light in the sky that was shaped in the image of Our Lady of the Miraculous Medal. Starting on December 15, 1988, when Patricia was in a state of ecstasy, the Virgin sometimes spoke through her to all those who had assembled to watch her.

The apparitions, which received widespread attention including coverage on national TV, are still under investigation by the Archdiocese of Cuenca. An initial commission appointed by Archbishop Luna in January 1989 issued a report on April 18, 1989. The report acknowledged the sincerity of Patricia but stated that there was insufficient evidence of a supernatural manifestation. As the apparition continued to attract national and international attention, the archbishop reopened the investigation in February 1990 and expanded the commission. Patricia's spiritual director, Fr. Julio Dutari Teran, S.J., rector of the Pontifical University in Quito, is now the auxiliary bishop of Quito.

Description of the Virgin

"She was barefooted and standing over a cloud. A blue veil covered her head and flowed down to her ankles. She wore a white skirt with a red blouse. Her eyes are big and long, the color of honey. Her hair, which comes out on both sides of the veil, is also honey-colored. Her nose is small and straight and her lips are thin. Her face is fine and her skin is golden. She had a crown of twelve stars vertically around her head. Her arms were extended outward and down, and she was holding the Rosary in her hands with the cross near her left hand. The Rosary is a brown color and the cross had a metal Christ."

Messages

A Summary of the Messages

"I am the Guardian of the Faith.

"Make your consecration to my Immaculate Heart and to the Merciful Heart of my Son.

"Put the Heart of Jesus in your homes.

"Pray the Rosary, which is a shield against evil. The Rosary is the most complete prayer; work to spread it.

"Use the scapular, which will protect you.

"Do penance and fast and with prayer, you will arrive at the Heart of my Son.

"Attend Mass and visit the Blessed Sacrament. The Heart of my Son is very wounded.

"Offer your sufferings and penances to the Lord.

"Do not fear, the reign of God is near. Listen to the divine call.

"I ask you for peace, peace in your hearts. My children, you know my way, follow me. I will know how to illuminate your ways, my little souls."

•

"Pray the Rosary, which is a shield against evil. Use the scapular which will protect you. Place the Heart of Jesus in your homes for it will keep you united and in peace. Do penance and fast, and with prayer you will reach the Heart of my Son. Go to Mass and visit the Blessed Sacrament. Pray to me and I will keep you under my mantle and in the Heart of my Son. I love you, my little daughter." (October 8, 1988, Mexico City)

"I put into your hands the great mission of the conversion and the turnabout of the world. I am now holding back the hand of my Son with the message I have given you, and if my children convert, the Heart of my Son will soften and the intensity can be diminished. If not, the great trial will come." (October 11, 1988, Tepeyac, Mexico)

"I am also here to reveal to you the date of the great chastisement which you can reveal to no one, to nobody. I love you very much. Now I leave you and remember that I will always be the Guardian of the Faith." (November 4, 1988, Cuenca)

"The Rosary is the most complete prayer. Do not ask yourself why you pray it. Let it be your shield against the evil one who is acting. Do not detach yourselves of it. The Spirit of God descends upon you. You have the great mission of the conversion of the world. Please little children, make evil disappear. It is in your hands that the hand of my Son be detained or that you suffer as strongly as the sorrow of His Heart. Fear not, for I am with you. I will pour out the necessary graces on you. I love you much." (December 25, 1988, Cuenca)

"All these Rosaries are under my mantle. Keep your Rosaries on you because in this way you will not have temptation. I love you very much, and do not abandon yourselves into the darkness. Feel the Spirit of the Father in the depths of your little souls. Do not permit the Kingdom of the Father to be blasphemed by the youth. Make them get away from drugs, alcohol, and music and fashions that insult the Divine Father." (December 27, 1988, San Roque, Ecuador)

The Third World War

"Pray much for the countries of Latin America. Pray very much for the countries of Central America. Pray for the Soviet Union, Russia, the United States, Czechoslovakia, and China. These are countries that will be involved in the Third World War.... Today, more than ever, I ask you for prayer. Transmit the peace of my Son, Jesus, because great catastrophes are coming upon humanity. Today, children, I am present and I am protecting you under my mantle. I have gathered up your faith and I have made of it a beautiful rose of peace."

Heaven, Hell, and Purgatory

Patricia: "Once when I was praying late into the night, the Holy Virgin appeared to me and said: 'My little one, I have kept you awake because I need to tell you and show you many things. Now I have told you before, the time is short, because you know there is condemnation for those who do not fulfill what God asks of them in His law.... For there is a Hell as there is a Heaven, but there is only one King, God the Father; for Satan exists who contains hatred, perversion, and all that does not give peace to your hearts.'"

Patricia: [Hell is] "a terrible place, like a big volcano where you see souls that hate each other. There are skulls and they don't have faces, but they hate and insult God. What are those little hats the bishops use? I could see some of those in Hell." [Purgatory was like coming out of the volcano with hands reaching out and crying, trying to get out.] "And while I was there, I heard a voice telling me to pray for them because they couldn't do anything without our help.... The Virgin] exhorted us to, 'Pray much for the souls in holy Purgatory. Pray much for those who wander through the world. Pray for the elderly, pray for the sick.'"

Patricia (on Heaven): "I didn't go in because I didn't deserve it. There were two choirs of angels at each side of the door. The Rosary, prayer, is the door, and the cross of the Rosary is the key to open the door to go into Heaven."

Fashions and Music

"Another great victory of Satan is fashions, styles, and the way young women dress for Mass, obscenely. They arouse temptation to sin. They should be respectful and dress in a way in which they will not be looked at sinfully, rather with honesty and respect. For you know that fashions and music are a great victory for Satan. For with fashions he moves people to become slaves of money and of sin. For those who exhibit their body and who do not repent will be judged, because the Father did not give the body to be exhibited, but to take care of it as a temple of God.... That music, in how many messages I have asked you to abandon it, for you know they are praises to Satan and they will remain engraved in your mind, for he infuses them and they will remain engraved in your life. He, through this music, makes mockery of the Father, of my beloved Son, and of the Spirit of God, and of me. His great victory is to be idolized to the point of offering rituals with human blood and other human elements and [they] have even offered the sacrifice of their life in order to give their soul to Satan. He has managed that images be made to adore him, and they have their book which they say is sacred, for they have great temples for his adoration."

On the Reason for Her Worldwide Apparitions

"The Heart of my Son is very wounded. Just as the Father one day gave me the mission of leading and guiding Jesus, my Son, for the world, now the Father wants me, your Immaculate Mother, to lead and guide the world for the Heart of Jesus. Know then, children, that your Father is merciful, and the Father loves you and wants you to love Him.

"Children, there is much sorrow in my Heart for many natural catastrophes and others created by man are coming. Hard times are already taking place. The Third World War threatens the world.... Do not frighten your hearts because the peace of God is with you.... The time is very short.... You must fill your hearts with the light of my Son, so that a desolation of faith will not exist.... Today more than ever, I ask prayer of you. Times of great tribulation have come, and the darkness of faith of my little ones inhabits the world.... Satan will tempt you. But do not be afraid, my little ones, I am with you. The times of darkness have begun, the darkness of your faith. The kingdom of God will come with justice.

"I am your Mother, remain in constant prayer. Earthquakes will come, hurricanes, the sky will shower fire, all this will come from the Father, the Son, and the Spirit of God. In those days men will be destroyed by their lukewarmness. You yourselves will create your own destruction. You do not know the sorrow I feel as I announce these natural catastrophes and those created by you. Man will destroy man. You are only a step away. Do not allow this to happen. Have more prayer groups; pray the Rosary as a family. Go to Mass frequently. I love you much, my children, and I am the guardian of your faith.... Little children, I need prompt conversion from a humble heart. Teach unity, love, peace. For he who is with God will be protected under my mantle, in the Heart of my Son and in my Heart." (January 1, 1989)

After 120,000 People Spent a Night in Prayer at El Cajas at the Request of the Virgin

"Little children, do not be anguished. Sow happiness and give joy to the world. My little ones, I love you much. I am happy with what you have offered today. Jesus is here in each one of your hearts that has been purified this day. We have begun the period of hard times. It will be in ten very sad years. Time is short. I am expecting you the first Saturday of March. My physical presence among you will end then. But I will always stay here to pour out my blessings upon you. Atheism and materialism are eating the world. My priests, religious, and lay people, work in the work of my Son, Jesus. I give my blessings to everyone in the name of the Father, and in the name of the Son, and in the name of the Spirit of God. Amen." (February 3, 1990)

Final Message

"My little children, small of heart, today I have brought you here so that you may love the Heart of my Son, Jesus. Little children, I love you so much. Today is the day of my physical departure, but my spiritual retreat will never be. I will be with you always, little children. I ask you for prayer, fasting, and penance. Help those most in need. Children, in the end God will triumph over all things.

"Remember the first commandment of my Son, Jesus: Love one another, and love God above all things. Little children, I ask you for peace, pardon, and conversion.

"Children, priests, and religious, help in the conversion in the world, the redemption of souls, and the purification. Children, the laity, help in the conversions. Young people, be examples of light. Carry the cross in your hearts. Put on humility. Children, white dove of peace, be the light. The sick are indeed chosen by God, chosen for the redemption of the world. Little children, I love you so much that even for me it gives great sorrow to say goodbye to you. Children, I am not going to leave you ever, because I will be here and I will wait for you always, just as each month, as each time that you have come here to leave me your sadness, your pains, and your anguishes.

"Little children, each representative of each country, I ask you to take the message of peace, love, and understanding.

"Children, I give you the blessing of the all-powerful God, Father, Son, and the Holy Spirit. Come always to visit me. Never abandon me little ones, because I love you so much, so much. At the end of all the apparitions in the world, I will leave a great sign in this place, in all those places where I have been. Goodbye, my little ones. Goodbye my children."

At this last apparition, the Virgin said, "Pray the Rosary. Go to daily Mass. Wear the brown scapular. Do works of mercy for others." (March 3, 1990)

(The main source for this account of the apparitions is *I am the Guardian of the Faith* by Sr. Isabel Bettwy.)

COMPREHENSIVE CATECHESIS

1. Amsterdam, Holland, 1945–84
Our Lady of All Nations

Amsterdam's theme of Our Lady of All Nations makes it one of the iconic apparitions of the century inasmuch as many of the modern apparitions seem to be converging on the theme of the Virgin's motherhood of all peoples: in Banneux, the Virgin spoke of the "spring for all nations" in Betania she said she is the reconciler of "all peoples and all nations." Amsterdam is important also in continuing the focus on the New Eve theme, which began with the Miraculous Medal apparition, was highlighted at Fatima, and reached its logical conclusion in Amsterdam in the doctrine of Mary as Coredemptrix.

It is also no coincidence that an image of Amsterdam's Our Lady of All Nations was later made into the very statue that was the source of the miracles at Akita. The messages of Akita, in fact, echo Amsterdam. Bishop John Ito of Akita informed Howard Dee, Filipino ambassador to the Holy See, that "the Akita miracle confirms the authenticity of the Amsterdam messages as the Akita statue that wept and bled was a sculptured image of 'Our Lady of All Nations.' Heaven would not have allowed the supernatural events at Akita to be focused on an image of 'Our Lady of All Nations' if her messages at Amsterdam do not represent the truth."

The link between Fatima, Akita, and Amsterdam is not often appreciated. One of the "mandates" of Fatima from Jesus, addressed to the Church, was to "put the devotion to this Immaculate Heart [of His Mother] beside the devotion to My Sacred Heart" (1929). This mandate was tied to the conversion of Russia. At Amsterdam, a dogmatic proclamation formalizing the title of New Eve (implicit in the Fatima mandate) is tied to future peace. Other connections abound. John Haffert, founder of the Blue Army, a Fatima apostolate, notes seven parallels: (1) Both at Akita and Fatima, a statue of the Virgin came to life; the Pilgrim Virgin of Fatima has shed tears like the Akita statue of Our Lady of All Nations. (2) An angel taught Sister Agnes the same prayer that was taught at Fatima. (3) At both Fatima and Akita, angels prepared the visionaries for the coming of the Virgin. (4) Eucharistic miracles preceded both Fatima and Akita, and the Amsterdam apparition took place on the anniversary of a famous Eucharistic miracle. (5) The Real Presence of Christ in the Eucharist was strongly affirmed in all three apparitions. (6) The importance of praying the Rosary was stressed at all three apparitions. (7) The Fatima and Akita messages include the observation that only the Virgin's intercession can save the faithful from certain chastisements (and this includes a call at both places for all the faithful to join in making reparation to prevent chastisement: the importance of our free responses to God is again made clear).

The bishop of Akita said that the messages of Akita were the same as those of Fatima. Bishop Ito of Akita in fact even said, "I made three trips to Rome to the Sacred Congregation for the Doctrine of the Faith. Cardinal Ratzinger finally put my fears to rest by telling me that the message was the same as the third secret of Fatima." Ambassador Howard Dee reports in his *Mankind's Final Destiny* that Cardinal Ratzinger, who has custody of the third secret, confirmed to him that the message of Akita was the same as the third secret of Fatima.

Finally, Amsterdam is notable for the many detailed and specific prophecies made by the Virgin in these apparitions, some of them prophecies that were later fulfilled, others still awaiting fulfillment. It is also not without significance that the apparitions started precisely on the same day that a great Eucharistic miracle had taken place in Amsterdam six hundred years before; the second series of messages are called "Eucharistic Experiences" because they were given while the visionary was praying before the Eucharist.

Amsterdam has none of the fascination of the nineteenth- and twentieth-century apparitions to children: there is no meeting of a luminous figure in the woods or on a hillside, no ongoing struggle to convince villagers and local clergy, no crowds watching the visionary in ecstasy. At Amsterdam, on March 25, 1945, the Virgin appeared to a forty-year-old single woman, Ida Peerdeman, in her living room. Information about this apparition was restricted to a few friends and clergy and the visionary herself remained anonymous for many years.

Nevertheless, the apparition made up for its lack of a glamorous setting with substance of a thrilling kind: it was concerned with momentous prophecies touching on world history and theological teaching. The "sign" that serves as evidence for the truth of the Amsterdam apparitions is the fulfillment of the prophecies made there. The Virgin had said that she would give no signs other than her words: "You are as yet unable to appreciate my words. My signs are inherent in my words" (May 31, 1955). "Now I will give a reply to those who have asked for a sign. To all of them I say: My signs are contained in my words. O you of little faith! You are like children who insist upon fireworks, whereas they have no eyes for the true light and for the true fire" (May 31, 1957).

On May 31, 1996, the bishop of Haarlem, Holland, Hendrik Bomers, officially approved the devotion and title of Our Lady of All Nations (also translated as "All Peoples") with a declaration that "there was no objection against public veneration of the Blessed Virgin Mary" under the title of Our Lady of All Peoples/Nations. Shortly after this approval, on June 17, Ida died; it had been prophesied that she would live to see the approval of the devotion. The prayer taught by Our Lady of All Nations had by then been received by millions of people around the world, and her messages had been translated into many languages. Bishop Bomers also reaffirmed the imprimatur issued by his predecessor for the Our Lady of All Nations prayer. The Virgin had specifically told Ida that the messages were intended for all peoples of the world.

The Virgin appeared to Ida sixty times from 1945 through 1959 with a variety of prophecies and messages. The messages of these years can be divided into two periods: the first from March 1945 to November 16, 1950, and the second from November 1950 to 1959. The messages of the first period explain why the Virgin has come to the world and also present prophecies for the Church and the world. In the second period, she predicts the proclamation of a new title for herself. In subsequent years, from August 15, 1970, to March 25, 1984, Ida had a series of supernatural experiences, including apparitions, visions, and locutions, before the Eucharist.

Ida recounts the beginning of the apparitions thus:

> It was March 25, 1945, the feast of the Annunciation. My sisters and I sat talking in our drawing-room, around the pot-bellied stove. The war was still on, and it was the year of that terrible "hunger-winter." Fr. Frehe [her spiritual director] was in town that day and called in for a brief visit. We talked about the war and about our experiences. We were in close conversation, when suddenly — to this day I don't know how or why — I felt drawn to the adjoining room. I looked in that direction and suddenly saw a light coming. I said to myself: where is this light from? And what a curious light! I got up and felt compelled to go toward it. There, in the corner of the room, I saw the light coming nearer. The wall disappeared before my eyes, and with it all the rest that was standing there. There was, instead, one sea of light and an empty space. And out of it I suddenly saw a figure move forward, a living figure, a female form. She was clad in white and wore a sash. She stood with her arms lowered and the palms of her hands turned outward, toward me. As I looked, a strange feeling came over me. I thought: It must be the Blessed Virgin, it can't be anything else. Then, all at once, the figure began to speak to me. She said: "Repeat what I say." I therefore began — she spoke very slowly — to repeat word for word what she said. . . . My sisters and Fr. Frehe had gathered around me. I heard Fr. Frehe say: "What is she going to do now? Playing the saint, is she?" But when he heard that I had begun to speak, he said to one of my sisters: "Write down what she says." My sister didn't care to do this; she thought it was all tomfoolery. But Fr. Frehe said: "Do write it down." [In all of the subsequent apparitions, the messages were given in this manner to the visionary and were then transcribed by one of those present.]

Messages

The messages of Our Lady of All Nations are a blend of moral exhortation, theological exposition, prophecy, and history because they are concerned with the link between our moral and spiritual lives and the state of the world. The messages focus on the need to come back to the Creator, the Cross (the crucified Christ) and the Holy Spirit. Without this, no true peace is possible and the world will sink into greater degeneration. "It is by dint of terrible strife and calamity that the world, with all those who have turned away from the Blessed Trinity, will come back to the Church. Bring all nations back to their Creator" (December 31, 1951).

In the present era, the Virgin has been sent by God to bring all nations back to their Creator in her ancient role as the New Eve who cooperates with the New Adam and is Mother of all the redeemed. Central themes in the messages include the mystery of redemption, thus the focus on the Cross, and also the conflict between the spirit of Satan and the Holy Spirit in the human mind. The Virgin makes many prophecies of future political and theological events, some of which have been fulfilled. She also gives explanations of her title as Our Lady of All Nations and a future dogma that will declare her Coredemptrix, Mediatrix, and Advocate (doctrines that were "contained" both in the biblical narratives and the New Eve teaching of the Fathers). At Amsterdam she also bestows a prayer to Jesus and an image of her before the Cross that are icons of her messages. She states too that "my sole purpose is to ensure that the will of the Son is obeyed in these times" (March 4, 1951).

The fulfillment of some of the major Amsterdam prophecies has been mentioned in an earlier section. Two of her prophecies are of particular interest.

Prophecy of the Second Vatican Council

One is her "preview" of the Second Vatican Council: "Then I see St. Peter's. The Lady says, 'Child, there you see the Pope in full pontificals. He holds up two fingers. Listen well, the doctrine is correct but the Pope is right in changing the laws.... Now I see a large council hall in which the Pope is seated. 'Child,' says the Lady again, 'The laws may be changed, some can and others must be changed' " (October 1, 1949).

"Then I hear the Lady say to me, 'Look carefully, these are the bishops of all countries.' All at once the Pope has a large book in front of him and the Lady says, 'Listen well, my child. Some changes have already been made and others are under discussion. I, however, will deliver the message of the Son: the doctrine is correct, but the laws can and must be changed' " (February 11, 1951).

" 'The Church, Rome, will have to face a terrible struggle. Before the year 2000 much will have changed in the Church, the Community. Nevertheless, the substance will remain" (March 19, 1952).

During the Council, the Lady warns, "Go to Pope Paul and tell him in the name of the Lady of all Nations: This is the last warning before the end of the Council. The Church of Rome is in danger of a schism. Warn your priests. Let them put a stop to those false theories about the Eucharist, sacraments, doctrine, priesthood, marriage, and family planning. They are being led astray by the spirit of untruth — by Satan — and confused by the ideas of modernism. Divine teaching and laws are valid for all time and newly applicable to every period" (May 31, 1965).

Prophecy of a Global Catastrophe

The other prophecy concerns a future world catastrophe. She prophesies many events that have since taken place: the rise of Communist China ("In China I see the red flag," October 7, 1945); the formation of Israel, the Korean, Vietnamese, and Balkan wars, the death of Pius XII, the threat of Russia ("Russia will try to deceive everyone in everything she does," May 7, 1949); and even the U.S.-

Soviet race to land on the moon ("Then I see all of a sudden two lines, each with an arrow at the end; on the one it says 'Russia' and on the other 'America.' Then I see the Lady before me and the moon. I say, 'There's something getting on to the moon,' " February 7, 1946). As the Lady of All Nations, she also gives specific prophecies about nations across the globe from Germany to America to Africa to Japan to India.

Finally, as in some of her other apparitions, the Virgin warns of a catastrophe in the distant future: "Then I notice that the Lady has stepped aside and from the other directions demons are coming toward me. I hear the Lady say, 'I predict another great catastrophe for the world' ["another" is significant here because the previous catastrophe implied by reference was the Second World War]. This she says very sadly and she keeps on making gestures of warning. She continues, 'If people would only listen!' and she keeps shaking her head — 'but they will not!' Then I sense a short span of time and hear, 'Things will apparently go well for a short time.' I see the globe and the Lady points to it and it looks as though the globe will burst asunder on all sides. Then the Lady points at the sky. She stands to my right, in the West, and points to the East. I see a great number of stars in the air. 'This is where it comes from,' she says. Suddenly I see a Cardinal's hat lying before me and above it an X-sign appears. There will be a struggle in Rome against the Pope. I see many bishops and I hear a voice say, 'Catastrophic!' Then the Lady disappears" (June 9, 1946).

Germ warfare and chemical weapons will be a feature of this war, and both were prophesied at Amsterdam: "Now I see something like a cigar or a torpedo flying past me so rapidly that I can scarcely discern it. Its color seems to be that of aluminum. All of a sudden I see it burst open. I feel with my hand and have a number of indefinable sensations. The first is a total loss of sensibility. I live and yet I do not live. Then I see faces before me (swollen faces) covered with dreadful ulcers, as it were a kind of leprosy. Then I am aware of terrible diseases (cholera and so on). Then tiny little black things are floating around me: I cannot distinguish them with my eyes, and it is as if I were made to look at them through something [a microscope] and now I see [what are now known to be] slides of extraordinary brilliance and upon them those little things enlarged. I do not know how to interpret this. 'Bacilli'? I ask. Then the Lady says, 'It is hellish!' I feel my face swelling, and it is swollen when I touch it, all bloated and quite stiff. I can no longer move. Then I hear the Lady again, saying, 'Just think! This is what they are preparing!' and then very softly, 'Russia, but the others as well.' Finally the Lady says, 'Nations be warned' " (December 26, 1947).

"Then the Lady says, 'Come along to Russia.' I see all kinds of people in glass buildings underground as well. . . . 'They are making chemicals. America be warned!' " (October 1, 1949).

This will be a world war: "She says: 'Disasters will overtake the world — from North to South, from South to West and from West to East. . . .' The Lady speaks again, 'The world is as it were going be torn in two,' and I see the world lying before me and a great rent appears diagonally across it. Black clouds are hanging over it and I feel great sorrow and misery" (December 26, 1947).

As at Fatima and elsewhere, the Virgin's purpose in making these prophecies is not to terrify her listeners. Like the Old Testament prophets, she points to the cause-and-effect relationship between human sin and its inevitable consequences in the natural order (divine chastisement is often simply a matter of letting nature take its course): "The Lady looks sadly on mankind and says very dejectedly, 'Righteousness, Truth, and Love are not to be found among men.' After that the Lady, gazing intently in front of her, says, 'Disaster upon disaster! For a second time I tell you: as long as these are missing, there can be no true peace' " (June 9, 1946).

Beyond pointing out the correlation between sin and suffering, the Virgin comes also to offer relief: she herself has been divinely ordained to assist humanity at this critical time. But, even here, humanity, especially as personified by the Church, must request, accept, and cooperate with God's messenger if she is to be effective. Free will sets the rules. This the Lady of all Nations explicitly reiterates, "I have let it become clear to all nations that obedience and free will were given precedence" (May 31, 1957). In this hour of crisis, when the full efficacy of her intercession is so urgently needed, she cannot be thus efficacious until her true role in salvation history is acknowledged and honored. Scripture records that strange incident in which the Son is unable to work miracles in a certain locality because of the lack of faith of its inhabitants. So it is with the Mother.

What then are the conditions to be fulfilled? In brief, her roles as New Eve at the Annunciation, the Presentation, and the Crucifixion; as Advocate at Cana; and as the Mother who is Mediatrix in Revelation 12 must be definitively proclaimed. Moreover, the divine command that all generations are to call her blessed must be truly fulfilled. If all of this is done, then she can intercede in the manner and mode demanded by the times. At Amsterdam, the prayer, the image, and the dogma embody the asking that precedes receiving, the knocking that comes before the gates of grace can be opened.

Below are the messages relating to the prayer and the image of Our Lady of All Nations and the prophesied dogma.

The Prayer

Ida: "Then the Lady says to me, 'Let all men return to the Cross! Only this can bring peace and tranquillity. Repeat this after me. Do say this prayer in front of the Cross:

> 'Lord Jesus Christ, Son of the Father,
> send now Your Spirit over the earth.
> Let the Holy Spirit live in the hearts of all Nations,
> that they may be preserved
> from degeneration, disasters, and war.
> May the Lady of all nations, who once was Mary,
> be our Advocate. Amen.

'My child, this prayer is so short and simple that each one can say it in his own tongue, before his own crucifix; and those who have no crucifix, repeat it to themselves.' " (February 11, 1951)

"And I tell the little ones, If you practice love in all its refinement among your-selves, the big ones will no longer have a chance to harm you. Go to the crucifix and say the prayer I have taught you and the Son will grant your request." (February 11, 1951)

"In these days I want to be the Lady of all Nations and therefore I require of you to get the prayer translated into all the principal languages and said every day." (March 4, 1951)

"Let everyone say this short and simple prayer every day! This prayer is pur-posely kept short and simple, so that every person may manage to say it, even in this modern and speed-crazed world. It has been given so that the coming of the Spirit of Truth may be implored for the world." (September 20, 1951)

"All of you, whoever or whatever you may be, ask that the Holy Spirit of Truth may descend. You shall beg this of the Father and the Son. The Blessed Trinity will reign over the world again. The Lady stands here as the Advocate. It is the Creator we are concerned with and not the Lady. Tell your theologians. Ask them to send this prayer over the world and the Lady will give them the ability and the strength to carry it through." (December 31, 1951)

"The prayer has been given for the salvation of the world. This prayer has been given for the conversion of the world. Let this prayer accompany whatever you do in your daily life. This prayer should be spread in the churches and through modern means of communication." (December 31, 1951)

"Satan is not banished yet. The Lady of all Nations is now permitted to come in order to banish Satan. She comes to announce the Holy Spirit. The Holy Spirit will only now descend over this earth. But you should say my prayer, the one I gave to the world. Every day and every moment you should think of the prayer the Lady of all Nations gave to this world at this time. How thoroughly Satan holds the world in his clutches, only God knows. He now sends to you, to all the nations, His Mother, the Lady of all Nations. She will vanquish Satan, as has been foretold. She shall place her foot upon Satan's head. Nations, do not be deceived by false prophets, listen only to HIM, to GOD, the Father, the Son, and the Holy Spirit." (May 31, 1955)

The Image and the Title

"I am the Lady — Mary — Mother of All Nations. You may say, 'The Lady of All Nations' or 'Mother of All Nations.' I wish to be known as this. Let all the children of men, of all the countries in the world, be one!" (February 11, 1951)

Ida: "I see the Lady standing clearly before me and she says, 'Look at my picture and study it well.... Have this picture of me painted and together with it spread the prayer I have taught you." (March 4, 1951)

"Now I will explain to you why I have come in this way: I am the Lady standing in front of the Cross. My head, hands, and feet are like those of a human being. The trunk, however, belongs to the Spirit because the Son came through the will of the Father. Now, however, the Spirit is to descend upon the world, and this is why I want people to pray for His coming.' Then the Lady pauses before she adds, 'I am standing upon the globe because this message concerns the whole world." (March 4, 1951)

"In these modern times, in this modern world, which knows so well how to act promptly and swiftly in material affairs, it is equally necessary in spiritual matters to act swiftly and without delay.... Do not be so frightened. Why be afraid of things which are coming from the Son? Make this devotion known. Otherwise the world will degenerate completely. Otherwise there will be war upon war and no end to destruction." (March 28, 1951)

Ida: "Then the Lady draws my attention to the globe on which She is standing. Snow is falling all around her.... And now I see the globe deep in snow.... The snow is melting into the ground." The Lady: "Now I will explain to you the reason for my coming today: Just as the snowflakes whirl over the earth and fall upon the ground in a thick layer, so the prayer and the picture will spread all over the world and penetrate into the hearts of all nations. As the carpet of snow melts into the ground, so will the fruit, which is the Spirit, come into the hearts of all those who say this prayer every day. For they are praying for the Holy Spirit to come down upon the earth.... A great movement has to be set on foot for the Son, for the Cross, and for the Advocate, the bearer of peace and tranquility: the Lady of All Nations. You child, will have to cooperate without fear or dread. Spiritually and physically you will suffer. Tell them that it is urgent. The world is becoming so degenerate, so materialistic, that it is high time to bring the simple faith again among the people. And this is all they need: the Cross with the Son of Man. You adults of this world, do teach your children to return to the Cross. I shall help them as the Lady of All Nations." (April 1, 1951)

"The Son came into the world as the Redeemer of men and the work of redemption was the Cross, with all its sufferings both of body and spirit. I repeat: the Son came into the world as the Redeemer of mankind. The work of redemption was the Cross. He was sent by the Father. Now however, the Father and the Son want to send 'the Lady' throughout the whole world." (April 15, 1951)

"I wish to be made known to those people who are being kept away from the Son. Do save the people who are forced to turn away from Him. You are duty bound to do so. The world is degenerating so much so that it was necessary for the Father and the Son to send me into the world among all the peoples." (April 29, 1951)

" 'My child, imprint this image deeply on your mind and transmit it correctly. The flocks of sheep represent the peoples of the world who will not find rest until they fix their eyes on the Cross, the center of this world. Now look at my hands and relate what you see.' I see in the palms of her hands what appear to be wounds already healed, and from these rays of light stream out, three from each hand, and diffuse themselves upon the sheep. Smiling, the Lady adds, 'These three rays are Grace, Redemption, and Peace.' Through the grace of my Lord and Master, and for the love of mankind, the Father sent his only-begotten Son as Redeemer of the world. Now they both wish to send the Holy Spirit, the Spirit of Truth, who alone can bring Peace. Hence: 'Grace, Redemption, and Peace.' The Father and the Son wish to send Mary, 'the Lady of all Nations,' as Coredemptrix, Mediatrix, and Advocate. — Now I have given you a clear and lucid explanation of the picture. There is nothing more to be said." (May 31, 1951)

"Now I wish to be the Lady of All Nations. Great and important events are drawing near — in the spiritual, economic, and material spheres." (September 20, 1951)

"I will comfort you. Nations, your Mother knows what life is like: your Mother is familiar with sorrow. Your Mother knows what the cross means. Whatever you suffer in this life, your Mother, the Lady of All Nations, suffered before you. She has shown you the way in her own person." The Lady waits a moment and adds very slowly, "But she went up to the Father, she returned to Her Son. You too, nations, go to the Father along the way of the cross; you too go to the Son along the same way of the cross; the Holy Spirit will help you to do this. Implore Him now. I cannot repeat this often enough to the world: have recourse to the Holy Spirit now. You will obtain help. Go back to the Church. When the time of the Lord Jesus Christ has come, you will see that false prophets, war, discord, and dissension will disappear." (July 2, 1951)

"Fear nothing! The powers of Hell will break loose, but they will not prevail against the Lady of All Nations." (December 3, 1953).

"Peoples of Europe, close your ranks. It is the Lady of All Nations who calls on you to do so — not as though you would want to destroy your enemy, but so that you might win him over to your side. Just as you are striving to achieve political unity, so you must also be of one mind in the True, Holy Spirit.... Your enemy is lying in wait.... It is modern humanism, realism, socialism, and communism that have the world in their clutches. Listen to the Lady who wants to be your Mother. Pray, nations, that your sacrifice may be acceptable to the Lord. Pray, nations, that the Holy Spirit of Truth may descend. Pray, nations, that the Lady of All Nations may be your Advocate." (March 20, 1953)

"This picture is however destined for all peoples: for everyone who wishes to come to the Lady of All Nations." (October 5, 1952)

"The Lady of All Nations has the power to bring the world peace. Yet she has to be asked for it under this title." (October 11, 1953)

"You will have to endure a great deal as yet in this century. You, nations of this era, do realize that you are under the protection of the Lady of All Nations; call upon her as the Advocate; ask her to stave off disasters; ask her to banish degeneration from this world. Degeneration breeds wars. You young people will see enormous changes. The world has lost its bearings. Well then, nations, put your trust in your Mother, who has never forsaken her children." (May 31, 1955)

The Dogma

Both the prayer and the picture prepare the hearts and minds of humanity for a new dogma about Mary, the proclamation that she is coredemptrix, mediatrix, and advocate. But the dogma is new only in the sense that it is only now being proclaimed as a dogma: it contains doctrines that go back to the very beginning of the Church, in particular the unanimous conviction of the Fathers that Mary was the New Eve. The Virgin says pointedly, "I am not bringing a new doctrine. I am now bringing old ideas." (April 4, 1954).

She provides both the scriptural and the theological foundations of this new dogma:

- She was coredemptrix from the beginning when she was chosen to be the handmaid of the Lord who would bear the Son.

- The will of the Father destined her to bring the Son of Man into the world along with the Church and the Cross and so she is necessarily allied to the Church and the Cross.

- She is coredemptrix, mediatrix, and advocate not only because she is the Mother of the Lord but also because she is the Immaculate Conception.

- She became coredemptrix at the Annunciation by the will of the Father.

- She became coredemptrix in giving a body to the Redeemer.

- She was predestined for sacrifice; a sword was directed at the heart of the Mother (Luke 2:3); she endured suffering, both bodily and spiritual, with her Son on Calvary.

- She was named coredemptrix, mediatrix, advocate at the sacrifice of the Cross in the last words of her Son when He gave her as Mother to all the world.

- She has crushed the snake with her foot.

- Just as she remained with the Apostles at the descent of the Holy Spirit, she comes now to bring the Holy Spirit to her apostles and all the nations.

- The true fulfillment of her prophecy "from henceforth all generations shall call me blessed" will come about in the proclamation of this dogma.

The dogma is to be proclaimed only now because all the other dogmas that concerned her earthly life had to come first before this final dogma that concerns her role in salvation history both during and after her earthly life. The Virgin says that there will be fierce resistance to the dogma but that "the outcome is assured." There is an urgency to the definition of this dogma because the Lady of all Nations can give "true peace to the world" only when the dogma has been proclaimed.

"I stand in oblation before the Cross. For I have suffered with my Son, spiritually and above all bodily. This will become a much contested dogma.... This brings the Marian dogmas to a conclusion. I have said that theology must yield to the interests of my Son." (April 1, 1951)

"This picture will precede a dogma, a new dogma." (April 15, 1951).

Ida: "Indescribable sorrow is written over her whole face and the tears run down her cheeks." (April 15, 1951)

Ida: "I see the Lady collapse beneath the Cross. She throws both her arms around the feet of her Son and weeps bitterly. After this the Lady rises and I see a sword coming from the right, its point directed against the Lady's heart. Then I hear the Lady say, 'That was the sword thrust that has been foretold.'" (April 29, 1951)

"This picture has only a preparatory function. Again I say, preparatory. It will be used as a preparatory work for peace and redemption. Later on they will use the picture for the Coredemptrix. In the sufferings, both spiritual and bodily, the Lady, the Mother, has shared. She has always gone before. As soon as the Father had elected her, she was the Coredemptrix with the Redeemer, who came into the world as the God-Man." (April 29, 1951)

"I have said that it will arouse much controversy. Once again I tell you that the Church, 'Rome,' will carry it through and silence all objections. The Church, 'Rome,' will become stronger and mightier in proportion to the resistance she puts up in the struggle. My purpose and my commission to you is none other than to urge the Church, the theologians, to wage this battle. For the Father, the Son, and the Holy Spirit will send the Lady, chosen to bear the Redeemer, into this world as 'Coredemptrix and Advocate.' I have said, 'This time is our time.' By this I mean the following: the world is caught up in degeneration and superficiality. It is at a loss. Therefore the Father sends me to be the Advocate, to implore the Holy Spirit to come. For the world is not saved by force; the world will be saved by the Spirit." (April 29, 1951)

"I know well the struggle will be hard and bitter but the outcome is already assured." (April 29, 1951)

"'It is the wish of the Father and the Son to send Me into the world in these times as the Coredemptrix, Mediatrix, and Advocate. Now look at my hands and relate what you see.' Now I see in the palms of her hands what appear to be wounds already healed and from these, rays of light stream out, three from each hand, and diffuse themselves upon the sheep. Smiling, the Lady adds, 'These three rays are Grace, Redemption, and Peace. Theologians, you should have no difficulty if you consider that the Lord and Master had predestined the Lady for sacrifice. For the sword had already been directed at the heart of the Mother (Luke 2:3). My meaning is that I have always gone before the Son in spiritual and physical sufferings.'" (May 31, 1951)

"Now watch well and listen. The following is the explanation of the new dogma: As Coredemptrix, Mediatrix, and Advocate, I am standing on the globe in front of the Cross of the Redeemer. By the will of the Father, the Redeemer came on earth. To accomplish this, the Father used the Lady. Thus, from the Lady the Redeemer received only — and I am stressing the word "only" — flesh and blood, that is to say, the body. From my Lord and Master the Redeemer received His divinity. In this way the Lady became Coredemptrix." (July 2, 1951)

"I have crushed the snake with my foot. I have become united to my Son as I had always been united with Him. This is the dogma that has gone before in the history of the Church. As Coredemptrix, Mediatrix, and Advocate I stand here, now in this time, in our time. The dogma of the Assumption had to come first. The last and greatest Marian dogma will follow it. The sacrifice stands and will stand at the center of the world, in this era." (August 15, 1951)

"Coredemptrix I was already at the Annunciation. This means that the Mother became Coredemptrix by the will of the Father. Tell your theologians this. Tell them, moreover, that this will be the last dogma in Marian history." (November 15, 1951)

"Transmit the following exactly: the Father, the Lord and Master, has willed the Handmaid of the Lord, to come into this world as 'Miriam' or 'Mary.' She was chosen from among all women as Coredemptrix, Mediatrix, and Advocate. Say to your theologians: She was made Coredemptrix already at the beginning." (December 31, 1951)

"Tell your theologians this! Christ the Son of the Father, brought with Him the Cross to the world. With the Cross came the sacrifice." Ida: "Now the Lady waits in silence for a long time. Then she resumes." The Lady: "The Lord and Master selected a woman, called 'Miriam' or 'Mary,' from among all the peoples of the world. She was destined, through the will of the Father, to bring the Son of Man into the world, together with His Church and the Cross. The Lady was the handmaiden of the Lord. She bore the Son of Man through the will of the Father and was thus necessarily allied with the Church and the Cross. This woman stands in front of you in this present time as the Coredemptrix, Mediatrix, and Advocate." (February 17, 1952)

"Pass on the following to the theologians: 'The Lady' came with the sacrifice of the Cross: The Son said to His Mother, 'Woman, behold thy son.' So you see, it was at the sacrifice of the Cross that the change came about. The Lord and Master chose 'Miriam,' or 'Mary,' from among all women, to become the Mother of His divine Son. At the sacrifice of the Cross, however, she became the 'Lady' ('Woman') — the Coredemptrix and Mediatrix. This was announced by the Son at the time that He returned to His Father.... The forthcoming dogma is the last Marian dogma, namely, the Lady of All Nations as the Coredemptrix, Mediatrix, and Advocate. At the sacrifice of the Cross the Son announced the title to the whole world." (April 6, 1952)

"Never has Mary been officially called Coredemptrix. Never has she officially been called Mediatrix. Never has she officially been called Advocate. These three thoughts are not only closely connected; they form one whole. Therefore this will be the keystone of Marian history; it will become the dogma of the Coredemptrix, Mediatrix, and Advocate." (October 5, 1952)

"I do not reproach the theologians if I say: Why can you not come to an agreement about this dogma? Once more I shall explain it and make it clearer still. The Father sent the Lord Jesus Christ as the 'Redeemer of all Nations.' The Lord Jesus Christ was this from the beginning. He became this in the sacrifice and in His going to the Father. Miriam, or Mary, became the handmaid of the Lord, chosen by the Father and the Holy Spirit. From the beginning she was in virtue of this choice the Coredemptrix, Mediatrix, and Advocate of All Nations. Only at the departure of the God-Man, the Lord Jesus Christ, she became the Coredemptrix, Mediatrix, Advocate. When leaving, in one final act, the Lord Jesus Christ gave Miriam, or Mary, to the nations, gave her as the Lady of All Nations. He spoke the words: 'Woman, behold thy son; son, behold thy mother — ONE act! — and by this, Miriam, or Mary, received this new title." (October 5, 1952)

"How is it that this new title — Lady of All Nations — only now enters the world? It is because the Lord reserved it for this present time. The other dogmas had to come first; just as her life on earth had to precede the Lady of All Nations. All previous dogmas comprised the mortal life and the living of this life by the Lady." (October 5, 1952)

"This picture must be spread all over the world. It is the illustration of the new dogma. This is why I have personally given this picture to the nations. The prayer will remain to the end. The prayer that Mary as the Lady of All Nations has presented to the world, will have to be said in all churches." (December 8, 1952)

"The Lord is the Redeemer of all nations. Mary, the Mother, was from the beginning chosen as Coredemptrix. She became Coredemptrix at the departure of the Lord Jesus Christ to the Father. She became the Mediatrix and Advocate of all peoples. Because Mary was destined to be the Coredemptrix, Mediatrix, and Advocate, she comes now into these times as the Lady of All Nations. Because Mary will be given the title of Lady of All Nations, she has come under this title in different places, in different countries.... The 'Lady of All Nations' is not destined for one country and one place, but is meant for the whole world, for all nations." (October 11, 1953)

"I am not bringing a new doctrine. I am now bringing old ideas. Because the Lady is Coredemptrix, she is also Mediatrix and Advocate; not only because she is the Mother of the Lord Jesus Christ, but — and mark this well — because she is the Immaculate Conception." (April 4, 1954)

"The Lady was chosen. She was also to be present at the Descent of the Holy Spirit. The Holy Spirit had to come down upon the Apostles — [and raising her finger, she adds with emphasis] the first theologians! For this reason the Lord willed that His Mother should be present there. His Mother, the Lady of All Nations, became at the departure of her Son the Lady of All Nations, the Coredemptrix, Mediatrix, and Advocate, in the presence of one Apostle, one theologian, to be witness to it. For he had to take care of 'the Mother.' She had to take care of 'her Apostles.' " (April 4, 1954)

"The Lady remained with her Apostles until the Spirit came. In the same way the Lady will come to her apostles and all the nations in order to bring them the Holy Spirit anew. Because — the Holy Spirit of Truth must always be invoked before great decisions. Again the Lady waits a while and then says in a low voice, 'My prophecy, From henceforth all generations shall call me blessed, will be fulfilled more than ever before, once the dogma has been proclaimed.' " (May 31, 1954).

The Lady: "From now on all nations will call me blessed. The Lady of All Nations desires unity in the Holy Spirit of Truth. The world is encompassed by a false spirit — Satan. When the dogma, the last dogma in Marian history, has been proclaimed, the Lady of All Nations will give peace, true peace to the world. The nations, however, must say my prayer, in union with the Church. They must know that the Lady of All Nations has come as Coredemptrix, Mediatrix, and Advocate." (May 31, 1954).

"Why do you not ask your Holy Father to pronounce the dogma the Lady demands? Once the dogma has been pronounced, the Lady of All Nations will give her blessing. Then the Lady of All Nations will bestow peace. She will help you when this dogma has been proclaimed." (May 31, 1955).

•

Two other themes sounded by the Lady of All Nations bear mention here. One concerns the battle for the human mind, which is the most dangerous battle in the modern world, and the other is the significance of the Eucharist.

The Fight for the Spirit

"This is the spiritual battle that is being carried on all over the world. It is much worse than the actual wars now being waged, because it is undermining mankind." (January 3, 1946)

"The Church must influence the mind. This is a most opportune moment; for mankind is seeking. The attack is no longer directed against nations, but against the mind of man." (February 14, 1950)

"There is at the moment a war of ideas. It is no longer races and nations that are at issue: the fight is for the spirit. Have no doubt about this." (February 11, 1951)

"The enemy of our Lord Jesus Christ has worked slowly but effectively. His posts are manned. His work is almost finished. Nations, take warning: the spirit of untruth, lies, and deceits is carrying many away. The churches will be undermined still more. A heavy responsibility rests upon the people of these times. Educators and parents, take care of the young. Do show them the way to the True Church. You have no idea how serious and how difficult these times are." (December 8, 1952)

"Nations, come back and try to find your simple faith. Acknowledge your Creator and be grateful. This is no longer to be found among mankind; a perverse spirit governs the world. A modern paganism, humanism, atheism, socialism, and communism control the world. Beware of the false prophets! The Lady of

All Nations cannot tell you this often enough, nor warn you sufficiently. Do listen, everyone! The Lord who sends me to warn you is the same Lord who once was sacrificed for mankind. Oh, you do not know what tremendous forces are threatening this world. I am now not speaking only of modern humanism, atheism, socialism, and communism; there are yet forces of quite a different nature that threaten this world. Nations, do search for the truth." (May 10, 1953)

"You, men who hold higher positions in this world, do not lead your children astray: do not misguide the least of my children; you are responsible before your Lord Jesus Christ." (May 31, 1955)

The Eucharist

The apparitions began on the six hundredth anniversary of the Eucharistic Miracle of Amsterdam. The Virgin states that the image of the Lady of All Nations should remain in Amsterdam because of the link to the Eucharist: "The Lady has her special reason for this. Amsterdam is the city of the miraculous Host. There the Lady of All Nations also will go" (October 5, 1952).

Other Significant Messages

"Before the Lord Jesus Christ returned to the Father — before the Sacrifice of the Cross began — the Lord Jesus Christ gave to the nations of the whole world the daily miracle." The Lady casts a searching glance over the globe and very slowly and questioningly says, "How many are there who experience this great wonder? They pass this great miracle by. The daily Sacrifice has to have its place again at the center of this degenerate world." (March 20, 1953)

"Before the Lord Jesus Christ died His bodily death; before the Lord Jesus Christ ascended to the Father; before the Lord Jesus Christ appeared in the world — moved anew among men — He gave you the great Mystery, the great Miracle of every day, every hour, every minute. He gave you Himself. No, nations, not merely a remembrance; no, nations, listen to what He said: not just an idea, but Himself, under the appearance of a little piece of bread, under the appearance of wine. This is how the Lord wants to come among you, day after day. Do accept it. Do act on it. He gives you the foretaste — the foretaste of eternal life." (May 31, 1957)

"Warn the clergy against heretical doctrines, particularly in the domain of the Eucharist." (May 31, 1958)

2. San Nicolás, Argentina, 1983–90
Our Lady of the Rosary

Since the creation of the Parish of San Nicolás de los Arroyos in the vicinity of Buenos Aires, Argentina, there has been a deep devotion to Our Lady of the Rosary. On September 25, 1983, San Nicolás played host to a phenomenon that aroused nationwide and even international attention: an ordinary housewife, a mother and grandmother who had no formal education (she had studied only up to the fourth grade) and no knowledge of either the Bible or theology, announced that she had seen the Holy Virgin on that day. The phenomenon lasted from the first apparition, which was silent, to almost daily apparitions with messages (most of them from the Virgin and sixty-eight from Jesus) until February 11, 1990. The bishop of the diocese, Monsignor Domingo Salvador Castagna, instituted an investigation of the phenomenon, which concluded that the visionary was of sound mental health and that her messages were doctrinally sound. The bishop approved the devotions associated with the apparition and authorized the construction of the sanctuary requested by the Virgin. From March 25, 1986, the bishop accompanied a procession held on the 25th of each month, at which up to one hundred thousand people are present. On July 25, 1990, the bishop said, "Undoubtedly this event of grace will continue to grow; it has proved its authenticity by its spiritual fruits." An image with a likeness to the Virgin as she appeared to Gladys is kept at the cathedral. San Nicolás is source of conversions, healings, vocations, and many groups of prayer in the country. Numerous healings, including the cure of a boy with a brain tumor, have been reported and documented.

A chronology of the phenomenon follows.

1983

- September 25: First appearance of the Virgin to Gladys Quiroga de Motta.

- On October 7, Gladys asked the Virgin what she wanted. Gladys: "I saw her and I asked her what she wanted of me. Then her image faded away and a chapel appeared. I understood that she wanted to be among us."

- October 12: Gladys discusses her experiences with a priest.

- October 13: The Holy Virgin talks to her for the first time.

- November 17: Gladys sprinkles holy water on the apparition.

- November 19: Gladys is informed of her mission: "You will become a bridge of union. Proclaim my words."

- November 24: A shaft of light in the darkness shows Gladys where the Church should be built — on a wasteland called Campito on the banks of the Parana river. The ray of light is seen by one other witness, a nine-year-old girl.

- November 27: Gladys recognizes the apparition when she sees an image of Our Lady of the Rosary relegated to the belfry of the diocesan cathedral because of damage. The Virgin referred to Exodus 25:8 in describing the church to be built. This passage says, "They shall make a sanctuary for me, that I may dwell in their midst." The significance of this passage is that it contains the instructions given by God to the Israelites for building the Ark of the Covenant by means of which Yahweh would be present to them. The New Testament and the early Church had consistently understood Mary to be the New Ark of the Covenant, who was the dwelling place of the Holy

Spirit and the Bearer of the Son. At San Nicolás, the Virgin was restating this ancient teaching.

1984

- November: Gladys is welcomed by the new bishop of San Nicolás, Domingo Salvador Castagna. The bishop has an audience with Pope John Paul II, at which he discusses the phenomenon.

1985

- April: A Commission of Inquiry is named.

1986

- February 25: First pilgrimage and celebration of the Holy Mass in El Campito, the location for the new sanctuary.
- May 25: Spreading of a medal introduced by the Virgin in the apparitions.
- September 25: Placing of the foundation stone of the sanctuary.

1987

- April 11: Bishop Castagna has an audience with Pope John Paul II in Rosario, the main city in his diocese. The bishop promises the Pope that he will direct a study of San Nicolás.
- October 13: The building of the sanctuary begins.

1989

- March 19: Moving of the image from the cathedral and blessing and opening of the sanctuary.
- November: Bishop Castagna has another audience with the Pope.

1990

- February 11: The end of the catechesis of Our Lady of San Nicolás.
- August 25: Bishop Castagna consecrates the sanctuary and the pilgrims to God through the Immaculate Heart of Mary.

Over eighteen hundred messages were received over the course of the apparitions. Distinctive features of this apparition and its messages include: the Virgin often specified particular scriptural references in her messages; the visionary Gladys "saw" the apparition of the Virgin when she closed her eyes after receiving a supernatural signal (unlike most other apparitions, where the visionaries saw the Virgin physically in front of them and were oblivious to their external surroundings); Gladys could hardly read or write before the phenomenon began but she was able to document the many messages she received with great clarity and precision; Gladys was the recipient of the stigmata (the wounds of Christ) on her wrists (with stigmata also on her feet, side, and one shoulder) and has been a "victim soul" uniting her suffering to that of the Lord. In some of the apparitions, Mary confirms that she is the New Ark of the Covenant as well as the Woman Clothed with the Sun of Revelation 12. In His messages, Jesus confirms that Mary is the New Ark of the Covenant and states that acceptance of Mary and her messages is necessary for the world.

(Provided courtesy of Patrizia de Ferrari Coronado of Argentina.)

Description of the Virgin

The Virgin's figure glowed with light. She had a blue gown and a veil and held the baby Jesus in her arms along with a large Rosary. She bore a close resemblance to a statue of Our Lady of the Rosary that had been left to languish in the belfry of a nearby cathedral.

Messages

Here is a synthesis of more than eighteen hundred messages that were given almost daily for a period of nearly seven years: Our Lady prepares Gladys for her mission. She teaches her a pedagogy of prayer and Christian life and asks that the sanctuary be a place of ecclesial gathering. She promotes a prophetic catechism for the people of today, with their anguish and sufferings, in order to give them back hope supported in Jesus Christ, the Savior. The words of Jesus (78 messages) are associated with the words of Mary (1816 messages) to create a dynamic of conversion and spiritual force. The Virgin invites everyone to restore their life with God inside the Church with the essential means of faith and the sacraments, the love and sacrifice they promote, and the development of the Christian virtues. She invites her children to go back to all that the Church had received from God. She invites us to consecration, the seeds of which have been received from God in Baptism but are blocked by materialism and secularism, because this "divinization" must take over all of our being and life. This is emphasized specially in her last messages, such as the invitation she makes on February 2, 1990, where she explains the real nature of the consecration:

> Gladys, I want my consecrated children to give the Mother whatever she asks: To dedicate at least one hour a day to prayer. To go to communion every day. To be humble. To be at the total service of Mary. To thank God for every day of consecration lived. To be united to the Son's love. To ask the grace of living under the Light of the Holy Spirit. The consecration must be made on a special day of the Mother. This is the consecration that I ask at my Sanctuary.

Five messages of special significance must be cited here as a prologue to the others.

"Father deliver us from all evil. With Your holy wisdom, Lord, save us from all sin. In the name of all those who love You, Lord, lead us on the right road. Amen. Read: Proverbs 2:1–11. He who says this prayer during nine consecutive days, together with a Rosary, will receive a very special grace from me." (December 12, 1983)

"You must have a medal cast with my image of the advocation of Mary of the Rosary of San Nicolás, and on the other side the Blessed Trinity with seven stars." (December 2, 1984)

"My daughter, I will tell you the meaning of the seven stars. They are seven graces that my Son Jesus will grant to those who wear it on their breast. Praise be to the Lord." (September 25, 1985)

"My daughter, because of a few good people, many bad people will be saved. I mean that with prayer, with the continual prayer of true Christians, many will reach salvation. Here, I explain the reason for my presence and the remaining of my messages, that are, in the final instance, the Lord's word. There must be conversion for the salvation of the soul to be possible." (December 15, 1986)

"My daughter, in this time, I am the Ark, for all your brethren! I am the Ark of peace, the Ark of salvation, the Ark where my children must enter, if they wish to live in the Kingdom of God. There is no obstacle for this Mother, and there will be none for the children." (February 6, 1987)

•

1983

"Beloved children, you are in need of me. It is time to pray; it is time to ask forgiveness and it will be given." (October 30)

Jesus: "I am the sower. Gather the harvest; it will be great." (November 15)

Jesus: "Glorious days await you. You will rejoice in me, my beloved children." (November 17)

I asked the Virgin whether she would like to be called "Mary of the Rosary of San Nicolás," and she replied: "It must be so. My wish is to be among you, to cover you with blessings, with peace, with joy, and bring you close to the Lord Our God. Read Col. 3:15, 4:15, 2 Cor. 4." (November 26)

"All humanity is contaminated. It does not know what it wants, and it is the evil one's chance, but he will not be the winner. Christ Jesus will win the great battle, my daughter. You must not let yourselves be surprised; you must be alert. For this reason, daughter, I ask for so much prayer, so much obedience to God. I say this for the whole world. Preach this! Amen." (December 27)

"Speak of my messages, you cannot hide them! It is your Father's will! He would not ask for something that cannot be done, nor say something that could not be spoken of. Read Matt. 10:26–28, 32–33, Mark 7:14–16." (December 29)

1984

"At these moments all humanity is hanging by a thread. If the thread breaks, many will be those who do not reach salvation.... Hurry because time is running out." (January 8)

"My children, do not disobey Christ Jesus, for His pure Heart suffers if He sees you sin. The Lord wants you to be as perfect as you can. He does not want anyone to fall into worldly temptations. My daughter, today open your heart to your neighbor. Make this known, for it is my will and that of your Father. Amen. Read 1 John 2:3–6, 17." (January 15)

"In all the places of the world, where my messages have been given, they would seem to be preached in cemeteries. There was not the response that the Lord wishes. That is why your people were chosen. Preach for your brethren to respond to the call of the Lord Our God. Amen, Amen. Read Ps. 107B:35–42." (February 18)

"The Lord will answer those who repent for their bad behavior. The Lord says: 'Repent and I will forgive you.' The enemy will not advance, the hand of God Our Father will stop him. When the time comes, He will uproot all evil, purify you, and you will become good Christians. Glory be to Heaven." (February 25)

"Do not provoke the wrath of the Lord — more than wrath, pain, on seeing the disobedience of His children. Prove that you love Him, giving all for Him. This is the chance. May He find truth in your hearts and may He glory in you. Amen, Amen. Read James 4:4–10, 5:19–20." (March 11)

"In other places where I have appeared, the Lord has been present. My children, without the hand of God, nothing is possible. I make you listen to things that you had listened to before, but did not practice. Now the Lord gives you a new chance. The answer is in you. Amen, Amen. Read 1 Chron. 22:19." (April 12)

Gladys: "I see a large city with many buildings and it is destroyed, as if there had been a war. Later I see a white pigeon flying. The Virgin says to me: 'Blessed are those who love peace, because war brings total destruction. It is horrifying to see that men cannot restrain their impulse of ambition and power. They do not know how to see where the true sense of life is that can lead them to complete happiness. Only God can achieve it, and only God has the power of making it possible.' " (May 7)

Jesus: "He who listens to My Word will be saved, and he who puts it in practice will live forever. Those who hope in God do not hope in vain." (June 15)

"Those who offend Christ Jesus are like those who scourged Him and crucified Him. That is how He feels it. He suffers offenses and injustices so intensely. Remember that the God who gives life is the same One who will comfort your sorrow and will grant you the joy of life everlasting. Amen, Amen." (June 18)

"Listen, children of God! You who proclaim peace, you are living in strife. You who love freedom are slaves, yes, you are the evil one's slaves. Although you may deny it, he is using you against the Lord. You know well that everyone who does not act as the Lord says is doing wrong. Do not surrender! Do not let yourselves be taken; pray and the Holy Spirit will make you see the way out. Be certain it will be so. Glory be to Heaven." (July 19)

"People are unaware of the poison that the evil one places in them, and they let themselves be tempted. Today they continue to crucify Christ with that behavior. That is why the Lord is instructing His children." (December 20)

1985

"Tears burn my eyes when I see such coldness in those that I try to save, because I know that if they do not convert themselves, they will go to death." (January 11)

Jesus: "I am not hiding. I want to save mankind. I am with my Ark, this time, on land. Blessed is he who surrenders to the Lord." (February 21)

"What value prayer has for the Lord, you cannot imagine! My children, that is why I ask for so much prayer! Say the Holy Rosary meditating! I assure you your prayers will rise like a true song of love to the Lord." (June 13)

1986

"You may ask yourselves. 'Can the Lord forgive those who forget His existence?' I tell you, yes, my children, the Lord can, because of His great mercy. But do not take excessive advantage of God's kindness. Cling to my mantle strongly, for it will really cleanse you and present you pure before the Lord. Glory be to the Most Holy of Heaven and the earth. Read Isa. 29:18–19, 30:18, 21." (February 28)

Gladys: "Today I have a vision. I see serpents, they move...." The Virgin: "Daughter, the Prince of Evil pours out his venom today with all his might, because he sees that his sorry reign is ending; little is left to him. His end is near. Amen, Amen." (March 7)

"My daughter, the evil one is triumphant now, it is true, but it is a victory that will last briefly. The Lord is only giving him time, the same time that He gives man for him to return to God. That is why vices and worldly madness increase every day. The weaknesses will have to become strengths and in this way will be able to get rid of evil. As yet, man's heart is not totally invaded. Glory be to God." (October 11)

Gladys: "I see her eyes full of tears." The Virgin: "My daughter, my love wants to touch the insensitive souls. I say insensitive because they are covered in ice; they have opposed everlasting clarity." (October 13)

"Daughter, the earth is inhabited, but it seems uninhabited, a very great darkness is over it. God's warning is over the world! Those who stay in the Lord have nothing to fear, but those who deny what comes from him have." (October 14)

1987

"Do not expect everything from God, if you do nothing for Him. Awaken and return to the Lord." (May 10)

"My dear daughter, how sadly lost youth is! Drug addiction and easy life is the picture the evil one has set for the young! Sin, committed in very different ways, makes them stray further and further from God! If only they turn their eyes toward the Mother of God, the Mother will make them find God again. If only they penetrate the Mother's Heart will they be able to hear the Lord's voice." (September 21)

1988

"Gladys, the mercy of my Son wishes to reach mankind. That is why souls must prepare to receive it, surrendering to the Mother's heart. My children: In the Cross of Christ, I have become your Mother and my continual watch over you will make you reach that mercy." (March 16)

Gladys: "I have a vision: I see the earth divided in two parts. One part represents two-thirds and the other one-third, in which I see the Blessed Virgin." The Virgin: "Gladys, you are seeing the world half destroyed. These rays of light are sent from my heart, which wants to save as many hearts as it can. My heart is all powerful, but it can do nothing if hearts are unwilling. The means to save souls are prayer and conversion. Every soul must prepare so as not to be imprisoned eternally by darkness." (March 21)

"My daughter: It was the blows that started His suffering; then the thorns, the nails, the lance. It was so painful for me to see Him suffer! Today, it is the sins, the hurtful words, the atheism. Yes, again they are crucifying Him, again my heart bleeds." (April 1, Good Friday)

"My dear daughter, today as never before, my messages must be spread! Today as never before, the world must know my words! All must know my urgent call to conversion, my request of consecration to the Sacred Hearts of Jesus and of Mary!" (August 26)

"There are at present serious offenses against God: murders, abortions, and all kinds of violence, are ways of attacking the Lord. I repudiate injustice, immorality, violence, lack of peace. I am a mother and I ask of my children: repentance, charity, confidence. Preach to all mankind. Blessed be the Savior." (September 13)

"In these times of so much confusion and so little light in souls, my most pure light will be the one to guide you in the midst of so much darkness. Many are the children who do not admit that the Mother is the Mediator before the Son; many resist going to the Son through the Mother. I tell all mankind: I will help you to overcome every uncertainty; this Mother will make your encounter with the Son possible. For this it is necessary to become little and abandon yourself in my heart. I assure you, do not doubt. Preach it daughter. Glory be to Heaven." (December 8)

"It is not mankind who is abandoned by God, but God who is abandoned by mankind!" (December 10)

1989

"Now the world must know that the Mother of Christ will overcome Satan, because by her side will be her Son's humble ones." (February 17)

"For these times, the Lord has marked a sign: The Woman Clothed with the Sun. She is the hope that the children must grasp. The Mother has set her eyes on you, set your eyes and your heart on God." (February 28)

"My daughter, as previously in Fatima, today my visits are renewed on earth. They are more frequent and more prolonged, because humanity is passing through very dramatic times. Has mankind not understood that they must be uniquely at the service of God? If they resist, their souls are going to perish. Many hearts do not accept my invitation to prayer and conversion. That is why the work of the devil is growing and expanding. My dear children, it is only through prayer and conversion that you will return to God. May He not find your hearts dry." (May 13)

"My children: I am the door of Heaven and the help on earth." (May 24)

Jesus: "All creatures should come to Me, because only with Me, the souls will live eternally. It is My Mother who will prevent them from going adrift, who will make them come directly to Me." (July 25)

"I am the Mother of the Savior; therefore, I am the only guide capable of guiding you to salvation. May this be known in all the universe." (September 1)

"My children, my Son has charged me with a mission: to be the guide of the souls who truly want to reach Him. Preach it." (December 7)

Jesus: "Before the world was saved by means of Noah's Ark; today the Ark is My Mother. Through her, souls will be saved, because she will bring them toward Me. He who rejects My Mother rejects Me! Many are letting the grace of God pass by in these days." (December 30)

(The initial commentary on the messages was provided courtesy of Patrizia de Ferrari Coronado; the text of the messages is taken from *Messages of Our Lady at San Nicolás* published by Faith Publishing Company.)

3. Naju, Korea, 1985
Queen of the Holy Rosary

Julia Kim of Naju in South Korea is one of today's most famous visionaries: she has been privileged to witness or participate in a broad spectrum of supernatural phenomena ranging from bleeding statues and messages from the Virgin to the stigmata and Eucharistic miracles. She is a visionary, stigmatist, and victim soul.

Below is a short history of the phenomena and a summary of the supernatural signs and messages of Naju. This information was provided by Mary's Touch, an organization distributing information on the Naju phenomenon.

Julia was born in Naju in Korea in 1947. Her father and grandfather were killed by Communist guerillas, and she and her mother lived in poverty. In 1972, she married Julio Kim and the couple had four children. A few years later, Julia was diagnosed with terminal cancer. While on her deathbed after multiple surgeries, her husband brought a priest to pray for her. The priest told her that her sufferings were blessings from God. Her body suddenly became warm and she started sweating. Shortly after she was completely healed and began a life of prayer.

One night, at 3 a.m., Julia saw a vision of Our Lord bleeding miserably, especially from His Heart, which was torn by human sins. Julia was deeply moved and promised a life of reparation for the sins in the world. Miraculously, she began suffering severe pains again. Julia also received the stigmata, the wounds of Our Lord. These stigmata usually last for several days and disappear. They reappear later. On June 30, 1985, Julia saw Our Lady's statue in her room weeping for the first time. Later, on July 18, she received the first message from Our Lady. On October 19, 1986, clear tears turned into bloody tears. Julia has continued receiving messages and suffering pain. Other miracles have also continued: fragrant oil from Our Lady's statue, the fragrance of roses, healings of incurable illnesses, and Eucharistic miracles.

A Summary of the Supernatural Signs in Naju

1. *Tears and tears of blood from Our Lady's statue.* For a total of seven hundred days between June 30, 1985, and January 14, 1992. Samples of the bloody tears were tested in a medical laboratory and were found to be human blood.

2. *Fragrant oil from Our Lady's statue.* For seven hundred consecutive days from November 24, 1992, to October 23, 1994.

3. *The external appearance of bread in the Holy Eucharist changed into visible flesh and blood on Julia's tongue.* Twelve times between May 1988 and October 1996. The miracle on October 31, 1995, was witnessed by Pope John Paul II during a Mass in the Pope's private chapel in the Vatican. Bishop Roman Danylak from Toronto, Canada, and Bishop Dominic Su of Sibu, Malaysia, also witnessed the miracles in Naju and Sibu, respectively, and wrote their testimonies expressing their belief in the authenticity of these miracles.

4. *The Sacred Host descended from above to the chapel in Naju.* Seven times between November 24, 1994, and August 27, 1997. The first two miracles were witnessed by the Apostolic Pro-Nuncio in Korea during his visit to Naju. On July 1, 1995, seven Sacred Hosts descended. They were consumed by two priests and five lay people, including Julia, according to the local archbishop's instruction. The external appearance of the Sacred Host that Julia received changed into visible Flesh and Blood on her tongue. A sample of this Blood was tested in the medical laboratory at Seoul National University and was found to be human blood. The descent of the Eucharist on June 12, 1997, was witnessed by Bishop Paul Kim of the Cheju Diocese in Korea. The Eucharist again descended on August 27, 1997, during Fr. Raymond Spies's visit to Naju. An intense fragrance is continuing (as of May 1998) from the spot on the floor in the chapel where the Eucharist came to rest.

5. *Spiritual and physical healings*. Numerous people have regained love and peace in their families and returned to the sacraments. Many were healed physically, especially while repenting their sinful lives after experiencing Our Lady's love.

6. *Julia's stigmata*. Bleeding occurred on Julia's two hands and two feet during their sufferings. Doctors examined Julia and stated that her wounds and bleeding had no medical explanation.

A Summary of the Blessed Mother's Messages

- Become little children (in relation to God and your Heavenly Mother). Do not seek to be higher than others. Live a life of self-denial and sacrifice.

- Offer up reparations for the conversion of sinners in the world. Repair the wounds in the Sacred Heart of Jesus and the Immaculate Heart of Mary with prayers and sacrifices.

- Pray fervently, especially the Rosary, to defeat the devil.

- Achieve peace and love in your family. Forgive one another.

- Be loyal to the Pope and his teachings. Respect, love, and support priests. Pray for them ceaselessly that they may be protected from the devil's attacks and be faithful to their mission.

- Let everyone know that the Lord is truly present in the Holy Eucharist with His Body, Blood, Soul, and Divinity. Make frequent and sincere Confessions so that you may receive the Lord more worthily.

- Respect human lives — especially the neglected, the sick, the elderly, and the unborn. Let everyone know that life begins at the moment of conception and that abortion is murder.

- Have complete trust in me. Love this Heavenly Mother wholeheartedly and seek refuge in her Heart. I am the shortcut to Jesus and the Helper in His Redemptive Work.

- Hurriedly spread and practice my messages of love.

As an ongoing phenomenon, the supernatural events in Naju are still under investigation by the Church, and no final verdict will be issued until after the end of the phenomenon. Nevertheless, as at Medjugorje and Akita, the worldwide impact of the events in Naju have resulted in a closer involvement of the Vatican in the ongoing investigation as well as positive affirmations from bishops across the globe.

Like at Akita, some of the more liberal local Catholic theologians have tried to discredit the phenomenon at Naju with criticisms that are essentially irrelevant. The chief critic does not deny the fact that unusual phenomena — witnessed by many people of sound mind and investigated by scientists — are taking place at Naju. He simply attributes these phenomena to preternatural rather than supernatural causes. But this attempted explanation does not address all the facts:

even if one holds that the tears and blood of the statue stem from Julia Kim's preternatural powers, there is no precedent in the history of the preternatural for a piece of what appeared to be bread turning into flesh and blood (a miracle that took place on numerous occasions before eyewitnesses). Also not explained here are the stigmata, the healings, and the descent of the Eucharist. The same critic said that the Eucharistic miracle contradicted traditional teaching on the Eucharist; he is apparently unaware of the many other similar miracles of the Eucharist that were actually accepted and celebrated by the Church. Finally, he charged that the Naju messages simply copy Fr. Stefano Gobbi's locutions. In response, we might ask why the messages in these two cases could not be similar if they come from the same source. As a matter of fact, however, there is a substantial difference between the whole tenor of the Naju phenomenon and Fr. Gobbi. Fr. Gobbi has many edifying messages but he is not generally associated with miraculous phenomena. At Naju, on the other hand, many of the messages are accompanied by supernatural manifestations (the suffering of the visionary, visions of Heaven and Hell, and the like).

About the involvement of the Vatican, a story by Jong-Chang Woo in the June 1998 issue of *Wulkan Chosun* reports:

> On November 24, 1994, when Archbishop Giovanni Bulaitis, the Apostolic Pro-Nuncio in Korea, was visiting Naju, a Eucharist with images of "A" and "W" on it came down. It was basically the same as the miracle in Fatima, Portugal, in 1917, when St. Michael the Archangel brought the Eucharist to three children. Archbishop Bulaitis broke the Eucharist into smaller pieces and gave Communion to about seventy people who were present in the chapel. Archbishop Bulaitis reported this event to the Holy See. In May of 1995, the Vatican sent Monsignor Vincent Thu, a private secretary of the Pope, to Naju. Msgr. Thu brought the Pope's words that he loves and respects the Blessed Mother of Naju. The news spread widely in many countries. Even though Naju had not been officially approved by the Church yet, more than a half million people, including many priests and religious, have visited Naju.... In October 1995, Julia made a pilgrimage to Rome. She was invited to the 7:30 a.m. Mass on October 31, celebrated by the Pope in his private chapel on the third floor of his residence. When Julia received Communion from the Pope, an amazing phenomenon of the Eucharist bleeding on her tongue occurred.... After the Mass ended, the Pope greeted all the people who attended the Mass, one by one, and gave everyone a Rosary. He gave two Rosaries to Julia. Julia still had the Eucharist in her mouth and, when the Pope came to her, opened her mouth and showed him the Sacred Host already turned into flesh and blood. The Pope looked and raised his hands as seen in a photograph.

In an August 20, 1998, letter, the Congregation for the Evangelization of the Peoples noted that "this Congregation is well aware of the questions concerning Naju as well as of the problems touching upon the faith and the form of Christian life in Korea and elsewhere, in the wake of Vatican Council II. You are invited to pray that the Holy Spirit may enlighten all the persons of the Church whose duty it is to watch over the purity of the faith. Relying on the divine grace of the Holy Spirit and the unfailing help of the Blessed Mother, the present problems will certainly be overcome."

Messages

The Struggle against Sin

"Now is the time. Stay awake and pray. Many souls are walking toward Hell because of the cunning violence of the devil, the enemy of the Cross, but I stretch out my mantle and am waiting for their return, because I love them all.

"My dear children! Listen to my words well. Look back at history, when people did not listen to the many warnings given by God. What will happen to this age, if people, like those of the past, remain indifferent to or reject the words of God and my messages of love? Keep in your heart the words of this Mother, who is the Helper in redemption, and offer up even the pains that cause bleeding inside of you.

"In this age of aridity, an age of an endless desert, the victory can be won only through love. When you love, you must also shed some tears. Tears will help the seeds to bear good fruit and also help the absorption of heavenly nutrition by the souls who are hungry and have been deprived of vitality because of delinquency.

"Children! All the souls reaching the bosom of God will enjoy eternal love, peace, and joy in the Lord's love. But those who betray the graces, are ungrateful, and insult the Holy Spirit will be cut off from the Lord forever.

"Satan is striving with all his power to promote a tendency of despising the Holy Laws of the Lord, but my burning Immaculate Heart will achieve victory, when the sounds of little souls' prayers to my Immaculate Heart soar high to Heaven. You will surely see my victory."

Julia: "I saw a man with an angel on his right and a black, hard-to-recognize object (devil) on his left. When he prayed sincerely from his heart, the angel offered a fresh rose to Heaven, whereas, when he prayed superficially, the angel offered a wilted rose. The angels stored the fresh roses and the wilted ones separately. When the man made sacrifices and reparations, forgave and reconciled with others, and offered all his life with a joyful heart, fresh roses were offered, but when he was only enduring (difficulties) and lacked love, wilted roses were offered. When he did good works, roses accumulated in Heaven, but, when he did evil and criticized others, the devil was overjoyed and threw the roses, which had been accumulated in Heaven, into the flaming fires of Hell, one after another.

"God can do everything Himself, but He acts through priests and lay people. Likewise, the devil also does his work through humans. Thus, he employs all kinds of methods in using people around us to make us angry, resentful, unable to forgive and to make us commit many mistakes."

The Blessed Mother: "Daughter! Did you see that? Good and evil always coexist inside you, because your guardian angel and the devil confront each other: the angel helping you to do good works and the devil afflicting you and tempting you to do evil all the time. The guardian angel stores roses one by one in the treasure warehouse in Heaven. Thus, when a soul offers many good works by offering prayers and making sacrifices and reparations, many roses accumulate. When that soul rises to Heaven, the angels make a garland with the roses and dance holding it. The saints also welcome the soul with majestic music.

"But even if good works have been accumulated, the devil will burn the roses in the fire of Hell by taking the roses out of the treasure warehouse when evil deeds are committed. Because one goes to Hell only when there are no roses left at all, the devil strives with all the available methods to win even one more soul over to his side and, thereby, to form his army.

"Therefore, daughter, do not give a chance to the devil! Arm yourself with love and win the victory. Do not forget my bloody merits and the power of the Lord's Sacred Blood, and knock at the door whenever your cross is too heavy.

"The souls who are elevated high on the Cross and offer themselves gracefully as victims to the Lord are truly the souls who glorify the Lord and are the little souls who are closest to me. I want all the children to become completely humble and to be tightly embraced in my bosom of love like the Baby Jesus. I will make you spread the strong fragrance of my Motherhood to all the corners of the world." (September 17, 1991)

Julia: "Many children continue to be controlled by the devils. The devils influence people's minds, making them criticize each other with jealousy and resentment; making them justify their actions by speaking ill of and cheating others and by pride, hatred, and selfishness; and making them confront each other with anger and indignation. They also make people live in disorder through lust and obscenity and make them accommodate evil through hatred and the inability to forgive each other." (July 5, 1989)

The Blessed Mother: "Now is the time for a huge battle between me and my enemy. Our enemy is the army of the Red Dragon, who looks like a terrible animal. All the devils are out to conquer this earth from Hell. They [try] to corrupt many souls of this world by making them reject God, commit sins with all kinds of selfishness, and defile everything. Daughter! See how they allure people into the traps of Hell."

Julia: "The Blessed Mother had hardly finished her words when the black animal figures of the devils began appearing with their carts. The carts were well decorated but were black. The devils looked somewhat like eagles. They were snatching many souls and loading them into the carts. Around the carts were the black devils and many souls attracted to the carts. In order to make the souls join them, the devils were chattering in an inscrutable manner. Many souls were giggling and having fun with the devils without knowing that it was the road to Hell and without running away from or rejecting it. Soon these souls, too, were turning black. I was so sad."

The Blessed Mother: "Daughter! Did you see that? A huge battle has begun like this already. Since it is a spiritual war, arm yourselves with me by entrusting everything to my Immaculate Heart. Also practice the messages of my love. Then, you will be able to escape from the terrible chastisement approaching the human race and the Church." (August 26, 1989)

"Let even those who are in despair, depressed, full of wounds, and in tribulations suffering under the heavy pressures from their arid hearts, sins, hatred, violence, and impure habits come aboard the Ark of Salvation of my love. I will wrap them with my warm mantle and help them even in the midst of a bitterly cold snowstorm.

"My beloved children! Now offer even those trivial things in your life to me gracefully. I will give you the power to transcend even the most trivial things. When you offer up everything and drink the painful cups of the cross and martyrdom with love, even those who are deserted in the middle of pains of death will repent and see the light in darkness." (November 4, 1991)

"I want to rescue this world into my Immaculate Heart, as it is facing the grave danger of being swept away by the storm and being destroyed....

"Therefore, my daughter, I, Mother of Love, will become the ark sailing toward Heaven. Help me by forming the Order of Mary's Ark of Salvation so that all the children may come aboard. I am the comforter and refuge. I am the Ark of Salvation that sails toward Heaven. To those souls who follow me, holding my hands, accept me, and put the messages of love into practice, I will become the Ark of Salvation for safe arrival at the heavenly harbor. I will hold their hands in all their tribulations, poverty, and adversities." (November 11, 1990)

"All the children of the world! Darkness can never defeat light. The devils are trying to strike down many of my children who are following me. But do not forget that the Lord does not refuse the pleas of those who call upon His Name with love and follow me.

"Daughter! You cannot win the victory without going through the Cross. You must understand the amazing mystery of the Holy Eucharist by which God comes down from Heaven through priests in order to be with you. Therefore make frequent Confessions to receive the Lord more worthily; open your heart widely, keep it clean and organized, and love one another so that it will become a palace and a tabernacle where the Lord can dwell. Then, the Lord will dwell in you, who are unworthy, and set a fire in you.

"My beloved daughter! Tell all the children of the world, I want all of you to wear the scapular with the intention of being with me: pray the Rosary fervently with all your body and mind and with love; live a completely consecrated life of prayers, sacrifices, and reparations; renew your life with the spirit of self-renunciation and poverty; and, thus, repel the violence of the devil.

"I am imploring you again and again, because I want to save you all from this dangerous world. Therefore, renounce your ego and follow my wishes well. Then darkness will retreat from this world, and the Kingdom of the Lord will come." (April 21, 1991)

"When you follow me without doubting that this is the perfect shortcut with no danger of slipping and falling off the cliff, my flaming Immaculate Heart will burn away all your sins. Thus, even falling into sins can be utilized for a greater good. Now, bring all those things that you think are worthless, miserable, and weak and gather around my great banquet, which has a sacred value. There will be a great blessing on all the children who are rushing to my bosom of love." (May 8, 1991)

Jesus: "Admitting your sins in a simple and humble way and in obedience, aspire ever more strongly for the little person's way of love, loving and trusting My Mother. Then your attachment to pleasures, reputation, social status, power, material goods, pride, and face-saving will be replaced by heroic deeds.

"Do not lay down your cross, even when it feels too heavy. If you lay it down, evil will enter your heart right away and take control of it with an explosion of passions. Wake up in a hurry and pray.

"Too many of My children loiter outside the door and are unable to meet Me, because they do not accept My Mother's messages of love while insisting upon their own way of faith that they have received and are giving to others.

"My dear children! Listen well. Keep in mind that My Mother only leads you to a life of intense love inside My noble Heart. Come to Me hurriedly through My Mother, who is the shortcut to me....

"My Mother prepares a safe refuge in her Immaculate Heart for all of you and leads you to Me. The hour of the pains and chastisement of Gethsemane and Calvary is approaching the children of the world. But the gate of Heaven will open through the prayers, graceful consecrations, and bloody efforts by you, My little children. Do not fear. Entrust everything to Me with faith and trust. I will be with you always." (December 8, 1992)

Visions of Heaven, Purgatory, and Hell

Julia: "At about 9 p.m., I suddenly lost energy in my whole body and fell down. I went upstairs to my room supported by others, where I was struggling with excruciating pains. A while later, I entered an ecstasy and saw Heaven, Purgatory, and Hell.

"It was a world of difference. Such a tremendous difference! The saved children were sharing peace, joy, and love in the flower garden, but the condemned ones were burning in the intense flames with resentment and hatred.

Heaven — Our True Home. "Countless angels were playing a beautiful and majestic symphony welcoming the saints who were entering Heaven. Also, numerous saints were welcoming them with loud cheers. Jesus was waiting for them with open arms, and the Blessed Mother was stretching out her hands to hold them. God the Father smiled, expressing a welcome with His eyes. St. Joseph was also welcoming them.

"It was a place without any jealousy or resentment. All were sharing love with one another. It was filled with love, peace, and joy. It was a place of heavenly banquet where one does not become hungry even without eating.

"The Blessed Mother prepared crowns of flowers and put them on people, who were then dancing holding each other's hands. In the flower garden, Jesus and the Blessed Mother together held up her mantle, and all were entering the inside of the mantle. All were humble to each other and were keeping order to avoid inconveniencing others. Their faces were full of smiles and were beautiful.

Purgatory. "It is a place where one must walk into the terrible flames of fire. There, one does the unfinished penance of this world and becomes purified.

"It is a place far away where those who die in grace but have unfinished reparations must walk the way of atonement. When they are completely purified, they are lifted into Heaven by the angels with the help of the Blessed Mother. The process can be expedited if we in this world pray for them. We can also help them by making sacrifices and doing penance for them.

"It will be too late to regret not having done penance in this world. So, while still alive in this world, one must offer love constantly through sacrifices for others."

Hell. "When the angels tie the hands of the condemned souls and drop them, the devils snatch them violently. Then, they fall into the flames of fire. It is a place of eternal perdition. It is useless, however hard one may regret and struggle. It is a sea of fire filled with hatred. Who will hold their hands? Nobody.

"People struggle like a person drowning and trying to grab even a straw, but only run around in the fire, tear each other down, and try to take food away from others, but all the food burns in the fire, and nobody can eat anything. So, they are growling with eyes that are sticking out. They become horrible devils.

"It was a terrible scene one could not even look at."

The Blessed Mother: "My little daughter, who rejoices in suffering pains for my Son Jesus and me! My Heart is hurt so much, because numerous children who have been called to Heaven are walking toward Purgatory and Hell.

"Even some of my priests, whom I love so much that I can put them in my eyes without feeling any pain, are going toward Purgatory and Hell....

"Even at this very moment, numerous souls are walking toward Hell. I wish to save them through your sacrifices and sufferings. Will you take part in the pains?"

Julia: "Yes, my Mother! How joyful it is to suffer with you for the conversion of many souls! Before I knew you, I had been so unhappy and miserable. But now I thank God and you for allowing me to take part in the sufferings despite my unworthiness.

Terrible Pains of Hell. "I was crying and screaming in extreme despair that cannot even be imagined with a human mind.

"The Blessed Mother is suffering and calling us incessantly to prevent us from going to the cursed abyss where the condemned souls separated from God are punished in many different ways under the just judgment by Jesus — bitterly lamenting, screaming, regretting, and struggling in vain. We must say yes to the endless calls by Our Mother." (July 24, 1988)

Abortion

"My Heart is broken because of the unlimited birth control. Prevent abortions and pray for those who carry out abortions." (July 18, 1985)

Julia: "The Blessed Mother shed tears from midnight to 8 a.m. I saw her eyes filled with tears.

"Mother, why are you weeping?

"Momentarily, I fell down and saw many souls. Some of them were walking with a cane; some did not have any legs; some were without shoulders or arms; some did not have eyes or ears; some had disfigured noses or mouths. They were going somewhere, pushing each other, fighting with each other in noisy and mean ways and falling again and again. I was astonished and screamed. I thought they were the souls in Purgatory."

The Blessed Mother: "Look! Many souls are going toward Hell because of abortions. I have to implore with tears like this in order to save those numerous souls. I intend to save them through you — through your sacrifices and reparations. How can I be unaware of the pains you endure? Now, would you participate in the pains of the little babies who have been abandoned by their ignorant and cruel parents?"

Julia: "Yes, Mother, I can do anything, if you stay with me."

"At that moment, my posture became that of an unborn baby — with arms and legs crouched. My face became red like blood. I suffered for four and a half hours. When these pains ended, pains of delivery began. My face became swollen like a pumpkin and I could not move myself. I suffered all day. The spiritual pains were harder to endure than the physical pains." (May 12, 1987)

The Blessed Mother: "Tell everyone that a little baby is not a bloody lump, but has a life flowing in it from the moment of conception in the mother's womb.

"I am overcome with sorrows, because these innocent lives, precious lives given by God, are cruelly trampled, brutally kneaded, crushed, torn, and killed by ignorant and indifferent parents." (July 29, 1988)

The Chastisement

The Blessed Mother: "The human feet should be used for rushing to adore God, but are, instead, being used for running toward evil things. Their mouths should be used for praising and admiring the Son of God, but are being used for blaspheming and judging God. As a result, the whole world is being covered with darkness and is provoking the anger of God. The punishment is imminent.

"You will be saved if you do not ignore my tears and tears of blood, accept my words well, and live a life based on the Gospels. But, if you do not, major calamities from the sky, on the ground, and in the seas will continue to happen. The world will experience all kinds of disasters. There will be moments of incredible distress in the near future. Therefore do not think these are accidental happenings. Be awake and pray.

"Children! I beg you. Like the Israelites who crossed the Red Sea and entered the fertile land of Canaan after the slavery in Egypt, you must also leave evil, practice my messages, and, thereby, walk toward Heaven. If not, you will not be able to escape the crisis of the Third World War. It will be too late to regret it.

"You must not forget that, as God called Moses to Mount Sinai to save the Israelites, I am calling you without ceasing, imploring with tears in order to save you.

"What might have happened, if Noah had not said yes and obeyed when Yahweh told him to build a ship to save him? Keep in your heart my words spoken with tears of blood. How can you be so blind and deaf?" (October 14, 1989)

"How can the worldly people understand that the agonies befalling you [the sufferings of Julia] are coming from the Lord's love? You must tell people that holy virtues cannot be attained without going through the Cross. Also tell them that only through numerous sacrifices will the messages of my love spread to the entire world....

"The gate to Heaven is small and, therefore, little children enter it. For this reason, little souls must unite with each other more solidly and follow me in order to save the world.

"The numerous souls who have brought about an imbalance in the universe because of their excessive pride will convert and world peace will be achieved through my fervent calls and tears and through the prayers, sacrifices, and reparations by the little souls.

"Thus, the walls of East Germany collapsed, the pagans will repent, the atheists will return, the Communist countries will convert, the barbed wires between South and North Korea will be cut, the devils will collapse, and a terrestrial paradise will be established on this earth. But if you do not accept my words and reject the Lord, the world will become seas of fire and perish through the Third World War. The God of love can also be a God of wrath. Pray harder and offer sufferings." (November 26, 1989)

"Daughter! My daughter, who entrusts everything to me even in the midst of sufferings! I want you to follow me with a greater love and without agonizing too much over your inadequacy. This world is decaying with corruption and degradation. The human race is facing a crisis under black clouds and the sins are spreading like a horrible cancer. The storm is already becoming violent. This world is exposed to a grave danger as the storm rages on. How would the Heavenly Mother feel in her mind as she watches all this? Follow me with courage even faced with serious tribulations and threats of violence, wars, and destruction. There isn't much time left before the incredible punishments will fall even upon those countries which have been protected and intensely cherished so far. Many people are inordinately rejecting God and the iniquities and corruptions are increasing every day, causing more violence and frequent wars.

"The darkness is even infiltrating the Church in cold-hearted and deliberate ways. Thus, the last hour of bleeding for purification is waiting for you. If you do not live according to the Words of Truth, you will soon suffer calamities and will surely have regret. What is the use of regretting after the justice of God is realized? In this way I am imploring my children, who have been called, as the time permitted [for the human conversion] is almost over. Be awake and pray without procrastinating. Also become simple as a child. Nobody knows the exact date and hour of the Lord's coming again to us. Preparations are in progress to defeat His enemies, destroy them, and establish His Kingdom on this earth. He will come to you on clouds displaying His power to build His glorious Kingdom. Prepare to greet Him with trust, love, and faith. He is coming to you through me, His Mother. As He was sent to you by God the Father through my virgin body, Jesus will be using my Immaculate Heart in returning to you as the King. Therefore, all the children of the world, open your mind widely without delay and return to me. Rekindle the fire in your heart that has been extinguished, achieve a unity among all, and practice my messages of love. Spread the messages all over the world fervently and filled with hope.

"If you do not reject my motherly love and practice love, my Immaculate Heart will achieve a victory in the face of the threat of a new, terrifying war, and there will be love and peace in the world. I will stretch and open my mantle and hide and save in the safe refuge of my Immaculate Heart all those souls who follow my words even in the midst of a huge darkness. But those who do not accept my words and reject the Lord will be thrown into the sea of an intense fire. Therefore, have trust in me, the Mother of Peace, and rely completely on my Immaculate Heart." (January 29, 1991)

"All the children of the world! How sad it will be if the fire falls upon you from the sky! Pray and pray again. This current age is extremely important for the whole human race. Shouldn't you find ways to protect yourselves from the many calamities? Your God looks down at your acts and is about to punish you. But He is still forgiving you. Repent hurriedly. Repent sincerely and come back to God who can save you. You must repent, because the sins of this world have reached an extremely high level. The world is mired in evil habits and delinquency. As order is disturbed, chaos is increasing and the spiritual world is being destroyed. All things are collapsing, provoking the wrath of God.

"My beloved children! Become little persons and follow me humbly and with hope and courage. When you follow me wholeheartedly in response to my messages of love, new buds will sprout even from the burnt ground, my love will flame up on the ruins, and a cup of blessing instead of a cup of wrath will be bestowed upon you by God." (March 10, 1991)

"The time when God the Father will speak with a stern voice of judgment is approaching. You must protect yourselves with prayers, sacrifices, penance, and consecration. My Heart has already been torn apart into pieces, and my bloody tears and bloody sweat are pouring down on the earth. I have already told you that the terrifying judgment of God will come down. As you know, that day will come like a thief at night. Destruction will come suddenly, when people are singing of peaceful and secure times. It will be like the pains of delivery to a pregnant woman, which are sudden and yet certain and cannot be avoided. The souls who accept my messages that you are spreading are accepting me. Those who reject them reject me and reject the Father in Heaven." (June 18, 1995)

"Become littler. I invite you to Heaven where only little souls can enter. Because the gate of Heaven is small and large souls cannot enter it, you must become littler continuously and bring many souls to me so that they may be nurtured with my spiritual milk of love and become little souls. My babies who have been invited to become little souls! The cup of God's wrath is overflowing, because the world has reached a saturation point with sins and great degradation. Expedite your efforts, remembering that the time of judgment is being delayed because of the little souls despite their small number. When the number of the little souls increases, God's voice of wrath and breath of anger will turn into blessing and this world will become the Kingdom of the Lord." (June 12, 1997)

Julia: "Jesus began speaking earnestly and sorrowfully with a very sad voice."

Jesus: "My beloved little soul! This world is now so filled with sins that I cannot even look at it with open eyes. People, who had been welcoming Me, crying out "Hosanna!" just a few days before My execution on the Cross, were saying, "He is a criminal who deserves to die. Crucify him!" But I resurrected in three days to manifest God's glory. Even at this moment, many clergy, religious, and other children are celebrating My Resurrection, but how many of them are truly remembering and consoling Me?

"Together with My Mother, Mary, who gave birth to Me and raised Me, I have been giving many messages of love and signs in Naju, Korea, but even many of my children who experienced the miracles of love are dispersing in all directions because of the devil's temptations. How sad and deplorable!

"All My beloved children in the world! Because it is not too late yet, hurriedly come to Me, following My Mother who is imploring sorrowfully, shedding tears and tears of blood. You should not face the approaching destruction unprepared. Remembering that God the Father's wrath has reached an extreme and a chastisement is inevitable but that He is still delaying the time because of the prayers of the little souls, wake up from sleep and pray. Hurriedly and humbly respond to My Mother's pleas by making your best, strenuous efforts so that the miracles of love may be fully realized. What use will it be to regret after the destruction comes? The proud people dislike the humble ones. When a rich person falters, his friends support him. But when a powerless person is in difficulty, people turn their faces away from him. You now feel much sadness in your hearts, but remember that I and My Mother are always at your side, and work in unity with each other, with high spirits, courage, and hope. There is not much time. Hurriedly and more gracefully offer up your current sufferings and achieve victory over the devil.

"Two thousand years ago, I could have come down from the Cross. However, without dying, there could be no Resurrection. Even at this moment, I can perfect everything. However, because I allowed free will to humans, sacrifices by little souls, including even death agony, are necessary. Remembering anew the truth that one must die to arrive at resurrection, at least you, who have responded to My call, should follow Me in unity and with a simple and upright mind, imitating the faith of the martyrs.

"Know that now is the time to separate empty heads of grain from good ones. Therefore, the prayers and sacrifices by My children who will gain the Kingdom of Heaven are so urgently needed. The so-called leaders are moving away from the truth and yet look so strong and overpowering. But the Kingdom of Heaven does not belong to them but to you who are working for Me. I have given up everything for your sake. As you recognize My voice and rush to Me and My Mother, you experience much difficulty and pain. But you who work for My Mother and Me will surely share love at My dining table in My Kingdom where there is no sorrow, pain, or suffering. The tears that you shed now will be completely wiped away before the throne in Heaven, where there is no thirst or hunger. You will be given a hundred-fold reward. Happiness will be yours. However, there will be nothing I and My Mother can do at the time of the Last Judgment for those who turn their faces away from Me and My Mother and reject Us to the end. My little souls! The prayers of my little children who are not shaken under any circumstances will wipe away the stains of blood on My clothes and My Mother's. They are the comforts and fragrant oil that wipe away the bloody sweat and bloody tears. The world, which is in such a shocking condition, will be reduced to ashes; this age will be destroyed by the devil's attacks. However, when there are more little souls, My Sacred Heart and My Mother's Immaculate Heart will surely triumph. Do not fear, but hurriedly perpetuate the Paschal Mystery of Resurrection. I will help you." (April 12, 1998)

The Eucharist

The Blessed Mother: "You must understand the amazing mystery of the Holy Eucharist by which God comes down from Heaven through priests in order to be with you." (April 21, 1991)

Jesus: "My real, personal, and physical Presence in the Mystery of the Eucharist is an indisputable fact. I have repeatedly shown the Eucharist turning into visible Blood and Flesh so that all may believe that the Eucharist, which is a Mystery of the Infinite Love, Humility, Power, and Wisdom, is My Living Presence." (July 1, 1995)

4. Medjugorje, Bosnia, 1981–Present
Queen of Peace

Medjugorje is without doubt the most influential apparition of the century after Fatima. The parish records of St. James Catholic Church in Medjugorje show that over fifty thousand priests and religious — among them hundreds of bishops and cardinals — have come to Medjugorje, inspired by the presence of the Virgin. Second, other than Guadalupe, no other Marian apparition in history has been the direct cause of as many conversions as Medjugorje. Guadalupe brought about the conversion of eight million Aztecs. Medjugorje has now attracted over thirty million pilgrims, the vast majority of whom have had their lives transformed or touched by their encounter with the Queen of Peace (not to speak of the tens of millions of others who have never visited Medjugorje but have been third-party recipients of the graces mediated by the Virgin).

The significance of these two facts will be evident to anyone who has studied the Church's time-tested canons for the discernment of supernatural phenomena. The Church's great doctors of the spiritual and the mystical life have said for centuries that an authentic supernatural revelation will bear two marks: it will attract the religious and it will cause conversions. Satan posing as an angel of light can bring about many extraordinary signs and wonders, but the one thing he cannot and will not do is bring about a conversion. Judged by these two criteria of an authentic supernatural revelation, Medjugorje has no parallel in Christian history beyond Guadalupe: it has attracted tens of thousands of priests and religious and it has caused hundreds of thousands, perhaps millions, of conversions (along with unprecedented levels of reception of the sacraments of Reconciliation and the Eucharist).

These two facts about Medjugorje no one can dispute since they have been so publicly chronicled. It is also to be noted that there are over a thousand documented cures attributed to Medjugorje.

The apparitions began much like many of the other famous apparitions of the last 150 years. On June 24, 1981, two peasant girls, Mirjana Dragicevic, seventeen, and Ivanka Ivankovic, sixteen, were walking from their village of Bijakovici past the hill of Podbrdo when Ivanka saw a luminous figure, a lady bathed in light, on the hill. She told her companion Mirjana to look at the Gospa, Croatian for "Our Lady," but Mirjana thought she was joking and refused. (Similarly the Beauraing visionaries initially dismissed Albert's urgent pleas to look at the apparition of the Virgin as a prank.) Nevertheless, Ivanka persisted, and when they reached the Pavlovic house, she persuaded Mirjana to return to the hill with Milka Pavlovic, thirteen. They had tried to bring their friend Vicka Ivankovic, seventeen, as well, but was told by her mother that she was asleep. When they reached Podbrdo all three now saw the Lady. They were soon joined by Vicka, who was too frightened to look but summoned two boys, Ivan Dragicevic, sixteen, and Ivan Ivankovic, twenty. Ivan Dragicevic, later to become one of the six principal visionaries, fled without looking, but the other five now saw a beautiful lady with black hair and a grey gown holding a baby and gesturing to them to come to her. The children were too scared to go up but prayed for some time and then returned home.

Although their friends and families were skeptical, Mirjana, Ivanka, and Vicka returned to Podbrdo the next evening at about 6 p.m. along with the younger Ivan, Milka's sister Marija, seventeen, and her cousin Jackov Cholo, ten. Neither Milka nor the older Ivan came with them. A few curious villagers followed them. They saw the Lady again and this time accepted her invitation to come closer. Although the adults present could not see the Lady, they were astonished by the speed with which the visionaries ascended the mountain. As soon as they reached the Lady, they were on their knees praying the Lord's Prayer; the adults noticed that they were all spontaneously looking in the same direction. Ivanka's mother had died quite recently, and she asked the Lady if she was in Heaven. The Lady said yes and told her that her mother wanted her to be obedient to her grandmother. She told them to pray seven Our Fathers, Hail Marys, and Glory Bes and the Creed daily. Like many visionaries before her, Mirjana said that she found it hard to convince people of the Lady's presence, to which she simply smiled. (On the 28th, when the visionaries asked why she wouldn't appear in the church so that everyone could see her, she said, "Blessed are they who have not seen and who believe.") She then said "Go in God's peace" and left.

On the 26th, thousands of people assembled at Podbrdo — not just from the five villages that made up the parish of Medjugorje but from neighboring towns. The visionaries and some of the others who had gathered there saw a glowing light at the top of the hill at 6:15 p.m. and on reaching the top saw the Lady there. Vicka brought some holy water which she sprinkled on the Lady, who smiled. When they asked her who she was, she replied, "I am the Blessed Virgin Mary." They asked why she had come there and she said, "I have come here, because there are many devout believers here. I have come to tell you that God exists, and He loves you. Let the others, who do not see me, believe as you do." She also said, "Peace, peace, peace. Be reconciled."

The Communist authorities were now becoming concerned about the situation. They interrogated the visionaries on June 27 and 28 and had them evaluated by a psychiatrist, who pronounced them normal and of sound mental health. Communist regimes often imprisoned dissenters in psychiatric wards on trumped up charges of mental instability. But this stratagem could not be applied here because of their own psychiatrist's report. On the 30th, two Communist social workers abducted the visionaries just before the time of the now-daily apparition. Although the visionaries could not therefore be at Podbrdo, they forced the workers to stop the car at the time of the apparition. They saw a light far away on Podbrdo. The light came to the roadside and the Gospa appeared to them there.

There is a curious footnote to this story: one of the most prolific critics of Medjugorje, who furnishes the source material for most of the other critics, is a Croatian priest in the United States whose cousin was one of these social workers; moreover his nephew was the high-level Communist official sent to Medjugorje with express orders to end the "disturbance"; apart from the conflict of interest issue here, apparently much of this Croatian critic's source material came from these two hostile "sources."

As if the visionaries didn't have enough problems with the civil authorities, they were soon to run into even worse problems with the clergy. Their parish priest, Fr. Jozo Zovko, was a skeptic from the beginning — and remained a skeptic although his bishop, the bishop of Mostar, the diocese to which Medjugorje belonged, urged him to believe. There was soon to be a role reversal, with the bishop turning hostile and Fr. Zovko befriending the visionaries. On the 30th, the authorities arrested their friend Marinko for helping with the crowds. On the same day the visionaries asked Fr. Jozo if the apparitions could be held in the church, but he turned them down.

On the next day, July 1, the authorities moved in. The police blocked off access to Podbrdo and then came to Bijakovici to arrest the visionaries. The visionaries made a quick getaway and headed for the parish church of St. James. Meanwhile, Fr. Jozo, who was praying in the church, heard a voice telling him, "Protect the children." This was the sign from Heaven he had been praying for. Stepping outside he saw the terrified visionaries running toward the church. He took them to the rectory, where the apparition took place on that day. Following the apparition, he celebrated Mass. Thus began a new era in the history of the Medjugorje apparitions. From that day, a regular pattern was established: the apparitions would be in the church or on church property, following which there would be the celebration of Mass.

Fr. Jozo, however, had to pay a price for the "protection" of the children. As at Lourdes and Marpingen and in so many other sites of Marian apparitions, the civil authorities decided to fight fire with fire: what better way to end an "outbreak" of faith than by persuading the perceived "guardian" of faith to do the dirty work? The initial reaction of the newly installed bishop of Mostar, Pavao Zanic (consecrated in 1980), to the apparitions was not just positive but exuberant: "The children are not lying," he said. "If there were just one child one could say: 'This kid is so hard-headed that not even the police can make him speak.' But six innocent simple children like these would have told all in half an hour if anybody had been manipulating them." The bishop's train of thought here was and still is formidable (although he himself has long since abandoned it). But his strong support for the apparitions soon came to the attention of the authorities.

On July 4, 1981, Branko Mikulic, the president of Bosnia-Herzegovina (one of six republics in the erstwhile Yugoslavia), had branded the alleged apparitions as counter-revolutionary. The State Security Police, the UDBA (the Yugoslavian version of the KGB), summoned both the bishop of Mostar and Fr. Jozo Zovko to their offices in Sarajevo, threatening them with imprisonment unless they stopped supporting the apparitions. The two reacted differently to the same threat. Fr. Jozo continued his support; the bishop kept silent. The bishop then called Fr. Jozo to his office and discussed both the threat from the UDBA and a warning he received from his own diocesan priests who said that the bishop's support for the apparitions was elevating the prestige of their rivals, the Franciscans. Fr. Jozo was imprisoned by the UDBA on August 17, 1981, and sentenced to three and a half years of hard labor, although this was reduced to a year and a half. Neither during his trial nor his imprisonment did he receive any support or communication from Bishop Zanic. Fr. Jozo's imprisonment convinced the bishop that the UDBA was serious, and he began reversing the positive stand he had initially adopted. On his release from prison, Fr. Jozo visited Bishop Zanic at his office. The bishop told him that he had no choice but to back off from Medjugorje in view of the threats from both the state and from his diocesan priests; he said even the local Franciscan authorities were advising silence on Medjugorje because they needed the help of the UDBA.

The bishop's silence about Medjugorje erupted into open hostility when he realized that the phenomenon was beginning to attract thousands of people from around the world and also the support of such eminent theologians as Cardinal Hans Urs Von Balthasar and Fr. René Laurentin. Also, the chief champions of the apparitions in Medjugorje were the Franciscans, who had engaged in a long and bitter feud with the secular clergy. As bishop, he had two advantages: one, it was he who would ultimately decide on the authenticity of the apparitions; and two, he was both the repository of all data relating to the case and its principals and the disseminator to the world of the interpretations of the data. He issued several statements attacking both the visionaries and the Franciscan supporters of the apparitions. He also instituted a commission made up of individuals he personally appointed to investigate the apparition.

It was well known that the commission's report would be negative but, shortly before the report was published, the Vatican stepped in and removed all affairs relating to the apparition from the jurisdiction of the bishop. Henceforth the view of the bishop of Mostar on any issue relating to Medjugorje was to be considered nothing more than a private opinion. A letter from the Vatican in 1998 confirmed that this was the case even on the question of whether or not pilgrimages could be made to Medjugorje; the Vatican has no objection to private pilgrimages. The responsibility for investigation of the apparitions was transferred to the Yugoslavian Bishops Conference. In an interim report in 1990, the Conference said that they could not confirm whether or not there was anything supernatural involved at Medjugorje but that they would provide pastoral support for pilgrims to Medjugorje. It was rumored that in a 1991 meeting to be held in Mostar the Conference was going to forbid transmission of the messages from Medjugorje. But this meeting never took place. Shortly before it was to be held, war broke out and Yugoslavia was not only divided into different republics but Bosnia-Herzegovina, the republic to which Medjugorje belonged, became the center of some of the most savage and bloody battles in Europe since the Second World War.

Medjugorje itself was miraculously untouched by the violence all around it. A number of media reports noted this puzzling fact: how is it that Medjugorje, which lay at the very center of the bloody war in Bosnia, was entirely untouched by the fire and fury all around it throughout the war? The *Wall Street Journal,* in a November 9, 1992, front-page story, reported, "The war has enhanced Medjugorje's fame as an oasis of peace and mystery.... The sole air raid on the town ended with a few bombs exploding harmlessly.... 'You have to believe that either we are very lucky,' he [Dragan Kozina, the town's mayor] said, 'or that someone is protecting us.' "

From the first apparitions in 1981, the visionaries continued to see the Gospa daily and were endlessly investigated by scientists and reporters during the apparitions. In judging the authenticity of an apparition, what matters ultimately (in addition to the theological content of the messages) is the actual state of the visionary during the apparition. At the beginning of the typical Medjugorje apparition, the visionaries would suddenly and simultaneously cease whatever they were doing, kneel down, and turn their eyes toward the same point on the wall facing them and move their lips without any sound; this naturally inexplicable coordination would be followed by the state of ecstasy. The scientists and psychiatrists who have rigorously studied the phenomenon almost from its inception and more recently in April and July 1998 in Bologna, Italy, are unanimous on two conclusions: (a) the visionaries are normal people, and (b) their physiological processes during the apparitions show no clinical signs of hallucination, hysteria, neurosis, catalepsy, or pathological ecstasy. Moreover, the visionaries are insensitive to pain and various other kinds of sensory stimulation during the ecstasy. The April 1998 study included a whole battery of tests from neurological examinations and computerized polygraph tests to numerous other physiological and psychological tests. This latter study confirmed that the visionaries still continued to experience the same state of apparitional ecstasy observed in earlier studies (such as in 1985).

As noted at the beginning, Medjugorje has been the direct cause of hundreds of thousands of conversions and over a thousand documented cures. In addition

to this, many of the pilgrims have reported a stupendous variety of other supernatural phenomena ranging from Rosary links turning to gold to the kind of
solar miracles witnessed at Fatima. It would seem that the modern age is so cut
off from all sense of the supernatural that Heaven, when it acts decisively, has
to bring the full spectrum of signs and wonders to the table. Thus Padre Pio, the
saint for the twentieth century, was endowed with every one of the supernatural
gifts — the stigmata, reading of souls, bilocation, aroma, healing — whereas
saints in previous ages received only one or two such gifts. Likewise, Medjugorje seems to be "equipped" with all of the charisms that the apparitions of the
past possessed singly: conversion and evangelization as in Guadalupe; healing as
in Lourdes; penance, mortification, and reparation as in Fatima and a host of
other apparitions; apocalyptic secrets again as in Fatima and La Salette.

It has often been said that Medjugorje is the fulfillment of Fatima. Whereas
Fatima was the herald of the dawn of Communism, Medjugorje was the herald of
its dusk. Both apparitions contributed to the demise of Communism, Fatima in
unleashing a worldwide campaign of prayer and the subsequent papal consecration of Russia and Medjugorje in bringing about a worldwide religious revival
from the middle of a Communist country (many of the most devout pilgrims
came from other countries behind the Iron Curtain). The Medjugorje messages
made the first direct reference to Fatima after the failed coup of August 22,
1991. In her August 25, 1991, message, the Gospa said, "I invite you to renunciation for nine days so that with your help, everything I wanted to realize
through the secrets I began in Fatima may be fulfilled." The relation between
Medjugorje and Fatima was most clearly discerned by the countries in which
Russia had "spread its errors." Cardinal Frantizek Tomasek, the late archbishop
of Prague and former Communist concentration camp inmate, said Medjugorje
"fills me with a great inner joy, fills me with a great inner power." In a 1988
interview with *Medjugorge Gebetsaktion,* he said, "Personally, I am convinced
that Medjugorje is the continuation of Lourdes and Fatima. Step by step, the
Immaculate Heart of Mary will triumph. And I am also deeply convinced that
Medjugorje is a sign for this."

Medjugorje has certainly inspired a torrent of polemic mostly directed at
individuals and events that are tangential to the only relevant datum: the phenomenon itself. The generation of such polemic will not surprise those who have
studied the history of apparitions. For instance, the Beauraing and La Salette
claims spawned storms of controversy both within and outside the Church and
succeeded in confusing many of the faithful. The principals of Lourdes and Fatima were both subjected to abuse. It is entirely possible that if the intrepid
psychiatrists who conducted such elaborate tests on the visionaries were to study
some of the critics they might end up detecting some of the pathologies and
neuroses they failed to find in the visionaries!

Concerning the Medjugorje critics, it may be said that they are not developing
arguments; they are painting a certain picture, creating a certain history of the
events of Medjugorje. If this picture reflects the reality, if this history is true
to the facts, then someone who has not studied the sources for himself would
understandably be inclined to think that there is a cloud over Medjugorje. What

is required is an intellectual exorcism: First, one must lay out one's biases and agendas on the table before beginning the discussion. Second, the narrator must admit that there is more than one *account* of the facts and must attempt to present other accounts. Third, he or she must acknowledge that there is more than one *interpretation* of the facts and here again attempt to present other interpretations. Finally, it must be acknowledged that a presentation of history is not an argument.

If we go by the key criterion instituted by the Congregation for the Doctrine of the Faith (see appendix), the absence of any "psychopathic tendency in the person which might enter into the alleged supernatural event; no psychosis or collective hysteria of some type," then Medjugorje is an authentic apparition of the Virgin.

The other relevant consideration is the theological content of the messages. Even Bishop Zanic did not criticize the theology of the Medjugorje messages, his only complaint being that they are banal. (It might be responded that the repetition of eternal truths is not likely to furnish much in the way of novelty.) The Medjugorje messages, in fact, seem so orthodox and sensible that the chief allegation of the critics is that they were doctored by the Franciscans.

The logical structure of the charge of theological editing seems to be the following:

> The messages are theologically sound.
> Therefore they were doctored by the Franciscans.

Now if the messages were coming from the Virgin, one would expect them to be theologically sound. So what does this argument prove? Should the messages be theologically unsound so as to prove they are not from the Franciscans? And if they are theologically unsound will the critics accept them as coming from the Virgin? No possible answer will apparently satisfy this class of critic.

Fortunately it is fairly easy to show that — quite apart from the question of theological soundness — the Medjugorje messages could not have originated with the Franciscans. Consider this:

1. Who "created" the original messages from the Gospa? At the beginning of the phenomenon, the parish priest, Fr. Jozo Zovko, did not believe that the visionaries were witnessing an authentic apparition. Both he and his assistant pastor were skeptical — and only the bishop of Mostar believed the visionaries. So which Franciscans did the editing?

2. Fr. Jozo was imprisoned for a year and a half after he decided to protect the visionaries. So who created the messages during this period?

3. The Franciscans at the parish were regularly transferred — yet the messages have retained a uncanny consistency from the beginning to the present. In other words, the messages before the Franciscans got involved, during the crisis of Fr. Jozo's arrest, during the many transfers of parish priests, during the chaos of the war, and to this very day have consistently focused on central Gospel themes.

4. One Franciscan who has been a spiritual adviser to the visionaries, Fr. Slavko Barbaric, came to Medjugorje at the request of Bishop Zanic in order to investigate the authenticity of the apparition. He came as a skeptical psychiatrist but was so impressed with the evident sincerity and veracity of the visionaries that he remained with them giving them the direction they required for their spiritual formation. Like all human beings, the visionaries also need spiritual directors — as did St. Margaret Mary and many other visionaries of the past.

5. Often the messages of the visionaries were antithetical to the views and background of the Franciscans. For instance, when the visionaries asked the Gospa who was the holiest person in the village, she responded that a good example was a Moslem lady who lived there. Considering the historical animosity between the Franciscans and the Moslems, this could hardly be viewed as a Franciscan-edited message. On one occasion, the Gospa chided Vicka for asking so many questions about the Franciscans. Moreover, with reference to the war between the Croatians and the Serbs, she said that Satan was on both sides.

6. The visionaries have always said that the Gospa has asked them to respect, love, and pray for their bishop, the bishop of Mostar. Some of the Franciscans, on the other hand, have been less than respectful in their relations with the bishop. Here an incident of July 20, 1984, is especially revealing:

> "Open your hearts to me, come close. Say in a loud voice your intentions and your prayers." Our Lady was very attentive to the prayers of the visionaries. While praying for Bishop Zanic of Mostar, Her eyes welled up with tears and she says: "You are my little flowers. Continue to pray; my task is lighter because of it." She then blessed the visionaries and the people with a crucifix and ascended back to Heaven crying.

7. Very significant also is the fact that the visionaries have sometimes received messages from the Gospa that the Franciscans were unwilling to publicize, resulting in tension between the Franciscans and the visionaries. An example is the Gospa's message of a special blessing that can be received in Medjugorje; this is a message that the visionaries maintain as coming directly from the Gospa and which the Franciscans have tried to downplay. (Historically speaking, this message cannot be considered an anomaly: in other apparitions, the Virgin has spoken of special graces coming from the Miraculous Medal, the Scapular, the Rosary, the healing spring in Lourdes, etc.)

The Vatican's current position on Medjugorje was clearly enunciated by Archbishop Tarcisio Bertone, secretary of the Congregation for the Doctrine of the Faith, in a published interview (*Maria,* March–April 1999) with Dr. Fernand Sanchez, moderator general of the Community of the Beatitudes, and Fr. François-Xavier Wallays, a member of the Community's general council (their meeting took place in Rome on January 12, 1999). In response to a question from Dr. Sanchez, "Can we remain in Medjugorje and continue our apostolate there of evangelization with the pilgrims?" the archbishop stated, "Not only can you do so, but you must remain in Medjugorje, at the service of the pilgrims!" Dr. Sanchez then asked, "Can we continue to accompany private pilgrimages there?" To this the archbishop replied, "It is necessary to accompany private pilgrimages! For the moment, one should consider Medjugorje as a sanctuary, a Marian shrine, in the same way as Czestochowa." The comparison with Czestochowa is surely significant!

The Gospa has said that each of the visionaries will receive ten secrets, and when the six of them have received all ten secrets, the apparitions will cease and the apocalyptic events revealed in the secrets will begin to unfold. Among the ten secrets is the promise that, at the end of the apparitions, Medjugorje itself will be the site of a lasting "Great Sign" that will convince the skeptics. To date, three of the visionaries (Mirjana, Ivanka, and Jackov) have received all ten secrets and the other three have received nine. The three who have received the ten secrets, no longer have daily apparitions. On the 25th of every month, the Gospa gives the visionaries a message that is intended for the world. (About the concept of secrets, we read this in St. Paul: "But I will move on to the visions and revelations I have had from the Lord. I know a man in Christ who, fourteen years ago, was caught up — whether still in the body or out of the body, I do not know; God knows — right into the third heaven. I do know, however, that this same person — whether in the body or out of the body, I do not know; God knows — was caught up into paradise and heard things which must not and cannot be put into human language" [2 Cor. 12: 1–4].)

In his brilliant book *Heaven Wants to Be Heard,* the British scholar Dudley Plunkett lists the following spiritual appeals of the Medjugorje messages as Heaven's message to the modern world:

- Attend daily Mass (March 30, 1984).

- Offer three hours of prayer a day (July 4, 1983).

- Pray three Rosaries each day (August 14, 1984) as well as seven Paters, Aves, and Glorias for peace.

- Go to monthly confession (August 6, 1982).

- Give time for adoration of the Blessed Sacrament (March 15, 1984).

- Read the Scriptures daily (October 18, 1994).

- Pray before the Cross (September 12, 1985).

- Observe family prayer (October 20, 1983).

- Make an act of consecration to the Sacred Heart of Jesus and to the Immaculate Heart of Mary (October 25, 1988).

- Undertake pilgrimages, penance, sacrifices, and fast on bread and water twice a week (June 27, 1981).

In the final analysis this is what Medjugorje is all about. This is why it has attracted fifty thousand priests and religious and converted millions of men, women, and children. Herein is set forth the banquet of grace to which the Mother of God who is the Mother of Humanity invites all her children — especially those most in need of the Divine Mercy.

Description of the Virgin

"She has black hair, a bit curly, blue eyes, rosy cheeks, slender, beautiful." She has a beautiful smile and her voice has been compared to music. She is three-dimensional and has often been embraced. She wears a grayish gown but on feast days she wears a gold gown. There is a crown of twelve stars over her head, and she appears on a cloud.

Messages

The Medjugorje Program:
A Formula for the Happiness of Heaven

Medjugorje is essentially a divinely designed program of conversion and consecration, purification and protection, sanctification and salvation, and finally human participation in the divine plan. The hundreds of messages received at Medjugorje form a blueprint for becoming and being a Christian in the modern world. Moreover, each component of the program in one sense is identical with every other component because they are all simply different ways of looking at the same fundamental reality of union/reconciliation/peace with God. Thus conversion = consecration = purification = protection = sanctification = salvation = participation in the plans of God.

It is quite apparent that the possibility of living a truly Christian life has never been as difficult — in terms of the temptations of the world, the flesh, and the devil — in any era as it is today. Evil, packaged in a thousand attractive and instantly gratifying incarnations, is all but irresistible, even to the very elect. The intellect, the will, and every one of the senses have been seduced and subjugated by the most ingeniously invasive vehicles of sin imaginable (from global cable television to widely used hallucinogens). Never has the soul been in such peril as it is today.

But just as she came "out of the blue" to the seat of the Enlightenment (Paris, France, in 1830) and the heart of the pagan New World (Tepeyac, Mexico, 1531), the Virgin initiated an innocuous but instantly effective counterattack against all that is evil in modernity in the country which triggered off this century's first great wave of destruction.

The Medjugorje messages can be classified under the categories that form its basic program: conversion, which literally means ripping out the root of evil in us implanted by original sin and hardened by the modern world; consecration, the complete surrender of all that we are and have to God, a letting-go that is as unsettling as it is comforting; purification, the eradication of the "habits" of sin and the allure of temptations through fasting and penance; protection from the world, the flesh, and the devil through prayer from the heart and the use of all the aids given us by God; sanctification, through the sacraments and again prayer;

salvation, with graphic portrayals of the consequences of our present choices in the life to come; and human participation in the divine plan, an unveiling of the impact of our actions and our prayers on God's scheme of salvation for the human race. In practical terms, the program calls us to daily Mass, monthly confession, daily prayer of three hours (this includes the time spent at Mass and praying the Rosary), and fasting on bread and water on Wednesdays and Fridays. The Medjugorje program is the divine Physician's life-support system for the patients who lie comatose in the intensive care units of the inferno of modern life; it is a formula for both sanity and sanctity in a world that knows neither.

In sum, the Medjugorje program if wholeheartedly embraced and applied, will set us on the path of salvation, and its sanctifying fruits will soon become evident in our personal experience (as millions can testify). But, warns the program director, any departure, any deviation from the program, no matter how slight or innocuous, can be disastrous, exposing us to the full fury of the world, the flesh, and the devil. We dare not make any exception lest we be defiled. "Satisfaction" is guaranteed, but only if the conditions are met.

Of these conditions, the one emphasized in almost every one of the messages is prayer, prayer that is all but constant, prayer from the heart. The heart is very important in everything about Medjugorje: it is a program of the heart from the Queen of hearts: she leads our hearts to her Immaculate Heart and through that to the Sacred Heart of her Son. There can be no earthly way to communicate the joy that comes from entering the life of prayer from the heart; it is so easy to enter and yet so easy to overlook for years and years and even throughout one's life. Hence the Gospa's constant reminder to "Pray! Pray! Pray!" But prayer to be fruitful must be undergirded by three other conditions that are again consistently taught at Medjugorje: utter humility, reconciliation with all our brothers and sisters, and total consecration to Jesus through Mary. Humility is fundamental: we can do nothing by ourselves; we have to let God do everything and be humble instruments in His Hands. This means we should not have any trust in our own abilities or our own spiritual strength: we must recognize that all we are and have comes from God and God has to continually sustain these (and the one good that God brings about from our falling into sin is this recognition). Then there is reconciliation: complete forgiveness of all those who may have hurt or insulted us is essential for us to start on the path to Heaven. Jesus' warnings about God not forgiving those who cannot forgive their brothers have to be taken seriously — and they are at Medjugorje. Finally, we have to be totally consecrated to Jesus through Mary. We must be consciously and constantly aware that we have entrusted our entire being to God through the hands of the Blessed Mother. There is no alternative to surrender of the self in its entirety. No part of us can be our own — because anything we own or control inevitably falls under the world, the flesh, or the devil. Once we make this consecration, once we give all that we own materially or spiritually, most especially the spiritual merits of any of our actions, to Jesus through Mary, we can be fully protected from our enemies.

The messages that embody the basic elements of the Medjugorje program are presented below.

Conversion

"I have come because there are many true believers here. I wish to be with you to convert and to reconcile the whole world."

"Peace, Peace, Peace! Be reconciled! Only Peace. Make your peace with God among yourselves. For that, it is necessary to believe, to pray, to fast, and to go to confession." (June 26, 1981)

"When God is with you, you have everything; but when you do not want Him, then you are miserable and lost and you do not know on whose side you are. Therefore, dear children, decide for God and then you will get everything." (December 25, 1991)

"Dear children, today I want to call all of you to decide for Paradise. The way is difficult for those who have not decided for God. Dear children, decide and believe that God is offering Himself to you in His fullness. You are invited and you need to answer the call of the Father, who is calling you through me. Pray, because in prayer each one of you will be able to achieve complete love. I am blessing you and I desire to help you so that each one of you might be under my motherly mantle." (October 25, 1987)

"Dear children, today again I am calling you to complete conversion, which is difficult for those who have not chosen God. I am calling you, dear children, to convert fully to God. God can give you everything that you seek from Him. But you seek God only when sickness, problems, and difficulties come to you, and you think that God is far from you and is not listening and does not hear your prayers. No, dear children, that is not the truth! When you are far from God, you cannot receive graces because you do not seek them with a firm faith. Day by day, I am praying for you, and I want to draw you ever closer to God; but I cannot if you don't want it. Therefore, dear children, put your life in God's hands. I bless you all. Thank you for having responded to my call." (January 25, 1988)

"Dear children, I, your Mother, love you; and I wish to urge you to prayer. I am, dear children, tireless; and I call you even when you are far away from my heart. I feel pain for everyone who has gone astray. But I am a Mother and I forgive easily; and I rejoice for every child who comes back to me! Thank you for your response to my call." (November 14, 1985)

"Dear children, today I want to wrap you all in my mantle and lead you all along the way of conversion. Dear children, I beseech you, surrender to the Lord your entire past, all the evil that has accumulated in your hearts. I want each one of you to be happy. Therefore, dear children, pray, and in prayer you shall realize a new way of joy. Joy will be manifest in your hearts, and thus you shall be joyful witnesses of that which I and my Son want from each one of you. I am blessing you." (February 25, 1987)

"Dear children, today I am grateful to you for your presence in this place, where I am giving you special graces. I call each one of you to begin to live as of today that life which God wishes of you and to begin to perform good works of love and mercy. I do not want you, dear children, to live the message and be committing sin which is displeasing to me. Therefore, dear children, I want each of you to live a new life without the murder of all that God produces in you and is giving you. I give you my special blessing and I am remaining with you on your way to conversion." (March 25, 1987)

"Dear children, I am calling every one of you to start living in God's love. Dear children, you are ready to commit sin, and to put yourselves in the hands of Satan without reflecting. I call on each one of you to consciously decide for God and against Satan. I am your mother and, therefore, I want to lead you all to complete holiness. I want each one of you to be happy here on earth and to be with me in Heaven. That is, dear children, the purpose of my coming here and it's my desire." (May 25, 1987)

"Dear children, today I bless you in a special way with my motherly blessing and I intercede for you to God for Him to give you the gift of the conversion of the heart. For years I have been calling you to encourage you to a profound spiritual life in simplicity, but you are so cold! Therefore, little children, accept with seriousness and live the messages for your soul not to be sad when I will not be with you anymore and when I will not guide you anymore like an insecure child in his first steps." (December 25, 1989)

"Dear children, today, as never before, I invite you to live my messages and to put them into practice in your life. I have come to you to help you, and, therefore, I invite you to change your life because you have taken a path of misery, a path of ruin. When I told you, 'Convert, pray, fast, and be reconciled,' you took these messages superficially. You started to live them, and then you stopped because it was difficult for you. Know, dear children, when something is good, you have to persevere in the good and not think, 'God does not see me, He is not listening, He is not helping.' And so, you have gone away from me because of your miserable interests. I wanted to create of you an oasis of peace, love, and goodness. God wanted you, with your love and His help, to work miracles and, thus, give example. Therefore, here is what I say to you, 'Satan is playing with you and with your souls and I cannot help you because you are far from my heart.' Therefore, pray, live my messages, and then you will see the miracles of God's love in your everyday life." (March 25, 1992)

"I invite you to decide for God, and He will protect you and show you what you should do and which path to take. I invite all of those who have said yes to me to renew their consecration to my Son, Jesus, and to His Heart and to me, so we can take you more intensely as instruments of peace in this unpeaceful world." (April 25, 1992)

"Dear children, today I am happy despite there being some sadness still in my heart for all those who began to take this path and then abandoned it. My presence here is, therefore, to lead you on a new path, the path of salvation. Thus, I call you day after day to conversion; but if you do not pray, you cannot say that you are converting. I pray for you and intercede before God for peace:

First for peace in your hearts, then around you, so that God may be your peace." (June 25, 1992)

"Dear Children! Today I invite you again to put prayer in the first place in your families. Little children, when God is in the first place, then you will, in all that you do, seek the will of God. In this way your daily conversion will become easier. Little children, seek with humility that which is not in order in your hearts, and you shall understand what you have to do. Conversion will become a daily duty that you will do with joy. Little children, I am with you, I bless you all, and I invite you to become my witnesses by prayer and personal conversion." (April 25, 1996)

"Dear children! Today I invite you to decide every day for God. Little children, you speak much about God, but you witness little with your life. Therefore, little children, decide for conversion, that your life may be true before God, so that in the truth of your life you witness the beauty God gave you. Little children, I invite you again to decide for prayer, because through prayer, you will be able to live the conversion." (July 25, 1996)

"Dear children, today, I call you to become my witnesses by living the faith of your fathers. Little children, you seek signs and messages and do not see that, with every morning sunrise, God calls you to convert and to return to the way of truth and salvation. You speak much, little children, but you work little on your conversion. That is why, convert and start to live my messages, not with your words but with your life. In this way, little children, you will have the strength to decide for the true conversion of the heart." (September 25, 1998)

Consecration

"Dear children, today I am calling you to a complete surrender to God. Everything you do and everything that you possess give over to God so that He can take control in your life as King of all that you possess. That way, through me God can lead you into the depths of the spiritual life. Little children, do not be afraid because I am with you even when you think there is no way out and that Satan is in control. I am bringing peace to you. I am your Mother and the Queen of Peace. I am blessing you with the blessing of joy so that for you God may be everything in life." (July 25, 1988)

"Dear children, I invite you to decide completely for God. I beg you, dear children, to surrender yourselves completely and you will be able to live everything I say to you. It will not be difficult for you to surrender yourselves completely to God." (January 2, 1986)

"Dear children, today also I am calling you to a complete surrender to God. You, dear children, are not conscious of how God loves you with such a great love. Because of it He permits me to be with you so I can instruct you and help you to find the way of peace. That way, however, you cannot discover if you do not pray. Therefore, dear children, forsake everything and consecrate your time to God and then God will bestow gifts upon you and bless you. Little children, do not forget that your life is fleeting like the spring flower which today is wondrously beautiful, but tomorrow has vanished. Therefore, pray in such a way that your prayer, your surrender to God may become like a road sign. That way, your witness will not only have value for yourselves, but for all of eternity." (March 25, 1988)

"Dear children, I am calling you to a complete surrender to God. Let everything that you possess be in the hands of God. Only in that way shall you have joy in your heart. Little children, rejoice in everything that you have and give thanks to God because everything is God's gift to you. That way in your life you should be able to give thanks for everything and discover God in everything, even in the smallest flower." (April 25, 1989)

"Little children, I am with you and unceasingly I desire to lead you into the joy of life. I desire that each one of you discovers the joy and the love which is found only in God and which only God can give. God wants nothing else from you but your surrender. Therefore, little children, decide seriously for God because everything passes away. God alone does not pass away. Pray that you may discover the greatness and the joy of life which God is giving you." (May 25, 1989)

"Dear children, I wish to tell you that I have chosen this parish. I guard it in my hands as a little flower that doesn't want to die. I am begging you to give yourselves to me so that I can offer you as a gift to God, fresh and without sin. Satan has taken one part of the plan and wants to possess it. Pray that he does not succeed because I desire to have you for myself so I can offer you to God." (August 1, 1985)

"Dear children, abandon yourselves to me so that I can lead you totally. Do not be preoccupied about material things." (April 17, 1986)

"Dear children, today I am calling you to give me your heart so I can transform it to be like mine. You are asking yourselves, dear children, why you cannot respond to what I am asking from you. You cannot, because you have not given me your heart so I can change it. You are speaking, but you are not acting. I call you to do everything I tell you. In that way, I will be with you." (May 15, 1986)

"Dear children, today also I call each one of you to decide again and to surrender yourself completely to me. Only that way will I be able to present each of you to God. Dear children, you know that I love you immeasurably and that I desire each of you for myself, but God has given to all the freedom which I lovingly respect and humbly submit to. I desire, dear children, that you help me so that everything God has planned in this parish shall be realized. If you do not pray, you shall not be able to recognize my love and the plans which God has for this parish and for each individual. Pray that Satan does not entice you with his pride and deceptive strength. I am with you, and I wish you to believe that I love you." (November 25, 1987)

"Dear children, my call that you live the messages which I am giving you is a daily one, especially, little children, because I want to draw you closer to the

Heart of Jesus. Therefore, little children, I am calling you today to the prayer of consecration to Jesus, my dear Son, so that each of your hearts may be His. And then I am calling you to consecration to my Immaculate Heart. I want you to consecrate yourselves as persons, families, and parishes so that all belongs to God through my hands. Therefore, little children, pray that you may comprehend the greatness of this message which I am giving you. I do not want anything for myself, but rather all for the salvation of your souls. Satan is strong and, therefore, you, little children, by constant prayer, press tightly to my motherly heart." (October 25, 1988)

Purification

Purification comes from mortification, for mortification defangs the desires of the flesh. In the Old and the New Testaments, fasting is the main vehicle of mortification. It is portrayed as a tool of cleansing and a weapon against the enemy. Jesus Himself fasted before facing trials and temptations. Medjugorje has brought back to the modern world the ancient Christian practice of fasting (on bread and water) on Wednesdays and Fridays. But to be effective as a means of purification, says the Medjugorje program, fasting must be complemented by prayer. In her earliest messages, the Blessed Mother asked for three hours of prayer a day. To the priests she said, "Each of you could pray even four hours a day" (April 24, 1984).

"The best fast is on bread and water. Through fasting and prayer one can stop wars, one can suspend the natural laws of nature. Works of charity cannot replace fasting. Those who are not able to fast can sometime replace it with prayer, charity, and a confession; but everyone except the sick has to fast." (July 21, 1982)

"I ask the people to pray with me these days. Pray all the more. Fast strictly on Wednesday and Friday. Say every day at least one Rosary: joyful, sorrowful, and glorious mysteries." (August 14, 1984)

"Persevere in fasting." (June 25, 1982)

To Ivan: "Observe the complete fasts, Wednesdays and Fridays. Pray at least an entire Rosary: joyous, sorrowful, and glorious mysteries." (August 14, 1985)

Ivanka after her annual apparition: "Our Lady pleaded with us to defeat Satan. 'The weapon to defeat him is prayer and fasting. Pray for peace for Satan wants to destroy the little peace you have.' " (June 25, 1992)

"Dear children! Also today I call you to fasting and renunciation. Little children, renounce that which hinders you from being closer to Jesus. In a special way I call you: Pray, because only through prayer will you be able to overcome your will and discover the will of God even in the smallest things. By your daily life, little children, you will become an example and witness that you live for Jesus or against Him and His will. Little children, I desire that you become apostles of love. By loving, little children, it will be recognized that you are mine." (March 25, 1998)

"Dear children, everything has its time. Today, I invite you to start working on your hearts. All the work in the fields is finished. You found time to clean even the least important places, but you have left your hearts aside. Work more, and, with love, clean every corner of your hearts. Thank you for your response to my call." (October 17, 1985)

"Excuse me for making you repeat, but I wish you to sing with the heart. You must really do everything with the heart."

    "[At the beginning of prayer] one has to be already prepared. If there are some sins, one must pull them out, otherwise, one will not be able to enter into prayer. If one has concerns, he should submit them to God. You must not preoccupy yourselves during prayer. During prayer, you must not be preoccupied with your sins. Sins must remain behind." (February 1985)

"Dear children, I am calling you to an active approach to prayer. You wish to live everything I am telling you, but you do not have results from your efforts because you do not pray. Dear children, I beg you to open yourselves and begin to pray. Prayer will be joy. If you begin, it will not be boring because you will pray out of pure joy. Thank you for your response to my call." (March 20, 1986)

"Dear children, today also, I invite you to prepare your hearts for these days when the Lord is about to purify you in a special way from all the sins of your past life. Dear children, you cannot do it by yourselves; and, for that reason, I am here to help you. Pray, dear children! That's the only way you will be able to recognize all the evil that dwells in you and abandon it to the Lord so that He may purify your hearts completely. So, dear children, pray without ceasing and prepare your hearts in penance and fasting." (December 4, 1986)

"Dear children, I invite you to surrender to God. In this season, I want you to renounce all the things to which you are attached but that hurt your spiritual life. Therefore, little children, decide completely for God, and do not allow Satan to come into your life through those things that hurt both you and your spiritual life. Little children, God is offering Himself to you in fullness and you can discover and recognize Him only in prayer. Make a decision for prayer." (February 25, 1990)

"Dear children! Today, in a special way, I invite you to take the cross in the hands and to meditate on the wounds of Jesus. Ask of Jesus to heal your wounds, which you, dear children, during your life sustained because of your sins or the sins of your parents. Only in this way, dear children, will you understand that the world is in need of healing of faith in God the Creator. By Jesus' passion and death on the cross, you will understand that only through prayer you, too, can become true apostles of faith, when, in simplicity and prayer, you live faith, which is a gift." (March 25, 1997)

"Dear children, today I invite all of you who have heard my message of peace to realize it with seriousness and with love in your life. There are many who think they are doing a lot by talking about the messages but do not live them. Dear children, I invite you to life and to change all the negative in you so that it all turns into the positive, and into life. Dear children, I am with you and I desire to help each of you to live and, by living, to witness to the good news. I am here, dear children, to help you and to lead you to Heaven. In Heaven is the joy through which you can already live Heaven now." (May 25, 1991)

Protection

To Mirjana: "Excuse me for this, but you must realize that Satan exists. One day he appeared before the throne of God and asked permission to submit the Church to a period of trial. God gave him permission to try the Church for one century. This century is under the power of the devil, but when the secrets confided to you come to pass, his power will be destroyed. Even now he is beginning to lose his power and has become aggressive. He is destroying marriages, creating division among priests, and is responsible for obsessions and murder. You must protect yourselves against these things through fasting and prayer, especially community prayer. Carry blessed objects with you. Put them in your house, and restore the use of holy water." (1982)

Mirjana Dragicevic, in an interview with Fr. Tomislav Vlasic:
    Q: "Tell me where the devil is especially active today. Did she tell you anything about this? Through whom or what does he manifest himself the most?"
    M: "Most of all through people of weak character, who are divided within themselves. Such people are everywhere, and they are the easiest for the devil to enter. But he also enters the lives of strong believers — sisters, for example. He would rather 'convert' real believers than nonbelievers. How can I explain this? You saw what happened to me. He tries to bring as many believers as possible to himself." (January 10, 1983)

"Dear children, these days you have been experiencing how Satan is working. I am always with you and do not be afraid of temptations. God is always watching over you. I have given myself up to you and I sympathize with you even in the smallest temptations." (July 19, 1984)

"Dear children, these days you have savored the sweetness of God through renewal in your parish. Satan is working even more violently to take away the joy from each of you. Through prayer you can totally disarm him and ensure your happiness." (January 24, 1985)

"Dear children, today I am begging you to put more blessed objects in your homes, and that every person should carry blessed objects on himself. Let everything be blessed so that Satan will tempt you less because you are armed against him." (July 18, 1985)

"Dear children, I want to shepherd you, but you do not want to obey my messages. Today I call you to obey my messages, and then you will be able to live everything that God tells me to relate to you. Open yourselves to God, and God will work through you and give you everything you need." (July 25, 1985)

To Mirjana, at Sarajevo: "My dear children! I come to you in order to lead you to purity of soul and then to God. Whenever I come to you my Son comes with me, but so does Satan. You permitted, without noticing, his influences on you, and he drives you on. Sometimes you understand that something you have done is not agreeable to God, but quickly you no longer pay attention to it. Do not let this happen, my children. Wipe from my face the tears that I cry in seeing what you do. Wake up to yourselves. Take time to meet with God in the church. Come to visit in your Father's house. Take the time to meet among yourselves for family prayer and implore the grace of God. Remember your deceased. Give them joy with the celebration of the Holy Mass. Do not look with scorn on those who beg you for a piece of bread. Do not turn them away from your full tables. Help them and God will also help you. Perhaps it is in this way that God will hear you, and the blessing that He wants to give you in thanks will be realized. You have forgotten all this my children. Satan has influenced you also in this. Do not let that happen! Pray with me! Do not deceive yourselves into thinking, 'I am good, but my brother next door is no good.' You would be wrong. I, your Mother, love you, and it is for that reason that I am warning you about this." (January 28, 1987)

At Ivanka's Annual Apparition: "Pray because you are in great temptation and danger because the world and material goods lead you into slavery. Satan is active in this plan. I want to help each of you in prayer. I am interceding to my Son for you." (June 25, 1989)

"Dear children, you know I promised you an Oasis of Peace here, but you are not aware that around every oasis is a desert where Satan is lurking. He wants to tempt each one of you. Dear children, only by prayer are you able to overcome every influence of Satan in your place. I am with you, but I can't take away your free will." (August 7, 1986)

"Dear children, today, also, I want to show you how much I love you. I am sorry that I am not able to help each and every one of you to fathom my love! Therefore, dear children, I am calling you to prayer and complete surrender to God, because Satan wants to conquer you in everyday affairs. He wants to take the first place in your life. Therefore, pray, dear children, without ceasing." (October 16, 1986)

"Dear children, Satan is strong and is waiting to test each one of you. Pray, and that way he will neither be able to injure you nor block you on the way to holiness. Dear children, through prayer grow all the more toward God from day to day." (September 25, 1987)

"Dear children, I am calling you to a complete surrender to God. Pray, little children, that Satan does not sway you like branches in the wind. Be strong in God. I desire that through you the whole world may get to know the God of joy. Neither be anxious nor worried. God will help you and show you the way. I want you to love all men with my love, both the good and the bad. Only that way will love conquer the world. Little children, you are mine. I love you and I want you to surrender to me so I can lead you to God. Pray without ceasing so that Satan cannot take advantage of you. Pray so that you realize that you are mine. I bless you with the blessing of joy." (May 25, 1988)

"Dear children, I am with you, even if you are not conscious of it. I want to protect you from everything that Satan offers you and through which he wants to destroy you. As I bore Jesus in my womb, so also, dear children, do I want to bear you on to holiness. God wants to save you and send you messages through men, nature and so many things which can only help you to understand; but you must change the direction in your life. Therefore, little children, understand also the greatness of the gift which God is giving you through me, so that I may protect you with my Mantle and lead you to the joy of life." (March 25, 1990)

"Dear children, today I invite you so that your prayer will be prayer with the heart. Let each of you find time for prayer so that in your prayer you discover God. I do not desire you to talk about prayer, but to pray. Let every day be filled with prayer of gratitude to God for life and for all that you have. I do not desire your life to pass by in words, but that you glorify God with deeds. I am with you, I am grateful to God for every moment spent with you." (April 25, 1991)

"Dear children, today I invite you to draw still closer to God through prayer. Only in that way will I be able to help you and to protect you from every attack of Satan. I am with you, and I intercede for you with God, that He protect you; but I need your prayers and your "yes." You get lost easily in material and human things and forget that God is your greatest friend. Therefore, my dear little children, draw close to God so He may protect you and guard you from every evil." (February 25, 1992)

"Dear children, today also I wish to tell you I am with you in these restless days in which Satan wishes to destroy everything which I and my Son, Jesus, are building up. In a special way, he wishes to destroy your souls. He wishes to guide you as far away as possible from Christian life as well as from the Commandments to which the Church is calling you so you may live them. Satan wishes to destroy everything that is Holy in you and around you. Therefore, little children, Pray! Pray! Pray! in order to be able to comprehend all that God is giving you through my coming." (September 25, 1992)

"Dear children, these years I have been calling you to pray, to live what I am telling you, but you are living my messages a little. You talk but do not live. That is why, my dear little children, this war is lasting so long. I invite you to open yourselves to God and to live with God in your hearts, living the good and giving witness to my messages. I love you and wish to protect you from every evil, but you do not desire it. Dear children, I cannot help you if you do not live God's Commandments, if you do not live the Mass, if you do not abandon sin. I invite you to become Apostles of love and goodness. In this world without peace, give witness to God and God's love and God will bless you and give you what you seek of Him." (October 25, 1993)

"Dear children! Today I invite you to come still closer to me through prayer. Little children, I am your mother, I love you, and I desire that each of you be saved and thus be with me in Heaven. That is why, little children, pray, pray, pray until your life becomes prayer." (August 25, 1998)

"If you pray, Satan cannot injure you even a little, because you are God's children and He is watching over you. Pray, and let the Rosary always be in your hands as a sign to Satan that you belong to me." (February 25, 1988)

"Dear children, I ask you to ask everyone to pray the Rosary. With the Rosary you will overcome all the troubles which Satan is trying to inflict on the Catholic Church."

    Marija: "Our Lady, what do you wish to say to the priests?"

    Our Lady: "Let all priests pray the Rosary. Give time to the Rosary." (June 25, 1985)

"Dear children, today I am calling you to pray against Satan in a special way. Satan wants to work more now that you know he is active. Dear children, dress up in clothes of armor against Satan. With Rosaries in your hands, you will conquer." (August 8, 1985)

"Dear children, today I am begging you to pray the Rosary with lively faith. Only in this way can I help you. Pray! I cannot help you because you don't want to be moved! Dear children, I am calling you to pray the Rosary. The Rosary should be your commitment, prayed by you with joy and so you will understand why I am visiting you for such a long time. I want to teach you to pray!" (June 12, 1986)

"Dear children, today, like never before, I invite you to prayer. Your prayer should be a prayer for peace. Satan is strong and wishes not only to destroy human life, but also nature and the planet on which we live. Therefore, dear children, pray that you can protect yourselves, through prayer, with the blessing of God's peace. God sends me to you so that I can help you if you wish to accept the Rosary. Even a Rosary alone can work miracles in the world and in your lives. I bless you and I stay among you as long as it is God's will. Thank you for not betraying my presence here, and I thank you because your response is serving God and peace." (January 25, 1991)

"Dear children! God gives me this time as a gift to you, so that I may instruct and lead you on the path of salvation. Dear children, now you do not comprehend this grace, but soon a time will come when you will lament for these messages. That is why, little children, live all of the words which I have given you through this time of grace and renew prayer, until prayer becomes a joy for you. Especially, I call all those who have consecrated themselves to my Immaculate Heart to become an example to others. I call all priests and religious brothers and sisters to pray the Rosary and to teach others to pray. The Rosary, little children, is especially dear to me. Through the Rosary open your heart to me and I am able to help you." (August 25, 1997)

"For the cure of the sick, it is important to say the following prayers: the Creed, and seven times each the Lord's Prayer, the Hail Mary, and the Glory Be, and to fast on bread and water. It is good to impose one's hands on the sick and to pray. It is good to anoint the sick with holy oil. All priests do not have the gift of healing. In order to receive this gift, the priest must pray with perseverance and believe firmly." (July 25, 1982)

Sanctification

"Dear children, I want to dress you from day to day in holiness, goodness, obedience, and love of God so that from day to day you can be better prepared for your Lord. Dear children, listen to my messages and live them. I desire to lead you. Thank you for your response to my call." (October 24, 1985)

"Dear children, today I invite you to holiness. You cannot live without holiness. Consequently, overcome all sin with love. Overcome every difficulty you meet with love. Dear children, I beg you to live love within yourselves. Thank you for your response to my call." (July 10, 1986)

"How must we pray?" "Continue to recite the Lord's Prayer, the Hail Mary, and the Glory Be seven times, but also add the Creed. Good-bye, my angels. Go in the peace of God." (June 27, 1981)

"Dear children, tonight your Mother wishes to call you, as I have before, to renew prayer in the family. Dear children, families need to pray today. It is my wish, dear children, that you would live my messages through family prayer." (January 1, 1990)

"Dear children, today I wish to tell you: Always pray before your work and end your work with prayer. If you do that, God will bless you and your work. These days you have been praying too little and working too much. Pray, therefore. In prayer you will find rest. Thank you for responding to my call." (July 5, 1984)

"Dear children, today I am calling you to prayer. Without prayer, you cannot feel me, nor God, nor the graces I am giving you. Therefore, I call you always to begin and end each day with prayer. Dear children, I wish to lead you evermore in prayer, but you cannot grow because you don't want it. I invite you to let prayer have the first place. Thank you for your response to my call." (July 3, 1986)

"When I say 'pray, pray, pray,' I do not only want to say to increase the number of hours of prayer but also to reinforce the desire for prayer, and to be in contact with God. Place yourself permanently in a state of spirit bathed in prayer." (June 26, 1984)

"Dear children, again, I invite you to prayer of the heart. If you pray from your heart, dear children, the ice cold hearts of your brothers will be melted and every barrier will disappear. Conversion will be easily achieved by those who want it. You must intercede for this gift for your neighbors. Thank you for your response to my call." (January 23, 1986)

"Dear children, today, again, I invite you to prayer. You, dear children, do not realize the preciousness of prayer until you say nothing else. Now is the time of prayer. Now, nothing else is important. Now, nobody is important except God. Dear children, dedicate yourselves to prayer with special love and, only in that way, can God give you graces. Thank you for your response to my call." (October 2, 1986)

"Dear children, today I am also inviting you to pray with your whole heart and to change your life day by day. I am especially calling you, dear children, to begin to live a life of holiness by your prayers and sacrifices. I wish that each of you who has come to this holy place, the spring of grace, may come into paradise with a special gift which He will give to me; and this gift is holiness. Therefore, dear children, pray every day of your life in order that you may become holy. I will be forever close to you." (November 13, 1986)

"Dear children, today I am calling you to prayer of the heart. Throughout this season of grace, I desire each of you to be united with Jesus; but without unceasing prayer, you cannot experience the beauty and greatness of the grace which God is offering you. Therefore, little children, at all times fill your heart with even the smallest prayers. I am with you and unceasingly I keep watch over every heart which is given to me." (February 25, 1989)

"I desire to lead you toward prayer with the heart. Only in this way will you comprehend that your life is empty without prayer. You will discover the meaning of your life when you discover God in prayer. That is why, little children, open the door of your heart and you will comprehend that prayer is joy without which you cannot live." (July 25, 1997)

"Dear children! Today I call you to comprehend that without love you cannot comprehend that God needs to be in the first place in your life. That is why, little children, I call you all to love, not with a human love but with God's love. In this way, your life will be more beautiful and without an interest. You will comprehend that God gives Himself to you in the simplest way out of love. Little children, so that you may comprehend my words which I give you out of love, pray, pray, pray, and you will be able to accept others with love and to forgive all who have done evil to you. Respond with prayer; prayer is a fruit of love toward God the Creator." (September 25, 1997)

"One must invite people to go to Confession each month, especially the first Saturday. Here, I have not spoken of it yet. I have invited people to frequent Confession. I will give you yet some concrete messages for our time. Be patient because the time has not yet come. Do what I have told you. There are numerous people who do not observe it. Monthly Confession will be a remedy for the Church in the West. One must convey this message to the West." (August 6, 1982)

"Dear children! Today I call you to prepare yourselves for the coming of Jesus. In a special way, prepare your hearts. May holy Confession be the first act of conversion for you and then, dear children, decide for holiness. May your conversion and decision for holiness begin today and not tomorrow. Little children, I call you all to the way of salvation and I desire to show you the way to Heaven. That is why, little children, be mine and decide with me for holiness. Little children, accept prayer with seriousness and pray, pray, pray. Thank you for having responded to my call." (November 25, 1998)

"Mass is the greatest prayer of God. You will never be able to understand its greatness. That is why you must be perfect and humble at Mass, and you should prepare yourselves for it." (1983)

"Dear children, I wish to call you to live the Holy Mass. There are many of you who have experienced the beauty of the Mass, but there are some who come unwillingly. I have chosen you, dear children; and Jesus is giving you His graces in the Holy Mass. Therefore, consciously live the Holy Mass. Let every coming to Holy Mass be joyful. Come with love and accept the Holy Mass." (April 3, 1986)

"I call you to be responsible and determined and to consecrate each day to God in prayer. May Holy Mass, little children, not be a habit for you, but life. By living Holy Mass each day, you will feel the need for holiness and you will grow in holiness. I am close to you and intercede before God for each of you, so that He may give you strength to change your heart. Thank you for having responded to my call." (January 25, 1998)

"Dear children, God wants to make you holy. Therefore, through me He is calling you to complete surrender. Let the Holy Mass be your life." (April 25, 1988)

"I would like to guide you spiritually, but I would not know how to help you if you are not open. It suffices for you to think, for example, where you were with your thoughts yesterday during Mass. When you go to Mass, your trip from home to church should be a time of preparation for Mass. You should also receive Holy Communion with an open and pure heart, with purity of heart and with openness. Do not leave the church without an appropriate act of thanksgiving. I can only help you if you are accessible to my suggestions; I cannot help you if you are not open. The most important thing in the spiritual life is to ask for the gift of the Holy Spirit. When the Holy Spirit comes, then peace will be established. When that occurs, everything changes around you. Things will change." (October 1984)

"This evening, dear children, in a special way, I am grateful to you for being here. Adore continually the Most Holy Sacrament. I am always present when the faithful are in adoration. Special graces are then being received." (March 15, 1984)

"Dear children, I wish to tell you these days to put the Cross at the center of your life. Pray especially before the Cross from which great graces are coming. Now, in your homes, make a special consecration to the Cross of the Lord. Promise that you will not offend Jesus and that you will not insult Him nor the Cross. Thank you for your response to my call." (September 12, 1985)

"Dear children, today I call you to read the Bible every day in your homes, and let it be in a visible place so as always to encourage you to read it and pray." (October 18, 1984)

"Put Holy Scripture in a visible place in your families, read it, reflect on it, and learn how God loves His people. His love shows itself also in present times because He sends me to call you upon the path of salvation. Thank you for having responded to my call." (January 25, 1999)

"Dear children, be humble. Live in humility. Thank you for your response to my call." (February 27, 1986)

"Dear children, I wish to thank you for your sacrifices and invite you to the greatest sacrifice, the sacrifice of love. Without love, you are not able to accept me or my Son. Without love, you cannot witness your experience to others. That is why I invite you, dear children, to begin to live the love in your hearts. Thank you for your response to my call." (March 27, 1986)

"Dear children, today I am calling you to a life of love toward God and your neighbor. Without love, dear children, you cannot do anything. Therefore, dear children, I am calling you to live in mutual love. Only in that way can you love me and accept everyone around you. Through coming to your parish, everyone will feel my love through you. Therefore, today I beg you to start with the burning love with which I love you. Thank you for your response to my call." (May 29, 1986)

"Dear children, today I am calling you to the love which is loyal and pleasing to God. Little children, love bears everything bitter and difficult for the sake of Jesus who is love. Therefore, dear children, pray God to come to your aid, not, however, according to your desires but according to His love. Surrender yourselves to God so that He may heal you, console you, and forgive everything inside you which is a hindrance on the way of love. In this way, God can mold your life and you will grow in love. Dear children, glorify God with the canticle of love so that God's love may be able to grow in you day by day to its fullness." (June 25, 1988)

"I desire to draw you ever closer to Jesus and His wounded heart that you might be able to comprehend the immeasurable love which gave itself for each one of you. Therefore, dear children, pray that from your heart would flow a fountain of love to every person, both to the one that hates you and to the one that despises you. That way, you will be able, through Jesus' love, to overcome all the misery in this world of sorrow, which is without hope for those who do not know Jesus. I am with you and I love you with the immeasurable love of Jesus. Thank you for all your sacrifices and prayers. Pray so that I might be able to help you still more. Your prayers are necessary to me. Thank you for having responded to my call." (November 25, 1991)

To Mirjana: "Dear children, as a Mother, for many years already, I am teaching you faith and love for God. Neither have you shown gratitude to the Dear Father nor have you given Him glory. You have become empty and your heart has become hard and without love for the sufferings of your neighbors. I am teaching you and I am showing you that the Dear Father has loved you, but you have not loved Him. He sacrificed His Son for your salvation, my children. For as long as you do not love, you will not come to know the love of your Father. You will not come to know Him, because God is love. Love. And have no fear, my children, because in love there is no fear. If your hearts are open to the Father and if they are full of love toward Him, why then fear what is to come? Those who do not love are afraid because they expect punishment and because they know how empty and hard they are. I am leading you, children, toward love, toward the Dear Father. I am leading you into Eternal Life. Eternal Life is my Son. Accept Him and you will have accepted love." (March 18, 1995)

"Dear children, I am calling you to peace. Live peace in your heart and in your surroundings, so that all may recognize the peace, which does not come from you, but from God. Little children, today is a great day. Rejoice with me! Celebrate the birth of Jesus with my peace, the peace with which I came as your Mother, Queen of Peace. Today I am giving you my special blessing. Carry it to every creature so that each one may have peace. Thank you for having responded to my call." (December 25, 1988)

"Dear children, today I invite you to peace. I have come here as the Queen of Peace, and I desire to enrich you with my motherly peace. Dear children, I love you and I desire to bring all of you to the peace which only God gives and which enriches every heart. I invite you to become carriers and witnesses of my peace to this unpeaceful world. Let peace rule in the whole world, which is without peace and longs for peace. I bless you with my motherly blessing. Thank you for having responded to my call." (July 25, 1990)

"Dear children! Today I call you to come closer to my Immaculate Heart. I call you to renew in your families the fervor of the first days when I called you to fasting, prayer, and conversion. Little children, you accepted my messages with open hearts, although you did not know what prayer was. Today, I call you to open yourselves completely to me so that I may transform you and lead you to the heart of my son Jesus, so that He can fill you with His love. Only in this way, little children, will you find true peace—the peace that only God gives you. Thank you for having responded to my call." (October 25, 1998)

Salvation

"Today many persons go to Hell. God allows His children to suffer in Hell due to the fact that they have committed grave, unpardonable sins. Those who are in Hell no longer have a chance to know a lot better. People who commit grave sins live in Hell while here on earth and continue this Hell in eternity. They actually go to Hell because they chose it in life and at the moment of death." (July 25, 1982)

To Mirjana: "Men who go to Hell no longer want to receive any benefit from God. They do not repent nor do they cease to revolt and to blaspheme. They make up their mind to live in Hell and do not contemplate leaving it."

"In Purgatory there are different levels; the lowest is close to Hell and the highest gradually draws near to Heaven. It is not on All Souls Day, but at Christmas, that the greatest number of souls leave Purgatory. There are in Purgatory, souls who pray ardently to God, but for whom no relative or friend prays on earth. God makes them benefit from the prayers of other people. It happens that God permits them to manifest themselves in different ways, close to their relatives on earth, in order to remind men of the existence of Purgatory and to solicit their prayers to come close to God who is just, but good. The majority of people go to Purgatory. Many go to Hell. A small number go directly to Heaven." (January 10, 1983)

"There are many souls in Purgatory. There are also persons who have been consecrated to God — some priests, some religious. Pray for their intentions, at least the Lord's Prayer, the Hail Mary, and the Glory Be seven times each, and the Creed. I recommend it to you. There is a large number of souls who have been in Purgatory for a long time because no one prays for them." (July 21, 1982)

"Dear children, today I would like to invite you to pray, day by day, for the souls in Purgatory. Every soul needs prayer and grace to reach God and His love. This way, you too, dear children, can find new intercessors who will help you in life to know that all things of the earth are not important for you. It is only Heaven which you need tend to. For this reason, dear children, pray without interruption so that you may help yourself and those to whom your prayers will bring joy." (November 6, 1986)

"You go to Heaven in full conscience: that which you have now. At the moment of death, you are conscious of the separation of the body and soul. It is false to teach people that you are reborn many times and that you pass to different bodies. One is born only once. The body, drawn from the earth, decomposes after death. It never comes back to life again. Man receives a transfigured body."

"Whoever has done very much evil during his life can go straight to Heaven if he confesses, is sorry for what he has done, and receives Communion at the end of his life." (July 24, 1982)

"Dear children, today also, I invite you to dedicate your life to me with love in order that I may guide you with love. I love you with a special love, dear children, and I want to bring you to Heaven with God. I want you to comprehend that this life is very short in comparison with that in Heaven. Therefore, dear children, today decide anew for God. Only in that way can I show you how much you are beloved by me and how much I want all of you to be saved and be with me in Heaven." (November 27, 1986)

Human Participation in the Divine Plan

"The sign will come; you must not worry about it. The only thing that I would want to tell you is to be converted. Make that known to all my children as quickly as possible. No pain, no suffering is too great for me in order to save you. I will pray to my Son not to punish the world; but I plead with you, be converted. You cannot imagine what is going to happen nor what the Eternal Father will send to earth. That is why you must be converted! Renounce everything. Do penance. Express my thanks to all my children who have prayed and fasted. I carry all this to my divine Son in order to obtain an alleviation of His justice against the sins of mankind. I thank the people who have prayed and fasted. Persevere and help me to convert the world." (June 24, 1983)

"Dear children, this evening, in a special way, I am asking for your perseverance in trials. Ponder how the Almighty is still suffering because of your sins. So, when sufferings come, offer them as your sacrifices to God." (March 29, 1984)

"Dear children, this evening I am especially asking you to venerate the Heart of my Son, Jesus. Make atonement for the wounds inflicted to the Heart of my Son. That heart has been offended with all sorts of sin." (April 5, 1984)

"Dear children, I have told you already that I have chosen you in a special way, the way you are. I, Mother, love you all. And in any moment when it is difficult for you, don't be afraid. I love you even when you are far away from me and my Son. I ask you not to allow my heart to cry with tears of blood because of the souls who are being lost in sin. Therefore, dear children, pray, pray, pray!" (May 24, 1984)

"Dear children, these days Satan is trying to thwart all my plans. Pray that his plan may not be fulfilled. I will pray to my Son, Jesus, that He will give you the grace to experience His victory in Satan's temptations." (July 12, 1984)

"Dear children, I continually need your prayer. You wonder what all these prayers are for. Turn around, dear children, and you will see how much ground sin has gained in this world. Therefore, pray that Jesus conquers. Thank you for your response to my call." (September 13, 1984)

"Today is the day when I wanted to stop giving messages because some individuals did not accept me. The parish has responded; and I wish to continue giving you the messages, like never before in history since the beginning of time. Thank you for your response to my call." (April 4, 1985)

"Dear children, I invite you to prayer so that, with your prayers, you will help Jesus to realize all of His plans. By offerings and sacrifices to Jesus everything that is planned will be fulfilled. Satan cannot do anything." (January 9, 1986)

"Dear children, today I invite all of you to pray in order that God's plan with you and all that God wills through you may be realized. Help others to be converted, especially those who are coming to Medjugorje. Dear children, do not allow Satan to reign in your hearts. Do not be an image of Satan, but be my image. I am calling you to pray so that you may be witnesses of my presence. God cannot fulfill His will without you. God gave everyone free will and it is up to you to be disposed." (January 30, 1986)

"Dear children, you are responsible for the messages. The source of grace is here, but you, dear children, are the vehicles transmitting the gifts. Therefore, dear children, I am calling you to work responsibly. Everyone will be responsible according to his own measure. Dear children, I am calling you to give the gift to others with love and not to keep it for yourselves." (May 8, 1986)

"Dear children, behold, also today I want to call you to start living a new life as of today. Dear children, I want you to comprehend that God has chosen each one of you, in order to use you in a great plan for the salvation of mankind. You are not able to comprehend how great your role is in God's design. Therefore, dear children, pray so that in prayer you may be able to comprehend what God's plan is in your regard. I am with you in order that you may be able to bring it about in all its fullness." (January 25, 1987)

"Dear children, today I invite you to pray for peace. At this time, peace is threatened in a special way and I am seeking from you to renew fasting and prayer in your families. Dear children, I desire you to grasp the seriousness of the situation and that much of what will happen depends on your prayers; and you are praying a little bit. Dear children, I am with you and I am inviting you to begin to pray and fast seriously, as in the first days of my coming." (July 25, 1991)

"Dear children, today also I invite you to prayer, now as never before, when my plan has begun to be realized. Satan is strong and wants to sweep away plans of peace and joy and make you think that my Son is not strong in His decisions. Therefore, I call all of you, dear children, to pray and fast still more firmly. I invite you to renunciation for nine days, so that, with your help, everything that I wanted to realize through the secrets which began at Fatima may be fulfilled. I call you, dear children, to grasp the importance of my coming and the seriousness of the situation. I want to save all souls and present them to God. Therefore, let us pray that everything I have begun will be fully realized." (August 25, 1991)

"Dear children, today, in a special way, I invite you all to prayer and renunciation. For now, as never before, Satan wants to show the world his shameful face, by which he wants to seduce as many people as possible onto the way of death and sin. Therefore, dear children, help my Immaculate Heart to triumph in the sinful world. I beseech all of you to offer prayers and sacrifices for my intentions so I can present them to God for what is most necessary. Forget your desires, dear children, and pray for what God desires and not for what you desire." (September 25, 1991)

"Dear children, today I wish to place you all under my mantle to protect you from every Satanic attack. Today is the day of peace, but throughout the whole world there is much lack of peace. Therefore, I call you to build up a new world of peace together with me, by means of prayer. Without you, I cannot do that and, therefore, I call all of you with my motherly love; and God will do the rest. Therefore open yourselves to God's plans and purposes for you to be able to cooperate with Him for peace and for good. And do not forget that your life does not belong to you but is a gift with which you must bring joy to others and lead them to Eternal Life. May the tenderness of my little Jesus always accompany you." (December 25, 1992)

"Pray in order to understand that you all, through your life and your example, ought to collaborate in the work of salvation. Little children, I wish that all people convert and see me and my Son, Jesus, in you. I will intercede for you and help you to become the light. In helping the other, your soul will also find salvation." (May 25, 1996)

"Dear children! Today I invite you to open yourselves to God the Creator, so that He changes you. Little children, you are dear to me. I love you all, and I call you to be closer to me and that your love toward my Immaculate Heart be more fervent. I wish to renew you and lead you with my Heart to the Heart of Jesus, which still today suffers for you and calls you to conversion and renewal. Through you, I wish to renew the world. Comprehend, little children, that you are today the salt of the earth and the light of the world. Little children, I invite you and I love you and in a special way implore: Convert! Thank you for having responded to my call." (October 25, 1996)

Philosophical, Scientific, and Theological Criteria in Assessing the Authenticity of Apparitions

Fundamentally, there are two kinds of objections that can be leveled against apparitions: one is philosophical in nature and the other scientific. The philosophical objection is simply that miracles and supernatural phenomena do not occur since these would be violations of the laws of nature and such violations are impossible. The scientific objection is that an apparition is a hallucination because the phenomenon witnessed by the visionary or visionaries cannot be witnessed by anyone else. If a given apparition can be defended against these two kinds of fundamental objections and can be shown to be authentic, then we are met with yet another kind of objection: the theological objection. Theological objections can be classified under two heads: the first denies the possibility of any authentic appearance by Jesus, Mary, or the saints and attributes all alleged apparitions to the devil; the second accepts the possibility of such appearances but wants confirmation that a given claim of an apparition indeed derives from one of these personages.

The Philosophical Objection: There Are No Supernatural Phenomena

The philosophical question here is whether miracles and supernatural phenomena *can* take place. Miracles have been defined as violations of the law of nature. A more neutral description may be that they are suspensions of the laws of nature. We may add that these suspensions are miracles if they are brought about by a supernatural agent and serve a "religious" purpose (e.g., to demonstrate God's power or to help bring about salvation).

The chief objections to miracles are the following: the laws of nature are universal and can never be violated; all claims of miracles depend on historical evidence and, since it is extremely improbable that the laws of nature can be violated, no amount of historical evidence will support the case for such violation. (Historical evidence rests on the testimony of witnesses and such witnesses could be deceiving us or themselves be deceived.)

These objections were given their classical formulation by David Hume, the fountainhead of modern skepticism, and continue to be propagated by his contemporary followers like Antony Flew. Professor Flew, who is the best-known spokesman for atheism in the English-speaking world, has kindly carried on a dialogue with me on many issues in the philosophy of religion, including the question of what constitutes evidence for apparitions.

Richard Swinburne, one of the most influential philosophers of the present day, lists four kinds of evidence that should be brought to bear in evaluating claims of supernatural phenomena: our own memory (and this applies to the memory of the recipient of an apparition) of which we can be certain; the testimony of others, and this testimony could be historical or contemporary; physical traces of what is said to have taken place; and our contemporary understanding of what is physically impossible or improbable.

In Swinburne's view, Hume's mistake was to focus strictly on the second and fourth kinds of evidence without saying anything at all about the first and third kinds. As Swinburne sees it, all four kinds of evidence — not just testimony and our understanding of scientific laws — are relevant in evaluating the case for a given miracle: every kind of evidence should be admitted before reaching a judgment. He takes Antony Flew to task for asserting that the only criterion to be considered in evaluating the evidence is the principle that there can be no exceptions to a law of nature. Just as a law of nature provides a simple and coherent description of a large number of observed data, the testimony of individuals to a miraculous occurrence or physical traces of such an occurrence can be considered reliable if they conform with established correlations between present and past phenomena. Both the laws of nature and the claims of testimonies and traces, says Swinburne, are essentially established in the same way: certain formulae described the data that is observed in a coherent manner. The evidence for miracles and supernatural phenomena that emerges from various independent testimonies and traces can cumulatively outweigh the objection that there are no exceptions to a law of nature — and, in fact, Swinburne even says that generalizations about the reliability of testimony are better established than many laws of nature. In correspondence, Professor Swinburne informed me that his "whole analysis of the cognitive status of religious experience in Chapter 13 of *The Existence of God* is highly relevant" to the claims of Marian apparitions.

The a priori objections to miracles characteristic of Hume and Flew depend obviously on their worldview. There is no logical basis for affirming that there is some inner necessity about the laws of nature that forbids any change in them. These laws simply describe certain regularities in the behavior of natural phenomena. The question is how did these regularities or laws develop. We have no reason to believe that there is anything absolute about the laws of nature.

On the contrary, our question must be how did nature come into existence and how was it endowed with these regularities. There are only two serious responses possible: either there is no explanation for the existence of nature and its laws or there is an Ultimate Explanation, the infinitely perfect Creator of all being. The next appendix will show why the second explanation — the existence of a Creator — makes more sense than the first option. Ironically, on the one hand, Hume denies miracles because they violate scientific observations about cause and effect while, on the other, as a skeptic, he denies that we can establish that there is a law of cause and effect. If he were to admit the existence of such a law, he would ultimately have to look to a Creator as the Ultimate Explanation for the universe. But he can't have his cake and eat it too: if he denies miracles because they violate a law of nature, then he must also affirm that there are such laws (which he does not).

If indeed nature was created by a Creator, and created with certain regularities, there is no logical reason why this Creator could not suspend these regularities to achieve a certain purpose. We cannot use science to argue against such suspensions because science itself is simply a description of such regularities and not an explanation of how they originated.

If a software program performs certain activities in a manufacturing plant because the relevant "rules" were embedded in it, there is no reason why the architect who wrote the program could not override some of these rules in exceptional situations. It is really a question of why the rules were embedded in the first place. If the program was written to meet certain objectives and the attainment of these objectives requires changes to the program on occasion, then such changes would be required — and the architect would know when and how to make such programming changes.

On the question of the improbability of miracles outweighing even the best historical evidence, the problem lies with the alleged improbability. If there is a Creator and if He directs nature and history to meet certain objectives, then there is a strong probability that He will intervene in nature and history to meet these objectives. Such interventions are especially to be expected if the program develops bugs or contracts viruses. The activity of debugging will be less or more intense depending on the virulence of the virus or bug. If operational activities in the manufacturing plant are changed or halted, the personnel could speculate that this has happened because the software is being overhauled or debugged. If some of them are taken to the computer room where they meet a software engineer who confirms the debugging hypothesis and shows them the debugging in progress, then there is no reason why their colleagues outside should reject their testimony.

Consider Marian apparitions in this context. We know that there is a God who is Lord of Nature and History. We know that in Jesus Christ He has intervened decisively in history and revealed His purpose in history. Part of this revelation included the promise that the Mother of Jesus is the Mother of His adopted brothers and sisters. We see that evil continues to have the upper hand in the world. We then see claims of the appearance of a messenger from God, the Mother of Jesus, arising from different cultures across the world since the time of the early Church. These appearances are especially prominent when there is some crisis or calamity. Hers is a call to conversion and a return to God — just what we would expect God to provide.

We note also that Marian apparitions follow certain common patterns and, we might even say, their own "laws." Such laws include the ecstasy of the visionary, "physical traces" of an apparition which are called "lasting signs" (the Guadalupe tilma, the healing spring at Lourdes, and the like). Although these laws are by no means applicable to every authentic apparition, they help us in evaluating new claims of apparitions — just as an acknowledged law of nature helps us in understanding new natural phenomena.

The Scientific Objection: All Apparitions Are Hallucinations

When someone claims to witness an apparition of the Blessed Virgin, three explanations are possible of this phenomenon: (1) it's a lie, (2) the visionary is witnessing something which is not there, i.e., he or she is hallucinating, and (3) the visionary is indeed a witness to an apparition of the Virgin. The question of whether the visionary is lying will be addressed in the next section (as also the question of whether apparitions are diabolic deceptions). Here we will consider hallucination as an explanation of apparitions.

The "hallucination" charge is often used loosely by critics. People do have hallucinations, but hallucinations have definite causes. They are caused by mental illness (neurosis, psychosis), drugs, an exaggerated tendency for wishful thinking, or such conducive circumstances as a strong desire and a favorable setting. Again, hallucinations do not introduce anything not already in the subject's mind: no new external information is generated. Finally, a hallucination theory will have to account for all of the data at hand, not just the visual portion of an apparition but all the other associated phenomena.

Once the various factors associated with hallucinations are listed, it should be obvious that none of the famous visionaries or apparitions can be subsumed under the hallucination category. Take the visionaries. The approved apparitions have — almost as a general rule — been witnessed by holy people, peasants and children. In no instance has there been a charge that any one of these visionaries was mentally unsound or on drugs. The peasants especially had the same hard-headed view of things as did the Apostles who witnessed the Risen Christ. Moreover, the apparitions were witnessed across the world by people in many different cultures; how is it that they all had a consistent and mutually compatible account of the Virgin and her messages? Wish-fulfillment, strong desire, and favorable circumstances can be ruled out as factors as well. Most visionaries initially reacted in fear and surprise and some even thought they were being deceived by the devil. Their status as visionaries meant that they would have to suffer for the rest of their lives. None of them had a favorable setting because they had to prove their veracity before skeptical authorities and sarcastic peers — a process that sometimes took years.

Regarding charges of hallucination, an expert in this area, Professor Emilio Servadio, writes, "Genuine hallucination (as distinct from optical illusions or mass hysteria), is always peculiar to one individual. It is not possible for a group of people to have repeated identical hallucinatory experiences, which they insist are real, without showing signs of psychic abnormality" (*Il Tempo*, December 12, 1984).

As for the content of the apparitions, in many cases the messages transmitted by the visionaries were not understood by them. Thus Bernadette reported that the Lady said she was the Immaculate Conception — whatever that meant. The secrets entrusted to the Fatima visionaries were spectacularly fulfilled in later history. In these and other instances, it is clear that the content of the apparition story could not have come from the mind of the visionary — and this again tells against the hallucination charge.

Finally, there is the need to account for the external phenomena related to each apparition: the tilma of Guadalupe, the spring at Lourdes, the dancing sun at Fatima. Hallucinations could not possibly have "generated" these. So the hallucination hypothesis has to be set aside when we evaluate the approved apparitions. We have also seen earlier that the scientific and medical authorities who examined the Medjugorje visionaries demonstrated the nonhallucinatory nature of that phenomenon.

As a footnote, we should mention here that one of many significant differences between Marian apparitions and reports of UFO sightings and alien abductions is the total lack of "public" evidence for the "alien" claims. No less a proponent of the search for extraterrestrial intelligence than the late Carl Sagan wrote,

> Where is the physical evidence? Some abductees allege that aliens stole fetuses from their wombs. This is something that would surely cause a stir among gynecologists, midwives, obstetrical nurses, especially in an age of heightened feminist awareness. But not a single medical record has been produced substantiating such claims. Some abductees say that tiny metallic implants were inserted into their bodies — high up their nostrils, for example. But no such implants have been confirmed by physicists or chemists as being of unearthly manufacture. No abductee has filched a page from the captain's logbook or a strange examining instrument, or taken an authentic photograph of the interior of the ship, or come back with detailed scientific information not hitherto known on Earth. These failures surely tell us something. (*Parade*, March 7, 1993, 7)

Contrast this dearth of evidence for aliens with the wealth of "public" evidence that accompanies Marian apparitions: the tilma, healing springs, spinning suns, mass conversions, and numerous other publicly experienced miracles.

Atheists and Apparitions: An Analysis of Professor Antony Flew's Critiques

Professor Antony Flew, the famous British atheist, is one of the few skeptics who has performed a serious analysis of apparition claims. As noted earlier, I was pleased to have the opportunity to carry on discussions with him on apparitions like Medjugorje and on the philosophy of religion in general. As best as I can, I will outline Professor Flew's critiques here and offer what I believe to be adequate responses.

In a nutshell, Professor Flew issues two challenges. First, he grants the possibility that witnesses to an apparition may indeed honestly believe that they have seen something. He holds, however, that the visionary cannot legitimately move from a claim about his or her experience in the private, limited sense to the conclusion that this experience is of something independent of the visionary and that it is experience in the public sense. He admits that the visionary speaks with special authority on the private experience because it is the visionary's own dream or vision and not someone else's. But this authority, in his view, cannot be extended to the claim that the visionary is indeed experiencing something that exists independently of the mind. While it is true that the experience may have been very vivid, he points out, a hallucination too could be just as vivid. Flew's second challenge relates to the alleged cultural conditioning involved in apparitions. Claims of apparitions, he says, would be more impressive if they referred to "deities not worshiped in the circles in which the claimants actually moved." He notes that apparitions of the Virgin Mary are usually reported in Catholic localities while apparitions of Shiva the Destroyer are reported in Hindu areas like Benares and Mysore and apparitions of dragons were reported in ancient China. The conclusion for him is that apparitions are obviously products of cultural conditioning.

Professor Flew's first challenge is really a challenge to the veracity and objective reality of any claim of religious experience — and this includes such claims of religious mystical union with God as are found in the writings of St. John of the Cross. The same challenge has, of course, been issued time and again by other skeptics and has been countered in a variety of ways by philosophers of religion. To my mind, a particularly significant though modest response came from Frederick Copleston, the great historian of philosophy, in two essays, "The Philosophical Relevance of Mysticism" (a chapter in *Religion and Philosophy*) and "Mysticism and Knowledge" (in *Religion and the One*). Although Copleston's arguments are mainly concerned with the "truth-value" of claims of mystical union with God, the arguments are essentially applicable to the issues raised by apparitions. In addition, claims of apparitions are somewhat easier to articulate and explain because they are not ineffable, as are experiences of mystical union with God. And whereas an experience of mystical union is a wholly inner experience, an apparition has something of a flesh-and-blood dimension and involves sensory experience.

Copleston admits that claims of religious experience cannot be cited as proof for the existence of God. By its very nature, as Flew mentions, these experiences are private and personal. They are not publicly available or repeatable at will. The central issue is whether or not these experiences are caused by an external agency acting upon the visionary. On this point, the atheist and the religious believer will have different perspectives. On the one hand, the atheist can say that the whole experience can be entirely explained in terms of psychological or physiological causes either today or in the future. The religious believer, on the other hand, is going to look at the whole phenomenon in the context of the theistic worldview. If the believer accepts the existence of a supernatural realm there is no reason to reject the possibility of some kind of interaction between the supernatural and the natural.

In the case of an apparition, the kinds of messenger and message involved are in principle compatible with a Christian frame of reference and with the personal experience of the spiritual world available to all Christians. Both the Old and the New Testaments themselves speak of apparitions of angels on various occasions. Even if some aspects of an apparition can be explained in terms of certain psychological and physiological causes, the believer can point out that these causes in turn could have been directed to produce the intended effects by a supernatural agency. Moreover, the fact that a religious experience like an apparition cannot be actually experienced, and thus be known "from the inside," by everyone is not an argument against its objective reality. A congenitally blind person cannot get the feel of visually experiencing color — but this does not cast doubt on the existence either of color or of the visual experience of color. The fact that an apparition is a private experience, therefore, does not automatically make it any less an experience of objective reality. Also, to say that some people could witness an authentic apparition is not to say that anyone who claims to have witnessed an apparition should be believed. We can accept the first claim — which is mainly a matter of our theological presuppositions — while admitting that some who claim to witness an apparition are either deluded or deluding. Whether or not an apparition is truly from a supernatural source can be determined not by adhering to the atheist's dogmatic restrictions but by paying attention to all the evidence cited and then making a judgment.

As remarked above, an apparition cannot be used as an argument for the existence of God because most people who decide that an apparition is authentic already believe in God and see the apparition as part of God's activity in the world and in history. It must be said, however, that strong evidence for an authentic apparition can sometimes lead a favorably disposed agnostic to full-fledged faith. When someone sees much in the world that seems to indicate the existence of a transcendent being but is hesitant to take the final leap, the kinds of supernatural phenomena associated with an authentic apparition could serve as the springboard for leaping to the light.

Professor Flew's second challenge is less serious than the first. To be sure, apparitions of the Blessed Virgin Mary have almost always taken place in cultures that are predominantly Catholic (although the Marian apparitions in Guadalupe, Mexico, Vailankanni, India, and Zeitun, Egypt, are famous exceptions). But this in itself is no argument against the authenticity of the reported apparitions. If there is a God and God chooses to reveal a special message through a special messenger, it is only to be expected that the message and the messenger will be manifested to individuals and communities whose minds and conceptual frameworks have been "prepared" to the degree necessary to make sense of the whole thing. Should the Fatima apparition have taken place before a tribe of cannibalistic animists, the messages that came with the apparition could hardly have achieved the intended effect; the emphasis on reparation for sin, for instance, would not carry much weight with those who have no knowledge of the rudiments of Christian theology. Presumably, the aim of each apparition is to achieve something. It does not take too much thought — let alone infinite intelligence — to see that nothing would be achieved by throwing pearls to swine. Professor Flew, of course, does not see any divine side to apparitions and confines himself exclusively to naturalistic explanations. That is his privilege as a naturalist, but such a perspective is by no means normative for those who recognize a Beyond and an Other.

It should be mentioned in this context that the mystery of the Incarnation was made manifest in a cultural environment which had been conceptually prepared to understand its implications. The Jews believed in a God who created the universe and was separate from it and who progressively revealed His nature and will through His messengers. Although our Lord's claim to be a divine Person united with a human nature shocked them, it shocked them because they could appreciate the implications of this claim. If the same claim was made in a Hindu environment, its dramatic significance would have been missed because of the pantheism that is often to be found in Hindu thought. It is significant too that the Incarnation came at a time when Greek philosophy had developed to a point at which it could be used to articulate the central concepts of Christian doctrine; this articulation was not conditioned by Hellenistic thought-forms but used these thought-forms to express the unique insights of the Christian faith. We can see in all of this a coincidence — or we can see the handiwork of Infinite Intelligence.

Professor Flew's second challenge is also flawed by rather shaky facts. As far as I know, reports of apparitions of Shiva are not common in Hindu areas. In fact, to my knowledge, there has not even been a single instance of such a claim being seriously made. Of course, there are some Hindu teachers who claim to have certain higher powers — but this is a different kind of claim altogether. This absence of claims of apparitions seems to be the case in cultures centered on other religions too — although there have been claims of other kinds of phenomena. Claims of apparitions of the Blessed Virgin are in a unique class and cannot easily be explained away as examples of cultural conditioning. And the extraordinary similarities in the reports of Marian apparitions that have taken place at different times and places to visionaries of different races and different cultures is a good reason for taking each claim seriously and examining it on its individual merits.

The Theological Objection:
Apparitions Are Deceptions of the Devil

Once an apparition is established as originating from a source external to the visionary, we have to ask whether it is from the Mother of Jesus or some other source. Not every claim of witnessing an apparition can be taken as originating from a divinely established source simply because the phenomenon cannot be explained in natural terms.

According to some Protestant Christians, all alleged apparitions of Mary are actually deceptions of the devil. Their argument is as follows:

1. All divinely guided supernatural revelation ceased once the canon of the Bible was fixed.

2. The Bible warns us that any claim of a supernatural revelation actually originates from a diabolic source.

3. Marian apparitions teach unscriptural doctrines and are therefore diabolic in origin.

These three objections to Marian apparitions are seriously flawed.

There is no passage in Scripture that states that supernatural revelation ceases after the fixing of the canon; in fact, the principle that there will be no further supernatural revelation is nonscriptural. For instance, 1 Thessalonians 5:21 and 1 John 4:1 tell us the very opposite: these verses assume that both the Spirit and good spirits will be communicating with us and that, in the case of communication from spirits, we should test them to see if they are divinely directed: "Never try to suppress the Spirit or treat the gift of prophecy with contempt; think before you do anything — hold on to what is good and avoid every form of evil." (1 Thess. 5:21); "It is not every spirit, my dear people, that you can trust; test them, to see if they come from God; ... you can tell the spirits that come from God by this: every spirit which acknowledges that Jesus the Christ has come in the flesh is from God" (1 John 4:1–3). Just from these verses, we see that claims of a supernatural revelation do not necessarily have a diabolic source and that we should instead expect there to be such communications from God and should exercise discernment when studying these communications. In addition, neither the verses cited here nor any other verse in the New Testament suggest that supernatural revelation ceases after the fixing of the canon.

Another verse often directed against Marian apparitions is St. Paul's warning to the Corinthians: "These people are counterfeit apostles, they are dishonest workmen disguised as apostles of Christ. There is nothing unexpected about that; if Satan himself goes disguised as an angel of light, there is no need to be surprised when his servants, too, disguise themselves as the servants of righteousness. They will come to the end that they deserve" (2 Cor. 11:13–15). Critics of apparitions cite only the "Satan himself goes disguised as an angel of light" verse. But it should be obvious to anyone who reads the entire passage that supernatural apparitions are the last thing Paul had in mind here. His concern is with false apostles. We are told that any teaching should be rejected if it goes against the true doctrines of the Gospel, and, of course, false teaching is to be rejected even if it comes from an angel of light.

Unlike 1 Thessalonians 5:21 and 1 John 4:1, this passage from 2 Corinthians is not concerned with messages from supernatural sources; its application to Marian apparitions is unwarranted at best. In any event, a Marian apparition is not the manifestation of an angel of light but purportedly an appearance of the Mother of Jesus. Scripture tells us to expect her to come to the aid of all Christians and, from the earliest eras of Christianity, Christians have universally accepted accounts of the intervention and intercession of the Virgin Mary in the life of the Church. Were they mistaken? Is it likely that Jesus would allow the devil to masquerade as His Mother and to mislead all those who belonged to His Church with such apparitions of the Mother of the Church from the very first days of that Church?

The charge that Marian apparitions should be rejected because they teach unbiblical doctrines is likewise mistaken because the messages common to most Marian apparitions are messages that have been doctrinally accepted by Christians from the beginning: for instance, the doctrine that Mary is the New Eve, a doctrine assumed by the New Testament and explicitly taught by all the Church Fathers and implicitly by the Councils, is graphically reinforced in most of the apparitions. Her role as the New Eve includes her office as the Mother of all Christians (portrayed in Rev. 12), another universal belief. Similarly her role as the Mother of God was defined by several Church Councils and was accepted by most Protestants. These doctrines, which are as old as Christianity itself, form a key part of the Marian messages. If they are rejected, we would have a difficult time salvaging other key Christian doctrines.

One feature of apparition sites that disturbs Protestant critics is the focus on Marian images and icons. This fear again is unhistorical. Icons and images of Jesus, Mary, and the holy ones of God (i.e., the saints) were approved as worthy objects for Christian veneration by the Second Council of Nicaea. There is no danger of worshiping such statues because almost all Marian devotees know that they are simply using such objects to turn their minds to Jesus and Mary — a practice that Martin Luther found reasonable and acceptable. When critics of icons watch a movie or play of Jesus' life they are indulging in the same activity as those who remind themselves of Jesus with a crucifix or Mary with a Rosary.

The charge of Satanic deception should not be lightly made. In the New Testament, we see two basic models or paradigms of this charge, one of them wrong and the other right.

The wrong model is shown in the Gospel of Luke, where the miracles of Jesus are attributed to the devil. Jesus' response to this charge deserves careful reflection:

> But some of them said, "It is through Beelzebul, the prince of devils, that he casts out devils." Others asked him, as a test, for a sign from heaven; but knowing what they were thinking, he said to them, "Every kingdom divided against itself is heading for ruin, and a household divided against itself collapses. So too with Satan: if he is divided against himself, how can his kingdom stand? — since you assert that it is through Beelzebul that I cast out devils. Now if it is through Beelzebul that I cast out devils, through whom do your own experts cast them out? Let them be your judges, then. But if it is through the finger of God that I cast out devils, then know that the kingdom of God has overtaken you." (Luke 11:15–21)

Later in the same Gospel, he says, "Everyone who says a word against the Son of Man will be forgiven, but he who blasphemes against the Holy Spirit will not be forgiven" (Luke 12:10).

Plainly nothing Jesus could have said or done in response to His critics would have proved sufficient for them because of the mental framework in which they were trapped. Any miracle he performed or magnificent doctrine he preached would be dismissed as a deception of the devil since, they would reason, the devil is more ingenious than men and could easily deceive them through such means. The critics' mistake was to leave no room for divinely directed activity in their minds; as a result they could not discern any such activity even if it took place before them. So it is with the critics of Marian apparitions. Their mental frameworks have locked out the possibility of such "God-sent" apparitions and so every such apparition has to be attributed to the devil no matter how good the doctrine or how real the miracle. But if the Holy Spirit acts through His

Spouse, the Virgin Mary, in such a manner as to make it unmistakable that He was thus active, then we should be cautious about peremptorily dismissing these phenomena as diabolic deceptions for reasons given in Luke 12:10.

The right model or paradigm in responding to supernatural phenomena is laid out in 1 Thessalonians 5:21 and 1 John 4:1. We are asked to expect and welcome apparitions, not to reject them wholesale. We are told to "test" each claim of a supernatural nature and then hold on to what is good. For the Holy Spirit does indeed continue to act through His chosen Messenger and good spirits do communicate with us.

The next question is how do we "test" an apparition, for we are also warned that we cannot trust every spirit. Historically, ecclesiastical authorities have taken the attitude of "testers." And we must admit that they, like any of us, cannot simply accept every claim of a supernatural nature at face value. These claims, if they are inexplicable scientifically, could still have a demonic background — and certainly there have been instances of such deception (for instance, Necedah, Wisconsin, where the alleged visionary had an occultic background; Bayside, Queens, New York, where there was evidence of paranoid behavior; Magdalen of the Cross of Spain in which the visionary confessed to a pact with the devil; and many other dubious contemporary cases). Apparition claims originating from children are in many respects easier to evaluate — simply because children are more transparent. When the claim is made by an adult the burden of proof is necessarily higher.

Essentially, any "test" of an apparition should consider the facts of the phenomenon itself (the ecstasy, the visionary), the doctrine that emerges, and the spiritual and other fruits. These three central criteria have been systematized by Catholic ecclesiastical authorities into the framework given below that has been traditionally utilized in assessing and approving the authenticity of an apparition. This framework from the Sacred Congregation for the Doctrine of the Faith replaced the guidelines drawn up at the Fifth Lateran Council in 1516. Once the three criteria of facts, doctrine, and fruits are accepted as sound starting points, this framework itself should be acceptable to most Christians. Moreover, since the Catholic Church was instrumental in assembling and authorizing the content of the public revelation — namely, the books of the Bible that we have today — its historical criteria for assessing claims of private revelation should be given serious consideration. This is the framework utilized by the Church in its evaluation of apparitions past and present:

Positive Criteria

1. That there be moral certitude or a high probability that the facts are consistent with what has been claimed.

2. That the persons involved be psychologically balanced, honest, living a good moral life, sincere, respectful toward church authority.

3. That there be immunity from error in theological and spiritual doctrine.

4. That there be sound devotion and spiritual fruits, such as the spirit of prayer, testimony of charity, and true conversion.

Negative Criteria

1. That there be no manifest error regarding the facts of the event.

2. That there be no doctrinal errors attributed to God, Mary, or a saint.

3. That there be no evidence of material or financial motives connected with the event.

4. That there be no gravely immoral acts by the person on the occasion of the revelations or apparitions.

5. That there be no psychopathic tendency in the person which might enter into the alleged supernatural event, no psychosis or collective hysteria of some type.

These criteria have been applied in evaluating the claims of apparitions described in this book and have been judged to be successfully fulfilled in all of the accredited apparitions. To the charge of diabolic deception, we should also ask how the fruits listed below are to be evaluated. Here are some of the things that happen to visionaries at apparitions and to those influenced by the apparitions: total conversion; increasing holiness; prayer; aversion to sin and Satan; evangelism. Physical healings and miracles are also associated with most of these apparitions but are less important than the spiritual and moral transformation that takes place. We would be well within our rights to ask whether Satan would bring about any of these spiritual changes. In point of fact, it cannot be denied that each one of these changes is fundamentally inimical to Satan and can be attributed to him only by someone who is lost without a compass in the moral universe.

A survey of the major apparitions will show that the ecclesiastical authorities who investigated them tended to be hostile and often alleged that the phenomenon was diabolic in nature. The accredited apparitions, then, were accepted only after rigorous scrutiny by hostile prosecutors.

Although the apparitions cited in this volume can easily meet the criteria laid out above, there are still some Christians who remain unhappy with claims of apparitions for yet other reasons. Their argument can be summarized as follows:

1. Those who are apparition enthusiasts tend to give more importance to messages from apparitions than to the Gospel message.

2. Apparitions have an unhealthy eschatological or apocalyptic side to them that can whip up hysteria in the mobs.

3. Because they receive messages from a supernatural source, visionaries have a temptation to ignore or disobey those who have legitimate authority.

4. If an apparition message simply comes from a this-worldly and not a heavenly source, then those who are followers of the apparition will be focused on messages that have no external validation.

5. If an apparition comes from a diabolic source, the followers will eventually be enslaved by Satan.

Each one of these concerns can be appropriately addressed when we are dealing with authentic apparitions:

1. The accredited apparitions actually center our attention on the Gospel message and remind us forcefully of its truth and current applicability.

2. The apocalyptic and eschatological dimensions of apparitions are also found in many biblical passages. These dimensions are simply illustrations of the hard fact that violations of the laws of the spiritual universe have consequences of a cause and effect nature: every evil act calls forth punishments and chastisements. But the apocalyptic and eschatological dimensions are usually conditional in nature: they are requests from a loving mother to her children to avoid putting their hands in flames or playing on a busy highway.

3. Disobedience to authority is almost always a sign that an apparition is either human or diabolic in origin — since disobedience is the original sin of both Satan and the human race. None of the visionaries of the accredited apparitions or of the apparitions described in this volume were guilty of such disobedience.

4. Before one accepts the claims of an apparition, one must first be satisfied that it comes from a good supernatural source. That is why it is important to "test" the spirits to see if they are from God, but one cannot reject them automatically without violating a scriptural command.

5. We have seen that it is possible to ensure that an apparition claim does not originate from Satan. Once we are sure that there is no satanic root in a given apparition, then we are not in any danger of being enslaved by Satan if we adopt the recommendations of the apparition. In fact all of the accredited apparitions help liberate us from the slavery of Satan.

With all this, it still remains true that every apparition claim must be rigorously evaluated and should be accepted only if it meets all the relevant criteria. The dangers of human fraud and diabolic deception are ever present as are the human tendencies to gullibility and an unhealthy obsession with signs and wonders. We cannot let down our guard in these areas. But neither should we be on guard to such an irrational extent as to close our eyes and ears to the Messenger and Message sent to us by God. This latter is as much a danger as the former, as we see in the Gospel accounts of the charges against Jesus.

An Interview on Apparitions with Cardinal Joseph Ratzinger, Prefect of the Sacred Congregation for the Doctrine of the Faith, the Vatican (1991)

Q: *Is it the case that the Church pronounces on the doctrinal soundness of the messages coming from an apparition but not on the validity as such of the apparition?*

The Church cannot and will not decide with absolute certainty if it was an apparition or not. [It deals] only with the "symptoms" and may conclude this must come from another source, but these are conclusions from the indications we have.

There can clearly be situations where we can say that "this is not an apparition." This is possible because indications can be so clear that it is possible to give this judgment. But it's not possible with absolute certainty to say, "This was an apparition."

It's spiritual and pastoral guidance that we must give in the light of authentic revelation. We will not give an absolute judgment about what is in this person. But we can and must give pastoral guidance in the light of the authentic revelation of Christ.

Q: *That would mean determining whether the message is compatible with orthodox doctrine.*

This is the essential criterion, but there are other criteria. The essential criterion is coherence with authentic revelation.

Q: *What role do the bishops' conferences and bishops play? Is the final decision on the authenticity of an apparition from the Vatican?*

It depends a little on the importance of a phenomenon. If we have only a local phenomenon it's not necessary that the Vatican intervene. If the bishops have sufficient evidence about the situation, it's sufficient if the bishops give guidance to the people. Only if we [have something] of universal importance do I think it's useful that the Vatican approves and confirms [it], studies it, and, after study, confirms the decision of the bishops.

Q: *But does the bishops' pronouncement have the authority of the Church as such if it is only an empirical judgment?*

I would distinguish. As pastoral guidance it has the authority of government in the Church. It is not a doctrinal authority in the strict sense, but it has the authority of the pastors of the Church, who give disciplinary guidance to the people.

Q: *Will the judgment on Medjugorje be made only after the apparitions are over?*

Yes. The final judgment. The Yugoslavian bishops gave a provisional judgment because it [Medjugorje] is in need of more guidance. But a definitive judgment can be given only if the phenomenon has ended.

Q: *The Church does not validate or invalidate apparitions (although it could invalidate some). But it will not proclaim apparitions as a matter of public faith.*

The Church is charged by Our Lord to interpret official revelation, and she is not charged to interpret with the same authority and authenticity other events. But this includes [the fact] that apparitions are never required for salvation. The Old and New Testament revelation have all that is necessary for salvation. So it is not necessary that the Church have a special, definitive charism about these things because they are not necessary for salvation.

SENT BY WHOM?
ON THE EXISTENCE OF GOD

The existence of God, of a transcendent eternally existent Reality that brought the world into being, has been regarded as a self-evident truth throughout history and in virtually every culture and society. Atheism, the denial of God's existence, is historically and sociologically an aberration and, from the very beginning, an intellectually preposterous fantasy. (By "beginning" we refer here to the Enlightenment Era, when skepticism started as deism and evolved into a reductionist reaction against revealed religion in the nineteenth century and finally ended up as the full-blown atheism of today.)

The greatest superstition of the twentieth century is the widespread idea that the conscious thinking experienced by all human beings at every waking moment was produced entirely from and by mindless matter and is in fact reducible purely and simply to matter. We have lost our minds in more senses than one!

Of this we are all certain: we are conscious and aware that we are conscious. The data of our consciousness ranges from sensations that reach us through one or more of the five senses; memories that "relive" sensory experiences of the past; images that we form in our imagination by extrapolating from our sensory experience; concepts that do not have any correlation with our sensory experience, such as the notion of liberty or mathematical entities and theories; intentions that we form and execute, such as planning to go for a walk or a vacation; and choices that we make, ranging from giving up our lives for our country to telling the truth in a conversation.

Not only are we conscious and aware of being conscious, but we are just as clearly conscious that our consciousness is dramatically different from anything material or physical. We know that thoughts and feelings do not have physical properties (size or shape). We know that our mental activities are accompanied by physical processes but also that we cannot "see" a thought if we open up the brain. (We may see neural activity, but that's not the same thing as "seeing" the thought as we *experience* it.) Conscious thought has a reality of its own that cannot be perceived as being physical in any relevant sense of the term. When we perceive a neural firing in the brain we perceive a physical process, not that which we experience "on the inside" as a thought. The argument that the thought and the neural firing are identical although they "look and feel" different quite clearly flies in the face of the only empirical evidence that will ever be available to us, namely, what we can know about the physiological workings of the brain and the sensation or thought of which we are directly and immediately conscious. Consciousness, as we experience it, is irreducibly nonphysical, although it interacts constantly with the physical.

Could these fundamental features of the human condition of which we are directly and constantly aware — and aware of as intrinsically immaterial — have arisen from lifeless, purposeless mass-energy, given not just a few billion years but an infinite period of time? It is almost as if we were to say that given an infinite amount of time, a pen and a paper, without any external intervention, would somehow give rise to the concepts embodied in the Gettysburg Address. We are not speaking of the words that constitute the address but the concepts of liberty and equality and justice represented by the words: concepts as such are so radically different in nature from the physical objects used to represent them that it is simply nonsensical to suppose that the latter could "produce" the former.

We think, and our thinking is so obviously distinct from the physical realm that we cannot conceive of it as having risen from the physical: certainly we cannot give any credence to the idea that a certain bundle of mass-energy that just happened to exist (without beginning or end) then evolved without any direction or guidance over time into *thought*. We cannot seriously believe that intellect sprang out of mindless mass-energy, consciousness out of lifeless matter, intelligence out of blind force fields. Once we truly recognize that we are conscious thinking agents, we can never again conceive of our coming to be from anything less than a conscious thinking agent. Only Mind can beget mind; only an infinite Intelligence, an intelligence that has no limitation of any kind, can create beings with any kind of intelligence. Descartes said, "I think therefore I am." It would have been more correct to say: "I think and therefore know that I cannot as a thinking being have come into existence from nonthinking matter." I think: therefore God exists.

Belief in God's existence was universal because it was rooted in the undeniable basic human experience we have considered here. Disbelief is possible only if we blindfold the mind and walk away from the raw data of experience.

This raw data includes not just the consciousness we spoke of above but the very existence of the universe. Almost instinctively our minds tell us that something cannot come from nothing. How then do we explain the existence of the universe? Was it always here or was it created by a Being that explains both Its own existence as well as that of the universe? To say the universe was always here does not address our question, because even if this were the case, we ask why and how there could be a universe with the property of always being here. What we are asking for is an explanation for the existence of the universe — not the length of time it has existed (even if it this were endless in extent). None of the entities in the universe can explain their own existence. The word "universe" simply refers to the sum total of these entities; it is not something over and beyond the entities themselves. And so to say that none of the entities in the universe can explain their own existence is to say that the universe cannot explain or account for its own existence. The only rationally satisfying explanation for the existence of the universe then is the existence of a Being that explains Its own existence by virtue of Its infinite perfection: and the universe exists because it was created from nothing by this Being whom all call God. Rejections of this train of thought require either mental contortions that contradict our everyday experience (there is no explanation for anything; something can spring out of absolute nothingness without rhyme or reason; etc.) or mere indifference to the question of existence.

A common error made in considering the ontological origin of the world is to look for answers in contemporary cosmology. This is an error primarily because our quest for explanation as it pertains to the ultimate origin of material reality goes beyond empirical and quantifiable causes as such since we are here concerned with the transition from nothing to something. Nothing is absolute nothingness: no laws, no vacuums, no fields, no physical entities. Science can get to work only once something exists. Consequently the transition from nothingness to something lies forever beyond the purview of scientific methodology.

The Power and the Glory manifest themselves in other dimensions of experience as well. Take the intricate and complex structures that constitute the natural world and their innate purposiveness: the precarious but optimal balance of the vast array of natural forces and laws that made human existence possible, the grandeur of the genetic blueprint, the architecture of the human eye. To explain these as instances of an underlying evolutionary mechanism or matter's power of "self-organization" is to beg the basic question: from whence came the powers and the mechanisms that are so undeniably purposive and "intelligent?" Surely no one can deny that the eye in its current state exists for a particular purpose — to see — and that reproductive systems exist in order to enable the replication of a species. Or as the physicist Stephen Hawking asked, "What is it that breathes fire into the equations and makes a universe for them to describe?" When some scientists try to explain away the wonders of the world as simply the blind results of evolutionary processes, we must ask them to step back to a more fundamental level: all of physical reality, as they will agree, is governed by the laws of nature; where did these laws come from and how is it that these laws were "written" so as to give us such breathtaking beauty and an environment that allows human existence?

Again, our moral experience cries out for an explanation that goes beyond sociocultural influences and psychological states. Why do all cultures have norms of right and wrong? Granted, not all these norms are common to all societies and cultures (although there is much more held in common than is normally supposed). But the universal sense that there are moral absolutes and taboos that we cannot infringe without invoking divine retribution is mirrored in our own experience. Sartre the atheist confessed that when, at the age of six or seven, he set fire to some lace curtains, "this incendiary act had no witness, and yet I was thinking: 'The Good Lord can see.' " Every day, in every choice, every one of us hears the Voice of God in our hearts. The moral law is written into the fabric of reality as clearly as the laws of science and logic.

Above and beyond all of these considerations is the conviction to which many are led of a Force at work in their lives that is both transcendent and all-loving. The medley of events and individuals in their lives is suddenly seen to form a pattern and a plan that work toward an end, the End who is God Himself. But this experience of the divine is so personal as to make its description meaningless to those who have not themselves experienced it.

Despite the weight of experience and the sound reasons that oblige sound minds to acknowledge the Godhead, in modern times atheism has become the establishment position of the academic world. Atheism for many has become a religion of faith in the irrationality of a universe that they in their everyday behavior assume is rationally ordered; it is a pious belief that there are no beliefs, a hallowed intention to show there are no intentions, an inspired exercise of intelligence to demonstrate the nonexistence of intelligence. We can with good reason say of many academic atheists what the physicist Wolfgang Pauli said of his atheist colleague Paul Dirac, "Well, our friend Dirac, too, has a religion, and its guiding principle is: 'There is no God and Dirac is His prophet.' "

The dominance of academic atheism has been matched by the triumph of militant atheism in the world at large. Although the Nazis could not build an enduring empire and the Marxists lost a good part of theirs, the governing assumption of modern politics and government is that there is no God and no divinely grounded moral law.

The question of God's existence was not one which needed to be addressed by Jesus in His teaching. It was taken as an obvious truth that needed neither exposition nor defense. In fact, once it was accepted, the teaching of Jesus gave us nearly fourteen centuries in which monotheism was accepted as the only serious intellectual position.

It was the eighteenth-century phase of the Enlightenment that severed the link with rationality and celebrated the ultimacy of the mindless and the random. The seat of the Enlightenment was France, and it was here that the Virgin Mary began the great apparitions of the modern era. In the apparitions of the Miraculous Medal, of Lourdes, La Salette, and Pontmain, she showed the reality of the supernatural to the naturalists. As a concerned mother, she pursued atheism from incubation through birth, from the conception of the deception in the minds of her children to its coming of age as an ideology of death and destruction.

APPENDIX C

"SENT" AS A WITNESS:
ON THE HISTORICAL REALITY
OF JESUS

Everything about Mary revolves around Jesus. She was chosen to bring Him to this world, and by her free choice she became the vehicle of His Incarnation. Her relationship to Jesus did not cease with His physical birth. At the anointing of Jesus, the prophet Simeon is divinely inspired to proclaim that she will participate in His suffering. Her suffering begins when she loses Him for three days in the Temple, perhaps prefiguring the three days she is to lose Him again. Jesus' ministry begins with the miracle He performs for His mother. She is with Him again on Calvary where He gives her as Mother to the beloved disciple, who in the Gospel signifies every believer. Moreover, every appearance of the Virgin bears witness to the historical reality of the Man who was God.

In history, we have five witnesses to Jesus.

The first is our very measure of history itself: history is divided into Before Christ and Anno Domini (the year of Our Lord). Contemporary attempts to take the sting out of "A.D." by calling it the Common Era still have to take the coming of the Lord as their starting point.

Second, we have the Gospel narratives. New Testament critics and Jesus Seminars have at best given us various interpretations of these narratives and armchair voyages of speculation into their origin without turning up a single definite fact on which there is a consensus. To determine the veracity of these narratives, we must turn from the armchair detectives to the third witness to Jesus in history: the claim of His Resurrection.

We know beyond doubt that Christianity has spread to every corner of the world, that it began its genesis in first-century Israel and that its initial "evangelists" were the Jewish followers of Christ. What needs explanation is the transformation of these evangelists from cowering fisherfolk and peasantry who had just witnessed the murder of their Master into death-defying, world-traveling messengers of the Good News. What made them, men who had never left the safety of home, take on the most powerful empire of their time and sacrifice their lives in distant lands? To the very last, in the face of horrible deaths at the hands of savages, they held firm and bore witness to one truth: Christ had risen from the dead. No other explanation for the change in the disciples — and of the changed lives of millions throughout history — is plausible without reference to the actual historical resurrection of Jesus Christ from the dead.

Ludwig Wittgenstein, one of the most influential philosophers of this cen-

234

tury and a non-Christian, gave eloquent voice to the significance of Christ's resurrection for all human beings in his *Culture and Value:*

> What inclines even me to believe in Christ's Resurrection? It is as though I play with the thought. — If he did not rise from the dead, then he decomposed in the grave like any other man. *He is dead and decomposed.* In that case he is a teacher like any other and can no longer help; and once more we are orphaned and alone. So we have to content ourselves with wisdom and speculation. We are in a sort of Hell where we can do nothing but dream, roofed in, as it were and cut off from heaven. But if I am to be *really* saved, — what I need is *certainty* — not wisdom, dreams or speculation — and this certainty is faith. And faith is faith in what is needed by my *heart,* my *soul,* not my speculative intelligence. For it is my soul with its passions, as it were with its flesh and blood, that has to be saved, not my abstract mind. Perhaps we can say: Only love can believe the Resurrection.... What combats doubt is, as it were, *redemption.* Holding fast to *this* must be holding fast to that belief. So what that means is: first you must be redeemed and hold on to your redemption (keep hold of your redemption) — then you will see that you are holding fast to this belief. So this can come about only if you no longer rest your weight on the earth but suspend yourself from heaven. Then *everything* will be different and it will be "no wonder" if you can do things that you cannot do now.

The fourth witness to Jesus in history is the very land in which He lived and preached and died. Those who visit the Holy Land can see for themselves the correlation between the New Testament narratives and the geographical locations described there. More important, over two-thirds of the churches in the Holy Land are built on the sites of events in the Gospels and every significant event is commemorated by a church purportedly built where it took place (and certainly the locations correspond closely with the narratives themselves). To an outside observer, one sees here the literal fulfillment of Christ's prophecy to those who would not believe in Him: if His followers keep silent, then "the stones will cry out." One wonders whether the archaeologists who diligently search for evidence of the biblical past and revel in shocking the public with their speculative pronouncements have thought of expending some of their energy on the witness to the past of the living present.

The fifth and final witness to Jesus in history is His Mother, who has appeared to all nations with the message of her Son. This is most appropriate not simply because it was she who brought Him to this world and continues so to bring Him but because we are told in Revelation 12:17 that she is the mother of all who bear witness to Christ. She who is the mother of the witnesses is herself the primary witness.

Mary's primary message in her appearances is about following the commandments of Jesus. She echoes her command in the Gospel, "Do whatever he tells you," and the command of Jesus that "anyone who does not carry his cross and come after me cannot be my disciple" (Luke 14:27).

Appendix D

Ever a Virgin?

In calling Mary the Virgin, we are explicitly affirming the traditional teaching that she remained a virgin before, during, and after the birth of Christ. Many of today's Protestant Christians, however, deny the doctrine of Mary's perpetual virginity although it was strongly affirmed by the Ecumenical Councils, all the Fathers of the Church, and even the Protestant Reformers. For these Christians, the main stumbling blocks to this doctrine are the references to the brothers and sisters of the Lord in the Gospels.

The first question the dissenters should ask is how the doctrine could have established itself in antiquity if the first bishop of Jerusalem and the most prominent Christian leader after Peter and Paul was James, the brother of the Lord. If James was indeed a blood brother of Jesus, and believed to be such, then the Christian community would be schizophrenic if it also affirmed that Jesus was the only child of Mary.

The second question is simply the textual evidence itself. It is clear in the Gospels that those who are called the brothers of Jesus (Matt. 13:55, Mark 6:3) are also called the sons of Mary, the wife of Clopas. In a recent study of the questions from the standpoint of literary forms ("The Brothers of the Lord," *Downside Review,* January 1998), Harold Riley notes that this other Mary "is described in Matthew as 'the mother of James and Joseph' [who are called the brothers of Jesus in 13:55], in Mark as 'the mother of James the Little and of Joses,' and in Luke as 'the mother of James' (Matt. 27:56; Mark 15:40; Luke 24:10)." As for the other brother of Jesus, Judas, "In the Epistle which bears his name, he is described as 'a servant of Jesus Christ and brother of James' (Jude 1)." The fourth brother, Simeon, is described in the second-century writings of Hegesippus, a Hebrew Christian, as a son of Clopas, the brother of James and his successor as the bishop of Jerusalem since he was "the cousin of the Lord." In Hegesippus also we have a clue as to why James, Joseph/Joses, Judas, and Simeon were called the brothers of Jesus. Their father Clopas was the brother of Joseph, and after the death of Clopas it is believed that Joseph took in Clopas's sons and daughters as foster-children. They were therefore not just cousins but foster brothers and sisters of Jesus, and it is wholly natural to refer to foster brothers and sisters as simply brothers and sisters. Hence Clopas's children are called brothers and sisters of Jesus although they are never called the children of Mary. Mark 6:3 even calls Jesus "the son of Mary and a brother of James ... " just to make the distinction evident. Another key piece of textual evidence, according to Riley, is John 19:25–27:

In his dying moments Jesus commended his mother to the care of "the disciple whom he loved," and ... "from that hour the disciple took her to his own home." It has often been recognized that what is here reported is completely inconsistent with brothers and sisters elsewhere mentioned in the Gospels being the children of Joseph and Mary. The death of Jesus would have left to the surviving children what Lightfoot described as "the paramount duties of filial piety." The brothers of the Lord are among the earliest members of the Christian Church, with "Mary the mother of Jesus" (Acts 1:14), and could not conceivably have avoided, or even have desired to avoid, the responsibility of caring for their mother, or could have left this to another disciple.

Finally, there is the unanimity of the Fathers of the Church. In "The Brothers of Jesus and His Mother's Virginity" (*The Thomist* 63 [1999]), José M. Pedrozo argues that

> the claim that the Helvidian position [the view of the fourth-century layman Helvidius that Mary gave birth to children after Jesus] enjoyed antiquity and widespread support cannot be sustained even under superficial scrutiny. Before the fourth century, exactly who was a supporter of the Helvidian position? There is not one single explicit witness in favor of it. Helvidius himself could produce only two potential witnesses: Tertullian and Victorinus of Pettau. I have shown that Tertullian need not be taken as a clear witness against Mary's virginity. As far as Victorinus is concerned, there is no reason to believe that his testimony is as Helvidius implied. In addition, ... Victorinus is still a fourth-century witness.

Moreover,

> From a historical point of view, it is hard to see how Mary's virginity post partum, if false, could have been asserted at all in the second century without an explicit denial. After all, the "brothers and sisters" of Jesus and their descendants are known to have occupied prominent places in the Christian community well into the second century. The Book of James is a product of that era. If belief in Mary's perpetual virginity was a falsehood promoted only by gnostic groups, then it seems unlikely that some of the early Christian apologists who wrote against the gnostics would not have denied such mendacity explicitly. Furthermore, since history did not stop at the close of the third century one has to explain why, if the Helvidian view enjoyed such antiquity and widespread support in the early Church, it was so widely and immediately rejected in the fourth century. Mary "ever Virgin" was taught by individuals coming from different parts of the world, with a variety of theological styles and agendas: Athanasius of Alexandria, Ephraem of Syria, Hilary of Poitiers, John Chrysostom, Ambrose of Milan, and Augustine of Hippo among several other lesser mortals. After some denials of Mary's virginity in the Arianized atmosphere of the fourth century, followed by the historical blips of Helvidius, Jovinian, and Bonosus

(all three within the last two decades of the fourth century), followers of the Helvidian opinion practically became extinct.

Significantly, "After the fourth century, Mary's virginity was seriously questioned only with the beginning of denials of Christ's divinity in liberal Protestantism" [with the rise of the Enlightenment].

This last point illuminates one other issue. John Henry Newman famously argued that Marian doctrine and devotion preserved faith in the divinity of Christ: "They who were accused of worshiping a creature [Mary] in His [Christ's] stead, still worship Him; their accusers, who hoped to worship Him so purely, where obstacles to the development of their principles have been removed, have ceased to worship Him altogether" (*An Essay on the Development of Christian Doctrine* [Notre Dame, Ind.: Notre Dame University Press, 1990). In the present context, the Reformer Ulrich Zwingli warned that denial of Mary's Perpetual Virginity would lead to a denial of the Virgin Birth:

> It was not enough that the conception of Jesus take place without a male role, for if a woman who had previously known a man had conceived him even through the Holy Spirit, "who would ever have believed that the child that was born was of the Holy Spirit? For nature knows no birth that is not besmirched with stain." For the same reason she had to be ever a virgin, she who bore the one in whom there could not be even the least suspicion of blemish. For the birth of Jesus to be absolutely pure of every stain, Mary herself had to be free of any pollution of normal child-bearing." (David F. Wright, ed., *Chosen by God: Mary in Evangelical Perspective* [London: Marshall Pickering, 1989], 170–71)

WORKS CITED

Messages of the Virgin

The following books have been cited or utilized in summarizing the messages and narrative accounts of the apparitions:

Bartholomew, Courtenay. *A Scientist Researches Mary.* 2 vols. Asbury, N.J.: 101 Foundation, 1995, 1998.

Bettwy, Sr. Isabel. *I Am the Guardian of the Faith.* Steubenville, Ohio: Franciscan University of Steubenville Press, 1991.

Brown, Raphael. *Saints Who Saw Mary.* Rockford, Ill.: Tan Books, 1994.

Connell, Janice T. *Meetings with Mary.* New York: Ballantine Books, 1995.

Delaney, John J., ed. *A Woman Clothed with the Sun.* New York: Image Books, 1990.

Durham, Michael S. *Miracles of Mary.* San Francisco: Harper, 1995.

Lord, Bob and Penny. *The Many Faces of Mary: A Love Story.* Westlake Village, Calif.: Journeys of Faith, 1997.

Messages of Love. Portland, Ore.: Mary's Touch by Mail, 1996.

Messages of Our Lady at San Nicolás. Trans. Eleonora O'Farrell De Nagy-Pal and Marie-Héléne Gall. Milford, Ohio: Faith Publishing Company, 1991.

The Messages of the Lady of All Nations. Amsterdam: Miriam-Verlag, 1987.

Odell, Catherine M. *Those Who Saw Her: Apparitions of Mary.* Huntington, Ind.: Our Sunday Visitor, 1995.

Plunkett, Dudley. *Heaven Wants to Be Heard.* Leominster, Eng.: Gracewing, 1997.

Rollings, Peter. *Walsingham: England's Nazareth.* Walsingham: R.C. National Shrine, 1998.

Santos, S. R. *The Shrine Basilica of Our Lady of Health, Vailankanni.* Thanjavur: Don Bosco Press, 1983.

Smith, Jody Brant. *The Image of Guadalupe.* Macon, Ga.: Mercer University Press, 1994.

Swann, Ingo. *The Great Apparitions of Mary.* New York: Crossroad Publishing Company, 1996.

Weglian, Miriam and Stephen. *Let Heaven and Earth Unite!* Milford, Ohio: Faith Publishing Company, 1996.

Zahlaoui, Elias. *Remember God.* Montreal: Association Notre-Dame de Soufanieh, 1997.

Other Works

Bertone, Archbishop Tarcisio. Interview. *Maria,* March–April 1999.

Blackbourn, David. *Marpingen: Apparitions of the Virgin Mary in Nineteenth Century Germany.* New York: Alfred A. Knopf, 1994.

Buby, Bertrand. *The Marian Heritage of the Early Church.* Vol. 3 of *Mary of Galilee.* New York: Alba House, 1996.

Burghardt, Walter J. "Mary in Western Patristic Thought," in *Mariology,* ed. Juniper B. Carol. Vol. 1, pp. 109–55. Milwaukee: Bruce Publishing Company, 1955.

———. "Mary in Eastern Patristic Thought," in *Mariology,* ed. Juniper B. Carol. Vol. 2, pp. 88–153. Milwaukee: Bruce Publishing Company, 1957.

Gumbinger, Cuthbert. "Mary in the Eastern Liturgies," in *Mariology,* ed. Juniper B. Carol. Vol. 1, pp. 185–244. Milwaukee: Bruce Publishing Company, 1955.

Jastrow, Robert. *God and the Astronomers.* New York: W. W. Norton, 1978.

Joyeux, Henri, and René Laurentin. *Scientific and Medical Studies on the Apparitions at Medjugorje.* Dublin: Veritas, 1985.

Macquarrie, John. *Mary for All Christians.* London: Collins, 1990.

Mascall, E. L. "Theotokos: The Place of Mary in the Work of Salvation," in *The Blessed Virgin Mary: Essays by Anglican Writers,* ed. E. L. Mascall and H. S. Box. London: Darton, Longman & Todd, 1963.

McClure, Kevin. *The Evidence for Visions of the Virgin Mary.* Wellingborough, Northants.: The Aquarian Press, 1983.

McInerny, Ralph. *Miracles: A Catholic View.* Huntington, Ind.: Our Sunday Visitor, 1986.

The Office of the Akathist. Trans. Edward F. James. New York: Montfort Publications, 1959.

Pelikan, Jaroslav. *Mary through the Centuries: Her Place in the History of Culture.* New Haven: Yale University Press, 1996.

Sheehy, Jeremy. *Mary and Locality.* Wallington, Surrey: Ecumenical Society of the Blessed Virgin Mary, 1999.

Trethowan, Iltyd. *The Absolute and the Atonement.* London: George Allen and Unwin, 1971.

Varghese, Roy Abraham, ed. *Trinitas, Christos, Maria.* Forthcoming.

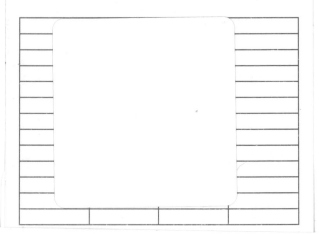